New Directions
in Comparative Politics

*Prepared under the auspices of
the Center for International Affairs,
Harvard University*

Revised Edition

New Directions in Comparative Politics

edited by
HOWARD J. WIARDA

contributions by

Douglas A. Chalmers
Ronald H. Chilcote
Lawrence S. Graham
Peter Lange
John D. Martz
Hudson Meadwell
Joel S. Migdal
Tony Smith
Sidney Verba
Howard J. Wiarda

WESTVIEW PRESS
Boulder • San Francisco • Oxford

Copyright © 1991, 1985 by Westview Press, Inc.

Published in 1991 in the United States of America by Westview Press, Inc., 5500 Central Avenue, Boulder, Colorado 80301, and in the United Kingdom by Westview Press, 36 Lonsdale Road, Summertown, Oxford OX2 7EW

Library of Congress Cataloging-in-Publication Data
New directions in comparative politics / edited by Howard J. Wiarda ;
   contributions by Douglas A. Chalmers . . . [et al.]. — Rev. ed.
      p.   cm.
   Includes bibliographical references.
   Includes index.
   ISBN 0-8133-0996-4—ISBN 0-8133-0997-2 (pbk.)
   1. Comparative government.   I. Wiarda, Howard J., 1939–
II. Chalmers, Douglas A.
JF51.N49   1991
320.3—dc20   90-45842
                                                                              CIP

Printed and bound in the United States of America

The paper used in this publication meets the requirements
of the American National Standard for Permanence of Paper
for Printed Library Materials Z39.48-1984.

10   9   8   7   6   5   4   3   2   1

Contents

PART THREE
Conclusion

Figures and Tables

Preface

Since the first edition of this book appeared in 1985, a great deal has happened in the field of comparative politics. The state-society approach, as represented in this volume in the chapter by Joel Migdal, has emerged as one of the major approaches in the field; and Migdal has gone on to publish a full-length book on the subject. Corporatism seems to have become ubiquitous in all political systems; meanwhile, the corporatist approach has been widely accepted in the political science literature, and the debate over it, as analyzed by Douglas Chalmers, has become less vociferous. The political economy approach, otherwise known as international political economy, or IPE, here exemplified in the chapter by Peter Lange and Hudson Meadwell, has similarly become one of the leading approaches to the study of comparative politics and development.

In other areas of the field greater flux has occurred. The dependency approach, analyzed here by Tony Smith, which enjoyed considerable popularity during much of the 1980s, has begun to fade somewhat, giving rise to methodologies that are more pragmatic rather than ideological and that stress interdependence as well as dependence. The idea of a nonethnocentric view of the world's political systems remains powerful, but the indigenous, Third World routes to development described in Chapter 7 have seldom worked out very well and, in the context of a renewed vigor of Western institutions, the debate about whether and how these should be exported to other nations has again been spirited. The Marxian approach described in Ronald Chilcote's chapter continues to be a source of inspiration to some, but Marxism has been gravely hurt by the manifest failures of Marxist regimes in the Soviet Union, China, Eastern Europe, Afghanistan, Ethiopia, Angola and Mozambique, Cuba and Nicaragua. Meanwhile, in this more moderate and pragmatic era, the public policy approach, as here represented in the essay by Lawrence Graham, has increased in popularity and number of adherents.

At the same time, some other and quite remarkable events have taken place in the comparative politics field. As the levels of economic development, literacy, and overall modernization of many of the developing nations have increased significantly in the last three decades, the political development approach, which earlier had been strongly criticized (including in this volume), has made something of a comeback. Similarly with political culture: What once had been a major approach in the field and was later criticized as

ethnocentric, biased, and even "racist" has recently been enjoying a renaissance. Moreover, the enormously encouraging democratic openings in
East Asia and Latin America in the last decade have resulted in a decline
in the earlier bureaucratic-authoritarian perspective and far greater stress
on theories of transition to democracy. The political culture, bureaucratic-
authoritarian, and transitions to democracy approaches are dealt with ably
in a new essay by John D. Martz. An overall perspective of recent trends
in comparative politics—including the revival of political development—is
dealt with in the concluding chapter by the editor.

The main trends stressed in the first edition of the book have been
confirmed by recent events. The field of comparative politics no longer has
the unity of approach that it once had. Instead, the field has fragmented
into a variety of approaches. When this book was first planned, these trends
were regarded in many quarters as dangerous and destructive; now such a
diversity is simply accepted as reflecting intellectual reality and the pluralism
within the discipline. Meanwhile, a great deal of empirical work and theory-
building, both called for by the first edition, have gone on *within* the various
subsets of the field; and there have been some notable efforts by scholars—
as exemplified in the new chapters here—to build connectors ("bridges" or
"causeways" are the metaphors we used before) among the various approaches
("islands of theory") analyzed here. Still, however, we do not have a single,
overarching *theory* of or approach to comparative politics; what is more,
scholars in the field are no longer convinced—as most of them once were—
that such a single approach is necessary or even desirable. Meanwhile,
comparative politics has once again, after being in the doldrums in the
1970s, become a vigorous, dynamic, diverse, and intellectually stimulating
field of inquiry.

The editor is grateful to Westview Press for its support in undertaking
production of this revised edition. He is indebted, too, to his contributors,
who have agonized over how and where their chapters needed to be changed
and updated and have arrived at different conclusions to those questions.
Once again, after spending several years in Washington, D.C., the author
is back at the University of Massachusetts and the Center for International
Affairs (CFIA) at Harvard University, where this book began in the early
1980s and where it continues now to be rethought and reinvigorated. The
editor is grateful to the CFIA for its generous hospitality. Longtime CFIA
director Samuel P. Huntington and new director Joseph S. Nye, Jr., have
provided sustained aid and encouragement to this undertaking.

One additional light note: The first foreign-language edition of this book
was published in Japan, the second in the Republic of Korea. The Asian
interest in this topic may also tell us something about the "new directions
in comparative politics."

Howard J. Wiarda

Preface to the
First Edition

The field of comparative politics, which involves the systematic and comparative study of nations and their political systems, is in a state of crisis. Few scholars are now able to define the field's parameters precisely, its methodology has been subjected to searching criticism, there is no longer a single integrating set of theories on which scholars in the field can agree, students are put off by the lack of a clear focus, and the field itself has become fragmented and disjointed. This crisis has come at a time of acute national need at the policy and popular levels to better understand the countries the United States must deal with, the political contexts in which they function, and the givens and dynamics of their political systems.

As a result of this crisis in the comparative politics field, a group of scholars, chiefly from the Cambridge area, began meeting in the spring of 1980 at, and under the auspices of, the Center for International Affairs at Harvard University. Chaired by the editor of this volume, the group was organized as a Center seminar for faculty and senior graduate students to explore new and future directions in comparative politics. The Seminar, which brought together some of the foremost senior scholars in the field— Gabriel Almond, Stanley Hoffmann, Samuel Huntington, Roy Macridis, Joseph Nye, Lucian Pye, Sidney Verba, Myron Weiner—along with a number of articulate, already published, somewhat younger scholars—Naomi Chazan, Douglas Costain, Jorge Domínguez, Elliot Feldman, Merilee Grindle, Douglas Hibbs, John Higley, Terry Karl, Bahgat Korany, Peter Lange, Terry McDougal, Kevin Middlebrook, Joel Migdal, Jerome Milch, Eric Nordlinger, Robert Putnam, Tony Smith—served as the nucleus for the present book. The Seminar met twice in the spring of 1980 and regularly on a biweekly basis during the 1980–1981 academic year.

The Seminar's focus was the past, present, and future of comparative politics. It explored the questions of where comparative politics has been as a field and subdiscipline, what it has accomplished, what the biases of the field and our approach to it have been, what the innovative approaches in the field are, and what lies ahead. Among the general issues we were concerned with in the Seminar and that find expression in this book are an evaluation and summing up of the work of the Social Science Research Council's (SSRC) Committee on Comparative Politics, a group of leading comparative politics scholars whose work long represented the dominant approach in the field; the absence at present of a single global and integrating theoretical framework and what might be substituted for it; the biases and ethnocentrism of the earlier approaches; the emergence of new theories and conceptual designs that are not always compatible with the earlier approach; the increasing assertion of indigenous models of development derived from the Third World; and the recognition of a diversity of approaches within the field and the implications of this new disciplinary pluralism.

The Seminar produced some interesting dynamics, not all of which can be fully recounted here. Some members saw the Seminar as a potential successor group to the now-disbanded SSRC Committee on Comparative Politics; others resisted that notion. There was spirited debate between some members who had been instrumental in founding the SSRC Committee and who defended its work vigorously and others, generally younger, who were often critical of that approach and preferred to strike off in new directions. Fascinating too were the comments of some of the SSRC Committee's earliest members concerning the assumptions, political as well as intellectual, that led the group to go in the directions it did. A number of these themes are discussed at greater length in Chapter 1.

The Seminar—and this book—explore both the older approaches in the field and the newer ones. Early on, however, we determined neither to rehash at length the stale debates of the past nor to dwell too long on retrospectives of past literature. We wished to give the older approaches their due, to emphasize what all conceded to be the positive contributions of the earlier development literature, but to concentrate on newer approaches. The book reflects that decision, which we believe makes it both stimulating and innovative. The introductory chapter (Chapter 1) and the retrospective by Sidney Verba (Chapter 2) deal primarily with the past: the accomplishments, main thrusts, and dominant paradigms of past decades. These chapters also provide an overview of the major transformations in the field in recent times. But the book's chief focus is the newer paradigms that have recently gained prominence or are currently being revived: the role of the state and state-society relations, corporatism and the corporatist approach, political economy, the dependency approach, non-Western conceptions of change, the Marxian paradigm, and comparative public policy analysis.

This list does not exhaust the inventory of new approaches in comparative politics, but we think most scholars would agree that it represents some of the more important, innovative, and provocative new directions in the field. Each of these approaches is treated analytically in an original chapter written by one of the major authorities on the subject. The contributions have the advantage of being formulated in the common Seminar setting or of deriving from a common set of concerns and main themes as developed in the Seminar, which ensures that the authors are operating more or less on a common wavelength. Most of the contributions have had the benefit of being analyzed, sifted, and criticized in preliminary fashion by fellow Seminar participants (although not all the papers given in the Seminar are in the book, and not all contributors to the book were members of the original Seminar). Where necessary and appropriate, the editor has gone outside the seminar group to get the best scholars possible on particular subjects. The Introduction and Conclusion by the editor help to further integrate these several contributions, place them in perspective, tie the book's main threads together, and ensure that this is a coherent book and not merely a loose collection of individual essays.

The subjects covered in the book are quite diverse; no common chapter outline can be rigidly or artificially imposed upon them. Each author approached his subject from his own point of view. However, each chapter contains, in varying forms, a brief statement as to why that particular focus is important, what the approach is all about in general terms, what constitutes the main literature on the subject, and what the contributions and limitations of that approach have been. These statements help provide the various chapters with a certain commonality of focus, theme, and purpose.

In the editor's introductory and concluding chapters, and in Verba's statement concerning past and future directions in the field, the themes briefly alluded to here are further elaborated. For although the SSRC Committee and the political development literature of the 1960s once served as the integrating focus in the field, that consensus no longer exists. Not only has the older approach been strongly criticized and, in varying degrees by now, rejected, but a variety of newer approaches has emerged to challenge, replace, or supplement it. From being dominated by a single integrating theory, the field of comparative politics has become dispersed into what we have called "islands of theory."

The contributors' chapters and the editor's Conclusion suggest that such varied approaches and diversity may be healthy for the field rather than detrimental. They reflect realistically the plurality of competing paradigms and the variety of approaches available, which is itself an accurate portrayal of the considerable diversity of the world's political systems and of the methods we must use to understand them. The next major task of theory, the editor suggests, is therefore not to construct or reconstruct some grand, universal framework into which all the world's political systems must arbitrarily and artificially be forced to fit. Rather we must seek to elaborate, clarify, sort out, and evaluate the several "islands of theory" through which we now approach the field, meanwhile seeking to build bridges between them. Comparative politics is unlikely quickly to recapture the unity of theory it once had, to find again a single common paradigm on which all or most students can agree. But we can constructively develop theory in the several islands of the discipline while we also work at building causeways among these archipelagos. That is, in any case, what theory is or ought to be, a point that receives major emphasis in the several contributions and in the overall focus of the book.

A book of this sort can be put together only with the assistance of individuals and institutions too numerous to name, but surely the greatest debt is owed to the Center for International Affairs (CFIA) at Harvard

University, under whose auspices it appears. The CFIA is surely one of the most high-powered, dynamic, and intellectually stimulating research centers anywhere in the world. The flow through the Center every day of prime ministers, former presidents, would-be presidents, foreign ministers, high-level policymakers, and intellectual elites and opinion molders of the various continents is nothing short of astounding. I know that in my own case my knowledge, understanding, insights, and perceptions were enormously broadened and deepened during the two years (1979–1981) I spent as a Visiting Scholar at the Center.

For this opportunity and for the encouragement and assistance in organizing the Seminar that formed the basis for the present book, I am particularly indebted to Samuel P. Huntington, Raymond Vernon, Benjamin Brown, and Grant Hammond; indeed, I am indebted to the entire CFIA-Harvard faculty and staff, who made my stay there so enjoyable and stimulating. Myron Weiner at MIT was also especially hospitable; he helped secure for me a visiting professorship at his institution during this period and, along with Professor Huntington, continued to cochair amicably and well that other ongoing, stimulating Cambridge-area Seminar with which ours occasionally overlapped, the Joint (Harvard-MIT) Seminar on Political Development (JOSPOD). To Janine T. Perfit I would like to extend many thanks for compiling the bibliography. Within this intellectually vibrant Cambridge setting, CFIA is a unique and a marvelous place to think about international affairs, do research, learn, dialogue, test ideas, and write, probably unsurpassed anywhere in the world.

H.J.W.

PART ONE

Introduction: The Field of Comparative Politics

1

Comparative Politics Past and Present

HOWARD J. WIARDA

THE RISE, DECLINE, AND RISE AGAIN OF COMPARATIVE POLITICS

Comparative politics has traditionally been thought of as one of the seven major fields in political science. The other fields are American politics, political theory, public administration, international relations, public law, and state and local government. Involving the study, analysis, and *comparison* (hence the name comparative politics) of the world's political systems, the field would seem to offer abundant attractions for research and study. The whole globe constitutes comparative politics' research laboratory. But in fact, comparative politics was long thought of as a kind of stepchild within the political science discipline. Perhaps the lack of interest historically was related to American isolationism and the sense of U.S. exceptionalism and superiority, perhaps to limited opportunities by scholars for foreign travel, perhaps to a lack of interest in other nations by Americans generally, perhaps to the sense that comparative politics was too "exotic," perhaps to other factors. Whatever the reasons, until the late 1950s comparative politics attracted relatively few students and scholars.

But then came the "boom" years, particularly the 1960s. It is probably safe to generalize that the distinct fields within political science tend to rise and fall in popularity depending on a great variety of circumstances. These include trends in U.S. and world history, new social and political currents, newspaper headlines, intellectual trends, and—not least—fads and fashions. In this period the most important trends seem to have been the sudden surge of a host of newly independent nations onto the world's stage, the internationalist flavor of the John F. Kennedy administration, a worldwide preoccupation with "development," the extension of the Cold War to the Third World, greater opportunities for rapid jet travel, and some very attractive social science theories of modernization aimed at the developing nations. These factors helped push comparative politics to the forefront of the discipline.

3

Since that time comparative politics has gone through a series of ups and downs. The 1960s was a high point, but the Vietnam War and a general undermining of numerous institutions during the 1970s cast a pall as well on the field of comparative politics. The field revived and became healthy again in the 1980s, probably corresponding to the end of the overall malaise of the previous decade, but it failed to recover the full élan and centrality within the discipline that it enjoyed in the 1960s.

Comparative politics may be defined as the systematic and comparative study of nations and their political systems. During the 1960s comparative politics had come to occupy an elevated position as, some claimed, the reigning field within the discipline of political science. Comparative politics theory, as articulated by such leading scholars as Gabriel Almond, David Apter, Karl Deutsch, Harry Eckstein, Samuel Huntington, Seymour Martin Lipset, Lucian Pye, Myron Weiner, and others,[1] seemed to provide some of the most interesting, innovative, and sophisticated new concepts and ideas in political science.

During that same decade, stimulated by the Kennedy style and enthusiasm, the Alliance for Progress and the Peace Corps, the idealistic desire not just to analyze development but also to bring its benefits to the less-developed nations, and doubtlessly encouraged also by the new scholarship programs for studying Africa, Latin America, and other Third World areas, many of the best young academic minds went into the comparative politics field. This trend had the added consequence, analyzed in more detail below, that the traditional European focus of comparative politics now shifted to the developing nations.[2] Comparative politics contributed some of the most innovative research strategies and approaches, and the comparative approach pervaded other areas of the discipline—for example, there were new studies of comparative foreign policy. Even American politics, a field that has traditionally kept aloof and been somewhat isolated from the comparative field, now began to be examined from a comparative perspective for the first time. There were even some elevated, almost imperial claims that comparative politics *was* political science, that as everything is comparative, comparative politics as a field therefore embraced the entire discipline.

Such imperial claims are still articulated from time to time, but less often than before. With the crisis that beset the field in the 1970s, comparative politics' claims are now somewhat more muted and modest. There have been enormous strides in the field, as Sidney Verba's chapter makes clear; but the sometimes exaggerated claims of premiership, ascendancy, and even "colonization" of the rest of the discipline are no longer often set forth. In fact, the field of comparative politics has had its good times and its bad times. As contrasted with the quite lofty plateau it occupied twenty-five years ago, comparative politics may now be somewhat diminished; but it remains a vigorous subfield within the discipline, with exciting concepts and a global research terrain, and in recent years it has staged a vigorous intellectual comeback.

CRISIS AND RENEWAL IN
COMPARATIVE POLITICS

From the elevated heights of the 1960s, comparative politics subsequently went into a period of crisis and decline. The reasons for this are still not entirely clear even today. Perhaps it had to do with some of the overstated claims to preeminence of some of the field's early leaders, perhaps with high but unfulfilled expectations about what the field could accomplish and the disappointments subsequently felt, perhaps with the strong method- ological attacks that were leveled against it in the 1970s, perhaps with the Vietnam War and the sense that the developmentalist strategies tried there not only failed to work but were misguided and inappropriate, perhaps other factors. Whatever the precise causes—itself a subject worthy of further exploration—for a time in the 1970s unhappiness and disenchantment with the field had set in. Comparative politics no longer held the leading or center place of prestige in the discipline.

The difficulties that critics and even neutral observers saw in the field were several. Few scholars any longer felt confident defining what the field was supposed to study, what its precise theory or approach was, or what its boundaries were. The claim that comparative politics was the leading field in political science—let alone that it *is* political science—was no longer ardently advanced. The methodology of much cross-national comparative analysis, especially that employing global categories, was strongly attacked by Peter Winch[3] and others as, in effect, adding up apples and oranges, of applying political-sociologist criteria and categories appropriate in one cultural context to others where they have but limited utility.

There no longer seemed to be any coordinating or integrating theory for the field (as "development" seemed to be in the 1960s) or even a set of agreed-upon concepts. Graduate students looking for a "central core" in comparative politics, a body of literature containing the field's fundamental concepts and definitions, were often disturbed and disenchanted by the lack of a clear focus, and in many graduate programs students were less attracted to the field than before. The field appeared to have become so large and all-encompassing, and at the same time so fragmented and dispersed, that in some quarters the question was raised whether comparative politics had sufficient unity to be called a field at all. The crisis and disenchantment in the field had come at a time, ironically, when there was an especially great need at the policy level to understand better the diverse national political systems of the world: their internal dynamics, how they change, the political- cultural and sociological contexts in which they function, their international connections and dependencies, and the value systems and ideologies that influence the way different nations perceive themselves and the outside world.

After living through and being participants in the turmoil and conflict that have characterized comparative politics in recent decades, the editor, the Harvard faculty seminar in comparative politics that provided the original inspiration for this book, and most practitioners in the field have by now reached some quite balanced assessments about it:

1. The early claims to preeminence and to centrality in the discipline made by some comparative politics writers in the 1960s were greatly exaggerated.
2. At the same time, the criticisms of the field strongly leveled in the 1970s, though accurate and telling in some respects, were similarly exaggerated and often overwrought.
3. After all these ups and downs, the field recovered its strengths in the 1980s and is presently healthy and vigorous and intellectually stimulating.

It has taken us a long time to arrive at this consensus, however, and in the meantime a great deal of vigorous debate and discussion has taken place. That is why we originally convoked the Harvard comparative politics seminar. All the members of this faculty group acknowledged the accomplishments of the field, most of us acknowledged that mistakes had been made and that at least some of the criticisms were valid, and all of us wished to know where we would go from here. Hence the seminar determined to explore the state and condition of comparative politics: past, present, and future. What is the history of the field and where do we stand now? What have been the field's major successes and its failures? What presumptions underlie the field, and are these valid? What will the future be like, and what are the field's prospects? These are some of the issues the seminar wanted to examine.

A memorandum, prepared by the editor, was therefore circulated to various Cambridge-area specialists in comparative politics. It suggested an examination of the following themes:

1. A summing-up, evaluation, and perhaps postmortem on what has come to be called the "development literature," and on the Social Science Research Council (SSRC) Committee on Comparative Politics (CCP). The Committee's series of volumes on developing nations largely set the tone and the agenda for comparative politics all through the 1960s.[4] The SSRC/CCP issued some of the most important books in the field, and its members were seen as the field's leading figures. The Committee's influence on a generation and more of scholars and graduate students was enormous.[5]

During the 1970s, however, this body of development literature was severely criticized, the SSRC/CCP series came to an end, and eventually the Committee itself was disbanded—even though many of its members remained active as individual scholars. Hence an evaluation was called for. What were the contributions as well as the biases, omissions, and limitations of this group; why did its writings so strongly influence both scholars and policymakers for such a long time; how valid were the criticisms leveled against the developmentalist approach; and could we expect the unity of focus and approach that the Committee provided to comparative politics for many years ever to be restored?

2. The possibility—or desirability—of a new, integrating "grand theory" for the field. There has not been, in the editor's view, a major, global, and comprehensive intellectual synthesis of the comparative politics/development field since Huntington's 1968 volume, *Political Order in Changing Societies*,[6] which represented both a summing-up and a powerful critique of the decade's previous studies of political modernization and development. The situation at present stands in marked contrast to that of the 1960s, when such major figures as W. W. Rostow, C. E. Black, K. Organski, Almond, Lipset, Apter, Deutsch, Pye, and others provided both a grand theory for the field and an intellectual approach and synthesis.[7] Today, there is no such grand, integrating theory on which all or most scholars can agree.

The absence currently of a single, overarching view and approach is not coincidental. The field has gone off in several different directions since the 1960s, several alternative schools of thought besides developmentalism have appeared, and there is no one single approach on which all comparative politics scholars can agree. The questions thus arise: Is there to be no more grand theory in the field; on what basis might such an all-encompassing approach to the field be grounded; is such a synthesis still possible or even desirable; does the lack of a single comprehensive approach help or hinder the field; how useful were the earlier global perspectives; and is it not the case that the present diversity of the field reflects healthily the plurality of approaches that scholars now use?

3. Theory at the middle-range or at the culture-area level. Many scholars are now arguing that the theorizing that occurs in comparative politics should be concentrated not at the level of grand theory but at lower levels, at the middle-range or culture-area level. The grand synthesis and consensus that undergirded the global models presented in the early development literature no longer exist, the argument runs; the field has fragmented into more specialized areas of interest, and we should deal with these facts realistically. Middle-range theory—dealing with comparative labor relations or comparative electoral behavior, for example—would therefore have us use theory and comparative perspectives that are significant and interesting but not necessarily global and all-encompassing. Theory at the culture-area level (on Africa, Latin America, and so on) is similarly more modest in its pretensions, concentrating on a single region consisting of similar or comparable countries rather than encompassing the entire universe of nations.

In Latin American studies, particularly, it is interesting to observe how the newer concepts generated initially at the culture-area level, such as dependency theory, corporatism, center-periphery relations, state-society relations, internal colonialism, and others have emerged as leading theoretical approaches and gained widespread acceptance from scholars studying in that area. By now many of these concepts have spread to other geographic or culture areas and have also infused the general literature. It seems as if the flow of ideas and concepts in comparative politics, historically from the Western European "core" area out to the "periphery" of developing nations, may be in the process of being reversed.

One recalls Zbigniew Brzezinski's argument that from a foreign policy perspective Europe may no longer be the center of international politics and power;[8] and, judging from the new ideas in the field, it may no longer be the center of our comparative politics models and the more exciting intellectual constructs either. Rather, it is from the study of the developing nations that most of the best new ideas in comparative politics in the last thirty years have come. After three decades of channeling some of our ablest students into Third World, development, and area studies, some of the area-study professional associations—such as the Latin American Studies Association—are several times larger in terms of membership and perhaps more stimulating of new and interesting ideas than their original parent organizations centered in Europe.

Keeping in mind the Eurocentric history and bias of traditional comparative politics (discussed more extensively in the following pages), one cannot help but be intrigued by the fact that concepts and theory developed in areas previously considered to be at the margins of the field have by now been applied and adopted in studying Western Europe and even the United States. We now apply the concepts of center-periphery relations, dependency, and others to Western Europe just as we would to various developing regions. Conceptually at least, the Third World "periphery" is now to a considerable degree capturing the "core," in that the rivulets of theory generated initially for the study of developing areas are now becoming part of the mainstream, and those who study Western Europe or the United States are beginning to learn from the concepts generated in Africa or Latin America instead of those "less-developed" areas always having to learn from the Western or First World example.

4. A reexamination of the terms "tradition," "modernity," and "development," and their implications. Much of the general literature in comparative politics, especially the development literature, was based heavily on the past experience of Western Europe and the United States and is therefore, many feel, biased, ethnocentric, and to a considerable degree irrelevant to the contemporary experiences of the developing nations.[9] The argument has been forcefully advanced that the conditions of the developing nations today are fundamentally different from those of Western Europe or the United States in the nineteenth century, when their great developmental leaps forward took place. Furthermore, the processes of change and even the institutions of the developing world are so much at variance with those of the developed that the former cannot be expected to and will not repeat the latter's earlier experience. But if this argument is valid and if the models based on the Western European or U.S. developmental experiences are only of limited utility, then we need to reexamine the precise meaning of those key terms that are often thrown around so glibly, such as "tradition," "modernization," and "development."

The question has recently been raised, for instance, as to whether we should now study indigenous and often non-Western institutions (such as India's caste associations, African tribalism, or Latin American organicism and corporatism) not as merely "traditional" and hence ephemeral institutions bound to disappear or be consigned to the dustbins of history as modernization proceeds. Instead, should not these Third World institutions be studied as potentially, or perhaps actually, viable, functional institutions in their own right? For we have begun to discover that rather than being superseded or overwhelmed as development goes forward, such traditional institutions as those noted have proved remarkably durable. They have adjusted to change instead of being cast off by it. Moreover, some of these institutions that we call "traditional" have themselves become instruments of certain kinds of modernization. They may provide an indigenous form of transition from traditionalism to modernity, an alternative to Western-style development rather than just a pale imitation of it.[10]

What does one make of these arguments, increasingly set forth by Third World leaders and intellectuals, for an indigenous as distinct from a Western model (or models) of development? How do they force us to reexamine certain basic assumptions concerning the universality of our social science paradigms? What is in fact universal and what particular in the European experience? To what degree can traditional and indigenous institutions adapt, shape, and condition the process of modernization without being submerged by it? Are such indigenous Third World institutions viable and functional? These are the questions that the Seminar sought to address and that comparative politics in the future must also answer.

5. Comparative politics as a reflection of changing world and international conditions. The decline in attractiveness and the receptivity accorded the Western developmental model in much of the Third World and the corresponding assertiveness of indigenous and nationalistic ones likely reflects in part a shift in power relations and realities in the world. It reflects, among other things, a certain diminution in admiration for the United States and things American, including the U.S. developmental model, during the 1970s and perhaps to the present; it reflects also the changed international configuration of recent years as compared with earlier times when the United States was overwhelmingly dominant in the world. The United States and Western Europe are no longer seen as the only or necessarily dominant group of nations. To an extent, dominant models in comparative politics reflect larger models of dominance; and with the perceived decline recently of Western hegemony in the political, economic, and military spheres, other nations and models of change (not necessarily Western) are gaining new prominence in the social sciences and in development studies as well.

Hence, we ask: To what degree are the models we use as scholars ethically, culturally, and politically neutral; to what extent do they mirror our own national or bloc prestige, power, and sense of superiority; was the earlier dominance of the development literature, largely written by Americans, as well as its earlier acceptance by many in the Third World, also a reflection of U.S. dominance as a nation—a product of both some degree of condescension toward the Third World and, as many spokespersons in the Third World itself now argue, a form of cultural imperialism? Is this now in the process of being changed or reversed as we have begun to talk of Third World models of development; and if so, how and to what extent? In short, do the models used by social scientists sometimes follow the flag overseas, just as at times the flag has sometimes followed the dollar?

6. What about the more recent alternative interpretations in comparative politics that in some quarters have been elevated almost to the level of new orthodoxies? One thinks, for example, of the receptivity afforded Immanuel Wallerstein's recent writings concerning capitalist expansion into a "world system" and its effect on many peripheral regions,[11] and of the popularity of the dependency approach. In some research institutes and among some faculty writing on social change in the Third World, Marxism has replaced developmentalism as *the* cognitive map from which virtually all interpretations follow. Among other scholars, new forms of determinism flourish. The comments offered are not meant to disparage these approaches but only to issue a preliminary caution against the elevation of often insightful and useful but still partial explanations into complete, all-encompassing ones. In this volume, then, we will be exploring both the contributions as well as the limitations of these new approaches, the biases and assumptions that undergird them, whether they are antithetical to the older approaches or reconcilable with them, and hence whether pluralism, pragmatism, and eclecticism still reign in the field or have been submerged beneath the new orthodoxies.

Moving from these large and philosophical issues to somewhat more concrete questions, and from the past in comparative politics to the present and future, the faculty seminar whose meetings served as the initial base for this book probed a series of related issues and set forth an agenda of problems with which we then wrestled:

1. Is there still a role for "grand theory" in comparative politics, for the universally applicable synthesizing volumes such as those written in the 1960s, or is the field now too diverse, too divided, and our confidence in fashioning a single model that fits all nations too shaken for that to be possible? Who might produce such a volume and what might its main synthesizing principle be? Or must we now concentrate on theory building at somewhat lower and more modest levels?

2. In the absence of very much acceptable "grand theory" at present, what are the implications of theory developing at middle-range and culture-area levels? Must we now be content with a more particular set of theoretical constructs for each subsection of the field, or can these lower-level theories be linked together at some point in a larger construct? Could this serve as the basis for a new, reformulated grand theory, or should we be content with theory development at less grandiose levels?

3. Given the biases and questionable assumptions of many of the earlier approaches, is a new general and nonethnocentric comparative politics of development still possible or must that goal be abandoned altogether? Shall we now have instead a Latin American social science of development, an Islamic social science of development, a sub-Saharan African social science

of development, a Confucian and a Hindu social science of development? What are the implications for both development and the social sciences of *that* kind of devolution and fragmentation?

4. What of the Marxist and class-based interpretations? Will they replace traditional political analysis or relegate political explanations to the status of "dependent variables?" Or are the two still reconcilable in terms of the recent focus on state-society relations, international political economy, or comparative public policy; and how might such new balances and combinations be fashioned? A third possibility is that Marxist explanations will have been so discredited by the manifest economic and political failures of a variety of Marxist-Leninist regimes (the Soviet Union, China, Eastern Europe, Afghanistan, Ethiopia, Angola, Mozambique, Cuba, Nicaragua) that the Marxist models will go into recession.

5. Is it still possible to combine a larger, global comparative politics with some of the more particular and narrower (middle-range) interpretations discussed above? What kinds of blends and fusions might be possible? Can theory building occur at several levels at once and then be fused into a more general approach, or are we now in a period when the more particularistic perspectives will supplant the more general but perhaps inevitably Western-biased views? What implications does such a redirection of emphasis on comparative politics carry both for the field and for U.S. policy toward the developing nations?

Obviously this is just a beginning, a preliminary listing of only some of the provocative questions and issues presently facing the comparative politics field that we discussed in our Seminar and that constitute the fundamental issues of this book. The questions serve to point up the simmering ferment in the field; to indicate some of the underlying reasons for the field's rise, decline, and then renewal; to suggest some of the major controversies and concepts that have undermined the field's earlier consensus; and to indicate the debates in the field and the new directions that it is presently exploring.

PAST AND PRESENT IN COMPARATIVE POLITICS: THE SEA CHANGES

Comparative politics has had a long and distinguished history as a field in political science. Here we provide a brief overview of the field and of its major shifts in direction, so as to put the current controversies into better perspective.

Aristotle was among the most eminent comparativists, with his informed study and discussion of the distinctive constitutional and political types to be found among the Greek city-states and his analysis of the socioeconomic and political-cultural conditions shaping, undergirding, and determining those forms. Plato and Cicero also used a comparative approach, as did Niccoló Machiavelli in his consideration of the comparative elements of power and politics in the Italian principalities and elsewhere. Thomas Hobbes, Jean Bodin, and Montesquieu could all be considered comparativists, and

Karl Marx drew upon comparative data derived in part from his studies as well as his living experiences in Germany, France, and England.

Some of the best early treatments of the United States, those by Alexis de Tocqueville[12] and Lord James Bryce,[13] were good precisely because these authors enriched their understanding of America by drawing upon comparative information derived from their European backgrounds. Examining this rich intellectual legacy, one would be tempted to say that political science has always been most illuminating as a discipline when it employed a comparative approach, that the foremost thinkers in the history of political philosophy have rather consistently been students simultaneously of comparative politics, and that all fields of the discipline, including American politics, have been greatly enriched when they have employed a comparative perspective.

However, as political science developed by the end of the nineteenth century as a distinct academic discipline within the social sciences—at least in the United States[14]—comparative politics emerged as only one, relatively minor field within the discipline. The reasons for this are complex and go to the heart of the American experience, to the deeply held belief that the United States is different from and superior to European and all other nations, the widespread conviction at the popular level that the United States had little to learn from the rest of the world, the near-universal belief of Americans in the superiority of their institutions and their attitude that the rest of the world must learn from the United States and never the other way around. Hence political science as it developed as a discipline in the United States was predominantly the study of American politics, for that is where the overwhelming emphasis and interest lay. Comparative politics was traditionally accorded one position—if that—in most major faculties and was sometimes considered an "exotic" field controlled by "old-fashioned" Europeans who had little to teach the numerically far stronger Americanists in the discipline. Those who studied and wrote about comparative politics were generally believed to have little to offer intellectually to other areas of the discipline.

Comparative politics in these early (pre–World War II) days concentrated on only a handful of countries in Western Europe (Britain, France, and Germany; eventually the Soviet Union was also included), and the chief teachers and scholars in the field were themselves often of European background. This served many times to isolate them further from the dominant Americanists in political science. Moreover, because in Europe political science had not yet emerged as a separate discipline but was predominantly a branch of law, comparative politics, too, had a more formalistic and legalistic orientation. It concentrated on the formal-legal aspects of politics, the constitutional precepts, the juridical rules, and the duly constituted institutions of government, as contrasted with the changing focus of U.S. political science, which came to concentrate more on informal political activities, interest groups, political parties, public opinion, decisionmaking, and the like. When European comparativists like Carl Friedrich or Karl

Loewenstein, who had been trained in law but also analyzed social and political forces, published their early studies in Europe, they were criticized by their legalistic colleagues as being "too sociological"; but when they later emigrated to the United States, their English-language books[15] were criticized by U.S. political scientists as being "too legalistic."

World War II had a profound effect on the field of comparative politics, a subject that has yet to be adequately studied. First, the war broke down U.S. isolationism once and for all, brought the United States fully and permanently into the world arena really for the first time, and made Americans aware of the need to study and understand foreign nations—allies and client states as well as those perceived as constituting threats. Second, the war and the genocidal policies pursued by the Nazis precipitated a new wave of European immigration, bringing to the United States thousands of intellectuals, artists, and opinion leaders, many with highly specialized knowledge of the European political systems and European modes of analysis—for example, German political sociology. The insights offered by these refugee scholars greatly enriched comparative politics, adding particularly to our knowledge of Europe and the totalitarian phenomenon.[16]

The war and the Nazi atrocities constituted a searing and horrible experience never to be forgotten. Among the first generation of leading comparativists in the postwar period—Friedrich, Loewenstein, Franz Neumann,[17] Hannah Arendt,[18] Herman Finer,[19] and many others—World War II had a profound ethical and moral effect on their writings, particularly in their efforts to dissect the Nazi system and to analyze the root causes of fascism. As some of these scholars began to study totalitarianism comparatively, encompassing both the Nazi system and Stalin's Soviet Union, it caused a tremendous controversy among the American Left, some of whom still viewed Stalin as a "progressive." In the aftermath of World War II, therefore, the comparative categories that scholars used became quite controversial in some intellectual circles, with implications also for U.S. foreign policy. In addition, comparative politics was concerned not just with the dispassionate analysis of distinct political systems; it was also justifiably infused with a profound moral and ethical sense conditioned by both the horrors of the Nazi period and the bloody excesses of Stalinist modernization.

World War II, the Nazi experience, and Stalinism continued to have a major impact on a second generation of post–World War II comparativists, those who rose to prominence in the 1950s and early 1960s and who were often instrumental in formulating the new theories regarding the developing nations. The motivations and underlying influences were of course complex; no single explanation is sufficient to account for the directions that comparative politics took during this period. The motives included excitement at the phenomenon of the new nations, a desire to see them succeed, the wish to extend the field outward from Europe to encompass these new areas, the hope that Third World development could be harmonized with U.S. foreign policy, and the sheer joy of working in new research terrains. There can be no doubt that, in part, comparative politics' new focus on the developing nations was also grounded in a strong ethical and moral sense. It is probably no coincidence that the modern nation—the model toward which the comparativists hoped the emerging nations would also develop— was pictured as moderate, socially just, middle-of-the-road, pluralist, and democratic. In short, it looked like a somewhat idealized version of ourselves or of what we wanted our own society to look like. In the literature on development, furthermore, more radical solutions that might produce either new Marxist-Leninist regimes or fascist backlashes to them were eschewed, to be resisted both politically and intellectually. The editor of this book shares these values politically and personally and is sympathetic to the agenda for the Third World as set forth in much of the development literature. But it must be pointed out, and is probably impossible to entirely avoid in any social science undertaking, that this approach was not entirely value-free, that there was a subtle moral and political agenda attached to the study of the developing nations as well as a purely social scientific one.

The generation that rose to prominence in comparative politics in the 1950s and early 1960s had also been strongly influenced by the emerging Cold War context of the postwar period. Most of these scholars had been thoroughly disillusioned with revolutionary socialism by the purges and mass killings of Stalin, by the Nazi-Soviet pact of 1939, and by the brutal practice of totalitarian communism in the Soviet Union. They had also witnessed the Soviet military occupation of Eastern Europe at the end of World War II, the communist push for power in Italy and Greece, the Berlin blockade of 1948, the Chinese Revolution and the similar practice of totalitarianism there, and the communist North Korean aggression of the early 1950s. The growing Cold War was considered almost universally, even after the efforts of later revisionists, to have been instigated by the Soviet Union. Soviet totalitarianism was thus to be resisted, as was totalitarianism's fascist form; it is indicative of the temper of the times that in W. W. Rostow's enormously influential book, *The Stages of Economic Growth: A Non-Communist Manifesto* (1960), communism was referred to, without blanching or further qualification, as a "disease of the transition."

The foremost students of comparative political development generally shared these Cold War sentiments, as did the American public. Those who would wish to comprehend the ethnocentric biases and the similarly anti-Marxist orientation of Almond and Coleman's path-breaking and enormously influential book, *The Politics of the Developing Areas* (1960, the same year Rostow's popular book was published), for example, must see it in the context of these times. Anyone seeking to understand the political and intellectual message of these volumes, as well as the corpus of work of the SSRC's Committee on Comparative Politics, which sponsored the Almond and Coleman book and whose views dominated the field for the next decade, should first read Almond's *The Appeals of Communism* (1954)[20] or Lucian Pye's *Guerrilla Communism in Malaya* (1956).[21] We don't wish to belabor this point but we do think it important to record that in this as well as, probably inevitably, other periods, comparative politics not only had a new scholarly approach but also sought to convey a political and foreign policy message.

Meanwhile, the field had been undergoing some other, quite fundamental transformations. The ferment began in 1952 with a meeting held at Northwestern University of the SSRC's Interuniversity Research Seminar on Comparative Politics, the forerunner of the Committee on Comparative Politics. Members of the seminar were Samuel Beer and Harry Eckstein of Harvard, Karl Deutsch of MIT, Kenneth Thompson and Richard Cox of Chicago, Robert Ward of Michigan, and George Blanksten and Roy Macridis of Northwestern, the latter serving both as host and chairman. Leading members of this group had begun to be strongly critical of the formal-legal focus of the older, European-centered comparative politics studies. These comparativists had been caught up in the broader revolution then sweeping political science, which called for an emphasis on interest group behavior, decisionmaking, and the more informal aspects of politics, rather than on the purely constitutional and formal features.[22] The early stirrings of what was called the "behavioral revolution" in political science were in the air, and the group at Northwestern wished to bring this to comparative politics.

The seminar group, or at least some of its members, was also interested in the incorporation of new sociological concepts into political science. Here the principal figure was Talcott Parsons of Harvard. Parsons had been the key person in translating and making known in the United States the work of the German sociologist Max Weber. Parsons expanded Weber's work and helped introduce into sociology and political science the approaches of structural-functionalism (which suggests that all societies must carry out similar functions even though the institutions by which they do so may be different). He also helped popularize the notion of an interrelated *system* of sociopolitical institutions and change, and introduced a series of "pattern variables" (ascription vs. achievement, particularism vs. universalism, tradition vs. modernity) that to some in the SSRC group seemed to offer a useful way to contrast developing and developed societies.[23]

The interuniversity group published a report in 1953 under the undramatic title of "Research in Comparative Politics."[24] But it was not until Roy Macridis dramatically and provocatively waved a flag in front of his comparative politics colleagues two years later[25] that the views of this group began to take hold. Macridis charged that in the past comparative politics had been parochial in focusing almost exclusively on Western Europe, that it had been descriptive rather than analytic, that it had been formalistic and legalistic rather than concentrating on more dynamic processes, and that it had been case-study oriented rather than genuinely comparative. The Macridis critique was strongly worded, posed the issue in stark either-or terms, and had an enormous impact on the discipline. His little monograph was probably read by every teacher and aspiring graduate student in comparative politics. The view that comparative politics should be non-parochial, nonformalistic, nonlegalistic, analytic, and genuinely comparative became the prevailing position among scholars.

In the meantime, Gabriel A. Almond had taken up the chairmanship of the newly organized Committee on Comparative Politics, and he soon emerged as the leading theoretician of political development. Almond had been wrestling with many of the same issues that Macridis and others had during these years, but from a somewhat different perspective. He was more strongly influenced, by way of a classic paper by F. X. Sutton,[26] by Parsons's structural-functionalism; he also employed Parsons's pattern variables and sought to incorporate them into an ideal-type model of the differences between developed and developing countries. That is, he viewed the emerging nations as characterized by ascription, particularism, and tradition and the developed ones as characterized by achievement, universalist criteria, and modernity. Most nations were of course strung out somewhere between these polar extremes; the dichotomies were used to categorize various nations on a continuum from traditional to modern.

Almond had also been strongly influenced, as he later wrote in an important autobiographical statement,[27] by the Chicago School of "scientific" politics and by the political activism of mentors such as Charles Merriam. In addition, Almond saw development not just as a phenomenon to be analyzed in a scientific way but also as a moral, ethical, and political "good" that he and his colleagues could bring to the developing nations. Like Macridis, he wanted to focus on the informal aspects of politics—political culture, interest group activity, and what came to be called "process variables." In a series of articles in the mid- and late 1950s Almond set forth these ideas forcefully, while also offering a new typology for the comparative politics field.[28] These writings served as a prelude to his later and very important edited volume, *The Politics of the Developing Areas.*

Other events during the late 1950s and 1960s, both intellectual and political, were instrumental in shaping the emerging consensus in the field. David Easton had begun to publish his general work on "the political system,"[29] which gave further impetus to the study of process, flow, and informal actors in politics; Easton also popularized an input-output systems analysis that was similarly incorporated into comparative politics. W. W. Rostow had just published *The Stages of Economic Growth,* which implied that all countries go through essentially the same processes of change on their route to development. He also suggested that with U.S. assistance the process of modernization that Western Europe and the United States had undergone could be replicated in the developing nations; showed that both communism and fascism were products of a certain stage of development that, with proper U.S. aid policies, could be avoided; and offered a hopeful and optimistic model in which the emerging nations would eventually look just like us—always a comforting view. During this period Karl Deutsch and others were doing parallel work on what they called "nation building."[30] Deutsch and Seymour Martin Lipset had both published influential articles,[31] and Lipset his provocative and insightful *Political Man* (1959), showing the close interrelations between social modernization and political democracy and suggesting (overly optimistically, as it turned out) that the two would march forward hand in hand. Their analyses implied that as countries achieved greater literacy, were more strongly mobilized, and acquired more radio and television sets, they would also become more democratic. Unfortunately, the wave of military coups that swept the developing nations later in the 1960s rendered this prediction wrong and helped discredit the Almond-Lipset-Rostow approach to studying development.

The actual political changes of the late 1950s and early 1960s were no less dramatic. First, by 1960 a large number of "new nations," chiefly in Africa and Asia, had burst onto the world's stage, not only significantly expanding the universe of comparative politics but also providing fresh and exciting new laboratories for the analysis of political development. Second, the election of John F. Kennedy and the reformist "Peace Corps mood of the time," as Almond referred to it,[32] seemed to provide vindication of the development literature's emphasis on democracy, pluralism, and social justice as the end points in the development process; it also appeared to give legitimacy to the idea that through foreign assistance programs, the United States could bring the benefits of its system, institutions, and accomplishments to the less-favored nations. As a result of the 1960 election and the presidency of Kennedy and, later, Lyndon Johnson, many of the scholars (and their friends and academic colleagues) who helped fashion the development literature and model—such as Rostow, who became head of the State Department's Office of Policy Planning—attained positions of considerable influence in the government that provided an unprecedented opportunity to put their scholarly analyses into practice.[33] Third, in Latin America, the Cuban Revolution was just occurring, revealing that the Western Hemisphere could no longer be taken for granted or be considered safe from communism, and stimulating—among other things—a flood of grants and fellowships designed to channel some of our most able young scholars into Latin American development studies, a field that had traditionally represented a lacuna in comparative politics.

For those attending graduate school during the early to mid-1960s, the development literature, particularly the Almond-Coleman volume on *The Politics of the Developing Areas*, was enormously attractive. Not only did this innovative book contain significant chapters by leading figures on the major developing regions, it also examined them using a common, global comparative framework. The common framework helped bolster the notion of a universal social science of development by which all countries could be analyzed. The literature also helped inspire U.S. scholars with the idea that by their analyses they could help bring development and democracy to the emerging nations. Development theory was therefore assumed to be not only "scientifically" sound, in accord with the prevailing systems theory and the Parsons-Almond categories, but it was thought to be ethically correct as well. It closely fitted the liberal internationalist thinking of most U.S. social scientists. It was this combination of apparent scientific validity, universal applicability, and moral correctness that helped make the developmentalist approach so appealing.

To be sure, not all scholars in comparative politics were attracted to the development literature. Among area specialists and those stressing the particular histories and traditions of distinct cultural regions or nations, there was often criticism of an approach that incorporated all the world's diverse societies into a single, all-encompassing framework.[34] In addition, many Europeanists (a dwindling number in the 1960s) and scholars involved primarily in quantitative comparative analysis were not greatly affected by the stress on political development, as their research concerns lay elsewhere.[35] Nor were Marxist scholars persuaded by the development literature, but in those days they were such a small minority within the profession that few gave serious attention to their criticism. Indeed, it had been in part to counter the Marxist appeal to the people in the emerging nations that the political development approach had been formulated in the first place.[36]

Among the first large wave of graduate students in comparative politics in the early to mid-1960s, however, the political development approach was enormously attractive. It was neat, coherent, and intellectually and emotionally satisfying. It provided an integrated and intellectually justifiable framework to fit the world's disparate nations and continents. It satisfied the liberal political requirement of providing a dynamic model oriented toward change, while at the same time giving students a vision of certainty and moral purpose. Armed with the categories and approach set forth in the development literature, a host of graduate students fanned out to the developing areas of Asia, Africa, and Latin America.

Their purpose was usually not just to find and study development but also to advance it. The latter quest was almost certain to be disappointing to the students who pursued it because the criteria used to measure development had been largely derived from the experiences of the United States and Western Europe, experiences that had only limited relevance in the Third World. Most students focused on the emerging newer groups in the developing nations, such as the middle class or the trade unions, since both those groups were assumed to be essential for the stable, moderate, pluralist, and progressive regimes that the Western (U.S. and Western European) experience had led scholars to expect and that their political preferences led them to want. Or they wrote theses on emerging peasant movements—again, with both scholarly *and* normative purposes in mind— and criticized those groups (usually referred to as "traditional," such as the armed forces, religious elements, or the landed elites) that seemed to stand in the way of this vision. The result was that we now have hundreds, perhaps thousands, of Ph.D. dissertations on peasant and labor movements but almost none on economic or political elites, who do, after all, still set the tone and govern in most developing nations. It was both the academic approach employed (developmentalism) and the political preferences of scholars that led to this imbalance and to the current situation in which we know a great deal about peasants and unions but very little about the people and institutions that actually run these countries. It is probably fair to conclude that our *wishes* for the developing nations got ahead of hardheaded analysis, and that part of the reason for this problem stemmed from the very developmentalist model that was being used.

In the same vein, literally thousands of theses were written on the new political parties in the developing nations, the single-party systems in Africa, for example, or the democratic left in Latin America, because parties were assumed to be *the* agencies of "interest aggregation" and "interest articulation," functions set forth in Almond's framework. Political parties were also assumed to be agencies of "modernization," leading to greater participation, pluralism, and democracy. Community development, agrarian reform, modern mass communications, and bureaucratic restructuring were the program areas that received a great deal of scholarly and official attention, in large part because it was thought that they would both advance development and bring about a desirable political system.[37]

We should clarify what exactly we are saying here. There may be nothing wrong in the developing nations with studying and having a political agenda in favor of agrarian reform, community development, expanded communications, bureaucratic reform, and a variety of other programs. Nor is there anything wrong with political parties, labor unions, or peasant associations. [Our purpose is not to criticize these programs or groups but only to show how those preferences led us to study (and often glorify out of proportion to reality) some groups at the expense of others and ignore some important groups and institutions because they were thought to be "traditional," and how these biases were *inherent* in the way that we conceived of development.]

The problem was that the political development literature presumed that these groups and policies both would and *ought* to be present in the emerging nations. If they were not, or these nations operated on a basis different from that analyzed in the literature, then it was often thought that it was the local developing nation, not the theory of development, that was wanting and problematic. Political and moral preferences and broader social science theorems that usually had but limited applicability in the non-Western world distorted scholarly analysis. Our desires and preferences with regard to the developing nations, as well as the continuing belief that the Western path of development was the only possible or acceptable one, impaired our assessments of the real situations in many nations.

An interesting study in the sociology of knowledge could be done based on the number of graduate students who went off to the developing nations during this period and came back to write Ph.D. dissertations pronouncing this or that institution or country "dysfunctional." At the time little thought was given to the fact they were often dysfunctional chiefly by the criteria established by the development literature, not necessarily in terms of the actual workings and indigenous dynamics of the countries studied. Because they had few and weak parties, trade unions, peasant associations, and similar organizations, these nations were frequently declared "dysfunctional." But such a designation ignored the fact that these political systems might nevertheless be quite functional in their own terms; they were only dysfunctional in terms of the particular institutional arrangements of the West, whose experiences and institutions had served as the model on which the developmentalist approach was based. By the Western criteria, the Third World was often deficient; but on the basis of their own or indigenous institutions, many developing nations were functioning quite well.

It would be a fascinating exercise to explore just how many graduate students returned disappointed from their fieldwork in Africa, Asia, or Latin America in the 1960s because, using the criteria set forth in the development literature, the countries they had studied didn't work or failed to measure up to the standards expected. An educated guess based on an informal survey of colleagues coming into the profession at that time would be that it was a very significant number. It should be reemphasized that at the time their Ph.D. dissertations were written, it was usually the countries studied and their lack of the developmental institutions expected and hoped for that were criticized and found disappointing, seldom the assumptions of the theoretical model used to study them.

There was, nonetheless, some important revisionist thinking already under way. Many who had earlier written dissertations or books using the development categories, after some time for reflection, had begun to question the assumptions of the model and its relevance for developing countries. So many countries or institutions had been pronounced "dysfunctional" that ultimately the issue began to be raised as to whether development theory itself was faulty. In 1968, in what was the last great integrating book on development, Harvard's Samuel P. Huntington weighed in with a telling critique of this literature and offered an alternative perspective. Huntington argued that social mobilization and modernization, rather than being supportive of or closely correlated with institutional development and democracy, in fact often served to undermine them in the emerging nations. Modernization led people to expect more from their political systems at a time when these lacked the institutional capacity to deliver in the way of effective programs, and the result was often decay and national breakdown. The Huntington critique of the modernization literature came to be generally accepted in the field, though his alternative proposal for an emphasis on orderly stable institutions such as armies or political parties as the key agencies in development was often criticized as an unexciting and politically conservative formulation.

By the late 1960s and early 1970s, criticism of the dominant developmentalist paradigm in comparative politics was widespread. The challenges were two: at the intellectual level and at the societal-political level.

Intellectually, the developmentalist perspective was criticized as being biased, ethnocentric, and considerably less universal in its applicability than its early advocates claimed.[38] The structural-functional approach was now subjected to the same searching criticism it had received some years earlier in anthropology, from which structural-functionalism in comparative politics had been derived. The approach was attacked as being vague, imprecise, lacking in theoretical sophistication, and bearing too close a resemblance to an idealized conception of the U.S. political system.[39] The developmentalist approach was accused by critics of ignoring the phenomena of class and class conflict, the influence of international market and political economy forces, and international dependency.[40] The Cold War origins and overtones of the developmental approach came under strong attack, and developmentalism was further criticized as perpetuating myths and stereotypes about developing nations that were downright destructive of cherished traditional institutions within these societies. The developmentalist model was associated with the dominant liberalism of the U.S. academic profession, which made it subject to attack by both the left and the right.[41]

These criticisms at the intellectual level were closely related to events occurring in the world and in U.S. society at the time. These included the Vietnam War and the mounting opposition to it, the student upheavals of the late 1960s and the general mood of rebelliousness, Nixon and Watergate, and the widespread questioning of all institutions and forms of authority. As Sidney Verba notes sardonically in the following chapter, at a time when all established verities were under attack—even motherhood and the family farm—it should not be too surprising that the dominant intellectual models in comparative politics were also questioned and criticized. This was especially the case as it was revealed that some of those responsible for articulating the developmentalist perspective were also among the government policy advisers who were helping or had helped to design and carry out what were now widely perceived to be ill-advised U.S. foreign policies with regard to the Third World and especially Vietnam.

It is not our purpose here to assess and determine once and for all the validity of the developmentalist approach or the arguments of its critics. Although many of the criticisms leveled were valid, they were also, in the editor's view, considerably overstated. Verba similarly notes in his chapter that the developmentalist literature was not as wrong and misguided as it is often pictured by critics, nor were its chief theoreticians unaware of the limitations of their approach or the utility of employing others. In fact, many of the early developmentalist scholars themselves had not always been happy with the particular approach of Almond; Almond, too, had continued to revise his views; and the developmentalist approach itself was always more varied and pluralistic than most of the blanket criticisms were willing to admit. As often occurs in academic disputes, the weaknesses of the developmentalist approach have been frequently and often gleefully pointed out, while its major positive contributions (the systematic approach, the focus on social change and political dynamics, the emphasis on informal actors and processes of politics, the attention now given to the developing nations and the efforts to study them comparatively) have been generally neglected. A balanced assessment of both the contributions and the limitations of the developmentalist literature and body of theory has yet to be written, although in Chapter 11 an updating and reconsideration of political development is presented.

By the 1970s it was apparent that the developmentalist perspective was no longer the only or even the dominant approach in comparative politics.

A variety of alternative approaches began to emerge in the late 1960s and early 1970s, often in response to the failures of or dissatisfactions that scholars had with developmentalism. At the same time some other approaches—Marxism and a focus on the state—were resurrected from earlier literature and given new emphasis. Initially, two main alternatives to developmentalism were offered that gained considerable influence within the field. One was the focus on corporatism and the corporate organization of society and politics both in the developing nations[42] and in the developed ones.[43] The corporatist approach is explained and its history and different schools of thought explored in a full chapter (Chapter 4) later in this book. The second new approach was a variant of Marxism, given new life by the seeming failure of the liberal-developmentalist approach and applied to the developing world in a form called "dependency theory." The dependency approach also receives chapter-length attention (Chapter 6) in this volume.[44]

These new approaches were not necessarily incompatible with one another or with the developmentalist perspective, although the often harsh disputes among these three schools of thought made it seem as if they were. Much depends on the precise meaning of the terms used and how strictly one is willing to assert the absolute correctness of one's own approach to the exclusion of all others. For example, the editor of this book was one of those who forcefully set forth the corporatist approach, probably overstating the case in order to make his point more emphatically and strongly criticizing the other main approaches in the process.[45]

But the intention was never to claim a monopoly on veracity or propose a new single-cause explanation to the exclusion of all others. Rather, the intention, sometimes drowned out in the heated debate that ensued, was to offer the corporatist approach as a necessary (and often neglected) but not a sufficient explanation, useful in enlightening some important research areas (labor relations, social policy, the relations of the state with various societal or "corporate" actors) that had not been adequately treated by the other approaches; but it was not intended as a substitute for them. The corporatist approach could be used, for example, to complement both the developmentalist and the dependency perspectives.[46]

These need not be matters of intensely ideological disputes, as they often were in the social sciences, but rather matters of pragmatic choice. Where such combinations of approaches are useful, by all means let us combine them. After all, there is no one single model that by itself can capture the full range and incredible variety of social and political behavior in all the world's nations, so such eclecticism of approaches would seem to be forced upon us by the very complexity of the universe that comparative politics seeks to explain. We return to this theme in the Conclusion, suggesting other permutations and combinations as well as the need to build connecting bridges among the various "islands of theory" that presently represent the field of comparative politics.

Meanwhile, other comparative politics approaches were either coming to the fore or were being revived. Political scientists rediscovered the state (what we used to call the "government") as a major variable and became aware of its importance in determining political outcomes. The new (or renewed) emphasis on the state was in contrast to the early systems approach, which pictured the state as a "neutral referee," umpiring the interest group struggle but itself not much influencing it. There was now, additionally, a resurgent interest in the phenomenon of state-society relations.[47] Mathematical modeling of comparative political systems and the greater use of computers to study these differences also became prominent in the field.[48] The approach in political science called "public choice theory" had a more limited effect on comparative politics, but its influence was felt there as well.[49] In terms of areas, European studies also enjoyed a spurt after nearly twenty years of concentration by comparative politics on the developing areas; Asia also attracted more attention, whereas first Africa and then Latin America received less.

The new ways of looking at both Western Europe and the United States were also quite distinct from the earlier perspectives that had posited the United States and Western Europe as *the* models toward which the developing nations both aspire and inevitably develop. A sober appraisal of the United States' prospects as a nation led scholars to be somewhat more modest in asserting the universality of its particular developmental experience. At the same time such events as the Iranian Revolution, the persistence of caste in India and of tribe in Africa, and the nationalistic assertion of new forms of Rousseauean organic statism in Latin America led some to begin to appreciate the value, continuance, and even viability of many indigenous institutions and models in the Third World, institutions that social scientists had previously been inclined to consign to the ashcans of the "traditional."[50] Comparative public policy analysis also flourished as a new area of scholarly focus in comparative politics.[51]

Among the new approaches, "international political economy," or IPE, became one of the most prominent in the late 1970s and on through the 1980s.[52] IPE borrowed from development theory, from the dependency approach, from corporatism, from Marxism, and from the state-society perspective. It generally focused on the impact of international structural or market forces (terms of trade, changing markets, international finance and capital, multinational corporations) in determining political outcomes. It thus eschewed the political-cultural explanations that had been so prominent in the 1960s (and that have since staged a comeback). IPE had its own journal (*International Organization*), and the IPE approach was strongly present also in other major journals in the field (*World Politics, Comparative Politics, Comparative Political Studies, Studies in Comparative International Development, Journal of Developing Areas*). IPE is well represented in this book in Chapter 5.

All these new or renewed approaches have provided a diversity to the field never experienced before. Comparative politics has fragmented since the 1960s, reflecting the uncertainties and upheavals in U.S. and world society more generally since that decade. The early 1960s was an era of relative national unity and optimism that was also reflected in comparative politics, but the 1970s in both U.S. society and the field of comparative politics was a period of disunity and apprehension. Some scholars have lamented the passing of the earlier unity and the supplanting of the once dominant developmentalist paradigm; in contrast, the orientation in this book has been to see the emergence of innovative approaches as healthy and invigorating for the field, as ushering in a period of refreshing reexamination and rethinking for comparative politics.

We have already spoken of comparative politics' being in crisis during the 1970s and early 1980s, and indeed it was. But from the vantage point of the 1990s, the crisis seems much less severe than it had appeared earlier; in fact, during the 1980s comparative politics was vigorous, alive, dynamic, and undergoing a revival. What had happened? Why had the field revived? As usual, there was a relationship between comparative politics and trends in the society and politics more generally.

To begin, by the 1990s the claims of comparative politics to universality and "scientific" certainty were more modest than they had been earlier; at the same time the criticisms of the field seemed no longer so central or so devastating as they once had been; and between the muted claims and the less intense criticism the field began to revive. A second factor was the decline of some of the other, more radical approaches, undoubtedly stimulated by the many failures of the more radical states (both on the left and on the right), which made the classic approaches of comparative politics again seem quite reasonable. A third reason was the relatively civil atmosphere that prevailed in academia and on campuses during the 1980s, which made the earlier charges of "imperialism," "racism," and "culturism" leveled against comparative politics less intense—or at least less listened to.

Fourth, many developing nations had achieved considerable success after some three decades of developmental efforts, which also made the approaches used to study these developments seem more positive. It may be that the Reagan era of jaunty self-confidence also had something to do with comparative politics' revival. The Reagan period, while also leaving a legacy of immense problems, helped restore economic prosperity, restored America's faith in itself, and gave a stimulus to Western institutions, which emerged from the 1980s in far better shape than did either "Eastern" (communist) or Third World institutions. These trends led in turn to a revival of the essentially Western approaches by which comparative politics interprets different societies, and even to revived self-confidence in the United States' ability, as compared with the cultural relativism of the previous decade, to export U.S. institutions to other nations, as in both the human rights (Carter) and democracy (Reagan) agendas.

By the beginning of the 1990s, therefore, the field of comparative politics seemed healthy and dynamic. It had recovered from the malaise of the 1970s, which had affected not just comparative politics but U.S. and European institutions more generally. There were new ideas in the field, new approaches, and a host of new investigators and scholars exploring new terrains. Moreover, the field seemed to have come to grips with itself and was no longer paralyzed by the sheer diversity of approaches. Rather, such pluralism was increasingly viewed as invigorating. No longer did very many scholars lament the passing of the earlier unity or the lack of a single overarching theoretical framework for the field. Most students and scholars treated these issues pragmatically, working in their own vineyards, selecting eclectically from a variety of approaches, building up both theory and data, and in the meantime continuing to fashion linkages among the various branches of the field. To most of us, that is what a field of inquiry ought to be.

Although the overall field of comparative politics seems to have settled down, the various approaches to it are in considerable flux—again, not necessarily an unhealthy condition. Some approaches seem presently to be waning while others seem to be thriving. At the moment, the Marxian and the dependency schools seem to be in a period of decline, probably reflecting the deterioration and lack of viability of various Marxist regimes and the resurgence of the West. At the same time, the political culture and political development approaches are enjoying a comeback—although the ultimate outcome of these trends is still very much in doubt. Meanwhile, the state-society relations and the corporatist approaches seem to have become solidly incorporated within the field and the literature; and the political economy and the public policy approaches are still rising in importance. The idea of a nonethnocentric or indigenous model of development for various Third World areas seems on hold for the moment: Their own ways have not worked out very well as a framework for development, and yet they are often reluctant to accept Western institutions.

It is a lively, provocative debate and discussion. As authors, we have tried to capture the diversity, the freshness, and the vigor of the comparative politics field in this book. Represented here are what we think of as some of the most dynamic and challenging "new directions" in comparative politics.

THE BOOK: A LOOK AHEAD

The following chapter, by Harvard University's Sidney Verba, provides a nice, careful, balanced overview of the comparative politics field—where we have been and where we are going. Verba's assessment, sometimes more positive and less critical than the views presented in this chapter, serves as a useful complement to this introductory statement.

The book then moves to a discussion of comparative politics' "New Directions." Joel Migdal, presently of the University of Washington but formerly a member of the Harvard Seminar, begins Chapter 3 with a reconsideration of the earlier political development literature but moves rapidly to a discussion of state-society relations, presenting a model of this new approach in the field and exploring its compatibility with a rejuvenated political development approach. In Chapter 4, Douglas A. Chalmers of Columbia University thoroughly dissects the corporatist perspective, exploring the different meanings and implications of that term and assessing the usefulness of the approach.

In the following substantive study, Peter Lange of Duke University and Hudson Meadwell of McGill University (Lange was part of the Harvard Seminar) use a sophisticated analysis to examine the gradual trend away from emphasis on political institutions in determining policy outcomes in Western Europe, and toward the greater importance of political economy variables. Taking a different tack, in Chapter 6 former Seminar member Tony Smith of Tufts University explores the new literature on dependency theory, recognizing its contributions while also being quite critical.

Chapter 7, by the editor, presents a strong criticism of the earlier development literature as biased and ethnocentric, and explores the newer and exciting indigenous theories of change as they have emerged in several Third World areas. In Chapter 8, Ronald H. Chilcote of the University of California at Riverside is also critical of the earlier paradigms, but his preferred orientation is toward a Marxist dependency approach.

Lawrence S. Graham's chapter combines comparative public policy analysis and comparative public administration. His stimulating contribution ranges across continents, encompassing socialist and capitalist systems, authoritarian and democratic regimes. It also provides a good example of how careful public policy research is done, from conceptualization to research design, to methodology and findings.

Chapter 10 is one of the new chapters. Written by John Martz, who is at Pennsylvania State University and is also editor of the important journal *Studies in Comparative International Development*, this chapter deals with bureaucratic-authoritarianism, transitions to democracy, and the role of political culture in explaining, or not explaining, these transitions. Chapter 11, by the editor, surveys the political development literature, explores the reasons for its rise, decline, and now revival, and at the same time offers a brief and provocative critique of the other main approaches in the field. This final chapter also discusses the task of building linkages among the several areas of theory presented by the book's contributors and considers whether some new and grand synthesis of these several approaches is still possible and desirable.

NOTES

1. Gabriel A. Almond and James S. Coleman, eds., *The Politics of the Developing Areas* (Princeton, NJ: Princeton University Press, 1960); David E. Apter, *The Politics of Modernization* (Chicago: University of Chicago Press, 1965); Karl Deutsch and William J. Foltz, eds., *Nation-Building* (New York: Aldine, 1963); Harry Eckstein and David E. Apter, eds., *Comparative Politics* (New York: Free Press, 1963); Seymour Martin Lipset, *Political Man: The Social Bases of Politics* (New York: Doubleday-Anchor, 1959); Lucian W. Pye, *Aspects of Political Development* (Boston: Little, Brown, 1966).

2. The causes, dynamics, and consequences of this trend away from European studies and toward studies of developing areas by at least two generations of comparativists merit further attention. To illustrate the dimensions of the change, by

1980 the Latin American Studies Association, the association of professional students of Latin America, had a membership of over 2,500; the comparable Council of European Studies had a membership of fewer than 500.

3. Peter Winch, *The Idea of a Social Science and Its Relation to Philosophy* (Atlantic Highlands, NJ: Humanities Press, 1970).

4. Social Science Research Council series, "Studies in Political Development": Almond and Coleman, *Politics of Developing Areas*; Lucian W. Pye, ed., *Communications and Political Development* (Princeton, NJ: Princeton University Press, 1963); Joseph LaPalombara, ed., *Bureaucracy and Political Development* (Princeton, NJ: Princeton University Press, 1963); Robert E. Ward and Dankwart A. Rustow, eds., *Political Modernization in Japan and Turkey* (Princeton, NJ: Princeton University Press, 1964); James S. Coleman, ed., *Education and Political Development* (Princeton, NJ: Princeton University Press, 1965); Lucian W. Pye and Sidney Verba, eds., *Political Culture and Political Development* (Princeton, NJ: Princeton University Press, 1965); Joseph LaPalombara and Myron Weiner, eds., *Political Parties and Political Development* (Princeton, NJ: Princeton University Press, 1966); Leonard Binder, James S. Coleman, Joseph LaPalombara, Lucian Pye, Sidney Verba, and Myron Weiner, eds., *Crisis and Sequences in Political Development* (Princeton, NJ: Princeton University Press, 1971); Charles Tilly, ed., *The Formation of the National States in Western Europe* (Princeton, NJ: Princeton University Press, 1975).

5. For a brief history of the Committee and a list of publications it helped generate, see Committee on Comparative Politics, *A Report on the Activities of the Committee, 1954–70* (New York: SSRC, 1971), mimeo.

6. Samuel P. Huntington, *Political Order in Changing Societies* (New Haven, CT: Yale University Press, 1968).

7. In addition to the volumes cited in notes 1, 4, and 6 above, see W. W. Rostow, *The Stages of Economic Growth* (New York: Cambridge University Press, 1960); C. E. Black, *The Dynamics of Modernization: A Study in Comparative History* (New York: Harper & Row, 1968); Kenneth Organski, *The Stages of Political Development* (New York: Alfred A. Knopf, 1965); and Myron Weiner, ed., *Modernization: The Dynamics of Growth* (New York: Basic Books, 1966).

8. Zbigniew Brzezinski, *Between Two Ages: America's Role in the Technetronic Era* (New York: Penguin Books, 1976).

9. Reinhard Bendix, "Tradition and Modernity Reconsidered," *Comparative Studies in Society and History* 9 (April 1967):292–346; Howard J. Wiarda, "The Ethnocentrism of the Social Sciences: Implications for Research and Policy," *Review of Politics* 43 (April 1981):163–97; and Chapter 7 in this book, by Howard J. Wiarda.

10. A. H. Somjee, *Parallels and Actuals of Political Development* (London: Macmillan, 1986); Howard J. Wiarda, *Ethnocentrism in Foreign Policy: Can We Understand the Third World?* (Washington, DC: American Enterprise Institute for Public Policy Research, 1985).

11. Immanuel Wallerstein, *The Modern World System: Capitalist Agriculture and the Origins of the European World Economy in the 16th Century* (New York: Academic Press, 1974); also by Wallerstein, *The Modern World System I* and *The Modern World System II: Mercantilism and the Consolidation of the European World-Economy, 1600–1750* (New York: Academic Press, 1980).

12. Alexis de Tocqueville, *Democracy in America*, 2 vols., ed. Bradley Phillips (New York: Alfred A. Knopf, 1944).

13. Lord James Bryce, *The American Commonwealth*, 2 vols. (Folcroft: Folcroft Library Editions, 1978 Reprint of 1891 ed.).

14. Political science in Europe was never so strictly separated from law, sociology, and economics as it came to be in the United States. This difference is related to

the lingering U.S. idea that politics can be considered autonomously from social, class, and other variables.

15. Carl J. Friedrich, *Constitutional Government and Democracy* (Boston: Ginn, 1941); Karl Loewenstein, *Political Power and the Governmental Process* (Chicago: University of Chicago Press, 1957).

16. H. Stuart Hughes, *The Sea Change: The Migration of Social Thought, 1930–65* (New York: McGraw-Hill, 1977); Walter Metzger et al., *The Cultural Migration: The European Scholar in America* (New York: Arno Press, 1977).

17. Franz Neumann, *Behemoth: The Structure and Practice of National Socialism* (New York: Oxford University Press, 1944).

18. Hannah Arendt, *The Origins of Totalitarianism* (New York: Harcourt, Brace, Jovanovich, 1951).

19. Herman Finer, *The Theory and Practice of Modern Government* (New York: Holt, 1949).

20. Gabriel A. Almond, *The Appeals of Communism* (Princeton, NJ: Princeton University Press, 1954).

21. Lucian W. Pye, *Guerrilla Communism in Malaya: Its Social and Political Meaning* (Princeton, NJ: Princeton University Press, 1956).

22. For example, David B. Truman, *The Governmental Process: Political Interests and Public Opinion* (New York: Alfred A. Knopf, 1951).

23. Talcott Parsons, *The Social System* (Glencoe, IL: Free Press, 1951); Talcott Parsons and Edward A. Shils, eds., *Toward A General Theory of Action* (Cambridge, MA: Harvard University Press, 1951).

24. Social Science Research Council, Interuniversity Research Seminar on Comparative Politics, "Research in Comparative Politics," *American Political Science Review* 47 (September 1953):641–765.

25. Roy C. Macridis, *The Study of Comparative Government* (New York: Random House, 1955).

26. F. X. Sutton, "Social Theory and Comparative Politics," prepared for the SSRC/CCP in 1955 and published in Harry Eckstein and David E. Apter, eds., *Comparative Politics* (New York: Free Press, 1963), pp. 67–81.

27. Gabriel A. Almond, *Political Development: Essays in Heuristic Theory* (Boston: Little, Brown, 1970), Introduction.

28. Gabriel A. Almond, "Comparative Political Systems," *Journal of Politics* 18 (August 1956):391–409; and "A Comparative Study of Interest Groups and the Political Process," *American Political Science Review* 52 (March 1958):270–82. See also Almond's comments in Henry W. Ehrmann, ed., *Interest Groups on Four Continents* (Pittsburgh: University of Pittsburgh Press, 1958).

29. David Easton, *The Political System: An Inquiry into the State of Political Science* (New York: Alfred A. Knopf, 1953) and "An Approach to the Study of Political Systems," *World Politics* 9 (April 1957):383–400.

30. Karl W. Deutsch, *The Nerves of Government: Models of Political Communications and Control* (London: Free Press, 1963); Deutsch and Foltz, *Nation-Building*.

31. Seymour Martin Lipset, "Some Social Requisites of Democracy: Economic Development and Political Legitimacy," *American Political Science Review* 53 (March 1959):69–105; Karl W. Deutsch, "Social Mobilization and Political Development," *American Political Science Review* 55 (September 1961):493–514.

32. Almond, *Political Development*, Introduction.

33. Robert Packenham, *Liberal America and the Third World: Political Development Ideas in Foreign Aid and Social Science* (Princeton, NJ: Princeton University Press, 1973).

34. The author recalls one of his mentors, Harry Kantor, objecting strongly to George Blanksten's efforts to put Latin America into the sometimes ill-fitting categories of the general theoretical approach in his contribution to *The Politics of the Developing Areas*, and adding it only reluctantly to our graduate seminar reading list. Other prominent Latin Americanists of the period, including Robert Alexander, Lewis Hanke, Robert Potash, Richard Morse, Kalman Silvert, and Arthur Whitaker, were similarly skeptical of the "developmentalist" framework.

35. This point was raised by Douglas Hibbs in our Harvard Seminar discussions.

36. The point is argued from a strong ideological perspective in Ronald H. Chilcote, *Theories of Comparative Politics: The Search for a Paradigm* (Boulder, CO: Westview Press, 1981). The point was freely acknowledged in our Seminar by several of the original members of the SSRC Committee on Comparative Politics.

37. There is room for a serious study of these changing emphases in development studies, and for studies of the types of institutions examined during this period and of those institutions and processes that were ignored.

38. Bendix, "Tradition and Modernity"; Wiarda, "Ethnocentrism"; Lloyd I. Rudolph and Suzanne Rudolph, *The Modernity of Tradition* (Chicago: University of Chicago Press, 1967); Clifford Geertz, *Negara: The Theatre-State in Nineteenth Century Bali* (Princeton, NJ: Princeton University Press, 1980); S. N. Eisenstadt, *Post-Traditional Societies* (New York: Norton, 1974); Clement H. Dodd, "Political Development: The End of an Era," *Government and Opposition* 8 (Summer 1973):367–74.

39. R. S. Milne, "The Overdeveloped Study of Political Development," *Canadian Journal of Political Science* 5 (December 1972):560–68; Robert T. Holt and John E. Turner, "Crises and Sequences in Collective Theory Development," *American Political Science Review* 69 (September 1975):979–95; Philip Coulter, "Political Development and Political Theory: Methodological and Technological Problems in the Comparative Study of Political Development," *Polity* 5 (Winter 1972):233–42; Geoffrey K. Roberts, "Comparative Politics Today," *Government and Opposition* 7 (Winter 1972):38–55; Philip H. Melanson and Lauriston R. King, "Theory in Comparative Politics: A Critical Appraisal," *Comparative Political Studies* 4 (July 1971):205–31; Ignacy Sachs, "The Logic of Development," *International Social Science Journal* 24, no. 1 (1972):37–43.

40. Especially in Chilcote, *Theories of Comparative Politics*; also A. R. Dennon, "Political Science and Political Development," *Science and Society* 33 (Summer–Fall 1969):285–98.

41. Packenham, *Liberal America and the Third World*; and Mark Kesselman, "Order or Movement? The Literature of Political Development as Ideology," *World Politics* 26 (October 1973):139–54.

42. Howard J. Wiarda, "Toward a Framework for the Study of Political Change in the Iberic-Latin Tradition: The Corporative Model," *World Politics* 25 (January 1973):206–35; and Wiarda, *Corporatism and National Development in Latin America* (Boulder, CO: Westview Press, 1981).

43. Philippe C. Schmitter and Gerhard Lehmbruck, eds., *Trends Toward Corporatist Interest Intermediation* (Beverly Hills, CA: Sage, 1979).

44. Barrington Moore, Jr., *The Social Origins of Dictatorship and Democracy* (Boston: Beacon Press, 1966); Theda Skocpol, *States and Social Revolutions* (New York: Cambridge University Press, 1979); Fernando E. Cardoso and Enzo Foletto, *Dependency and Development in Latin America* (Berkeley: University of California Press, 1979). There are of course a variety of Marxist and of dependency approaches; and not all dependency writers are Marxists. See the essay by Tony Smith, Chapter 6 in this volume.

45. Wiarda, "Toward a Framework" and *Corporatism and National Development*.

46. John D. Martz and David J. Meyers, "Understanding Latin American Politics: Analytical Models and Intellectual Traditions," *Polity* 16 (Winter 1983):214–41.

47. Alfred Stepan, *The State and Society* (Princeton, NJ: Princeton University Press, 1978); and the special issue of *Daedalus* devoted to "The State" (Fall 1979).

48. For example, Hayward R. Alker et al., *Mathematical Approaches to Politics* (New York: Elsevier, 1973); Anthony Downs, *An Economic Theory of Democracy* (New York: Harper & Row, 1965).

49. Mancur Olson, *The Logic of Collective Action* (Cambridge, MA: Harvard University Press, 1965).

50. See the references cited in note 37 above.

51. For example, Arnold J. Heidenheimer et al., *Comparative Public Policy: Policies of Social Choice in Europe and America* (New York: St. Martin's Press, 1975).

52. Warren F. Ilchman and Norman T. Uphoff, *The Political Economy of Change* (Berkeley: University of California Press, 1969).

2

Comparative Politics: Where Have We Been, Where Are We Going?

SIDNEY VERBA

The world has changed a great deal in the last few years. The developments in the Soviet Union, Eastern Europe, East Asia, Latin America, and the Islamic Middle East have been nothing short of remarkable. Other areas seem not to have changed so significantly. All of these changes, as well as the continuities, carry immense implications for the field of comparative politics.

The purpose of the faculty seminar on comparative politics that was convoked at Harvard's Center for International Affairs—and of this book, which grew out of the seminar—was to consider the past, present, and future of comparative politics. Most of the individual seminar sessions dealt with specific aspects of the current state of the field, and the contributions collected in this book focus on some new directions in the comparative politics field. My task has been to deal with the field more generally, to assess what and how much has been accomplished in comparative politics in the last three decades, to evaluate where we in the field have been and where we are going.

The assignment is not particularly or necessarily congenial. It is generally considered a sign of maturity and self-confidence in a discipline or a field when one no longer has to ask, What is political science? or, more specifically, What is comparative politics? What has it accomplished? and Where is it going? These questions are almost too general and too vague to answer; moreover, they imply that the burden of proof is on the respondent to demonstrate that something has been accomplished and that the field is *worthwhile* by some moral or pragmatic measure.[1] Such exercises in demonstrating self-worth always leave one vaguely uncomfortable; it is in any case preferable for students of comparative politics to pursue the substance of their work and let the answers to these larger questions emerge from the results, from what students of comparative politics have produced.

Nevertheless, it is useful from time to time to raise some general questions about the nature of the discipline and its various subfields: What is it; where has it been; how is it changing; what is its shape likely to be in the future?[2] For one thing, the self-awareness that comes from pondering such questions may have a salutary impact on our work. We do need to know the assumptions and biases of past work in the field, to be apprised of current research work both empirical and theoretical, to be aware of both past accomplishments and future directions. Second, such self-conscious consideration of what we are about affects the nature of the links among practitioners of comparative politics and between that field and other fields. A common understanding of the nature of our enterprise should foster communication among scholars, a greater accumulation of knowledge, and the cumulative development of the discipline as a genuinely "scientific" enterprise.

Third, though as practitioners we can sometimes ignore the questions of the overarching philosophy and direction of our discipline—safely ensconced as we are in our own areas of research and specialization—it is difficult to educate students in political science and train future scholars without some conception of the shape of the field. The usual practice is for graduate students to infer the nature of the discipline, sometimes by mysterious and circuitous processes, from the specific examples of it they encounter during their student years. But that is often unsatisfying both to instructors in the field and to students struggling to get a handle on an often elusive and fragmented discipline. A little more explicit help from their teachers cannot be all bad.[3]

Finally, a more self-conscious consideration of the present, past, and future of comparative politics may be useful in dealing with the complex issue of the division of labor in the field. I refer here to the division of labor among the broad fields of political science—international relations, comparative politics, and so on—as well as to the division of labor within each of the fields. Most professionals are overwhelmed with the amount of material produced in the field of comparative politics. We find it hard to keep up with the literature in our own research areas of special interest, let alone in other areas or in the field as a whole. One reason for this difficulty is that in comparative politics it is difficult to know the "boundaries of relevance" within the literature: what we have to know and read about for the kind of research work and writing we wish to do. An exercise of this sort helps us delineate those boundaries and determine more precisely (though not absolutely) what our division of labor should be. Hence the utility of a general commentary on the "state of the art" in comparative politics as provided here.

COMPARATIVE POLITICS: THE STATE OF THE FIELD

One of the most significant changes in political science in the last three decades has been the growth of a comparative perspective in virtually all areas of the discipline. Issues and subject matters that were once treated in isolation are now commonly examined in the light of a comparative approach or comparative data. Indeed, to talk about comparative politics might be now to talk about virtually anything and everything. Politics is everywhere, so the argument runs, and all understanding requires comparison; therefore, everything is comparative politics. Even studies of the U.S. political system are now frequently carried out within a comparative framework, perhaps reflecting the decline of the U.S. sense of "exceptionalism" and the dawning sense that the United States is, more or less, like other nations— or at least comparable to them. Certainly all of empirical political science, to carry the argument one step further, could be thought of as comparative politics.

This discussion, however, will focus on comparative politics as the branch of political science concerned with comparing nations—an easy and convenient definition for our purposes here. In this light, comparative politics is basically a macro social science. If a particular project deals with micro phenomena such as the political behavior of individuals, we can still classify it as part of comparative politics as long as national variations are part of the explanatory scheme. Thus we are interested in that branch of political science that tries to generalize—using that term loosely—about nations or to generalize about subnational entities like bureaucracies, parties, armies, and interest groups in ways that use national variations as part of the explanation.

What, then, is the current state of the field of comparative politics? As one with a background in public opinion survey research, I decided to ask people what they thought: How does the field look to practitioners? My survey was not rigorous and would hardly stand up to the canons of scientific objectivity. It was an informal survey of my friends and colleagues in the comparative politics field, conducted in the corridors of the annual meeting of the American Political Science Association and other such settings.

The results were, nevertheless, stunning and the responses all but unanimous: The state of the discipline is rather like the state of the world— appalling. Almost universally, scholars and practitioners complained of the division, fragmentation, and atomization of the field. There are too many special interests, too many narrowly focused research concerns, no center of intellectual gravity. My respondents agreed that the field lacked clear direction, leadership, or a commonly held and agreed-upon set of theoretical underpinnings. The need was widely expressed for greater unity in the field and for new works of synthesis.

There was disappointment as well in what might be termed the "unfulfillment of past promises." The great social science programs and models of the past seem to have delivered fewer results than had been expected. We have been studying development for a long time but we are no longer confident of what it is or our ability to understand it. We have been studying democracy even longer but do not fully understand that either—let alone its relations with development. We have by now built up a considerable fund of verified or verifiable knowledge in comparative politics, but we are less certain than we once were as to the inevitability of causal relationships or of the universality of many of our major concepts. The general sense we have of recent social science programs and undertakings is rather similar to the belief that has grown about many governmental programs: that we cannot create a social science—if that is what comparative politics is—by throwing money at it.

Given the accomplishments in the field (discussed more fully below), one may well question why the discontent with it is so great. Some possible explanations are as follows:

1. *The Age.* This is a time of discontent with many aspects of life: moral, religious, political, economic, intellectual, familial. Why should we be surprised to see the general malaise spill over into comparative politics as well?

2. *My Age.* Perhaps it is simply that I, like many others who participated in the new comparative politics in the 1960s, have reached the midlife years, when we must face the unfulfillment of past promises and the possibility that things may begin to go downhill. Most of my respondents were about my age and may face the same prospects. Bitterness, disillusionment, or simply the recognition of one's own limits and the limits of one's profession may merely be part of the life-cycle, "passages" in comparative politics as in other parts of life's unfolding. Perhaps it is the negativism of a generation still holding to a set of concepts fashioned some three decades ago while a younger generation is clambering over our barricades.

3. *The Problems of Progress.* There is a third possible explanation: Things are in fact getting better and there has indeed been progress in the social sciences and in comparative politics in particular, but, like affluence, one never has enough of such progress, and progress brings new problems and frustrations.

The third answer is the one I think most accurately describes our present situation. Comparative politics is and has been disappointing to some, but it is disappointing in comparison to past aspirations and hopes, not disappointing in terms of its accomplishments or in comparison to where we were two and a half decades ago. Like the Great Society of Lyndon B. Johnson, recent social science and comparative politics developments have not created a new utopia or a major new plateau of understanding (though a strong case could probably be made for the latter), but they have certainly led to some real improvements. These changes and accomplishments should not be underestimated.

The situation of comparative politics today might perhaps best be contrasted with that of the mid-1950s. It was only in the late 1950s and early 1960s that many of the major works were written that formed the beginning of what we might term the *new* comparative politics. One thinks of such works as Daniel Lerner's *The Passing of Traditional Society*,[4] Gabriel Almond's and James Coleman's path-breaking volume on *The Politics of the Developing Areas*,[5] Seymour M. Lipset's *Political Man*,[6] David Apter's *The Gold Coast in Transition*,[7] Lucian Pye's *Guerrilla Communism in Malaya*,[8] or W. W. Rostow's *The Stages of Economic Growth*,[9] a book that, though written by an economic historian, had a major impact on comparative politics. The period immediately prior to the publication of these key studies, the mid-1950s, was also a time of confusion and questioning concerning the nature of comparative politics. The ferment was exemplified in some early works by the Committee on Comparative Politics,[10] by Roy Macridis's critical review of the field,[11] and by some early articles by Gabriel Almond.[12] These critiques suggested that comparative politics to that point had been in reality the study of foreign government—and concentrated exclusively in northern and western Europe at that. These studies were rarely comparative; they were descriptive rather than analytic; and they emphasized formal structures of government rather than the more informal ways in which these systems actually worked. There were some large, somewhat idiosyncratic syntheses, such as the works of Herman Finer,[13] Carl J. Friedrich,[14] and Karl Loewenstein.[15] But the norm was for studies of individual countries in a generally atheoretical context.

ACCOMPLISHMENTS IN THE FIELD

It is useful to remember where comparative politics was thirty years ago in order to appreciate better the changes that have occurred since then. The discussion that follows is but a partial list of the more significant of those changes.

The Scope of Comparative Politics

Comparative politics now encompasses not only those Western European nations that formed the center of attention in an earlier period but the full range of states and political institutions in all parts of the world. The major texts in the field were once limited to the "Big Four": Great Britain, France, Germany, and the Soviet Union. Now texts may cover southern European as well as Scandinavian and Benelux countries,[16] Eastern as well as Western Europe.[17] And in many texts it has become acceptable, even commonplace, to consider developing nations alongside industrialized ones, new nations as well as old.[18] This expansion has of course been fueled by the quantum expansion in the number of new nations since the 1950s and by their emergence as important actors upon the world stage.

The earlier focus on a limited number of countries appears to have had several justifications. First, it was considered especially important to understand the governmental systems of those countries designated as major powers. Second, they were the nations many Americans understood best because of their European roots. They are Western nations; there was already extensive literature about them; European languages were generally easier for Americans to learn. In the light of more recent approaches, it should also be emphasized that these were assumed to be the nations whose developmental models the newer nations would emulate. But to make comparative politics more universally applicable and more scientific required a broader search for uniformity and a wider number of cases. Expanding the scope of comparative politics was crucial to its integrity as an intellectual enterprise.

The scope and range of comparative politics also changed as the foci, emphases, and perspectives of scholars in the field altered, becoming less parochial and ethnocentric and more multifaceted and relativistic. No longer are polities evaluated solely in terms of the Anglo-American model, the English "mother of parliaments," the German bureaucracy, or French republicanism (or Bonapartism). No longer is the Soviet Union *the* paradigm case of twentieth century revolution; China, Yugoslavia, Cuba, and other nations may also be considered. Scholars now draw evidence and illustrations of comparable political events from a much broader range of countries. The British model of democracy has in part been replaced by the Dutch one[19]— which, upon closer examination, seems to work no better than the British version. An understanding of bureaucratic behavior is now as likely to come from South Asia[20] as from France or Germany. In the first wave of studies that looked at the developing nations, Western models and yardsticks were the measures used almost exclusively. Now, not only are scholars more inclined to take such non- or semi-Western countries on their own terms and in their own developmental context, but in recent years models derived from non-Western societies have been increasingly applied to Western ones.[21]

Greater Depth Within Individual Countries

The new comparative politics introduced a variety of new approaches and considered a host of new variables. More attention was paid to the societal input into political decisions, and the hybrid discipline of political sociology was born. More recently, students of comparative politics turned their attention to the economic constraints on political action, and the field of political economy has been reborn. Instead of studying only the formal institutions of government, scholars have turned their attention to more informal agencies of government, the attitudes and perceptions of mass and elite publics, and nongovernmental institutions such as interest groups and political parties. The simplistic notions of the old-fashioned national character studies have given way to more sophisticated and discriminating studies of comparative political culture; and students of comparative politics have begun to reexamine the political cultural constraints on development and public policy. In looking at such informal political groups as clans, cliques, castes, tribes, and extended families, we have helped stimulate the growth of still another hybrid, political anthropology.[22]

These are significant accomplishments, but there were also costs involved. One important cost of the focus on informal actors, for example, was a temporary diversion of interest from the comparative study of the state itself and its institutions. For reasons that are somewhat obscure in retrospect, the state was considered for a time to be a "black box" into which "inputs" (influences, pressures, attitudes) went and out of which authoritative decisions flowed, but which was itself mysteriously neutral as a major influence.[23] This tendency is currently being rectified, however, in the new emphasis on the role of the state in public policy, decisionmaking, and in the key arenas of state-society relations.

An Expansion of Methods

The new comparative politics developed in the 1960s incorporated a set of methods involving survey research, analyses of aggregate data, content analysis, systems analyses, and a number of other approaches. The growth of this type of research in the comparative politics field coincided with the behavioral revolution in political science more generally, and the two served to enrich each other. The development of comparative politics as a major subfield was also closely associated with the growth of systems theory in political science, and it helped focus attention on the interrelated aspects of the newer political systems being studied. These new methods and approaches led to a considerable enrichment of the data base and suggested a variety of new concepts and relationships.

One might well point to methodology as an area in which comparative politics has experienced some of its greatest gains. In contrasting earlier work that attempted quantitative comparisons across nations with much of the more recent work—with its grounding in econometrics and other quite sophisticated techniques—the differences are readily apparent.[24] Research in the past two decades has made many earlier efforts look crude, but it has also built on the important innovations that these earlier works introduced.

The methodology of comparative politics has become both more sophisticated and more flexible. More studies employ quantitative methods such as opinion surveys and aggregate analysis, and the use of time-series data has also increased. Comparative politics has developed a greater awareness of the usefulness of combining quantitative and nonquantitative materials. Students no longer feel obliged to replicate the particular and quite sophisticated techniques used in the study of the U.S. polity in foreign field situations where their utility is dubious. The battle over the relative value of broad functional studies and in-depth studies in particular cases has abated as more scholars recognize the usefulness of both.

An Interest in Generalization

For the first time, comparative politics has become genuinely comparative. Przeworski and Teune[25] aptly called this process "the elimination of proper names" in comparative politics; they recognized that generalizing across a set of social and political units requires general and comparative knowledge. The goal is not particular information about specific countries.

This debate is often thought of as a methodological one between the idiographic and the nomothetic modes of understanding, between the in-depth case study and the more general and comparative statistical study. But the difference goes deeper, to the issue of what constitutes the most desirable form of knowledge and understanding. Do we want specific information about and comprehension of particular places or generalizations about how politics works? The answer depends on the purpose to which the work is directed, for there is clearly room for both kinds of studies. Why apply a set of research categories appropriate for one cultural setting to another society that they fit at best uncomfortably? In general, our studies have surmounted these difficulties, and the growth in generalization and genuine comparison is undeniable.

Theoretical Richness

In the last thirty years comparative politics has become much richer theoretically. The early post–World War II work in comparative politics, as Macridis emphasized, was atheoretical,[26] and was not primarily concerned with developing comparative concepts and approaches. Since that time the field has changed considerably.

Much early work in the new comparative politics was linked to functionalism. The functionalist approach, derived from anthropology and sociology, especially from the work of Talcott Parsons, seemed particularly appropriate in the 1950s because it enabled scholars to examine the newly emergent nations in ways that traditional approaches, derived largely from Western Europe, did not. It is thus no accident that the functionalist approach was strongly represented in the work of editors Almond and Coleman and that of the many contributors to The Politics of the Developing Areas.[27]

Regarding the debate over the appropriateness of the functionalist approach, I would suggest merely that functionalism was never a comprehensive and closed theory but rather a loose set of guidelines. It was never as bad as its critics thought. Almond himself recognized this when he subtitled a volume of his early writings "Essays in Heuristic Theory."[28] This open-ended, tentative quality was functionalism's strength and its weakness.

In the 1970s and 1980s there has been a proliferation of approaches— to the point where both graduate students and some professional practitioners in the field have at times seen the diversity as anarchy. A number of alternative theoretical approaches—one in political economy adopted from macroeconomics[29] plus various versions of neo-Marxism[30]—have emerged. Wiarda and Schmitter have offered various updated models of corporatism.[31] In addition there are what we referred to in our seminar as "islands of theory" dealing with specific subject areas such as voting behavior, political participation, bureaucratic behavior, value change, the role of the state and state-society relations, and public policy analysis.

Comparative politics is not economics—at least not yet, despite some imperialist designs from that direction. Comparative politics has no central paradigm guiding the work of most practitioners, as economics does. This lack is clearly a weakness in terms of the desire for scientific rigor, agreed-upon concepts and understandings, and the cumulativeness of findings within the field. The absence of a single integrating model and body of assumptions is disappointing. Yet there is strength in this diversity as well;

it keeps the field open to new and often unorthodox ideas and to a variety of approaches. Diversity, even some confusion, is not entirely inappropriate given the complexity of political phenomena and the variety of nations and subject matters involved—to say nothing of the still limited state of knowledge in the field. The proliferation of different approaches is a sign of health; it indicates that the field has not become ossified. And I agree with Abraham Kaplan[32] that the choice of which approach or approaches to use should be a pragmatic rather than an ideological decision.

Refinement of Explanations

Another area that shows considerable improvement over earlier work is in the refinement of what we seek to explain. An intellectual field is usually defined by a problem—that is, something students wish to explain. Much of the early theorizing in comparative politics was much too general to explain anything. Functionalism, for instance, or the various typologies that sometimes passed for theory in the 1950s and 1960s, really *explained* nothing at all.

An overarching theory of comparative politics is much too general to work. It cannot possibly hold for all nations at all times and places, or for all political phenomena within these nations. Even when the phenomenon to be explained was specified, it was usually so general that very little was explained at all. It was often on the basis of such single—but vastly simplified—notions that theorists tried to explain political development or the interrelations between economic development and democracy. Such explanations were too big to allow for accurate and satisfactory empirical work. Recent work in the discipline has been far more precise.

The Logic of Comparative Inquiry

A greater self-consciousness has developed over the years about the logic of comparative inquiry. Earlier work in the new comparative politics provided a general framework for analyzing political systems, but there was little concern for a logic of comparison that would enable scholars to test out theories and hypotheses in cross-national contexts. These early works have since been joined by a second wave of work much more specifically concerned with problems of research design and methodology. Apart from the increase in methodological thinking already discussed, this applies to considerations of general research strategy, scope, approach, and logic.[33] In this area as in others, comparative politics has come a long way.

A SUMMING UP

My assessment may seem a rather Pollyannaish view of the state of comparative politics, but with all that has been accomplished, much also remains to be done. Even the positive comments offered above require a good deal of qualification. Despite the large number of new and innovative studies, there is too little work that leads to cumulative knowledge. This is one drawback of the bustling and variegated comparative politics field.

The problem, I believe, is not so much the diversity of work in the field. Such diversity is welcome. Nor is it that methods and even theories vary. In this complex world, the proliferation of new approaches and insights should be applauded. The difficulty is that the definition or articulation of the problem or research terrain to be explored differs so greatly from researcher to researcher and from school of research to school of research. If scholars were to approach the same problem—i.e., a phenomenon to be explained—with different methods or different theories, there would be a fruitful clash of alternative approaches. But when the questions asked differ so markedly, works tend to follow separate tracks, rather than presenting true alternatives for comparison.

The new approaches, perspectives, and accomplishments noted here may all be thought of as general trends and characteristics of comparative politics. They do not imply a single, specific program of research, and they leave a good deal of flexibility for change and growth. In this way they differ from some of the earlier works in the new comparative politics, which from the perspective of the 1980s often seem naive in their assertions of a single and all-encompassing approach to various issues and overambitious both theoretically and methodologically. This is to be expected in a newly developing and rapidly evolving field, but these early works may now appear more naive or unidimensional than in fact they were. Current complaints about these early and path-breaking works—that they presented a false dichotomy between tradition and modernity, that they expected development to produce an inevitable and unilinear march to democracy, that they neglected the role of state institutions, that they ignored international economics—do not always reflect the subtleties and qualifications of much of the work.

Another problem is the proper division of labor within the field. Without more effective problem definition, it is difficult for scholars to know where their interests begin and end and how they can delimit a field or subfield to screen out irrelevant issues. The expansion of comparative politics into political sociology and political economy compounds the division-of-labor problem.

In the absence of a comprehensive theory and more precise problem definition, comparative politics remains dependent upon knowledge in depth of the particular systems being studied. This poses a problem for the comparative researcher. Most studies of particular locales or particular cases do not add up to much in a scientific and comparative sense and are not germane to a coherent program of generalization. Yet more general works that deal with data across a large number of nations often seem to be superficial and inadequate in their treatment of individual nations or actors— or worse than inadequate, sometimes they are outright distorted. The researcher in comparative politics who attempts to deal with a number of political systems is inevitably at a disadvantage compared with the true specialist. Clearly a better blend and overlapping of theoretically interesting case studies and broader comparative ones is called for.

For the future, one can expect to see more of the same in the comparative politics field. It will remain fragmented and appear disorganized. One hears a great deal of talk about the need for some major breakthrough, a new, all-encompassing theory or paradigm. It seems unlikely, however, that a new Newton, Einstein, or Keynes of comparative politics waits on the horizon. There are potential candidates to achieve such a new synthesis: Among the most potent are economic modeling and the neo-Marxist theory of the state. My guess, nonetheless, is that the discipline will maintain its heterogeneity of styles and theories and that most of its practitioners will continue to view that as healthy.

NOTES

1. The need for such self-justification in a field or discipline would itself be a worthwhile subject for comparative inquiry.

2. I have earlier addressed some of these issues in "Some Dilemmas in Comparative Research," *World Politics* 20 (October 1967):111–127; and more recently in "On Revisiting the Civil Culture: A Personal Postscript," in Gabriel A. Almond and Sidney Verba, eds., *The Civic Culture Revisited* (Boston: Little, Brown, 1980), pp. 394–410.

3. See also Howard J. Wiarda's comments on this theme in Chapter 1.

4. Daniel Lerner, *The Passing of Traditional Society* (New York: Free Press, 1958).

5. Gabriel Almond and James Coleman, eds., *The Politics of the Developing Areas* (Princeton, NJ: Princeton University Press, 1960).

6. Seymour M. Lipset, *Political Man: Essays on the Sociology of Democracy* (Garden City, NY: Doubleday, 1959).

7. David Apter, *The Gold Coast in Transition* (Princeton, NJ: Princeton University Press, 1955).

8. Lucian Pye, *Guerrilla Communism in Malaya* (Princeton, NJ: Princeton University Press, 1956).

9. W. W. Rostow, *The Stages of Economic Growth* (Cambridge: Cambridge University Press, 1960).

10. See the report prepared by Roy Macridis and Roy Cox of the deliberations of the SSRC Interuniversity Research Seminar on Comparative Politics, "Research in Comparative Politics," *American Political Science Review* 47 (September 1953):641–675.

11. Roy Macridis, *The Study of Comparative Government* (New York: Random House, 1955).

12. Gabriel A. Almond et al., "A Suggested Research Strategy in Western European Government and Politics," *American Political Science Review* 49 (December 1955):1042–1049; Gabriel A. Almond, "Comparative Political Systems," *Journal of Politics* 18 (August 1956):391–409, and "A Comparative Study of Interest Groups and the Political Process," *American Political Science Review* 52 (March 1958):270–282.

13. Herman Finer, *The Theory and Practice of Modern Government* (London: Methuen, 1961).

14. Carl J. Friedrich, *Constitutional Government and Democracy* (Boston: Ginn, 1950).

15. Karl Loewenstein, *Political Power and the Governmental Process* (Chicago: University of Chicago Press, 1958).

16. Roy Macridis, ed., *Modern Political Systems: Europe* (Englewood Cliffs, NJ: Prentice-Hall, 1978).

17. H. Gordon Skillings, *Communism National and International: Eastern Europe After Stalin* (Toronto: University of Toronto Press, 1964); or Arnold J. Heidenheimer and D. P. Kommers, *Governments of Germany* (New York: Harper & Row, 1975).

18. Gabriel A. Almond et al., eds., *Comparative Politics Today: A World View* (Boston: Little, Brown, 1980); Karl W. Deutsch et al., *Comparative Government: Politics of Industrialized and Developing Nations* (Boston: Houghton Mifflin, 1981).

19. Arend Lijphart, "Typologies of Democratic Systems," *Comparative Political Studies* 1 (April 1968):3–44.

20. Fred W. Riggs, *Administration in Developing Countries* (Boston: Houghton Mifflin, 1964).

21. Howard J. Wiarda, "The Ethnocentrism of the Social Sciences: Implications for Theory and Research," *Review of Politics* 43 (April 1981):163–197, as well as Chapter 7 in this book. The literature on dependency, center-periphery relations, and corporatism are examples of themes developed in studies of Third World countries now applied to the West. For illustrative purposes see Howard J. Wiarda, "The Latin Americanization of the United States," *New Scholar* 7 (1979):51–85.

22. S. Lee Seaton and Henry J. M. Claessen, eds., *Political Anthropology: The State of the Art* (The Hague, Netherlands: Mouton, 1979).

23. This notion grew out of the influential writings of David Easton, *A Framework for Political Analysis* (Englewood Cliffs, NJ: Prentice-Hall, 1965).

24. For example, David R. Cameron, "The Expansion of the Public Economy: A Comparative Analysis," *American Political Science Review* 72 (December 1978):1243–1261; and Douglas A. Hibbs, Jr., "Political Parties and Macroeconomic Policy," *American Political Science Review* 71 (December 1977):1467–1487.

25. Adam Przeworski and Henry Teune, *The Logic of Comparative Social Inquiry* (New York: Wiley, 1970).

26. Macridis, *Study of Comparative Government*.

27. Almond and Coleman, *Politics of the Developing Areas*.

28. Gabriel A. Almond, *Political Development: Essays in Heuristic Theory* (Boston: Little, Brown, 1970).

29. See Cameron, "Expansion of the Public Economy"; and Hibbs, "Political Parties."

30. For example, Barrington Moore, *Social Origins of Dictatorship and Democracy: Lord and Peasant in the Making of the Modern World* (Boston: Beacon Press, 1966); Immanuel Wallerstein, *The Modern World System* (New York: Academic Press, 1976); Theda Skocpol, *States and Social Revolutions: A Comparative Analysis of France, Russia, and China* (Cambridge: Cambridge University Press, 1979).

31. Howard J. Wiarda, *Corporatism and National Development in Latin America* (Boulder, CO: Westview Press, 1981); Philippe C. Schmitter and Gerhard Lehmbruch, eds., *Trends Toward Corporatist Intermediation* (Beverly Hills, CA: Sage Publications, 1979).

32. Abraham Kaplan, "Systems Theory and Political Science," *Social Research* 35 (July 1968):30–47.

33. Przeworski and Teune, *Logic of Comparative Inquiry*; and Robert T. Holt and John E. Turner, eds., *The Methodology of Comparative Research* (New York: Free Press, 1970).

PART TWO

New Directions in Comparative Politics

3

A Model of
State-Society Relations

JOEL S. MIGDAL

INTRODUCTION: IMAGES OF THE
IMPACT OF STATE ON SOCIETY

The incredibly quick unraveling of empire in Asia and Africa following World War II suggested to many the hidden political strength of poor, subjugated peoples. Daring leadership, such as that of Mahandas Gandhi, Kwame Nkrumah, and Gamal Abdul Nasser, together with imaginative political organization, such as that found in India's Congress, Algeria's National Liberation Front (FLN), and the Vietnamese Communist party, could topple the rich and powerful. An imperial state could be reduced to a Gulliver among the Lilliputians. Even to Third World leaders who eluded fiery anticolonial struggles, events in distant India or Algeria lent confidence about the important role that centralized, mobilizing politics could play in their countries after independence.

Western imperial powers were not only the bêtes noires in the transition from colony to statehood; they were models to be emulated as well. The aims of the founders of new states were taken largely from already successful states and the dominant European nationalist ideologies of the nineteenth century.[1] New political leaders of Asia and Africa came to believe, like leaders in the West and the socialist bloc, in their states' potential to shape their societies. Even in Latin America, where many state organizations were exceedingly weak and corrupt throughout the 1950s, a new "can-do" spirit gripped many who aspired to state leadership and to the creation of an effective bureaucratic state organization. In fact, the organization of the state became the focal point for their hopes of achieving a new social order, a unified channel for people's passions that until now had run in countless different directions. The state was to be the chisel in the hands of the new sculptors.

Great expectations in Third World countries about what the state organization could create were reinforced by another cultural artifact of their former masters, Western social science of the 1950s and 1960s. Images in scholarly works of integrated centers swallowing hapless peripheries, of

Great Traditions subsuming little traditions, of modern states and allied organizations shaping heretofore traditional societies, all had reverberating effects. Over and over again, articles, books, and lectures bolstered the belief that the impact of policies upon populations would be fairly close to what the policymakers had in mind as they devised their new laws, programs, and organizations. The notions of Western thinkers helped generate anticipation about the capabilities of new and renewed states in the Third World.

In the last decade, though, social scientists have begun to reassess the character and capabilities of states, both in the West and in the Third World. If events have not made eager researchers any wiser, they certainly have made them more wizened. The shining image of states has begun to appear tarnished. For some scholars, the state has retained its awesome capabilities, but the uses to which the state has been put have given them a more jaundiced view of this potential. Others have doubted whether the touted capabilities of states have indeed been so great. They have noted how infrequently potential strength has been translated into effective action. True, even weak states have had continuing and profound effects on numerous aspects of social life, but few have been able to channel that influence to create centralized polities and highly integrated societies. The character of social fragmentation into tribes, linguistic groups, ethnic communities, and religious blocs has changed in character in countries such as India or Zaire, but the actions of state leaders notwithstanding, the net result has often been only heightened communal tension and violence. The political issue is not simply one of political instability—in fact, some leaders of weak states have discovered wily methods that have kept them in office for years on end—but of the severely limited capability of states to regulate and transform their societies as had been expected.

The earlier images of modern states shaping formerly traditional societies were based on presuppositions about the overall role of politics in the organization of society and the dynamics of social and political change. The next section will examine some of these important premises about order and change—many of which have survived in contemporary research in one way or another. The chapter will then present an alternative understanding of the role of politics in society and a model of how to approach the question of overall societal change.

EXPLAINING ORDER AND CHANGE
THROUGH DICHOTOMOUS MODELS OF SOCIETY

Oddly, theories in the 1950s and 1960s that addressed what in the 1980s and 1990s we call state-society relations rarely mentioned the state at all. The state was more assumed than explained. Social scientists subsumed it within a broader array of organizations linked by similar ideas—the Great Tradition, urban society, the modern sector, or the center. Whether the state is truly autonomous—seeking its own course rather than the goals of another social group or mix of groups—was not a meaningful question. It was generally assumed that the members of a modernizing leadership (political, economic, social, and religious elites) share values and aims. Differences between the modern and traditional sectors (or between the components of similar dichotomies used by social scientists, such as center-periphery or elite-mass) represented the major contour in the landscape for theorists. Societal change, many assumed, comes in the gathering strength of the modern sector, enabling it to overcome stubborn beliefs and structures in the traditional sector. The images suggested a beachhead from which the center's modern elites would move outward to transform the hostile terrain of the traditional periphery. The political institutions would meld with churches and industries to form the advance force—the imposing modern center.

The Center-Periphery Model

Given the unassuming role of the state in most writings, it is not surprising that a sociologist, rather than a political scientist, carefully laid out many of the premises dealing with order and change in such a model. Drawing on Max Weber and Talcott Parsons, during the course of thirty years Edward Shils penned a large number of essays on aspects of this model.[2] These are worth looking at not only because of Shils's own impact upon the social sciences, but also because in them he spelled out what were for others implicit assumptions about the relations between center and periphery, modern and traditional, and other dichotomous models.

What did Shils mean by center and periphery? In fact, he never gave a precise definition, but from several scattered statements we can sketch a picture of the modern center. Three primary components constitute the center—values and beliefs, institutions, and elites—and these combine in a seamless weave.

Values and beliefs—what Shils called the central value system—form the core of what people in society hold sacred and the foundation that the elites act upon. Shils saw the center not simply as a random collection of stated and unstated preferences, but in regularized and harmonious terms as the *"order* of symbols, of values and beliefs, which govern the society."[3] Thus, besides giving society a recognizable configuration by differentiating center from periphery, Shils was eager to set forth the internal structure of centers, making them comparable in form if not in content. It is this form, this order, that is irreducible, connecting the center's values and beliefs.

A second component of the center is institutional. This is the critical realm of action. The offices, roles, and organizations express the order inherent in the central value system. No group of people has completely homogeneous values; the institutional component implements the values of the center throughout society. Its authority is the motor of social change. Shils's center is activist and aggressive; its institutional network both embodies and propounds the center's values and beliefs. "The center," he wrote, "consists of those institutions (and roles) which exercise authority—whether it be economic, governmental, political, military—and of those which create and diffuse cultural symbols—religious, literary, etc.—through churches, schools, publishing houses, etc."[4]

Besides the components of values and institutions (or symbols and offices, as Shils would have put it), those who fill the offices and play the roles act as elite custodians of the central value system. The standards of the elites form their authoritative decisions. The elites are thus intimately connected to the central values (their standards) and the institutions (their means). At one point, Shils simply equated an elite (or a single member of an elite) with authority; at other times, he spoke more broadly of the center as a repository of society's authority. A center must have the all-important ingredient of authority; it must be able to enforce its decisions despite differing tendencies and preferences in other parts of society.

The activism of the center, its unrelenting drive to spread its values and beliefs, and its overpowering strength—which derives from the integration of its elites and their organizations—combine to mold the periphery. Indeed, the need for authority implies that the center's values are *not* universally shared. The periphery contains dissenting habits, values, and beliefs. Authority expands the center into the periphery. Through its institutions, the center uses a smorgasbord of rewards and sanctions to facilitate the acceptance of its decisions and values.

The periphery plays a dutifully peripheral role in Shils's analysis. Although he described the periphery as highly differentiated, these differentiations were of little interest to him. It never occurred to him that change generated in the periphery might affect the very nature and capabilities of the center. Shils's understanding of society rests upon the dynamism and activism of the center; the periphery remains a passive recipient. There is an implied sameness, then, to processes of social change; the nature of structures and beliefs in the periphery seems to matter very little. Centers are of primary interest to social scientists because they have a coherence, a unity, an agenda-setting capability that peripheries lack.

Although the degree of consensus varies from society to society, the essential point for understanding a stable society is the center that brings together elites from disparate sectors, each with its own organizations and rules. Only a consensus on the essential order of values among these elites can result in united sufficient authority to bind the society together, and it is the integration of society that concerned Shils. The center integrates the society through a consensual pattern among the elites that assimilates the diverse persons, rules, and roles into a center. The elites constitute a ruling class, and the state is the political arm of this class.

The element of consensus or affinity is a powerful assumption on Shils's part, for it explains to us not only how society is held together but also how the entire society changes. The rules spewed out by the political institutions and the norms demanded by other center organizations constitute the limits of acceptable behavior; habits and ways that lie outside those boundaries must be altered by judicious use of the rewards and sanctions available to the center's institutions.

Problems with the Model

The center-periphery models of society and macro sociological change proposed by Shils and others were accepted by social scientists from a variety of disciplines. These models have a parsimony and elegance that continue to attract numerous researchers, though scattered writings have meanwhile made thrusts at various aspects of the models. Many authors have questioned some deep-rooted Western biases in the dichotomous models. Shils was more direct in his biases than many others: For him, the course of "historical development or evolution" is toward modernity. "Modernity," wrote Shils, "entails democracy and democracy in the new states must above all be equalitarian. . . . To be modern is to be scientific. . . . Modernity requires national sovereignty. . . . 'Modern' means being Western."[5] Modern values form the consensual basis for the center, which is the modern sector. Increasingly, students have become uneasy with such notions, which ultimately equate macro-level change with a necessary move toward Western ways. They have faulted Shils and others for a myopic view of social and political change.

Scholars have also questioned whether accepted images of strong, modernizing centers depict Third World and other countries accurately. Shils recognized the paradox of virile centers in applying his model to societies in which things fall apart. It is true, he admitted, that many states in Asia and Africa "have *not yet* become societies in a modern sense because they do *not yet* have effective centers."[6] Besides introducing an unwarranted teleology—which provides final answers before the questions are fully posed—an emphasis on the "not yet" grants that the center-periphery model is inadequate to depict the here and now. We are left with a tool, the center, which assumes a situation that, Shils tells us, is inapplicable to the societies being studied. The consensus and integration so important to the modernizing model are often lacking in Third World societies—which, according to Shils, are not real societies at all but only protosocieties. Others have added that even in contemporary Western Europe, a jumble of different value systems continue to survive, suggesting that centers may not be that effective and dominant in modern societies either.[7] Historically, Charles Tilly wrote, "the Europeans of 1500 and later did not ordinarily expand from a highly organized center into a weakly organized periphery."[8]

By the 1970s, criticism of the center-periphery or modern-traditional models also mounted over their supercilious treatment of the state. Social scientists pointed to the special, perhaps even autonomous, role that the state organization plays in making and enforcing rules and in influencing the very structure of society. Differing components do not mesh into a center as effortlessly as Shils and others had suggested. Indeed, there is a stealthy reemergence of the state in Shils's work. Unexpectedly, and only after his three major essays on center and periphery, he refers to the "prominence of the governmental center."[9]

STATES AND SOCIETIES:
ORGANIZATIONS IN A MELANGE

In the cautious move away from modern-traditional and center-periphery models, political scientists have given renewed attention to the state, focusing not on its formal legal mode but on its actions in society. They have noted the leading role the state has tried to take in numerous areas relating to national development. Yet recent writings have produced a Janus-faced image in confronting the reality of the state. Those writing on corporatism and bureaucratic-authoritarianism in the Third World, for example, have portrayed states as autonomous and effective, even as creating major social groupings in the society,[10] while others have portrayed the activist state as more illusory than real. The latter have remarked on the hapless, bumbling nature of states, emphasizing their instability and their ineffectiveness in carrying out their grand designs.[11] Detailed case studies more concerned with events and trends at ground level than with speculation about what has "not yet" occurred have harped on the disorganization and weakness of many states.

To examine the role that states actually play requires an overall approach to the maintenance of particular types of order and the process of change in society as a whole. Following Shils's example, we must build a new model—while avoiding, of course, the pitfalls he encountered. An understanding of how societies persist and change must start with the organizations that exercise social control, that subordinate individual inclinations to the behavior these organizations prescribe.[12] These informal and formal organizations, ranging from families and neighborhood groups to mammoth foreign-owned companies, use a variety of sanctions, rewards, and symbols to induce people to behave according to the rules of the game. These are the norms and laws that define the boundaries of acceptable behavior, and they may include what age to marry, what crop to grow, what language to speak, and much more.

At the top of the list of critical changes in human affairs during the last half-millennium has been a radical change in many societies' distribution of social control. The diversity of norms within areas—one set for this tribe and another for a neighboring tribe, one for this region and another for that—has been attacked by the state. Those running (or seeking to run) the state organization have striven to have *it* provide the predominant, often exclusive, set of rules. To be sure, the goal of uniform rules is not totally novel; one need only think of the monism of certain city-states. The difference in the modern era has been how state leaders have tried to impose one set of rules over so large a territory, and how universal this goal has become. There have been few universals in the processes of social change, yet on this issue one can generalize very broadly. By the middle of the twentieth century, in practically every society on earth, political leaders were trying to create a state organization that would either make the rules that govern the details of people's lives itself or determine which other organizations might establish these rules.

Success in achieving this goal has been elusive. Political leaders have faced tremendous obstacles in their drive, obstacles that they have often failed to overcome. Leaders of other social organizations have been unwilling to relinquish their prerogatives, their ability to devise rules governing some aspects of people's lives, without a fierce struggle. Indeed, the central political and social drama of recent history has been the battle between the state and other social organizations. The dispute is over who makes the rules, who grants the property rights that define the use of assets and resources in the society.

Scholars dealing with the maintenance of order and change in society as a whole need an approach that brings this struggle for social control into stark relief. The model I am suggesting depicts society as a mélange of social organizations rather than a dichotomous structure. The state is seen as one organization among many, which singly or in tandem offer individuals strategies of personal survival and, for some, strategies of upward mobility. Individual choice among strategies is based on the material incentives and coercion organizations can bring to bear and on the organizations' use of symbols and values concerning how social life should be ordered. These symbols and values either reinforce the forms of social control in the society or propose new forms of social life.

To be sure, there are cases of the state's overcoming the dogged resistance of other social organizations and achieving predominance. In such instances, the state may make and enforce nearly all rules in the society or may choose to delegate some of that authority to other mechanisms, such as the church or market. There are other societies, however, where social organizations actively vie with one another in offering strategies and in proposing different rules of the game. Here, the mélange of social organizations is marked by an environment of conflict, an active struggle for social control of the population. The state is part of the environment of conflict. In these cases, political leaders have not yet achieved predominance—the ability to fashion rules and force their broad acceptance—but they believe that the state *should* predominate. The state's battles may be with families over the rules of education and socialization; they may be with ethnic groups over territoriality; they may be with religious organizations over daily habits. In the early twentieth century, Mustafa Kemal of Turkey locked horns with religious organizations over whether men should wear hats with brims or without. As with so many other skirmishes, the issue was not as inconsequential as it may appear; the conflict was over who had the right and ability to make rules in that society.

In many Third World societies, where these struggles are most evident in the 1990s, states face a multitude of social organizations that maintain and vie for the power to set rules. Families, clans, multinational corporations, domestic businesses, tribes, political parties, and patron-client dyads may be among those actively engaged in the environment of conflict. Why have state leaders taken on all these foes to struggle for the ultimate rule-making capability? After al', central political organizations have not always taken such an aggressive stance. This sort of multifront war can easily sap the state's strength and eventually topple it.

The answer can be found by considering the special character of the world system that has been the backdrop for these struggles, forming a second tier of relationships for each state. Each state is not only one organization in a domestic mélange but is also one among many states globally. Its role on one tier, the society, is highly interdependent with its place in the other, the system of states. Since the fifteenth and sixteenth centuries, when modern states began to appear in Western Europe, they have presented dire threats to all other existing political forms. Their fantastic comparative advantage in mobilizing and organizing resources for war and other purposes brought the survival of other political entities into question. Only societies that developed state organizations themselves had a chance to resist being conquered and swallowed up by other states. A prime motivation in expanding the state's rule-making domain at the expense of other social organizations within its boundaries—even with all the risks that entails—has been to build sufficient clout to survive the dangers posed by those outside its boundaries.

How does increased social control by the state improve its prospects in the international arena? A state's ability to survive rests on a number of factors, including the organizational capabilities of its leaders, population size, available and potential material resources, and the larger international configuration. Probably none is more important in marshaling strength for the state, though, than the ability to mobilize the population.[13] Mobilization is the channeling of people into specialized organizational frameworks that enable state leaders to build stronger armies, collect more taxes, and complete any number of other complicated tasks.

It is not surprising that the growth of the very first modern states in Europe involved building three essential tentacles of the state—a standing army, a vastly improved tax-collecting mechanism, and an expanded set of courts. The imposition of state law in place of customary or feudal law through the extension of the court system was the essential ingredient in inducing people to behave as state leaders wanted them to behave and not according to dictates of local lords or others. In other words, the courts—along with the police and all others who fed into the workings of the courts—were an essential mechanism for shifting social control to the state. Mobilization of the population to serve in and financially support a standing army (or for other tasks) could only grow out of the increasing social control by the state made possible by the expanded domain of the courts.

Social control, then, is the currency for which social organizations compete. With high levels of social control, states can mobilize their populations effectively, gaining tremendous strength in facing external foes. Internally, state personnel can gain autonomy from other social groups in determining their own preferred rules for society; they can build complex, coordinated bureaus to establish these rules; and they can monopolize coercive means in the society to ensure that other groups do not prevent the enforcement of state rules. Increasing levels of social control are reflected in a scale of three indicators.

Compliance. At the most elementary level, the strength of the state rests on the population's conforming to its demands. Compliance is often compelled by the most basic of sanctions, force. Who controls the local police is often one of the most important questions one can ask about the distribution of social control in a society. The ability to control the dispersal of a broad scope of other resources and services also determines the degree to which the state can demand compliance.

Participation. Leaders of the state organization seek more than compliance. They also gain strength by organizing the population for specialized tasks in the institutional components of the state organization. In practical terms, leaders may want peasants to sell produce to the state cooperative or to employ state-licensed clinics instead of unauthorized healers.

Legitimacy. The most potent factor determining the strength of the state, legitimacy, is more inclusive than either compliance or participation. Legitimacy involves an acceptance of the state's rules of the game, its social control, as true and right. Whereas compliance and participation may be a practical response by individuals to an array of rewards and sanctions, legitimacy means accepting the symbolic component that the rewards and sanctions embody. It is the popular acknowledgment of a particular social order.

The strength of the state organization in an environment of conflict depends, in large part, on the social control it exercises. The greater the social control, the more currency—compliance, participation, and legitimacy—is available to state leaders to achieve their goals. Leaders of other social organizations reject the state's claim to predominance, and they too desperately seek social control. They can use the same currency of compliance, participation, and legitimacy to protect and strengthen their enclaves, in which they will try to determine how social life should be ordered, what the rules of the game should be.

THE CONSTRAINTS ON STATES

Many current students of macro-level political and social change have been mesmerized by the power of the state, much as earlier scholars were taken with capabilities of modern sectors or centers. Where threats to state dominance have been woven into analyses, there has been a tendency to focus on the constraints imposed by the rivals to *central* power, those who constitute an alternative state leadership.

With the tremendous comparative advantage that states have, it is little wonder that many social scientists have assumed the predominance of the state without carefully analyzing the outcomes of struggles with other organizations, even those in a nook of society whose leaders harbor no hope for central power. The state leaders, after all, can draw succor from norms in the international environment (led by those propounded by the UN) that exalt the role of the state in setting the rules on the status of women, treatment of children, issues of health, questions of reproduction, and much more. Also, the state is almost invariably the largest employer and accounts for a greater share of the gross national product (GNP) than any other organization in society. Not only are the rewards at its disposal many, but the portion of its budget devoted to maintaining armies and police is substantial.

Survival of Local Control

Yet the very character of the state and the substance of its policies can be shaped by a vicious cycle created by an environment of conflict. To enhance its strength and autonomy, states must increase their social control. But without the ability to mobilize human and material resources into specialized, task-oriented frameworks that come with already existing social control, states encounter grave difficulties in offering viable strategies of survival to individuals throughout the country. A potpourri of other social organizations may organize resources into selective incentives and sanctions, constituting alternative strategies. In brief, state leaders may find that despite all the seeming riches at their disposal, their organization—the state—lacks the wherewithal to dislodge people from the existing strategies offered by organizations with rules different from the state's. The "periphery" is far more important in shaping the future of a society than either Shils or later writers on the state imagined.

The bounty of state resources and personnel does have a tremendous impact on the rest of society, but often in ways unintended and unanticipated by state leaders. Social control by other organizations, gained from their mobilization of portions of the population, gives them a strength that can be very threatening to the state's local political representatives or bureaucrats. The state official is caught in a vise, with clear instructions from state superiors on how to use resources but with counterpressures from other social groups to employ different priorities. To avoid the damage local authorities might inflict upon their chances for advancement or even their political survival, many strategically placed state employees accommodate these local figures. State resources in many cases have had a deep impact on local society but in ways that have strengthened local social organizations at the state's expense.

Whole portions of states have been captured by people enforcing guidelines on how to use state resources that differ from those propounded by state leaders. State leaders' rules are contained in the official policies designed to regulate and monitor strictly the flow of state resources. It is tempting to see any deviation from these rules as corruption, as if the problem involved only a deficiency in monitoring distribution. In fact, much of what is commonly called corruption is not simply a single individual stuffing his or her pockets with state resources. It is behavior according to dissenting rules, established by organizations other than the state. Nepotism, for example, though against state law, may be a cardinal norm within the family or clan. How people are recruited into state jobs is an indication of whose rules of the game are being followed. The issue goes beyond technical monitoring of state functionaries to guard against nepotism or other infringement of state rules. Such transgressions reflect pockets of social control outside the domain of state leaders, which have been able to shape how the state acts—or, at least, how one tentacle of the state acts.

Even in the most remote parts of a country, states have had a huge impact. At times, it is difficult to imagine how a given place might have evolved without state penetration. Remote villages have state-financed police, roads, potable water, state tax collectors, credit, marketing cooperatives, schools, subsidized contraceptives, electricity, health care, and more. The distribution of state "goodies," collection of taxes, and application of force, however, may not be at all what state leaders had in mind—not to mention the resulting social structure, the effective rulers in the village, or the distribution of social control.

Lack of a Strong Political Base

Without the strength provided by the mobilization of the population in villages and towns across the country, the state faces two additional difficulties. First, it may lack a sufficiently strong political base to pursue, even at a gross level, policies that run counter to the existing distribution of power among sectors in the society. Michael Lipton, for example, found that despite rhetoric to the contrary, most Third World states had a clear urban bias because the urban sector has more "articulateness, organisation and power" than the rural sector.[14] State policies on taxing, pricing, capital investment, and welfare favor the most powerful sector, and without sufficient social control the state has insufficient autonomy to break this pattern.

Second, an inadequate power base for the state makes it a tempting prize for those who do have some organizational backing, either in society at large or even within one of the state's many tentacles. But the prize is often chimerical, for what aspiring leaders seize is not the capability to transform their societies in accordance with their goals, but simply seats coveted by others. Just to preserve their seats, they must adopt means that foreclose the use of power to fulfill their original purposes. Instead, substantive policy issues are pushed to the back burner. Lacking the means to mobilize sustained and organized internal support, leaders of weak states must increasingly turn their attention to staying in power, lest others develop the means to unseat them. In these circumstances the political life of leaders, though not necessarily short, is certainly nasty and brutish. When the head of state does not attend to the course of policy, it is little wonder that the tail—the state functionary assigned far from the state capital—may find the most compelling pressures coming from strong local figures and organizations with rules very different from the state's.

CONCLUSION: NEW DIRECTIONS FOR RESEARCH

Even in societies where other social organizations exercise significant social control, the state is still a major presence. In certain areas, such as negotiating with other states, dealing with transnational actors, and maintaining peace among different sectors of society, the state usually has built-in advantages for playing a major role. Other tasks, such as taxing exports and making particular kinds of transfer payments, may be performed even without achieving predominance. Social scientists focusing on these sorts of issues have stressed the state's prowess, pointing to its growing bureaucracy, its role in funneling private foreign capital to local entrepreneurs, and its ability to maintain social peace through corporatist measures. When social policy demands changes in behavior among broad segments of the population, however, states can be far less effective.[15] The same Mexican government that had considerable success in regulating the share of equity and the operations of foreign-owned firms repeatedly failed to execute a fair-price-for-the-poor policy in rural areas.

In brief, states are not always the unfettered prime movers of macro-level societal change they are sometimes portrayed to be. To be sure, the strength they draw from an international environment that continuously thrusts them into critical roles and offers resources to play those roles bolsters their position, particularly on issues such as diplomacy, war making, and transfer payments. At the same time, states are often severely constrained by their domestic environments from achieving an independent reordering of society. The autonomy of states, the slant of their policies, the preoccupying issues for their leaders, and their coherence are greatly influenced by the societies in which they operate.

Social organizations in a mélange, including the state, coexist symbiotically. In an environment of conflict, especially, the social control exercised even by small social organizations tucked away in remote areas constrains the state tremendously. The state is hemmed in—indeed transformed—by these internal forces, just as it is by international forces. But society is also transformed by the state. Social organizations, and the structure of society as a whole, are molded by the opportunities and impediments that the state presents, just as they are affected by other social organizations and by the openings and limitations posed by the world economy.

The model presented here—a mélange in which the state is one organization among many—focuses attention on the crucial battle for social control. In the modern world system, the state is at center stage in this struggle. Yet this central position in the limelight does not necessarily spell victory. Many societies remain in an environment of conflict in which order and macro-level change must be understood in terms of two tiers of forces. The first includes the effects of society on the state and vice versa. The second involves the impact on state and society of other states and of the world economy.

A partial research agenda based on this approach might include the following issues.

1. Under what circumstances has the distribution of social control in an environment of conflict altered? How can one explain variations in social control from society to society?
2. Can one generalize about the impact of transnational forces on the distribution of social control? How have these forces affected the role played by domestic social organizations in maintaining a particular order or in fostering certain types of societal change?
3. How has the form of politics—democracy, single party authoritarianism, etc.—been affected by the distribution of social control?
4. When social organizations besides the state exercise significant social control, how has the state's ability in different issue-areas been affected?
5. What has been the nature of the struggle between state and other social organizations in the post–World War II period? Which social organizations have been the most successful in maintaining and extending social control? Has this pattern changed over time? Does the pattern hold across cultures?
6. What are the implications of the changing balance between state and society not only in the developing nations but in the Soviet Union and Eastern Europe as well?
7. How have states and other social organizations accommodated one another in societies in which states have not achieved predominance?

NOTES

1. See, for example, two articles by Benjamin Neuberger: "The Western Nation-State in African Perceptions of Nation-Building," *Asian and African Studies* 11 (1976):241–261; and "State and Nation in African Thought," *Journal of African Studies* 4 (Summer 1977):198–205.

2. Many of those essays are collected in Edward Shils, *Center and Periphery* (Chicago: University of Chicago Press, 1975). Also, see his *Political Development in the New States* (Paris: Mouton, 1966).

3. Shils, *Center and Periphery*, p. 3, my emphasis; see also pp. 48–49.

4. Ibid., p. 39.

5. Shils, *Political Development*, pp. 8–10.

6. Shils, *Center and Periphery*, p. 44, my emphasis.

7. Suzanne Berger and Michael J. Piore, *Dualism and Discontinuity in Industrial Societies* (Cambridge: Cambridge University Press, 1980).

8. Charles Tilly, "Reflections on the History of European State-Making," in Charles Tilly, ed., *The Formation of National States in Western Europe* (Princeton, NJ: Princeton University Press, 1975), p. 24.

9. Shils, *Center and Periphery*, p. 74.

10. See, for example, Frederick B. Pike and Thomas Stritch, eds., *The New Corporatism: Social-Political Structures in the Iberian World* (Notre Dame, IN: University

of Notre Dame Press, 1974); and David Collier, ed., *The New Authoritarianism in Latin America* (Princeton, NJ: Princeton University Press, 1979).

11. See, for example, Samuel P. Huntington, *Political Order in Changing Societies* (New Haven, CT: Yale University Press, 1968); and Gerald A. Heeger, *The Politics of Underdevelopment* (New York: St. Martin's Press, 1974).

12. "Social control" is used in a broad sense and is interchangeable with a concept such as "power." It refers to "situations in which A gets B to do something he would not otherwise do." David A. Baldwin, "Power Analysis and World Politics: New Trends Versus Old Tendencies," *World Politics* 31 (January 1979):162–163. Baldwin notes that it is important to denote both the scope and domain of such concepts. The issue of domain (who is influencing whom) is at the heart of the rest of the discussion. The domain (influence in respect to what) involves the social behavior of individuals in a given society.

13. Krasner has made the point quite well. A state's strength in external relations rests on its strength in relation to its own society. Stephen D. Krasner, "Domestic Constraints on International Economic Leverage," in Klaus Knorr and Frank N. Trager, eds., *Economic Issues and National Security* (Kansas City: Regents Press of Kansas, 1977). To be sure, the state is dealing in two different domains and internal social control is not totally and immediately fungible to power in the world of states. Nonetheless, such social control is a necessary, if not sufficient, condition to exercise power internationally.

14. Michael Lipton, *Why Poor People Stay Poor: Urban Bias in World Development* (Cambridge, MA: Harvard University Press, 1977), p. 13.

15. Baldwin, "Power Analysis," p. 164, makes a point that should lead those writing on corporatism and bureaucratic-authoritarianism to some caution. "The so-called 'paradox of unrealized power' results from the mistaken belief that power resources useful in one policy-contingent framework will be equally useful in a different one. . . . The theme of such explanations is not 'he had the cards but played them poorly,' but rather 'he had a great bridge hand but happened to be playing poker.'"

4

Corporatism and Comparative Politics

DOUGLAS A. CHALMERS

After World War II, scholars in comparative politics came to share a belief that pluralism was a necessary bulwark against totalitarianism. Nazi totalitarianism had brought on that war, and one of the war's most terrible products was the spread of totalitarian Stalinism. Pluralism was set against communism and the contrasts sharply drawn; prior to the 1980s almost no one talked about pluralism *within* communism. Pluralism also provided a way to describe the historical process of change that had already taken place in Europe and was under way in its former colonies. This historical movement, which came to be represented by the concept of development, was described in terms of specialization, differentiation, and integration, pluralism's central concepts. A link was established between normative concerns (pluralist democracy) and historical changes that people saw, such as the growth of bureaucracy. Pluralism did not provide comprehensive explanatory or causal theories any more than did other approaches, although it pointed usefully to the pressures of groups as a way of explaining many outcomes such as election results or policies. Its main contribution was interpretive. Pluralism successfully provided a meaningful framework for a wide range of important phenomena. Considerable scholarly energy was generated based on the concepts of pluralism, sufficient to organize and inspire a vast amount of research.

The intellectual history of comparative politics in the 1960s and 1970s was dominated by the criticism and transformation of the pluralist approach. Marxism in one form or another was the most prolific source of criticism, particularly after the political movements of the 1960s, but many of the ideas in corporatism also played an important part in transforming the pluralist vision.

One attraction of corporatism is its frequent emphasis on several alternative historical patterns in place of the single dichotomy of pluralist differentiation or totalitarian force, which was both ethnocentric and simplistic.[1] Corporatism is also an ideological alternative. In the past it had opposed liberalism (which had much in common with pluralism), most prominently in the

1920s and 1930s, when corporatism was associated with fascism. That fascism is currently politically anathema does not alter the fact that it *was* an alternative. At other times corporatism has been linked with nothing more terrible than, say, papal social thought.

Unlike pluralism, corporatism paid attention to political structures and variables that analysts have since identified as dynamic and highly influential in shaping current affairs. In pluralism, the importance of the state was largely disregarded. Pluralists were locked into a view of multiple groups held together by a regulatory state. The drive, the energy, and the initiative in society came from groups that were organized and operated in the private sphere. Corporatism, in contrast, starts with the state and defines group interests in terms of their relations to the state.

What does corporatism have to offer as an alternative to the pluralist research paradigm? Could corporatism shape a school of thought as pluralism has done? Of course, one concept cannot substitute exactly for another: A concept at this level is too complex to serve precisely the same function as another concept. Yet corporatism and pluralism do play similar roles. Both are explanatory and interpretive, serving analytical and ideological purposes. Within the small world of comparative politics, corporatism does not yet serve as a major organizing idea for research and theory building, but it has considerable potential.

This review of what corporatism has to offer begins with a look at the process of theory construction in comparative politics. The first part of this chapter will consider the meaning of "corporatism." The second part will discuss what role corporatism plays in theory construction and research design. The last section will evaluate corporatism's potential contribution to comparative politics.

THE MEANINGS OF CORPORATISM

"Corporatism" is an ambiguous term. This is to be expected because it serves many purposes. It provides guidance for research, plays a part in political discourse, and contributes to theory. In each one of those contexts it picks up diverse meanings. Ambiguity, however, is not always a drawback. If we were constructing a tightly wrought proposition or theory, it would be, but corporatism is far from doing that. In pointing a way or suggesting approaches, ambiguity can be positive. The corporatist concept is a frame through which we may tentatively enter a new domain. It is not a precise template for drawing conclusions, but a rough map that guides scholars in exploring the major features of the new terrain.

Like many terms in political science, corporatism is used by political movements and activists to rally support and define a political position. As such it is the object of scrutiny by political scientists as a symbol that plays a role in political affairs independent of the scholar. Corporatism also has an analytical role as an instrument used by scholars in understanding politics. This double level of symbolism is the normal state of affairs for political scientists, but it complicates the job of theory construction.

The concept's twofold character is particularly relevant because "corporatism" as a political symbol is much more highly charged (negatively so) than, say, "pluralism." Many scholars writing on the subject find it necessary to open their analysis with a disclaimer. Because of corporatism's association with fascism in most readers' minds, a scholar's first task is to establish his or her detachment. Corporatism may never play a very strong role in "pure" analysis because it is so negatively charged. Many U.S. scholars have similar problems with using "communism" as an analytical concept. The associations of the term "corporatism" gave it a certain shock value in the 1960s that made its use vivid and interesting, but if it is to play an important analytical role, the concept may need a new name.

State-Group Relationships

Probably the most commonly assumed meaning of corporatism concerns the relationship between interests and the governing apparatus. The image of a corporatist relationship that comes most readily to mind is that of a formal organization representing a major economic or professional interest before state officials within the framework of an official institution. Take, for example, a business association in an official government consultative council. The group is *corporate*, and is *incorporated* into the state.[2]

Philippe Schmitter's definition, which is centered on the state-group relationship, is often cited despite its complexity. It seeks to achieve the widest possible application.

> Corporatism can be defined as a system of interest representation in which the constituent units are organized into a limited number of singular compulsory, noncompetitive, hierarchically ordered and functionally differentiated categories, recognized or licensed (if not created) by the state and granted a deliberate representational monopoly within their respective categories in exchange for observing certain controls on their selection of leaders and articulation of demands and supports.[3]

Although Schmitter does, in this definition, refer to a "system of representation" all of the distinguishing characteristics of this definition of corporatism concern the way individual groups relate to the state.

A central aspect of Schmitter's definition is the definite legal (or conventional) form that corporatist relationships take. These forms set the general terms of an exchange relationship that defines the interdependence of the interest organization and the government officials. The content of the exchange specifies the relative power of the group and the state and defines the degree of mutual autonomy. The legal quality of this relationship is crucial to corporatism. This is not to say that corporatism dwells on mere legal formalities, laws on paper that are often ignored in practice. It also includes customary and informal patterns as well. But it insists on drawing attention to whatever specifies rights and obligations and norms of behavior. More than pluralism and Marxism, corporatism emphasizes the direct connection between law and power and between law and interest.

As compared to the pluralist view, the distinctive quality of corporatist studies is their attention to the state. Pluralism places the bargaining and confrontation between groups at the center of its analysis, but corporatism does not see interest groups mainly in terms of their relationship to other interest groups. Those relations (conflictual or cooperative) are controlled by the formal requirements of the law, and the group's life is shaped by its exchange relationship with the state. This relationship determines the power of the state over the group and, conversely, the ability of the group to exploit its privileged position vis-à-vis state authorities to its own advantage. The pluralist view conceives of the state in essentially regulatory terms. Few pluralists would limit the state's actual behavior to the watchdog role posited by early liberals, and most recognize the importance and extent of regulation. But in a pluralist model the state is not a constituent part of interests, as it is in corporatism. Rather, it remains external to those interests, setting boundaries, rules, and incentives.

The Marxian, or class model does place more emphasis on the importance of the relationships between the state and societal groups. Class analysis pays close attention to the exchange or power relationship, which determines whether the state is being used to control one group on behalf of another.[4] However, it considers formal relationships to be merely changeable forms for establishing domination. Corporatism, on the other hand, makes those formal relationships a topic of central concern, for they are seen as the building blocks of the whole structure.

One of the qualities of a state-group relationship that gives it a corporatist character is suggested by Schmitter's use of the term "monopoly." Only one group is given the right to speak for a specified category of people. Schmitter is referring most particularly to the identification of a single organization to represent that category on various councils of state, such as an official trade organization or a labor union.

The "monopoly" associated with corporatism also can refer to the exclusive authority from the state to regulate a specified sphere of social activity. For example, in most societies the state gives doctors the exclusive right to practice medicine and gives their professional association the right to determine who can be a doctor and what standards they should uphold. In some contemporary authoritarian states, official labor organizations have a different, but related form of status, in that only one labor union organization is tolerated and all workers must belong to it. The union organization acquires the power to determine who can work, and who shall benefit from state services related to the members' status as workers.

"Monopoly" may be an unfortunate choice of words, however, to describe either the representational or social regulating function of corporatist organizations. It suggests broad control over a relatively stable set of people. In modern societies diverse and rapidly changing social structures imply that the boundaries of any particular occupational category are overlapping and constantly shifting. Courts and legislatures are constantly arbitrating between them and redrawing their boundaries. Sometimes college professors are workers and sometimes they constitute a separate profession. Farmers are sometimes considered part of the business community and sometimes a sort of self-employed working class. Even in one of the best defined spheres, the practice of medicine has its boundary problems. Legally, chiropractors are partly in and partly out of the practice of medicine.

The shifting boundaries mean that monopoly status in the sense of exclusive control over a fixed group is always problematical.[5] For corporatism the most relevant sense of the phrase "granting a monopoly," however, is rather the active state role in defining and redefining both the powers of these organizations and the group they control and represent. The state creates "official" or "legally recognized" organizations. In a highly authoritarian corporatist society, the government may carry out this active role one step further by actively suppressing any competing claimants, but even in nonrepressive corporatist societies, the notion conveyed by the term "monopoly" lies in the official grant of rights and privileges, rather than the total control of a fixed social category.

The most important subdivision of corporatism is based on variations in the power relationship between interest groups and the state. There are state-dominated groups and group-dominated states. Schmitter refers to "societal" and "state" corporatism. The state-dominated version is associated with authoritarianism and dependent developing countries.[6] The "societal" form is more an evolution—perhaps a corruption—of liberalism.

Sometimes, unfortunately, this distinction is ignored. On the one hand, the association of corporatism with fascism has encouraged many to write about corporatist relationships as if their defining characteristic was the dominance of the state. On the other, one can also find "corporatism" used to emphasize—reasonably enough—the importance and dominance of corporations. As with all typologies based on power relationships, it is questionable how clear and stable these types are in practice. Societal groups have different degrees of power over different dimensions of their relationship to the state, and this balance varies with time.

Corporatism as a Regime

"Corporatism" is also used to refer to a comprehensive organization of political society beyond state-group relationships. This is the conventional application of the term for, say, Italian Fascism, which sought to replace the system of parties and parliament with a system of corporatist bodies, in which "all" interests would have a firm and fixed role in the political decisionmaking process. In fact, although much of the legal apparatus for this was constructed, corporatism was never completely implemented in Italy. This is not unusual. Incomplete implementation is a major finding in almost every study about almost every corporatist experiment.[7] On these grounds, it would be easy to dismiss all corporatist pretensions to describe regimes, especially if one assumes that the only form that corporatist relationships may take is that of constitutionally established councils of corporations. This was how constitutional theorists of the nineteenth and early twentieth centuries spoke of corporatism.

This vision of corporatism as a regime is unduly restrictive, however. It is more useful to apply "corporatism" to any comprehensive set of relationships in which the major interests in society have been brought into a formal, specified set of exchange relationships with the state.

Almost no modern state has a council of corporations, yet several qualities are central as criteria for labeling some of them "corporatist." The first two are extensions to the entire system of relations that hold between one corporatist group and the state. One may say that a corporatist regime exists when most major groups in society are corporatist, that is, defined in legal terms with specific sets of rights and duties. The regime would not be corporatist if there was a constant redefinition of groups based, say, on negotiating power. To be corporatist, a regime must also have a relatively fixed pattern of representation, in which some definition of the important interests in society is established, maintained, and changed only with deliberation. If the groups relevant to policymaking were redefined on every issue, the system could not be considered corporatist.

Although these two criteria are clearly satisfied by a council of corporations or by other traditional corporatist deliberative bodies, they would also be satisfied by a stable but more informal pattern of comprehensive consultations, indicative planning bodies, and the like.[8] The regularity of ties, resting on a certain explicitness and stability, distinguishes them from pluralist arrangements. Obviously, this is a matter of degree. If regulatory agencies develop fixed clienteles, with—by custom or by law—privileged status for some groups, this is a move toward corporatism. Similarly, if corporatist institutions become more fluid in ways that bypass administrative decision, they are becoming pluralist.

On another level, corporatism implies something about how a system handles conflicts between groups. In the pluralist model, the primary form of interaction between groups is negotiation or bargaining. The class model of politics assumes either solidarity (between similarly placed groups) or irreconcilable conflict, with the first case represented by the marketplace, and the latter by war. In the corporatist model, the interaction between groups is carefully regulated by the instrumentalities of the state, and some planned, rational outcome is to be expected. If bargaining is the model for pluralism, and military conflict the model for class theory, then bureaucratic planning seems to be the model for corporatism. Like liberalism, corporatism assumes that interest groups do not stand in hostile contradiction, but rather postulates a regulated framework in which groups resolve conflicts guided by representatives of the community, the servants of the state. Corporatism has much in common with socialism's understanding of society after the end of class conflict. In that utopia, a fundamental harmony of groups within the state would presumably be achieved. Corporatist theory holds that this harmony is possible in the short run, and need not wait for the transformation of society.[9]

The need for methods to reconcile the bitter conflicts of the early twentieth century was one of the main impulses for the ideology of corporatism. Because corporatism has often been formulated as an explicit alternative both to the "chaos" and "greed" seen as products of the liberal model and to the bitter struggle foreseen by theorists of class conflict, it is not surprising that the controlled, nondestructive character of corporatist relationships is emphasized by corporatist theorists, particularly conservative ones.

Two problems remain with these definitions: (1) specifying what interests are representable and (2) determining whether there is any implied equality in the representations of various groups.

What sorts of interests are represented in a corporatist regime? Corporatism, like pluralism and Marxism, makes "interest" a central concept, but like them, never succeeds in defining it operationally. Thus, a definitive listing of legitimate interests to be represented in a corporatist regime is not available. In root versions of corporatism, these interests were associated with specific functional roles, prominently including the army, the church, and commercial and artisans' guilds. These versions apply to pre-absolutist days in Europe and to the colonial period in Latin America, when (at least in retrospect) the organizations in question were well developed and the boundaries between them clearly defined.

In contemporary societies the application is more difficult. Pluralists and Marxists begin with interest groups that are generated in society and explore their interaction. Pluralists assume no fixed definitions of interests; Marxists build primary definitions of interests around relationships to material production processes. In corporatism, however, interests are assumed to be limited and given—in contrast to pluralism—and are assumed to be determined by their function for the community as a whole, not by their dialectical confrontation around production or any other process. There is, however, no widely agreed-upon set of functions, and therefore no established set of corporatist interest groups. Most self-consciously implemented schemes in this century (for example, in Portugal and Italy) appear to begin with a quasi-Marxist definition of classes, broaden the definition to include all major economic interests, and add the professions. There seem to be no specifically corporatist interests. The lack of precision here is a real problem for corporatism, and I shall return to it in our evaluation.

Does a regime qualify as corporatist if restrictions are sharply imposed on some segments of the population and privileged access granted to others? In many states—Latin American bureaucratic-authoritarian regimes, for example—no broad-based councils exist, yet labor is caught in a state-dominated legal structure and certain economic interests have privileged legal status. Should these be denied the label "corporatist"? It has been argued with much justification that corporatist language was used in these cases as a smokescreen for the implementation of strong governmental controls over labor and dissident political groups.[10]

Evenhandedness does *not* seem to be part of a definition of corporatism. Rather, the very diversity and specificity of ways in which different groups establish links with the state and are treated by the state is the hallmark of corporatism. In many cases that concerned scholars in the 1970s and 1980s—the imposition of authoritarian controls in military takeovers in Latin America and elsewhere in the Third World—the imposition of unequal controls was clearly the product of a particular historical situation. With whatever justice, the military could claim that their unequal treatment of various groups in society was to correct the imbalances of the prior regime. In other words, the contrast in treatment accorded different segments of the population under corporatism is not only possible, but expected. There must, however, be some criteria of "appropriate inequalities," presumably based on the quality of a group's contribution to the community good. The nature of the interests represented would, one imagines, dictate the sort of link (including the power and exchange relationship) that the group has with the state. And since the specification of the appropriate interests is already problematic in corporatism, there is not much to help us in dealing with this question.

Clearly the concept of a corporatist regime is highly normative—more a matter of ideals than ideal types. The good things that would result from a successful corporatist regime substitute for a concrete description of just what that society would entail. One is left with a utopian picture in which there is a place for everything and everything is in its place. In this imagined regime, all important groups are represented in the formal structures of the state, and the state monitors and guides their interactions to avoid violent or otherwise illegitimate conflict and to secure stability and peace, appropriate rewards, and collective effectiveness. This is an image of an organic state.[11]

In the corporatist utopia, there is a formal structure that (in specific contrast to an ideal of equality) accords recognition to members of society based on the quality of their contributions, mediated through groups and institutions. Political interaction is regulated by a notion of the common good, and institutions enforce that notion. The spheres of life are carefully delimited.

Corporatism as an Ideology

As the suffix of the word implies, "corporatism" is often used to denote not only a form of relationship, but a set of beliefs about those relationships. In other words, it may be used in the way we have been discussing so far, to identify and explain a set of practices and institutions, but it also may refer to a set of beliefs held by people who value those practices and institutions and seek to bring them about. When theories are used politically in this way, they become ideologies, and corporatism has most certainly been an ideology. In order to understand the meanings of "corporatism," then, we must look at the political purposes to which it has been put.

The corporatist ideology has always served an established interest or institution (although not necessarily the dominant one). It has never been consistently used by or for the alienated or isolated. Efforts—for example, in Fascist Italy—to adapt corporatism to aggressively pro–working class movements have all failed. Despite this element of consistency, corporatism's political role has changed dramatically over the years.[12] In the early nineteenth century, corporatist theory was applied in the political disputes over the roles of the church and the state in society, and the corporatist ideology was a bulwark for the church against the encroachment of the state. Corporatism asserted the rights of established entities to govern themselves and their members. Later in the nineteenth century, with the rise of the "spectre of socialism," the corporatist ideology was applied to protect the church and the state against the encroachments of the working class.

Liberalism, while decrying the role of the state in matters touching on business, actively encouraged it to take over many of what the church considered its essential functions. Corporatism was used to defend and legitimize the privileged autonomy of the corporation—in this case, the church. Against socialism, which posed a different kind of threat, corporatism had an almost contrary function (although there were elements of the traditional threat to the church's functions when socialism was in power). Until the Russian Revolution, the socialist threat perceived by corporatists was the radical claim to autonomy presented in socialist theory, which went far beyond the claim of the corporatists. The socialists represented the proletariat, a class, they argued, that had no ties to the existing community that were to be valued. Against this radical claim to separateness, corporatist theory insisted on the integral nature of the community. The emphasis during this phase of corporatism's political role was on the harmony of classes and on the fundamental interdependence of the parts of society.

With the rise to power of the fascists and their preemption of corporatist ideology for political purposes, the emphasis changed once again, this time perhaps a bit more subtly, from the natural harmony of the community to an insistence on the duty, obligation, and right of the state, now conceived as an active force, to suppress fragmentation and enforce unity. Corporatism had come full circle, from an ideology that defended the rights of autonomous organizations against the state apparatus to the ideology of that apparatus as it sought to suppress independent organizations. Although such shifts in political meaning are not unique to corporatism, it is striking how large the reversals of its political role have been.

Corporatism is now rarely invoked as a political ideology. The association with fascism was so strong and so negative that it would take a daring political leader (or one blinded by political hatreds) to adopt the term willingly. It has been used more as a term of invective than as a proud identification of the guiding ideas of a regime, although there are some exceptions. Salazar in Portugal hung on to the term to the end, reflecting the profoundly conservative bias of that regime. The Peruvians apparently sought to adopt corporatism for their own purposes during the regime of the "progressive military."[13] By and large, however, the term is now used negatively. Governments are called corporatist in political discourse to identify an undesirable characteristic, particularly to establish an association with the fascists and to emphasize the aggressive use of the state to repress dissent—particularly dissent stemming from the lower classes.

CORPORATISM AS PART
OF THEORETICAL DISCOURSE

What contribution can corporatism make to progress in comparative politics? This is not an easy question to answer, because the notions of "contribution" and "progress" in the field have not been clarified. To simplify the task of applying the many criteria, I shall put them into two clusters. Corporatism has contributed to *explanation* on the one hand, and to *interpretation* on the other. In the positivist tradition of social science, the contribution of a concept is measured by the degree to which it furthers explanatory theory. This might take the form of building axiomatic theory, developing supported, falsifiable causal propositions, identifying simpler, more basic independent variables, or simply formulating clear, testable hypotheses and operational concepts.

A less commonly discussed form of contribution a concept can make is in building interpretive theory. Here, the contribution is measured by the extent to which a concept provides a coherent normative basis and an understanding of (usually) historical trends. Does the concept provide a way of measuring how well societies (or some part of them) fulfill those norms? Can it determine what stage in history a society has reached, and what basic dynamics or dialectical processes are involved? Interpretive doctrines are more oriented toward action. We should look at both dimensions before coming to a judgment about the utility of corporatism in political science.

Corporatism as an Explanation

Corporatist theorists make little pretense of presenting a comprehensive theory. Unlike most versions of Marxism, for example, but much like pluralism, corporatism points to important dimensions and suggests distinctions and underlying factors. It does not claim to explain events. It is often assumed that there is a claim to explanation from "culture," that is, the ideology of corporatism is handed down as part of tradition, and induces corporatist solutions to problems. Yet I know of no theorist who articulates this position. It is true that a culture of corporatism, that is, norms and beliefs congruent with corporatism, plays an important part in defining historical patterns in the work of Howard Wiarda,[14] but this is not the same as proposing that culture "determines" that pattern. The identification of historical patterns will be discussed later, because it plays an important role in interpretive theory.

Corporatism is therefore to be taken principally as a heuristic. "Heuristic" is often used very loosely to mean merely something less rigorous than a theory, but I am using the term in the sense of a "rule of thumb" that provides very specific rules to simplify a task that might be overwhelming in its complexity and demands for information.[15] A concept's heuristic value in explanatory theory depends on whether it provides efficient clues to useful theories, propositions, and causal factors. The efficiency of the clue (how clearly, quickly, and precisely it gets us to the idea) and the utility of that idea determine the value of a heuristic contribution. Because there is almost always more than one route to an idea of this kind, the competition among heuristics can and should be severe.

How could a general cluster of concepts such as we have discussed in the first part of the chapter serve as a heuristic in this more rigorous sense? The most important means is through focusing the attention of scholars. The range of political factors relevant in explaining any political fact is so large and so complex, and could be organized in so many ways, that identifying areas in which to look constitutes a major service to a scholar searching for explanations. Concepts might also provide clues to the structure of an explanation. There are many ways of ordering causal chains, and productive clues about which types of variables might fit into which slots can be very useful. Corporatism's heuristic contribution has been to emphasize (1) the central importance of state-group ties for explaining a variety of outcomes; (2) the importance of differentiation within the state apparatus; and (3) the importance of "design" and "choice" in explanation.

Probably the central heuristic rule which one can tease out of the corporatist framework concerns the importance it gives to structural-legal relationships in state group ties. In corporatist theory, the first question in almost any political explanation schema is, How are the interests linked to the state apparatus? Corporatism requires one to look not only at the interests of the state, but also at the structure that defines the relationships between various interests, the organizations that represent them, and the bureaucracy.

If the explanatory task is to indicate the causes of, say, the adoption of a particular policy, the corporatist heuristic directs the investigator to consider not only the relative power of the interest groups measured by the resources at their command (as pluralists would do), but also the interests of the actors in maintaining or changing their formally defined position within the state, and the way in which the formally defined patterns of representation affect the utilization of resources.

These issues have become central in policy analysis and other forms of political investigation in the 1970s and 1980s, although probably not through the prompting of corporatists. Studies of "bureaucratic politics" focus on the structure of the bureaucratic elements and the interests generated by that structure as significant in shaping policy outcomes.[16] Such studies have been particularly common in analyses of foreign policy decisions, presumably because in that arena, a relatively high percentage of actors (State Department and National Security Council members, for example) have obvious bureaucratic goals, and the interests of their constituencies are hard even to define. Corporatism is a more general approach to the problem of explaining policy outcomes, which has in general been dealt with rather parochially. It states the basic proposition that the rights and privileges determined by an individual's position in the state structure are important in shaping all sorts of political processes.

Corporatists also consider the "state" not as a single entity with a single interest, but rather as a "naturally" divided entity, made up of particular relationships with the major economic groups and professions (or however interests are defined). The state cannot be isolated from civil society: It is defined by the series of links that form both the state and the societal groups. On the one hand, there cannot be any single state interest, because the state is so complex. On the other hand, one cannot talk about state interests as opposed to those of society when the state is in fact made up of ties with interests in civil society. One can easily employ paradoxical notions in discussing these sorts of relationships, but the point is very simple. The corporatist framework instructs us that simpler and more accurate explanations of such things as policy decisions must begin with a description of the complex and multiple formal and informal legal relationships between the state apparatus and interests.

Another dimension of the heuristic provided by corporatism is highlighted by Charles W. Anderson.[17] By focusing attention on the importance of state-initiated structuring of group-state relationships, corporatism draws attention to the choices being made by those who design those links.

Political actions and their results are shaped by the institutions and laws that govern the system in which they take place. Those institutions and laws are the product of conscious design by constitutional conventions, legislatures, dominant leaders, triumphant revolutionary parties, and military juntas. Designing institutions implies making big choices. Although there are many small modifications made in any institution or law over the years, there are moments when a single great decision has to be made, providing a strong incentive for legislators to think about the whole institution and make even smaller choices in the light of its overall functioning. In other words, a major determinant of the outcome of political actions lies in the singular, conscious choices being made by those who are periodically called upon (or seize the opportunity) to design the political framework.

Political analysis often pays great attention to the actions of rulers, but the canons of the scientific method as applied to the social sciences were often said to require the rejection of the attempt to explain individual and unique occurrences and to focus instead on repeated patterns. Choice became the concern of political (and other social) scientists when the choice was repeated many times, as in voting. The study of major policy decisions, which clearly represent a sort of macro choice, was treated either as "merely history," as just one instance of the class of choices of a similar type, or as something to be explained as the outcome of many more stable causes.[18] When the results of a single choice are very influential in determining the course of political events that the political scientist wishes to explain, the choice is often assumed to be a given, say, as the fixed preferences of those making the decision.

Students of public policy are concerned with legislation drawn up by a government, and one might expect them to use an explanatory scheme based at least in part on choice. Yet they often do not go beyond the notion of given, fixed preferences of groups. They may use a simple model of choice that describes the outcome of policy choices as the result of pressures put on the decisionmaker. These pressures are the combination of established preferences (the direction) and the relative power of the group (the force). This reduces choice to a mechanical interaction.

The cognitive elements of choice are returning to the center of concern, however. By "cognitive elements" I mean the way in which preferences are shaped and decisions made on the basis of knowledge, information, and various symbolic forms. No one ever denied that these were important (except, perhaps for some cynics) but there appeared to be no way to enter cognitive elements into a systematic analysis. The rules governing cognitive behavior were either related to the "irrational" or based on logic. Logic, however, never got very far in explaining human behavior. It produced, rather, a general cynicism about the lack of education and culture among both common people and political leaders. What is needed is a more rigorous analysis of design and choice that takes into account the rapidly expanding knowledge of the structure of choice that lies between the rarefied elements of logic and the subterranean elements of the irrational. There is much being explored in the various divisions of cognitive science that is relevant.[19]

What is being "designed" in the cases with which corporatism is the most concerned is, of course, not policies but the larger structures of decisionmaking in a system: the regime and the state-group links. The choices involved in designing a regime are to be found in many aspects of political life, but are epitomized in the process of writing constitutions. Yet the study of constitutions and the writing of constitutions have not been very popular in the field of political science, and more particularly in comparative politics (in which it used to find a very comfortable home). Corporatism's emphasis on the importance of the structure of decisionmaking points toward a reinvigoration of the field.

This heuristic of corporatism, then, consists in a broad admonition to assess the design choices that have gone into the situation at hand. The factors that shape the outcomes will be a complex interaction of direct physical determinants as well as the conscious recognition, backed up by state authority, of the intentions of the designers of the system.

Corporatism and Interpretation

Evaluating the contribution of corporatism to interpretation requires a different set of criteria. What is important is the help corporatism can provide in assessing the significance of political events, not why they occur. Generally, corporatism is probably more effective at interpretation than it is at explanation. This is not surprising for a theory born in political action, not political science. The interpretive point of view involves much less "hard science" than explanation, but to people faced with making choices, interpretation is more relevant. People need some way of deciding the significance of what they are called on to do, and for this they need to know more than the latest causal explanation.

The first step in interpretive theories establishes a normative standard to allow direct evaluation. A norm is an elemental form of interpretive theory; it allows the observer to measure a polity against this norm and make an evaluation. The norm may be relatively simple—for example, "income is divided unequally"—or exceedingly complex—as in the statement, "human potential for realization is frustrated in this society." Evaluation may be used, of course, for assigning blame, estimating salvation, or as a basis for acting in order to achieve the ideal.

The second step, more intricate than the first, is to link general causal theory with these norms. This creates a complex I shall call "historicist theory."[20] It establishes a historical trajectory against which one can assess both current progress toward the ideal future state and the effectiveness of the current structure in establishing a historical path that will lead to the ideal. Beyond a simple evaluation of events, one gains insight about their significance by placing them in the flow of history. Political events can then be understood as a stage in the growth of a social structure, or as steps on the road to liberation from a besetting evil.

The most important modern models of historicist theory are Marxist socialism, in which the importance and significance of events is derived from the relationship of those events to the process of social revolution, and pluralist development, which establishes a link to an evolutionary pattern. The stages of growth in development theory are defined by reference to the end point of a fully developed, pluralist and democratic society. Development theory identified key steps and obstacles along the way and employed measurements of modernization to establish just where country X was in the process. Studies of obstacles looked at the relationship between, for example, urban poverty and traditional cultures and the grand historical process of development. Marxism, of course, has a similar range of elements.

Corporatism is also a historicist doctrine. It provides two bases of interpretation, which are in fact at least partially contradictory. First, corporatism suggests the possibility of an alternative path of historical change, which some countries take while others follow pluralist or socialist paths. Secondly, corporatism refers to a stage in development shared by all or most societies.

The Corporatist Path

Corporatism represents an alternative model of history. Of all the possible variants of historical experience that countries might go through, there are a limited number of types, and corporatist evolution is one of them. Philippe Schmitter presented this argument in his article, "Paths to Political Development in Latin America," and Howard Wiarda has been an indefatigable proponent of this point of view. Wiarda's position is most evident in his recent book, *Corporatism and National Development in Latin America,* in which he strongly emphasizes the role of corporatism in counteracting U.S./ European ethnocentrism in evaluations of change in Latin America.

Schmitter explicitly (and others by implication) postulates three main paths.

1. A pluralist path, in which societies proceed by gradual differentiation and specialization to a more and more integrated and presumably liberal-democratic society
2. A totalitarian path, in which an ideologically committed elite pushes through a comprehensive program
3. A corporatist path, usually linked with some form of authoritarianism

The notion of alternative paths of development has been important because of the general attack on development theorists, who have been accused of forcing the U.S. pattern of evolution (modified somewhat by their understanding of British history) on the experiences of Latin America and other Third World areas. The best-known alternative to the image of development is, however, not corporatism, but the dependency perspective, which is generally anchored in some form of Marxism. According to dependency theory, the later industrializing countries could not follow the same path as Great Britain or the United States because they had to deal with these already powerful states. The new countries had to adapt, and dependent development was the result. How one describes this form of development is a matter of perspective. A pessimist would characterize dependent development as stunted, or at the very least, distorted; a Marxist might suggest that a new, North-South revolutionary dynamic is occurring; a new realist would focus on particular variations in the patterns of production, distribution, and debt.

Wiarda's interpretation of corporatism takes a different perspective on the problem from that of the dependency theorists. In Wiarda's view, differences in development paths stem not only from the different environments of the new countries, but also from their distinctive historical traditions—in other words, their culture. "Culture" in this context refers not merely to a set of ideas, but to a set of practices and formal structures that result from the distinctive situation—including distinctive material conditions. The lines in the debate over the significance of culture are drawn not between "ideas" and "material conditions" but between the impact of history—through the accumulation of institutions and practices—and the impact of current demands. The dependency perspective is a historicist vision that views the behavior of societies as principally an ongoing adaptation to current external demands. Wiarda's view of historical trajectories emphasizes the momentum of the artifacts, institutions, norms, and ideologies. He argues that the accumulation of earlier adaptive responses and imposed practices in the southern European Latin cultures established a corporatist outlook and set of institutions. These were reflected in literature and education, which in turn reinforced corporatist practices and structures.

Schmitter and others criticize this view by noting that corporatist institutions are not continuous, but this is not a convincing argument against the existence of an effective corporatist culture. That culture could be so deeply embedded, for example, that it persists as a model and preferred form even though external forces or domestic calamities might impose a temporary alternative might suggest that the culture is even more relevant.[21] The corporatist historical trajectory, interpreted fundamentally as a culture, remains important. Discontinuity in corporatist institutions does highlight the problem of specifying the sources of corporatist institutions. If culture is only one determinant, what are the others?

Schmitter[22] speaks of the "elective affinity" of some countries, particularly in Latin America, for corporatism. Beyond culture, he attributes this to some of the factors that figure prominently in the discussions of economic growth. He discusses the impact of late development, that is, situations in which countries have to "catch up." This induces a high level of concerted state effort to speed up the developmental process, and the deals struck with the major economic interests push these countries toward corporatism. Similarly, the dependency of these countries on foreign markets and technology leads to state actions to break or weaken the dependency link and give the domestic economy the space to grow. The sorts of controls the state must impose are related to those that form the basis of corporatism. Dependency theorists do not normally postulate a corporatist path of development. They are more likely to view some new form of socialist revolutionary dynamic as the essential historical movement. But some of the same factors do fit in with a corporatist model.

The vision of a distinct corporatist path is potentially an important interpretive framework with which to understand the development of some parts of the Third World in a way that avoids the ethnocentrism of assuming that they will all inevitably follow the path toward liberal, capitalistic democracy, or that they will have to follow the revolutionary Marxist path. It poses important and interesting questions. The debate between the cultural and economic determinism of this path is one set of questions. Another set asks how closely such countries, presumably concentrated in southern Europe and Latin America, have approximated the ideal path of corporatism, and the consequences of the effort to impose pluralistic institutions in "essentially" corporatist countries.[23]

Corporatism as an Evolutionary Stage

A problem emerges, however, for observers who see signs of corporatism in places such as the United States.[24] The cultural argument would pretty well rule out a country without corporatist traditions becoming corporatist, as there is no underlying structure to which it can relate, and dependency does not help. The increasing evidence of corporatist institutions in such societies has therefore engendered a new form of historicist theory for corporatism. In this interpretation, corporatism is not an alternative path of development, but a stage in the evolution of political society. In response to the turmoil of late nineteenth-century Europe, corporatism offered an explicit counterproposal to the socialists' vision of the coming stages of history. Instead of the triumph of the working class over the bourgeoisie, the corporatists envisaged a future stage of harmony achieved through the reconciliation of the classes. This would be a corporatist era, or, as M.

Manoilescu called it in the title of one of the better known of corporatism's texts, "century of corporatism."[25]

If corporatist society is a stage in the "normal" evolution of societies, there must be a common underlying dynamic—a process they all go through to shape a common history. The internal forces of change in Marxism are dialectical, and in pluralist theories of development, technological and attitudinal change provides the dynamic force, but in corporatist theory there is no commanding, comprehensive treatment of the dynamic that produces corporatism. There are, however, a number of possible theories. A conservative variation understands the corporatist dynamic as the drive to restore the harmony of society that was shattered by industrialization. This suggests a very long-term equilibrium model, in which modernization is a powerful disruption and either complex social forces or conscious efforts to restore the balance provide the homeostatic force. Corporatism as a critical doctrine aims to transform society to restore the premodern harmony that existed before the "fall" into modern chaos. The central norm of this interpretation is the integrality of the community.

An alternative hypothesis in corporatist interpretive theory links the rise of corporatism to that of the state. In the 1920s the moving force that often promoted corporatism was nationalism. Linking nationalism and the state is one of the central points of corporatism, which treats them, along with community, as essentially overlapping aspects of the same reality. The forces leading to nationalism could be linked to corporatism on the grounds that they created the vehicle through which society could be organized and harmonized.

The growth of the state itself, irrespective of its links with nationalism, has been an obvious characteristic of the post–World War II period, and several implications of this trend are relevant to corporatism. One might begin with a rather developmentalist argument that the sheer expansion of governmental size and responsibilities leads to increasing specialization and differentiation of the governmental apparatus, and these units increasingly attract and then institutionalize relationships with interest groups. Regulation, planning, and coordination, made necessary by this expansion, may be seen as forcing an organization of procedures and institutions that is essentially corporatist. Alternatively, growth in the techniques of domination may lead elites in a position to influence state policy to promote controls over their competitors. Critics of corporatism see it as an ideological position justifying repression of workers, and the tools for repression as well as more subtle forms of control are increasingly easy to find. Over time, competing groups may take the reins of government and create more controls. The web of relationships that emerges may take on the character of corporatism.

A clear analysis of the basic dynamics of corporatism has not yet taken shape. Some scholars might object that such a large-scale and ambitious analysis is not feasible, and remain content merely to describe trends. Without some theory of the underlying dynamics, however, corporatism will never have the analytical power to become a major interpretive theory.

Another way of analyzing corporatism as interpretive theory is to ask about the envisaged historical scenario. Where does corporatism fit in? What stages are involved? Manoilescu and other scholars writing in the 1920s and 1930s thought of corporatism as an emerging dominant form of political organization, if not the culmination of historical political development. Among contemporary scholars of comparative politics in the United States, where residual liberalism is very strong, the tendency has been to consider corporatism, for all of its plausibility and important goals, as an intermediate stage in history. In his interpretation of Latin American and southern European corporatism, Howard Wiarda has clearly implied that despite its successes and appropriateness to the culture of the area, corporatism is a schema that must be transcended in order to achieve real development.[26] Schmitter, a bit playful with ideas, perhaps, ended his article on the "century of corporatism" with a hint that corporatism may be giving way to syndicalism.[27]

EVALUATION

Before considering corporatism's role in the practice of comparative politics, a few notes about corporatism's potential political role are appropriate. It is very unlikely that corporatism, named as such, will reemerge as politically important, given its legacy of association with the fascist regimes of the interwar period. However, this prediction does not hold for the concepts associated with corporatism. Some of these concepts will no doubt play an important role in politics, even though they may surface under another name.

There is no shortage of political advocates of a strong state, both among those who find democracies "ungovernable" and among those who feel that strong state action is required in developing the poorer countries. An ideology like corporatism could become the rallying cry of a new generation of politicians concerned with strengthening the state. I would expect, however, that the opposite might occur, with corporatism returning to the much earlier political role of limiting state power. Elements of corporatism may appeal to the conservative and neoliberal groups that have emerged in the 1970s and 1980s in countries such as the United States.

Although twentieth-century corporatist analysis has stressed the importance of an active role by the state, corporatism is also identified historically with limiting the state to protect the established privileges of important groups and institutions. The new conservatives of the 1980s tend to see private enterprise, the family, and local communities as entities that can and should exist completely separate from the bureaucracy, government officials, elected politicians, and the whole apparatus of the state. It seems almost inevitable that this generally conservative point of view will come to emphasize the protection of the established legal and political status of these groups—not their separation from the state in general, but insulation from the sort of arbitrary changes, restrictions, and disciplining that tends to be carried out by either authoritarian dictators or by political majorities in liberal societies. Corporatism, or at least these elements of it, might easily become a focus for those who wish to stabilize and retrench, to protect societal groups against populist policies without threatening their privileged position in, and their protection by, the state.

Corporatism's ability to serve as an important research paradigm in comparative politics is more promising than its political prospects. The concept packages a set of heuristics that are becoming steadily more important. Designing relationships to specify particular rights and duties for the various interest groups in society seems appropriate for the 1980s. In contrast to the pressure/bargaining models of pluralism or the Marxist effort to find a reductionist dynamic, corporatism seems to point scholars in the right direction.

As the state expands, links between official bodies and social groupings of all kinds have also proliferated. Analysts need concepts that will catch this type of increased "webbing" between the various elements of society, and corporatism does this better than liberalism or Marxism, both of which tend to reduce the relationships to ones of power. The expansion of the state is not the expansion of a single entity, but the increasing density of relationships that center on the official apparatuses of the state. Corporatism catches this better because of its focus on the links of the groups with the state apparatus, not on the distribution of power between a state interest and a societal interest.

The regulatory, consultative, and other sorts of relationships that are constantly being constructed and reconstructed between groups and the government have become a very active part of government. The image of governments simply making and then implementing policy foreshortens the process. Establishing bureaucratic instruments through which to implement and monitor policy is a major activity, and such acts of "bureaucratic creativity" have meaning not only for the specific policy, of course, but for the whole range of exchanges between the government and the affected interests. In other words, corporatist design has become more and more evident in the contemporary practice of statecraft.

There are, however, major problems with corporatism as a serious contribution to interpretive theory. Anderson points out, for example, that a major problem in implementing a corporatist design for a political system is that corporatism fails either to specify which interests should be represented in the state or to provide the means to make that specification.[28] This is not just a matter of applying a general analysis of such interests to the specifics of a particular country and time. That would be bad enough, but the problem is worse. No meaningful criteria have yet been established. As noted above, the corporatists of the 1920s and 1930s apparently accepted a quasi-Marxist definition of classes as at least one set of interests. The workers and the managers, suitably divided among a few general sectors of the economy, constituted the basic elements of corporatist schemes, although the logic of this was not convincingly spelled out. If corporatism does not begin from the quasi-Marxist definition of interest, it is apparently forced to accept any and all interest groups as legitimate and thereby becomes only marginally distinguishable from pluralism. If corporatism is to identify a certain kind of regime, then it must be able to determine which interest groups deserve the sorts of rights and privileges corporatism specifies. Otherwise, corporatism provides no way of assessing how well particular state relationships fit the mold and, therefore, no way of guiding action. This reduces corporatism to merely a post hoc justification that does not satisfy the requirements of interpretive theory.

Perhaps an even more damaging weakness of corporatism as an interpretive theory is its difficulty in specifying dynamic factors that would bring about the changes it projects. The reestablishment of equilibrium after the "disturbance" of modernism, nationalism, and the expansion of the modern state is so general as to be unconvincing. A truly powerful interpretive theory enables one to assess the value of certain actions in conforming to, countering, or making way for the operation of basic historical dynamics. In seeking the integration of group-state links, corporatism cannot afford to be vague about what causes integration or disintegration.

Finally, corporatism has paid little attention to the nature of conflict between groups. Some conservatives see corporatism as promoting depoliticized patterns of conflict resolution, with the interpretation that conflict must be resolved through the arbitration of experts. But the connection between the expert's opinion and the good of the community, which is the central part of the ideal, is not well explicated. Without further specification along these lines, the mechanics of progress toward harmony will remain unclear.

Corporatism has had a very important role in comparative politics as part of the critical attack on the pluralist-developmental thinking that dominated the field in the 1960s and 1970s. As a non-Marxist—even anti-Marxist—conception that has some affinity to the state-heavy authoritarian forms of government, it has opened up new ways of seeing. Particularly attractive is its perspective on the dominant fact of political life in the late twentieth century: the ramifying, interpenetrating network of state-society relationships. It is not yet, and may never be, a genuinely powerful research and theory-constructing paradigm. This would require not just elaboration of detail and empirical applications, but rather a thoroughgoing inspection and strengthening of its analytical foundations. And, given the political liabilities of the term, the constituent concepts of the ideology might emerge after such an overhaul under new names. Corporatism is full of interesting ideas and suggestions, but it is unlikely to survive in its present form.

NOTES

1. This emphasis appears, for example, in Philippe Schmitter's article, "Paths to Political Development in Latin America," in D. Chalmers, ed., *Changing Latin America* (New York: Academy of Political Science, 1972). Also see the collection edited by Frederick B. Pike and Thomas Stritch, *The New Corporatism: Social and Political*

Structures in the Iberian World, (Notre Dame, IN: University of Notre Dame Press, 1974); and Howard Wiarda, *Corporatism and National Development in Latin America* (Boulder, CO: Westview Press, 1981).

2. One sees references to the "corporate state" or the "corporate society" referring to the prominence of business corporations in political affairs, or, perhaps, the similarity of the state apparatus to a business corporation. This is not the meaning here. It may be a peculiarly American usage, in fact, to identify "corporations" only with business corporations.

3. Philippe Schmitter, "Still the Century of Corporatism?" in Pike and Stritch, *The New Corporatism*, pp. 93–94.

4. For this reason, class analysis and corporatist approaches both seem more relevant than pluralism to areas such as Latin America and the Third World in general, where the state is called upon to play a central role.

5. The more common meaning of "monopoly" remains applicable, of course. Firms still get monopoly profits by a variety of techniques ranging from a clever use of patents to coercion. Even this seems to be more difficult, however, with so many marginally different products. In any case, monopolies of representation are far more difficult to maintain.

6. See Schmitter, "Still the Century of Corporatism?" Note the association of corporatism with authoritarianism in the studies of the phenomenon in Latin America, as in James Malloy, ed., *Authoritarianism and Corporatism in Latin America* (Pittsburgh: Pittsburgh University Press, 1977).

7. For Italy see A. Aquarone, *L'organizzazione dello stato totalitario* (Turin: Guilio Einaudi, 1965).

8. Charles W. Anderson argues that parliaments are the typical institutional form of corporatism, and he is clearly right in that the ancient corporations met in bodies that evolved into modern parliaments. The modern typical form of corporatism would be, however, the administrative/consultative committee. Parliaments are too much the loci of bargaining among individuals (at least in the United States) or groups representing party factions that are not clearly interest linked to be significant as corporatist institutions. See his comments in Charles W. Anderson, "Political Design and the Representation of Interests," in P. Schmitter and G. Lehmbruch, eds., *Trends Towards Corporatist Intermediation* (Beverly Hills, CA: Sage, 1979), pp. 271–298.

9. Alfred Stepan, in *The State and Society: Peru in Comparative Perspective* (Princeton, NJ: Princeton University Press, 1978), discusses the "organic state" tradition, which emphasizes the integral nature of the community. He distinguishes this tradition sharply from corporatism generally on the grounds that the latter refers only to the institutions that relate individual interest groups with the state. This may be clarifying, but the two concepts have been used together, and depend on each other too much to make the separation permanent.

10. See Guillermo O'Donnell, "Corporatism and the Question of the State," in Malloy, *Authoritarianism and Corporatism*.

11. The term is central to Stepan's analysis in *The State and Society*.

12. Particularly useful in showing these changes are two volumes on the history of corporatism: R. Bowen, *German Theories of the Corporative State* (New York: Whittlesey, 1947); and M. H. Elbow, *French Corporative Theory: 1789–1948* (New York: Columbia University Press, 1953).

13. See Howard J. Wiarda, *Corporatism and Development: The Portuguese Experience* (Amherst: University of Massachusetts Press, 1977); and Stepan, *The State and Society*.

14. See particularly his collected articles in Wiarda, *Corporatism and National Development*.

15. For an example of the looser use, see Wiarda's last chapter in ibid. The more rigorous use of the term *heuristic* is common in writings on problem solving in such fields as "artificial intelligence." See for example A. Newell and H. Simon, *Human Problem Solving* (Englewood Cliffs, NJ: Prentice-Hall, 1972).

16. Well-known works in this bureaucratic politics school include G. Allison, *The Essence of Decision: Explaining the Cuban Missile Crisis* (Boston: Little, Brown, 1977); and M. Halperin, *Bureaucratic Politics and Foreign Policy* (Washington, DC: Brookings Institution, 1974).

17. Anderson, "Political Design."

18. The influence of the power and success of economic analysis is evident here, to the point that "theories of choice" as currently formulated in political science seem more often than not to be formulated as probabilistic theories of repeated choices, modeled on consumer choices. Voting studies are one example.

19. See, for example, Herbert Simon's immensely stimulating *The Sciences of the Artificial* (Cambridge, MA: MIT Press, 1969). For a collection of recent contributions, see D. F. Norman, ed., *Perspectives on Cognitive Science* (Norwood, NJ: Ablex, 1981). For an interesting review of some major concepts in perception and choice as they relate to international politics, see Robert Jervis, "Political Decision Making: Recent Contributions," *Political Psychology* 2, 2(Summer 1980):86–101.

20. The term "historicist" distinguishes this interpretive theory from that focused on less time-oriented concepts, such as theories based on the realization of an individual's potential during his or her lifetime or on a static moral ideal. As a static moral imperative toward harmony and integration, corporatism might conceivably function as a nonhistoricist interpretive theory, but this is not its most important use for comparative politics.

21. This seems to be one conclusion that might be drawn from Stepan's emphasis on the tradition of the organic state in Peru. At the very least, one should consider the "organic state" as an available option no matter what form of regime exists. See Stepan, *The State and Society*.

22. For example, in Schmitter, "Paths to Political Development."

23. There is much work, particularly in the 1950s and 1960s, that interpreted Latin America's political difficulties as rooted in the conflict of liberalizing trends with the traditions of the area. See, for example, Kalman Silvert, "The Costs of Anti-Nationalism: Argentina," in *The Conflict Society* (New York: American Universities Field Staff, 1966); and Richard Morse, "The Heritage of Latin America," in L. Hartz, ed., *The Founding of New Societies* (New York: Harcourt, Brace and World, 1964).

24. Howard Wiarda, for example, has noted a number of such features in "The Latin Americanization of the United States," in *Corporatism and National Development*, pp. 323–339. He does not, in that essay, seem aware of the problem for theory being considered here, i.e., that corporatism may be considered either an alternative path or a common stage, but not both, without a much more complex version of history than has been developed.

25. M. Manoilescu, *Le siècle du corporatisme* (Paris: Felix Alcan, 1936).

26. This seems to be the implication, for example, of the last paragraphs of Howard J. Wiarda, "Toward a Framework for the Study of Political Change in the Iberic-Latin Tradition: The Corporative Model," *World Politics* 25 (January 1973):206–235.

27. See Schmitter, "Still the Century of Corporatism?" I interpret Schmitter's use of "syndicalism" as referring to the growth of communes, grass-roots labor unions, and various forms of "collectives," which was a popular theme with observers in the 1960s. I wonder whether Schmitter would still suggest this direction for social change in the 1980s.

28. Anderson, "Political Design."

5

Typologies of Democratic Systems: From Political Inputs to Political Economy

PETER LANGE
HUDSON MEADWELL

INTRODUCTION

In the years between the two world wars, several European experiments with democratic institutions succumbed to authoritarian overthrow. Each of the cases shared certain critical features. The societies were deeply divided along organized, ideological lines. The party systems, reflecting these divisions, were composed of several highly contentious and ideologically oriented parties. And the breakdown of the democratic regime was preceded in each case by signs of decaying social, political, and economic order, including increased political violence, labor unrest, government instability, and high rates of inflation and unemployment.

In light of this experience, democratic stability became the "dominant concern of contemporary studies of democratic systems" (Lijphart 1968:8). A variety of typologies were proposed, and it was from "efforts at explanation [of democratic stability] that the typologies of democratic systems derive[d] their theoretical significance" (pp. 8–9). Despite important differences among them, these typologies share three important features. First, they emphasize the explanatory importance of variables on the input side of the political system—individual attitudes and political culture, societal and political role structure, political parties treated as input structures—or on the linkages between these. Second, the social and political divisions they focus on are culturally or ideologically defined, subjective rather than objective. Third, their overriding normative concern is democratic stability, and dependent variables are selected for their relevance to the stability of a regime.

These typologies—which together can be said to reflect a "liberal" approach to democratic systems—have left a profound mark on the postwar study of democracies and remain a primary reference point for scholarly work. Yet as early as 1968, Arend Lijphart noted that they required "substantial modification . . . because the generalizations that are explicitly or implicitly based on them are not entirely satisfactory" (Lijphart 1968:8). Drawing on his research on patterns of accommodation primarily among religious groups in the Netherlands, Lijphart successfully challenged the pluralist argument that societal consensus on fundamental values was a prerequisite for political stability. His reservations led him to shift his focus from mass toward elite values and behavior, without abandoning the liberal approach.

Especially since the 1970s, many studies have suggested that the liberal approach, in all of its variations, may be misplaced when trying to explain the politics of the contemporary advanced industrial democracies. In these studies—some of which are discussed in more detail below under "The Political Economy Approach," the factors identified as determining political outcomes have shifted from society to state, from individuals and their values to groups and their interests, and from the institutions of individual representation to the bureaucratic and administrative structures for policy formulation and implementation. Four specific implications, each of them relevant to the shared features of the liberal approach, can be culled from this literature. First, the stress is shifted from inputs to "withinputs" (Easton 1965), from variables outside the bureaucratic-administrative structures to features and processes of those structures themselves and of their relationship to organized social interests. Second, the emphasis is less on culturally or ideologically defined divisions in society and the polity than on functionally or structurally (class) defined divisions. Third, some studies have focused on the relative political power of functionally defined groups in the state and society, especially in the market. Fourth, the major interest of these studies is to explain a variety of aspects of system performance that are less aggregative than stability and that range beyond the kinds of variables central to the liberal studies to including political economic outcomes. The basic question has become not how stable each type of democracy is, but how the different types perform with regard to a broad range of political and political-economic variables, and what kinds of trade-offs are involved. It is sometimes implicit in these studies that poor performance overall will lead to instability, but this is neither an inherent characteristic of this work nor a critical assumption in undertaking it.

Students of democratic systems are thus confronted with two divergent—although not necessarily contradictory—approaches. There have been few systematic attempts to compare their relative usefulness in explaining different types of system outcomes, aggregated or disaggregated or even to compare the relative merits of different typologies within the same approach. For the most part, each study proposes a different scheme for classifying democratic systems, and the schemes often reflect a political system the author is particularly familiar with. The typology is then used to explain those outcomes with which the author is particularly concerned.

The absence of a systematic comparison of approaches and typologies is unfortunate because the evaluation of their strengths and weaknesses has potentially important implications for normative and empirical democratic theory. Each typology, with its attendant premises and assumptions, represents a (generally implicit) statement or theory about how democratic systems operate and about the trade-offs between different democratic values. Compared and correlated, they could help in identifying what the really important factors are in explaining different types of performance and what choices and trade-offs citizens of democratic systems may be confronted with.

Despite their sometimes different explanatory purposes, many of the dependent variables employed by different typologies are similar, providing a convenient basis for comparison. Typologies can be judged by their explanatory breadth, the extent to which they enable scholars "to make the maximum number of prophecies and deductions" (Huxley 1940, cited in Hempel 1952:53; see also Lakatos 1970), and this breadth could be the criterion for evaluating relative worth.

It might be argued that rather than compare different typologies, one should abandon typological analysis entirely and move toward sophisticated multivariate analyses employing the variables that have been incorporated into the different classifications of systems. There is significant merit in this viewpoint. It would permit a more flexible mix of independent variables and would avoid the problems of arbitrarily treating continuous variables as if they were ordinal. Nonetheless, there are reasons to proceed as we do here. Typologies have been an integral feature of postwar analysis of democratic systems, and abandoning them without a thorough evaluation would involve an unnecessary loss of the information recorded in a vast literature. In addition, despite the problems, there is an obvious attraction in being able to characterize whole systems with the related implication that different systemic features "hang together." It seems worthwhile, therefore, to compare typologies even if there may be some loss of information and analytic specificity.

This chapter is a first step toward a comparative analysis of postwar typologies. After a brief discussion of some methodological issues we discuss five typologies, three that reflect the liberal approach and two from the political economy school. We then suggest the type of outcomes or dependent variables the different typologies might be expected to explain, discuss the problems of focusing on stability, and propose other measures of performance. We identify a number of recent trends in comparative research on democratic systems and describe the theoretical and analytical trade-offs associated with the use of different typologies, dependent variables, and outcomes.

METHODOLOGICAL PREAMBLE

What criteria determine the boundaries of relevant country cases? What constitutes a typology? What can we expect typologies to explain? These issues are taken up briefly in this section.

The Selection of Typologies for Comparison

What countries are appropriate subjects for the kind of comparative study we are interested in? The answer depends on the definition of democracy and the historical, geographical, and developmental criteria used to identify relevant cases.

A rather broad and widely accepted definition of functioning democracy ("polyarchy") is that of Robert Dahl:

> I assume that a key characteristic of a democracy is the continuing responsiveness of the government to the preferences of its citizens, considered as political equals. . . .
>
> I assume further that in order for a government to continue over a period of time to be responsive to the preferences of its citizens, considered as political equals, all full citizens must have unimpaired opportunities:
>
> 1. To formulate their preferences.
> 2. To signify their preferences to their fellow citizens and the government by individual and collective action.
> 3. To have their preferences weighed equally in the conduct of the government, that is, weighed with no discrimination because of the content or source of the preference.
>
> These, then appear to me to be three necessary conditions for a democracy although they are probably not sufficient. (Dahl 1971:1–2)

This definition has the merit of incorporating the institutional features of democratic systems as they are popularly understood. It accords with the typologies we have chosen to examine, providing a shared terrain.

The most promising group of cases for our purposes are the post–World War II advanced industrial democracies. Confining the analysis to this group, while it limits the number of cases, has both practical and theoretical advantages. First, it allows us to assemble data on a wide range of indicators of performance for all the countries under consideration. Second, in opting for a "most similar systems design" (Przeworski and Teune 1970:32–34), we control for two variables, economic development and historical period.

Of the countries included in our study (Austria, Belgium, Canada, Denmark, Finland, France, Italy, Netherlands, Norway, Sweden, Switzerland, United Kingdom, United States, and West Germany), all have highly developed industrial capitalist economies today, and most were already relatively more advanced industrial economies by the early 1950s. Numerous studies have suggested that the performance of democratic regimes is affected by the degree of economic development (Lipset 1963). Recently, Powell (1981, 1982) has shown significant effects of levels of per capita GNP on several indicators of system performance; in some cases, these were sufficient to eliminate any net effects of the typology he was utilizing. Limiting our study to postwar systems also removes the possible impact of historical period. Our justification for excluding systems like Weimar Germany and the First Austrian Republic, which have often played an important role in the development of hypotheses about the factors promoting democratic stability, is that pre– and post–World War II Europe are qualitatively different contexts, with great significance for the stability and performance of democracies. As an example, the impact of international system variables, both political and economic, on the probability that already democratic systems would remain so was markedly different in the two periods. It then seems advisable to treat the two periods separately when testing for the effects of domestic variables on system performance. This does not exclude comparisons between the two periods at a subsequent stage of analysis.

The Selection of Cases for Comparison

All five cases to be discussed satisfy the basic requirement of a typology: Their categories are mutually exclusive and jointly exhaustive of the selected range of cases (see Hempel 1952:51). Typologies vary in their ability to fulfill two other functions: mapping and explanation. Mapping refers to the typology's usefulness in identifying important characteristics of the system based on "highly *visible* and *elemental* information" (Sartori 1976:291, his emphasis). Typologies must also go beyond the classification stage to establish empirical propositions and explain or predict features of system behavior that are logically independent of the type-defining characteristics (see Sartori 1976:290–91; Lijphart 1968:6).

Lijphart, drawing on earlier work in the philosophy of science, has offered appropriate guidelines for the explanatory function of typologies. A typology, he argues, following Hempel (1952), should strive for naturalness: "The more it aids in the discovery of empirical relationships, the more natural it is" (Lijphart 1968:7). Unlike artificial classifications, which are useful only for the limited purpose for which they were constructed, a natural classification can be used for a wide range of purposes. This means that when we compare typologies, we need not do so solely on the basis of the specific issues, and in terms of the specific dependent variables, which the author of any particular scheme sought to explore; explanatory breadth should be a criterion for the evaluation of the relative explanatory power of different typologies as well. More specifically, when comparing the merits of different typological schemes, the following questions seem appropriate.

1. Which typology best explains the set of phenomena the typologies were originally intended to explain?
2. Which best explains the broader set of phenomena that are relevant and significant in evaluating the performance of democratic systems?

TYPOLOGIES

Typologies of democratic systems are the independent variables in our study. They should, as indicated, provide parsimonious criteria for mapping. A number of typologies that meet this condition can be identified or developed from arguments in the literature. Those that fall within the liberal tradition reflect the interwar experience and stress the importance of societal, institutional, cultural, and ideological factors on the input side of the system. Their primary normative concern has been democratic stability. The political economy typologies, which reflect the development of the postwar advanced industrial democracies, are more diffuse in focus but stress, inter alia, withinputs, functional and class divisions, the distribution of political power along functional or class lines, and the importance of the administrative-bureaucratic structures of the state. Explicit normative concerns have played a smaller role in this literature, disaggregated measures of performance a larger one. Those normative concerns that have been important are questions of equality and economic growth, and aggregated measures of performance have been replaced by more specific measures such as unemployment and inflation rates.

We will present the basic outline of three typologies within the first tradition and two within the second. For each we will discuss the basic focus around which they are constructed, and what outcomes they have been used to explain. For each we will also illustrate where specific countries fit within the types identified by the classifications.

The Liberal Approach

Almond and Lijphart

In 1956, as part of a broader effort to develop a typology of political systems sensitive to differing levels of political development, Gabriel Almond proposed that democratic systems were of two types: the Anglo-American and the Continental European. The labels were used for convenience. What differentiated the types was not their location but the degree of homogeneity of the political culture and the extent of role differentiation. The Anglo-American systems were said to have homogeneous political cultures and highly differentiated role structures; the Continental European systems, segmented cultures and less differentiation of roles. The relationship between citizens and political organizations was also different. In the Continental European systems, "the organized political manifestations . . . take the form of 'movements' or sects, rather than political parties. This means that political affiliation is more of an act of faith than of agency" (Almond 1956:63). The Anglo-American systems were considered more developed and more stable. Almond argued that the stability of democratic systems could best be explained by the values and structures *in society* that fundamentally conditioned the inputs to the political system.

Almond's typology was, by his own admission, preliminary and tentative. Although it opened a discussion of different types of democratic systems, his typology excluded, for instance, the smaller European democracies and therefore fell short of becoming a major classificatory scheme for the broad, systematic analysis of cross-system differences. Over a decade later, Arend Lijphart (1968) made some significant modifications of Almond's formulation. In doing so, he created a typology that has become a major point of reference in the comparative politics literature (for a critique, see Steiner 1981).

Lijphart retained Almond's concern with stability and subcultural loyalties, but he observed that a number of European democracies with segmented cultures and low role differentiation were nonetheless stable. This led him

Figure 1
LIJPHART'S TYPOLOGY OF DEMOCRATIC SYSTEMS

Structure of Society

		Homogeneous	Plural
Elite Behavior	**Coalescent**	*Depoliticized* Austria (1966–)	*Consociational* Belgium Netherlands Austria (45–66) Switzerland
	Adversarial	*Centripetal* Finland Denmark Norway U.K. Sweden U.S. W. Germany	*Centrifugal* France Italy Canada

Source: Lijphart (1977): 106.

to hypothesize that "segmented or subcultural cleavages at the mass level" (Lijphart 1977:16) could be overcome by elite cooperation. This appeared to be the case in countries like the Netherlands, Belgium, Austria, and Switzerland, where elites worked together to reduce the potentially destabilizing effects of societal divisions. At the same time, elites used the values of the subcultures to bolster their own authority and thus increase the likelihood that elite bargains would be accepted at the mass level.[1]

On the basis of this analysis, Lijphart proposed a typology based on the structure of society—homogeneous or plural—and the behavior of elites—coalescent or adversarial. The resulting fourfold scheme is depicted in Figure 1, which employs the names Lijphart assigned to each of the types and indicates which European systems fall into which category.

Lijphart assigned great importance to the kinds of cultural divisions in society that Almond saw as a primary determinant of democratic instability. In systems with homogeneous political cultures, democracy was likely to be stable whether elites were coalescent or adversarial, although Lijphart raised the possibility that too much coalescence at all levels of society (the depoliticized democracies) could breed new forms of protest. In systems with heterogeneous and segmented cultures, however, the cultural divisions were assigned a double valence. They were sources of *potential* dissent and even system breakdown, but they could also help in the process of stabilization, *if* the elites of the subcultures chose to cooperate. This might suggest that Lijphart's scheme emphasized both inputs and withinputs as determinants of stability. Yet as Heisler and Kvavik (1974) have pointed out, Lijphart's analysis stresses not the structures and processes of the state through which elites cooperate, but rather the values they bring to their encounters. These values can be taken as formative of, rather than formed by, the political structures and processes through which policy is formulated and implemented.

This emerges clearly in Lijphart's summation of the consociational democracy type, which is the keystone to his entire classificatory scheme.

> Consociational democracy entails the cooperation by segmental leaders in spite of the deep cleavages separating the segments. This requires that the leaders feel at least some commitment to the maintenance of the unity of the country as well as a commitment to democratic practices. They must also have a basic willingness to engage in cooperative efforts with the leaders of the other segments in a spirit of moderation and compromise. At the same time they must retain the support and loyalty of their own followers. (Lijphart 1977:53)

The typologies developed by Almond and Lijphart represent a systematic attempt to use mass and elite values, and therefore societal and cultural input factors, to map democratic system types. Lijphart has also explicitly stressed the explanatory purpose of his typology. "Contrary to the view of some critics . . . it links the independent variables of the plural or non-plural character of society and of elite behavior to the dependent variable of political stability" (1977:108–9). Because Lijphart has emphasized the importance of "naturalness" in typologies, it is most appropriate that his typology be examined alongside others in terms of its relative ability to explain system outcomes.

Sartori's Typology

Despite its focus on political parties and the party system, Giovanni Sartori's typology of party systems (Sartori 1966, 1976) represents perhaps the most important and oft-cited alternative to Almond and Lijphart's scheme for the liberal analysis of democratic systems, for "the scheme is commonly used not only to distinguish between *party systems* but between entire *political systems*" (Lijphart 1968:6; emphasis in original). Sartori, too, concentrates on the input side of the system and takes democratic stability as his ultimate concern. He also gives an important role to political values. Yet his approach is quite distinct. On the one hand, Sartori's focus is not on how the distribution of mass and elite values affects stability, but rather on how the structure of the party system and the dynamics of party competition affect a democratic context in which the competition for votes is necessarily paramount. Sartori describes this difference between his approach and those that stress societal divisions bluntly: "Cleavages are not 'givens' coming out of the blue sky: they may mold and be reflected in the polity; but they may equally be polity molded" (Sartori 1976:291). On the other hand, Sartori is interested only in those values that are institutionally embedded in political parties in the form of political ideology. In contrast to the approach shared by Almond and Lijphart, therefore, Sartori is fundamentally concerned with the institutions (political parties) that he views as critical to the processes affecting political inputs and with how the structured and necessarily competitive relationship between them affects the probability of stable democratic life.

Figure 2
SARTORI'S TYPOLOGY OF PARTY SYSTEMS

Party System Fragmentation

Ideological Distance			
	Low	*Two-Party* Canada United States Austria United Kingdom	*Moderate Multipartisan* W. Germany Switzerland Netherlands Denmark Belgium French V
	High	*Predominant* Norway Sweden	*Extreme and Polarized* Finland Italy French IV

Source: Sartori (1976): 314.

Critics of Sartori have treated his typology as an elaboration of the traditional institutionalist interest in "the number of parties" as an explanation of the dynamics of democratic systems. In *Parties and Party Systems* (1976), the extended treatment of his overall approach, Sartori has vigorously denied this, maintaining instead that his typology employs two dimensions, one an independent variable and the other the most important intervening variable. The former is the "fragmentation of the party system," indicated by the number of politically relevant parties (with additional weight given, in some cases, to the balance of strength between the parties). Sartori establishes four categories: (1) one party predominant; (2) two-party; (3) three to five parties—moderate pluralist; and (4) more than five parties—extreme pluralist. The ideological distance variable is continuous, rather than ordinal, although Sartori uses the presence of an "antisystem" party as the chief indicator of great ideological distance. The party system fragmentation and ideological distance variables tend to covary directly: the larger the number of parties, the greater the ideological distance. This may explain why many have concluded that the number of parties is the defining characteristic of his typology. Nonetheless, a close reading of Sartori's discussion makes clear that the explanatory power of his scheme rests, for him, in the combination of the two variables. As he states, "with two predictors only (the independent and the major intervening variable, ideology) the scheme already accounts for a large number of dependent variables and already predicts a variety of trends and outcomes" (Sartori 1976:291). The combining of the two produces the fourfold classification presented in Figure 2.

What does Sartori hope to explain with this typology? Most directly, he seeks to explain the "direction of competition" (1976:293) among the parties. In their search for votes, do the parties move toward the political center (centripetal competition) or instead toward the extremes (centrifugal competition)? The prevailing tendency is indicated both by how the parties compete and, ultimately, by whether parties at the center of the political space are gaining or losing votes relative to parties at the extremes. Predominant, two-party, and moderate pluralist systems are characterized by centripetal competition, extreme pluralist ones by centrifugal competition. The former exercises a constant moderating pressure on party behavior, as all parties seek to increase their electorate by gaining votes in the center at the expense of rival parties. In polarized pluralist systems there is, instead, an "enfeeblement of the center" (p. 136) as "all the parties fight one another with ideological mentality" (p. 137). These contrasting patterns of competition are not necessarily a function of the will of party leaders, although they may be; instead, they are the necessary consequence of the systemic properties described above, and of the parties' drive for votes.

The direction of competition interests Sartori not only because it corresponds to other behavioral traits of the parties and party system, but also because it is "the one element that surely is of decisive consequence on the overall performance of the polity" (p. 293). The direction of competition has implications for government stability, for the ability of government to undertake effective policy (and sometimes any policies at all), for the legitimacy of the polity, and for the polity's capacity "to cope with explosive or exogenous crises" (p. 140). Sartori explicitly states (pp. 317–18) that the direction of competition affects the overall stability of the system, yet he also recognizes that even polarized polities can endure, for they can develop "invisible" mechanisms such as brokerage and clientistic systems to promote their survival (p. 143). It is, therefore, entirely appropriate to test his model at the level of specific measures of system outcomes and system performance.

Powell's Typology

The third of the liberal typologies is a recent one, proposed by G. Bingham Powell (1981 and 1982). Powell's typology is explicitly designed to explore the relationship between the "strength of the party system" and the performance of the political system. Like the other liberal typologies, it assumes that input factors are the most important in determining how well the system performs. Furthermore, Powell incorporates (but modifies) aspects of both the "number of parties" and societal cleavages arguments into his framework. He makes no assumptions about how well each type of system can be expected to perform. His intention, instead, is to evaluate the variables whose impact on performance has been debated in the parties' literature.

With one important qualification (concerning extremist parties), Powell's typology has two dimensions. First, does the party system produce parliamentary majorities? The issue here is: Which leads to better government performance, a party system with few, highly heterogeneous and aggregative parties producing clear legislative majorities, or one with parties that are more homogeneous but also more coherently representative and producing fewer legislative majorities? As Powell notes, this dimension parallels in several ways the "number of parties" criterion. His approach, however, emphasizes not the number of parties but rather whether or not majorities are produced. It also incorporates the long-standing debate in democratic theory about the possible trade-off between the representativeness of the party system and the effectiveness of government.

The second dimension is party-society linkage: whether or not there are strong and distinct linkages between different parties and social groups (Powell 1981:861). The issue here is whether system performance is better when strong, affective institutional ties between parties and subcultures provide the parties with high mobilizational capacity and enable them to have "disciplined governmental authority and policy-making ability" (1981:863) or when weak linkages produce much cross-cutting of cleavages and greater policy flexibility for parties in government. Despite a parallel emphasis on the importance of political culture, role structure, and, in the case of Lijphart, elite attitudes and links to their followers, Powell's argument stresses institutional linkages more than values, makes no assumptions about the views of elites regarding cooperation, and in principle although not operationally, includes functional as well as subcultural groups. Figure 3 uses Powell's typology to categorize some apposite advanced industrial democracies.

As mentioned earlier, Powell introduces an important qualification into his overall scheme. He notes the widespread agreement in the literature that the presence of "extremist" parties, i.e., "parties challenging the legitimacy of the regime itself, demanding some sort of fundamental change in the nature of the political order" can be taken as a sign of weakness of the party systems as well as a "threat to democratic regimes" (Powell 1981:861). This can be expected to affect system performance, regardless of the values of the other party system variables.

> [S]ubstantial popular support for extremist parties is believed to threaten a democracy's ability to generate a stable government, to contain conflict within democratic bounds, to manage responsive and responsible transfers of power. (Powell 1981:862)

In light of this argument, Powell treats party systems that include significant extremist parties separately when examining system performance, effectively creating a fifth type. This approach certainly has merit when viewed in the context of the existing literature. It ties in directly to Sartori's arguments about antisystem parties and indirectly to his stress on ideological distance. Furthermore, Powell's own findings suggest a strong relationship of extremist party representation with government instability and, less strongly, with rioting (Powell 1981, 1982).

At least one cautionary remark seems in order. The positive identification of extremist parties is difficult, as the extensive debate over the role of the Italian Communist party in the postwar Italian political system indicates (Tarrow 1977; Lange 1980). Powell has, by his own admission, used a broad operational understanding in defining extremist parties. He has treated as extremist not only parties that represent a "wide range of issue positions,

Figure 3
POWELL'S TYPOLOGY OF PARTY SYSTEMS: 1965–1975

Strong Linkages Between Groups and Parties

		No	Yes
Majority Producing	**In half of the elections**	*Aggregative Majority* Canada United States	*Responsible Majority* Austria United Kingdom
	In less than half of elections	*Fractionalized* Ø	*Representational* W. Germany Netherlands Norway Switzerland Sweden

Extremist Party Systems: 1965–1975*

Linkage

	Ø	Ø
Majority Producing	Ø	Belgium Finland Denmark France Italy

Source: Powell (1981): 866.

Those party systems having an average vote for extremist parties over 15% for elections in this period.

but also a substantial variety of positions regarding change in the political structure of society" (Powell 1981:865). Communist parties have been included simply because they are communist, even though Powell acknowledges that there are major disagreements about how antiregime some of these parties are. He has also treated tax protest parties, like the one in Denmark, as extremist. It is thus questionable whether the party systems Powell treats as extremist are accurately classified as such.

To address this problem, the explanatory power of Powell's typology can be examined both with his "extremist" systems treated as a separate type and with these systems included within their appropriate cells in the broader typology.

The Political Economy Approach

If the typologies just reviewed have left a profound mark on the discipline, it is because parties and party systems occupied a central place in the pluralist model dominant in comparative politics in the 1950s and 1960s. In this model, the party system was seen as the central institutionalized form of interest organization, representation, and mediation, and party representatives were important—if not crucial—sources of political leadership. The party system was a central arena for raising and settling issues among social interests and was the mechanism by which political leaders were held accountable. Finally, parties were socializing agents, providing the electorate with relatively enduring, affective, and cognitive orientations on political issues. In short, the party system was assumed to be the basic structuring principle for democratic politics. The turn in the 1970s and 1980s to a political economy model, however, has placed party systems in a broader institutional and systemic context, sharply qualifying this assumption.

A dominant substantive focus of the new political economy has been the relation between capital and labor—each defined essentially as a functional group sharing "objective" political-economic interests. The theoretical issues of this model are how such relations are institutionally structured; the types of strategies and resources each brings to bear in their relationship; the effects of constraints (and opportunities) in the broader national and international economy; the role of the state in mediating the relationship; and finally, how these broadly construed considerations can lead to varying patterns of conflict and consensus between capital and labor and to varying patterns of systemic outcomes.

One general change in the political economy of industrial democracies can be singled out as a contributing factor to the reemergence of capital-labor relations as a theoretical focus and research agenda. This was the end of the easy economic growth and expansion of the 1950s and 1960s in the advanced industrial democracies. This period of relative prosperity had been made possible in part by U.S. subsidies (Maier 1977:629), and at least among scholars, it had produced expectations of an emergent social consensus. With lower rates of growth, proportionately smaller social products for distribution, and accompanying threats to the fiscal effectiveness and redistributional capacities of national states, conflicts between labor and capital that had been "settled" in varying ways in different states in the immediate postwar period reemerged (Hirsch and Goldthorpe 1978; Goldthorpe 1984).

Consequently, new interest developed in analyzing the strategies of labor in different national settings, especially the relation between economic and political action and the interaction between their organizational forms—trade unions and political parties. The variation across cases in those systemic outcomes most obviously related to political economy concerns—rates of strikes, rates of growth, inflation, unemployment, distribution of income—and their seeming association with different types of capital-labor relations and labor strategy, also caught the attention of researchers. Both typologies considered in this section focus on the place of labor in national political economies.

Two themes from the literature on the political economy of advanced industrial democracies bear directly on the relation of parties and party systems to systemic outcomes. The first theme is the corporatist stabilization of capital-labor relations, and the first typology draws heavily on research on neocorporatism. A second theme is the relation between labor's power and bargaining position in the economic arena, labor's political power, and systemic outcomes favorable to the working class. Our second typology draws on research related to this theme. Although our presentation is not a detailed treatment, we believe it is both representative of the concerns of the broader literature on political economy and directly relevant to the larger theoretical and empirical issues raised in this chapter.

A Labor Inclusion Typology

Schmitter (1974), Panitch (1979), and others have identified structures of interest organization and representation that exist alongside and interact with party systems but have their own independent institutional dynamics. These organizational structures "add a second circuit . . . to the machinery of the democratic representative polity. The institutional order of which periodic elections, political parties and parliamentary government are the main element is supplemented by a political arrangement consisting of major organized interest groups, their relative procedural status [the extent of their state-sanctioned role in legislation and policy planning], and bodies of consultation and reconciliation" (Offe 1981:141; compare with Panitch 1980:173).

Several points seem to follow. First, some systemic outcomes are better explained by institutional arrangements in this corporatist circuit than by arrangements in the parties-cabinet-legislature nexus. Second, institutional arrangements and associated outcomes in the parties arena could be in disarray—with a large number of ideological parties with strong social linkages and high executive turnover, for example—and the political system remain intact, and even perform well on some measures, as a consequence of stabilizing arrangements in other arenas of interest intermediation. Finally, the association between historical periods or cases of apparent social peace and good economic performance on the one hand, and characteristics of party systems on the other, may be misleading if corporatist arrangements are also in place. Schmitter has investigated, in fact, the consequences of corporatist structures for a broader range of performance indicators. His approach is noteworthy because of its explicit emphasis on withinputs, and he also uses a very broad range of performance measurements, including both political and political-economic variables. Despite the necessarily provisional character of his findings and the limited time period involved, Schmitter's work suggests that corporatist patterns have a marked impact on system performance, generally of a positive nature (Schmitter 1981).

An emphasis on the independent dynamics of corporatist arrangements, however, must be balanced by a recognition of interaction between such arrangements and political parties and party systems. Several authors have argued that corporatist arrangements tend to be instituted when social democratic parties are in power (see Panitch 1979:129–30; Headey 1970).

Figure 4
LABOR INCLUSION TYPOLOGY: 1950–1980

Left Party Government Presence

		Low	High
Corporatist Inclusion	**High**	Netherlands Switzerland	Norway Belgium Sweden Austria
	Low	U.K. Canada Italy France W. Germany U.S.	Denmark Finland

Source: Constructed by the authors.

Government Presence: *High:* occupation of 20% of Cabinet Seats for at least 50% of the period 1950–1980.

Corporatist Inclusion: *High:* 7–9 on a 10-point Union Centralization Scale.
Low: 1–6 on the Union Centralization Scale.

There is, furthermore, evidence that government partisanship affects a number of systemic outcomes. Parties of the left, for example, appear to be associated with lower unemployment rates and stronger redistributive efforts (Hibbs 1977; Hewitt 1977; Cameron 1979; see also the articles collected in Castles 1982).[2] Crouch, however, refers to the state's responsiveness to working-class demands, downplaying the specifically partisan composition of the state's elected officials (Crouch 1979:27).

Based on theories about the centrality of corporatist structures and the effects of labor presence in government, we have constructed a two-dimensional typology that designates labor's institutional inclusion or exclusion in the national political economy. The first dimension is "corporatist inclusion" (C.I.); the second, "presence in government" (G.P.). The former would ideally be measured by the extent of institutionalized bipartite or tripartite centralized bargaining between unions, employer associations, and government. In practice, however, researchers have used a centralization index that measures the extent to which authority within the national union movement resides with the national confederations. This index is considered a reliable proxy for the broader concept of corporatist inclusion (Schmitter 1981; see Cameron 1985 for a more elaborated index). The second dimension is measured by the percentage of cabinet seats held by the left (Figure 4).

The resulting typology is admittedly a simple one. We recognize its limitations, especially in the corporatist inclusion dimension (assumed to be invariant over the postwar period) and in the arbitrary distinction between high and low categories for both dimensions.[3] The analysis for all typologies we are proposing, however, is designed to explain trends, both within and across cases, rather than variations around trend lines. This focus is less demanding empirically and, given the range of cases and measures, quite appropriate. The underlying logic of the typology is therefore worth testing, even in its present form.

Concerning the relative explanatory power of the labor inclusion typology compared with the pluralist typologies, we expect a more successful explanation of political-economic outcomes such as unemployment, inflation, and economic growth. The results may also help clarify issues internal to the political economy approach. For example, the relationship between left-wing governments and specific performance measures might be partly attributable to the existence of corporatist structures. By specifying this two-dimensional table in Figure 4, we can in effect evaluate the independent contribution of corporatism and of government composition in explaining outcomes.

A Labor Power Typology

In contrast to the labor inclusion typology, this typology downplays the independent effects of corporatist arrangements on systemic outcomes. It is developed from research on why such systems of interest intermediation are instituted in the first place. According to Korpi and Shalev, whose work has substantially influenced our arguments,

> rather than seeing institutions of industrial relations as crucial and independent factors for the extent of industrial conflict, [we should treat these institutions] primarily as intervening variables, which are themselves dependent on the power structure in society. . . . The institutions of industrial relations can be regarded as the residues of previous social conflicts and as reflecting attempts by the parties to routinize exchange relationships and to economize on power resources. (Korpi and Shalev 1979:170–71; see also Korpi 1983)

Although these institutions have some importance once in place, their continued presence depends on the power resources of labor, which vary in turn with the degree of integration of the labor movement (Korpi and Shalev 1979:170). Although Korpi and Shalev have focused on a specific outcome, industrial conflict, their approach is clearly more broadly applicable (Korpi 1980, 1983).

The argument that the strength of labor is an underlying cause of corporatist arrangements and, more broadly, that labor strength affects systemic outcomes such as levels of state redistribution and the rate of unemployment (see Stephens 1980:89–128; Madsen 1981:278) conflicts with a Marxist interpretation of corporatism, and of outcomes that offer short-term benefits to the working class, as a capitalist strategy for averting economic crisis in late capitalism by buying off labor (or at least labor's representatives). From this point of view, corporatist arrangements are inherently unstable (Panitch 1980:175) and the welfare state is a social democratic sellout of the working class. From the labor power viewpoint, however, corporatist structures should be stable as long as labor's relative strength is maintained. The continued presence and effectiveness of corporatist arrangements would instead vary with labor strength: If labor weakened, so would corporatist arrangements;

Figure 5
LABOR POWER TYPOLOGY: 1946–1976

Political Capacity
(Left votes as percentage of electorate)

		Low	33%	High
Economic Capacity (Union members as percentage of non-agricultural labor force)	**High**	Belgium	Sweden Austria Norway Denmark	United Kingdom
	40% **Low**	France Canada United States Netherlands Switzerland W. Germany		Finland Italy

Source: Constructed by the authors from Korpi and Shalev, 1980: 308, Table IV.

Political Capacity: *High:* 33 percent or greater of the electorate.
                   Low: 0–32 percent of the electorate.

Economic Capacity: *High:* 40% unionization rate.
                  Low: 0–40% unionization.

if labor became stronger, it might be able to move beyond corporatism to a bolder strategy (Stephens 1980:123). Proponents of this type of argument are also more likely to view "welfare capitalism" as a possible transition to socialism (Korpi 1978:1–5; Stephens 1980) and thus arguably in the long-term interests of the working class.

The labor power typology measures the mobilization capacity of the working-class movement but not the actual participation of left-wing parties in government. We preferred to treat the latter as a possible outcome of mobilizational capacity, although we realize that left-wing governments can have a reciprocal effect on mobilization capacity, by supporting union organization and by aiding union centralization (Stephens 1980:99; Korpi 1983; Castles 1978). The utility of the work on labor power, however, lies in its distinction between the social distribution of power and specific patterns of participation in political institutions. To bring government participation directly into the typology would be to beg the relationship between social power and these political patterns. Therefore, this typology measures mobilization capacity along two dimensions: *economic capacity,* measured by the ratio of union members to the nonagricultural civilian labor force, and *political capacity,* measured by the proportion of the electorate voting for the left (Korpi and Shalev 1979:179; Korpi 1980:35). See Figure 5 for an application of this typology.

The labor power typology places much less stress on withinputs and institutions than does the first political economy typology. Yet even with its emphasis on societal inputs, it still stands apart from the pluralist typologies already reviewed. Unlike the pluralist emphasis on values and political culture, the labor power typology stresses conflicts of interest between groups generated by the production process, and it treats relations between groups as a bargaining process in which resources are strategically mobilized to protect political-economic interests.

Several points seem to follow. First, if the labor power arguments hold, the relationship between corporatism and political and economic performance that underlies the labor inclusion typology should be weakened when we consider the effects of labor strength. With the small number of cases, and with obvious problems of covariance between labor strength and corporatism, this possibility is difficult to determine.

Those cases in which a relatively weak labor movement occurs with corporatist institutions would be of value in sorting out the relationship of labor strength and corporatism. The Netherlands may again emerge as one critical case because it ranks high on the union centralization index and low on both labor power and left presence. Another set of cases that would be of equal theoretical importance are cases in which labor strength and low corporatism occur together. One way to answer these questions is through dummy variable regression, using different cell typologies as the reference category and varying the composition of dummy variable categories in order to compare how well different typological arrangements of the cases explain political and political-economic outcomes.

Second, the relationship between social democratic presence in government and a range of performance measures may be weakened, once we control for labor strength (see Madsen 1981:289). Again, this would cause our labor power typology to behave differently from our labor inclusion typology; these differences should show up in the relative ability of these typologies to explain a number of systemic outcomes.

Class Compromise and Wage Restraint in Political-Economic Approaches

Underlying political-economic approaches is an argument about the presence and importance of class compromise in capitalist democracies. An economic exchange between capital and labor is the basis of class compromise. Workers accept capital's retention of profit on the assurance that the material welfare of workers will improve in the future. Compromise transforms a zero-sum into a positive-sum cooperative relationship, making consent to compromise rational for both collective actors. Labor and capital may maneuver to improve their relative positions but, at the same time, they have a shared interest in contributing to the expansion of the material basis of exchange (Przeworski 1985; Przeworski and Wallerstein 1982). Exchange relations between capital and labor are mediated in tripartite arrangements that include the state. The institutional capacities of the state both strengthen the material bases of compromise and help to assure that the terms of compromise are maintained.

Attention to voluntary wage restraint within the working class has been a natural extension of the interest in class compromise. The willingness of workers to accept limits on wage demands and to accept lower wages than could be gained under full employment is said to be conditioned by several sets of factors. First are the terms of trade of the exchange itself. It is typically assumed that workers will agree to restrain wages when they expect some form of nonmarket compensation, such as an increased social wage, or when the short-term sacrifice of a higher wage holds some promise of material benefits in the longer term. This is associated with the expectation that some portion of the profits produced by restraint is to be invested in the national economy for purposes of economic rationalization. Two kinds of uncertainty are present in this arrangement: mutual uncertainty whether the other actor will live up to the terms of the bargain and unanticipated changes in the economic environment that make the exchange less attractive for either actor.

Second, explanations of wage restraint also point to position in the international economy. Export-dependent, small economies are disciplined by the importance of maintaining competitiveness in international markets (Cameron 1978; Katzenstein 1985). The organization of labor is a third factor accounting for wage restraint. When trade unions organize a high proportion of the work force and are associated in a single peak confederation able to control rank-and-file behavior, wage restraint is more likely to occur. Under these conditions, the monopoly position of the peak association provides a nonmarket means of providing wage restraint. The association acts as an implementor of public policy, where implementation in this case means maintaining rank-and-file adherence to a policy of restraint. From the perspective of state administrators, this arrangement represents a devolution of public authority to a corporate body and a means of monitoring activity in civil society (Cawson 1986). Wage restraint, then, becomes possible precisely because of the monopoly power of labor organizations. Further, trade unions that are "encompassing organizations" are more likely to prefer efficiency to redistribution as a means of enhancing the welfare of their members (Olson 1982, 1986).[4] Where wage restraint is stably present in these circumstances, we would expect comparatively low rates of unemployment and inflation and comparatively high rates of economic growth.

The work force can also be disciplined and wage restraint involuntarily induced directly through the market. The pattern of economic performance will be different by this path. Although growth rates may be comparatively high and inflation rates low, unemployment will be higher than by the first path, which works through the organization of labor. This market strategy may also be coupled with political intervention to weaken the position of labor associations in labor markets.

Features of the party system, too, affect the emergence of wage restraint. A social democratic party, able to govern alone or in coalition, can ease fears within the working class about the exchange that underlies wage restraint by, for example, assuring that the state will promote the domestic investment of profit. A social democratic party that has this extended access over time to government office also will likely have resolved the electoral dilemma analyzed by Przeworski and Sprague (Przeworski 1985; Przeworski and Sprague 1986). The success of a "supraclass" strategy will vary with the linkages between party and trade unions. A well-organized trade union movement can continue to deliver the working-class vote and thus minimize the losses associated with this electoral orientation. This joint combination of organizational power in labor markets and political power is especially conducive to economic growth. A politically powerful labor movement that lacks organizational power will be unable to implement wage restraint. The presence of organizational without political power will make wage restraint a riskier choice for labor. In both cases, the consequences for economic performance, including growth, are negative. (See Hicks 1988; Lange and Garrett 1985; Garrett and Lange 1986; Jackman 1986.)

Wage restraint can also occur without this social democratic connection in societies in which the working-class vote is divided among several parties representing well-organized, cohesive subcultures. Under these circumstances, the class compromise institutionalized in class-specific organizations in the social democratic path (as in Sweden) is achieved within subcultures and is maintained through intergroup accommodation. The Netherlands combines these features of consociational and corporatist politics (Golden 1986:284). Because of this pattern of subcultural organization, wage settlements are not negotiated directly between peak associations of labor and capital within a tradition of free collective bargaining. Instead, the state plays a larger, more direct role and supervises a formal incomes policy (Katzenstein 1985:50). Consequently, religious and ethnic cleavages need not weaken class compromise through their effects on the organizational capacity of capital and labor and the ability of a social democratic party to mobilize its potential constituency. Further, when subcultures are most segmented along class lines than the Dutch *zuilen*, or pillars (as in Austria), the politics of wage restraint will more closely resemble the corporatist model. The grand coalitions of Austrian governments from 1949 to 1966, although often identified with consociationalism (Lijphart 1977) more directly express class compromise (Esping-Andersen and Korpi 1985: 190–194; Marin 1987) than the coalition governments and proportionality principle of Dutch politics in the same time period.

Although Schmitter (1974) emphasized the durability of corporatism, other studies have emphasized the fragility of wage restraint. Some of the causes of the breakdown of restraint can be grouped into four categories: unfair exchange, free-riding, rank-and-file revolt, and business-worker collusion. Changes in the terms of the exchange underlying restraint can adversely affect its maintenance over time. The inability of the government to control prices as the quid pro quo of restraint, or to provide promised nonmarket compensation (such as better pensions and improved sickness benefits) produce perceptions that the benefits of restraint are not commensurate with its costs. Such problems often arise out of international economic pressures that, in particular periods, work to transmit inflation or weaken the fiscal base of public policies.

Even when the exchange is considered fair, however, there are other sources of instability. There are problems of collective action (Olson 1965) nested within the exchange, as the business and labor organizations that negotiate collective bargains are collective actors. Rational, self-interested workers would prefer to demand higher wages and free-ride on the collective benefits produced by the wage restraint of other workers (Lange 1984; Schwerin 1981; Boston 1985). Some factors that allay this problem of free-riding are an identification with other workers (Lange 1984; Offe and Wiesenthal 1985 [1980]:183); centralized trade unions that sanction defectors from wage restraint (e.g., Marks 1986); industrial unions that are not subject to interunion conflict at the factory level, are less prone to rivalry around wage differentials, and are less likely to have the traditions of autonomy associated with skill/craft-based unions (e.g., Markovits 1982; Mommsen and Husung 1985); and repeated rounds of centralized wage bargains that can create the basis for contingent wage restraint as workers weigh the risk of loss (if one restrains demands and others do not) in the short-term against the possible long-term rewards of cooperation if it is sustained (Lange 1984).

When wage restraint is negotiated through centralized trade unions, another kind of problem can develop over time. Trade unions committed to wage restraint and class compromise are both implementors of public policy and representatives of the rank and file, and union leaders must balance these sometimes contradictory roles (Przeworski 1985:164; Panitch 1980). Too much autonomy for local unions can make implementation difficult; too little might alienate parts of the membership. Rank-and-file revolt, expressed as demands for increased autonomy for union locals at the firm or factory level, is a conceivable consequence of the bureaucratization of industrial relations (Martin 1984). Finally, the cohesion of class-specific organizations can break down, with negative consequences for wage restraint, when segments of business and labor break away from centralized wage bargains to negotiate at the sectoral or firm level. This can occur when producers face a buoyant market and are willing to offer wages above the norms established through wage restraint in order to meet their labor requirements and production schedules (Lash 1985).

The presence of class compromise stabilizes capitalist democracy in the specific sense that, under compromise, democracy will not be replaced by "capitalist dictatorship" or "labor autocracy" (Masters and Robertson 1988:1184). Compromise makes democracy more governable as well (Schmitter 1981), through class-based organizations and subcultures. At the same time, unanticipated consequences of compromise can introduce new political problems and issues.

Economic growth is both a goal and precondition of class compromise. The latter is mediated through extensive state regulation of the domestic economy. Under these conditions, the party system and interest organizations not only share a consensus but lower the opportunities for opposition to growth-oriented, bureaucratized political-economic management to be expressed in existing institutions of interest intermediation. New social movements with roots in local grass-roots organization, committed to values of decentralization, small-scale community, and environmental awareness and with links to new political parties may arise as a consequence (Kitschelt 1988; Offe 1985).

The extensive welfare states associated with compromise may also produce in response forms of protest organized around issues such as the distribution of the tax burden and the size, efficiency, and programmatic bases of states and public policy (Hibbs and Madsen 1981; Esping-Andersen 1985). To the extent that compromise is achieved in part through the use of foreign workers to protect the employment of the indigenous work force, political mobilization can develop to protect the privileged access of citizens to the state-supplied benefits of compromise. This latter process illustrates one kind of boundary to the inclusionary logic of compromise and corporatism (Freeman 1986) and the possible tension between domestic regulation and international liberalism in open economies (Keohane 1984).

Class compromise is argued to be a systemic attribute of society. This perspective has meshed nicely with the early work on corporatism, which also examined society-wide systems of interest intermediation. These two bodies of work converged on the analysis of relations between capital and labor in industrial settings. Recent work has begun to disaggregate corporatism. More attention has been paid to "meso-level" corporatism in which "the relevant collective actors are not peak class associations, but organizations which close around and defend specific interests of sectors and professions" (Cawson 1985:9). This work is much less closely tied to a union-centric perspective or to industrial contexts, although some of what is described under a (qualified) corporatist rubric also resembles forms of clientelism. (See Cawson 1985 [especially the piece by Atkinson and Coleman], Suleiman 1987; Keeler 1987; Scholten 1987; Jacek 1986).

DEPENDENT VARIABLES

No matter how elegant and descriptively satisfying, typologies are only as good as what they enable us to understand and explain. At the end of the section on methodology, we suggested two questions to be explored in analyzing the relative explanatory power of the different typologies. To explore these questions, we need to identify dependent variables that at least some of the classifications were intended to explain, that retained empirical interest, that varied from country to country, and that were potentially significant in evaluating the performance of political systems in the advanced industrial democracies. This section considers which kinds of variables a comparative analysis of typologies might (and might not) usefully employ. Because our selection is necessarily somewhat arbitrary, the variables discussed below are not the only ones that might be appropriate. They do all satisfy the designated criteria while capturing the recent change in focus in the comparative study of democratic systems.

The Concept of Stability

As already noted, the postwar literature on democratic systems has focused on the association between different regime types and political stability. Yet the concept of stability is, for both empirical and theoretical reasons, a most difficult and inopportune starting point for selecting dependent variables.

Intuitively, the stability of a regime refers to the "system's ability to survive intact" (Lijphart 1968:8) or the probability that it will do so, which, in turn, "depends on its capacity to deal effectively with the problems confronting it and to adjust flexibly to changing circumstances" (Lijphart 1968:8). To make this sense of stability empirically meaningful, however, we must develop boundary definitions (to give empirical substance to "intact") and identify phenomena (and ways of measuring them) that indicate a greater or lesser probability of survival. The first task is not overly difficult, especially for the advanced industrial democracies. The second presents serious difficulties, especially when dealing with "continuing" and not "historic" democracies (Eckstein 1971:25).

For historical regimes that have come and gone, durability can simply be measured by duration. For continuing democracies, however, the problem is not so simple. Even if we measure durability in terms of how long they have already lasted within certain parameters (Eckstein 1971:25–28), we find that all but one (the French Fourth Republic) have already outlasted the regimes that broke down in the interwar period. Furthermore, only one (again, the Fourth Republic) has suffered breakdown. At best then, we have only limited variance on this measure if stability is to be understood as the probability that the regime will endure.

Another common research strategy has treated stability as a multidimensional concept, "combining ideas that are frequently encountered in the comparative politics literature: system maintenance, civil order, legitimacy and effectiveness" (Lijphart 1977:4). Expanding the number of indicators, however, raises other measurement problems. If, for example, measures of cabinet stability, decisional efficiency, and civil order (see Eckstein 1971) indicate an underlying stability factor, we would expect them to correlate. Yet Hurwitz (1973) found only very weak correlations among indicators presented in the literature as constituting a "multifaceted definition" of stability. This suggests that there may be no underlying systemic characteristic (see also Powell 1982:25–29, 201–8).

The multidimensional interpretation of stability is premised on an implicit theory of how democratic systems operate and what factors are conducive to their stability. The assumption is that democratic regimes with higher levels of civic violence, lower levels of legitimacy, and less effective performance are less likely to remain democratic. Based on the experiences of the interwar years, these hypotheses seem plausible, but they raise theoretical issues, as there are other plausible starting points for the analysis of democratic stability. Two brief examples can be cited.

First, according to some Marxist theorists, the most fundamental condition for democratic stability is the maintenance of the structural underpinnings of capitalist accumulation. Lacking this, capitalist elites are more likely to abandon their commitment to democratic practices and to express their lack of "business confidence" through market behavior that undermines economic and eventually political performance with (supposedly) predictable consequences for the stability of the democratic regime (Block 1977). This view, which is certainly not wholly at variance with the interwar experience, would suggest that the indicators commonly used are not necessarily, or at best only indirectly, indicative of stability. Other indicators would be more appropriate.

Second, other theorists have suggested that legitimacy and effectiveness can be rather low, and levels of civic violence somewhat high, but the regime nonetheless stable. This could happen if the democratic state were the source or mediator of extensive exchange relationships among a large number of the more powerful groups in the society, or if the major social, economic, and political groups did not see that a change of regime would be to their advantage (Rustow 1970). The postwar Italian political system has been treated as an example of the former (Farneti 1973; Tarrow 1977), the Fourth French Republic as an example of the latter (Siegfried 1956:123–252). Our purpose here is not to judge which of these theories is correct, but only to point out the theoretical complexities of the stability concept, especially considering the relative durability of the postwar democracies despite significant differences among them in terms of supposed indicators of stability.

We are led to the following conclusion: The concept of democratic stability, despite its intuitive, historical, and normative appeal, does not at present constitute a promising starting point for a systematic, comparative analysis of the performance of democratic systems. The concept of stability confuses threats to the political and economic status quo with threats to the persistence of the liberal democratic order (compare with Kaase and Marsh 1979b:31). In turning to system performance as a dependent variable, we hope to provide a series of measures of political and political-economic outcomes that better indicate how political influence and economic goods are distributed in advanced industrial democracies.

System Performance

In place of system stability, we will use system performance as our theoretical focus, asking how well different typologies explain different aspects of the performance of the democracies, as measured by a variety of political and political-economic outcomes. Four things should be noted about this shift. First, it does not imply an abandonment of the dependent variables employed in earlier studies. Many of the same variables can still be employed; they are just viewed in a different light. Second, the shift from a concern with stability does not mean that normative concerns are missing. Each of the less aggregative variables suggested has normative implications. They relate to different themes in democratic theory rather than just to the maintenance of the democratic rules of the game.

Third, we propose a focus on system outcomes, not system outputs (Almond and Powell 1978; Chaps. 11–12). The dependent variables refer to aspects of system performance and not to the specific policies undertaken by government. The drawback is that factors other than governmental performance can be expected to affect the dependent variables being examined. If, however, the question is how well different types of democratic systems perform (or how stable they are, for that matter), then a unique focus on governmental policy is inadequate: An effective democracy should be able to adjust its outputs to meet the challenges it faces and thus achieve desired outcomes. The appropriateness of a focus on outcomes is all the more clear when we remember that the advanced industrial democracies all have similar levels of economic development. Finally, we will be looking not only at the relationship between system types and performance outcomes, but also at the relationship between different outcomes. This allows us to judge the validity of a number of common hypotheses—for example, the theory that aspects of governmental performance such as cabinet stability have an important impact on other dimensions of system performance.

The evaluation of system performance has become a major theme of research in recent years. A large number of variables have been utilized as measures, and a large number of rationales have been offered to explain their utility. On the basis of these studies, and considering our limits of data and space, we have selected a number of useful dependent variables. The variables, which can be considered measures of system outcomes, fall into two major categories: political and political-economic.

Political Outcomes

Government stability. Taylor and Herman and others have questioned the empirical significance of the stability of government for other aspects of government performance and regime stability (Taylor and Herman 1971:29). Yet, as they acknowledge, this question remains open pending further research. Along with the other system performance variables we suggest using, simple curiosity would seem to warrant including government stability in the set of dependent variables, for one can then examine its association with other aspects of performance. There is also, however, an important normative issue that is partially addressed through examining the extent of government stability in any system.

Two measures of government stability are commonly found in the literature on democratic systems: the "duration of government" and the degree of "executive control." The former measures the stability of governments by their length of stay in office; the latter indicates whether the government has majority or minority status in the legislature (see Strom 1984 for a discussion of minority government). Both measures have important implications for the ability of citizens to hold their government accountable. A government that is in office for only a short period of time is difficult to hold accountable for policy outputs and outcomes: It can mostly be held responsible for its inability to remain in office. Yet a government that lacks a legislative majority can also blur its responsibility, arguing that its policy ineffectiveness, or the specific content of its actions, was heavily conditioned by its lack of legislative dominance. The general importance of accountability in a theory of democratic government is a good normative reason for including measures of government stability in the set of dependent variables.

Political violence. One of the basic signs of a well-functioning political system is the restriction of political disagreements and protests within legally sanctioned channels. This is the case even in authoritarian regimes, although one may well disapprove of the narrowness of the legal definition of permissible protest and of the sanctions brought to bear on those who violate the legal norms or who simply engender the disapproval of the authorities. Democratic systems presumably give wider berth to political protest, apply less severe sanctions, and do not permit extralegal coercion of dissidents. The extent of extralegal protest in democratic regimes can therefore be taken as an important indicator of system performance.

The identification and measurement of extralegal political protest, however, is fraught with methodological difficulties (Eckstein 1971:32–50), and thus any particular indicator must be treated with caution. Nonetheless, one measure on which there appears to be widespread agreement is the extent of political violence in the system. The lower the incidence of violence, the better the system is performing. Two indicators are often employed: the number of protest demonstrations and the number of riots.[5] A broader specification of the kinds of collective action available in the mobilization of interests should also be considered. In delineating repertoires of collective action, we can therefore shift attention to the strategic place in interest articulation of protest demonstrations and riots, for example, and thus move away from the assumption that these kinds of behaviors are always indicators of instability or of anomie (on political repertoires, see Kaase and Marsh 1979a and Tilly 1978:142–59).

Political-Economic Outcomes

A basic measure by which to evaluate a political system is how well it provides for the economic, and not just the political, well-being of its citizenry. Whatever definitions one gives to these two dimensions of well-being, both are frequently used in judging how well a particular political system, or type of system, performs. In the democracies of the post-Keynesian era, citizens have come to expect their governments to actively promote their economic well-being. And at least until the very recent neoconservative shift in policy and ideology, most visibly evident in the United Kingdom, the United States, and Canada, governments accepted this as their responsibility.

It is perhaps surprising, therefore, that until the turn to political economy little systematic attention was given to how well different types of democratic systems were able to promote economic well-being. This is obviously treacherous empirical terrain, but probably no more treacherous than political stability. A system's performance with respect to the economic standing of its citizenry may be just as important for regime stability as more directly political outcomes. This has certainly been suggested in much of the recent literature on the so-called "crisis of democracy" (Crozier et al. 1975). Political-economic outcomes have not been dealt with by most of the liberal typologies, but to the extent that these typologies are intended to be "natural" and relevant, they should also have explanatory power in this dimension of system performance.

Of the many possible political-economic outcomes that could be used as measures of system performance, we have confined ourselves to those that have been used elsewhere. They are simple and direct: the annual average rate of growth in gross domestic product, the annual average rate of unemployment, the annual average rate of growth in consumer prices (inflation), the average annual "discomfort index" (rate of unemployment plus rate of inflation), the volume of strikes, and the annual extent of net government borrowing (see Schmitter 1981 for an extensive use of these). For the first of these, higher rates are assumed to indicate better performance; for all the others, lower rates indicate better performance.

These measures certainly do not exhaust the meaning of system performance. The concept of performance will need to be systematically unpacked in ongoing research. Our focus, however, indicates some of the central issues that have been posed in the political economy literature to date.

In using this set of measures, a few brief comments are in order. First, our primary concern is with how well different typologies of democratic systems explain performance as indicated by each of these measures. This will not determine which type of system best provides for the overall economic well-being of its citizenry. One can only evaluate systems in terms of different patterns of well-being and their distributional consequences; exploring such patterns and consequences has become an increasingly frequent and interesting feature of the cross-national work in political economy in recent years (see, for instance, Cameron 1985).

In contrast, the issue of distribution is notably absent in the liberal focus on stability and on social values (see, however, the discussion of policy responsiveness and of tax policies in Powell 1982:186–97).

Second, we recognize that no system can maximize performance in all areas simultaneously. However, the trade-offs involved can occur at different absolute levels and are likely to reflect different distributional outcomes and perhaps government preferences. The index of "discomfort" is intended, in a relatively crude fashion, to capture this possibility with respect to the most commonly discussed, if now much disputed, trade-off—that between unemployment and inflation. Third, the measures all indicate performance in a relatively short time horizon. They do not capture the possibility of policy trade-offs over time, especially the acceptance of poorer short-term performance for better performance in the long term. Fourth, the volume of strikes is a particularly interesting measure of political-economic performance. On the one hand, it indicates the extent to which the political economy is subjected to disruption due to the power of labor. On the other hand, a number of recent studies have shown that the volume of strikes, and of labor conflict more generally, may not simply reflect conditions in the economy such as the level of unemployment. Political factors such as the percentage of gross national product passing through public hands and the particular partisan composition of government may also influence labor unrest (Hibbs 1978; Korpi and Shalev 1979).

Finally, it must be noted that political-economic outcomes, even more than political outcomes, are not only a function of domestic factors. The state of the international political economy and the role of any national political economy in it will have a major impact on system outcomes. This has several implications. Performance may vary significantly during different "eras" of the international economy. For instance, one might expect a significant shift in performance before and after the early 1970s. Furthermore, systems that are more exposed to the international economy (e.g., have a higher degree of export dependence) should, *ceteris paribus*, be more affected by the state of the international economy (Katzenstein 1983). If these systems do well when the international economy is doing poorly, this might be an indication of particularly good performance. If open economies do well when the international economy is itself healthy, we may also need to reconsider the net effects of domestic outcomes on system performance, independent of the impact of the international economy (see Madsen 1981:274–75 and Katzenstein 1983).

To summarize, we propose a focus on system outcomes as measures of system performance. These measures constitute the dependent variables in terms of which the relative explanatory power of different typologies of democratic systems can be evaluated. The specific measures fall into two categories, political and political-economic. The political variables are the duration of governments, the degree of executive control, the number of protest demonstrations, and the number of riots. The political-economic variables are the annual average rates for growth, unemployment, inflation, and net government borrowing; the volume of strikes; and a discomfort index. Each of these measures has been used in previous studies of democratic systems, but no study has employed all of them. All can be argued to have normative significance. Combining these two characteristics in the selection of measures retains a linkage to the standpoint adopted in the earlier studies of types of democratic systems while extending the analysis to other, more recent theoretical frameworks employed in the study of the advanced industrial democracies.

CONCLUSIONS

This chapter has identified the very different assumptions and arguments underlying the "liberal" and political economy approaches to democratic systems. Researchers in the field need to recognize these differences in their research designs and to undertake tests to identify the strengths and weaknesses of each approach more fully. We hope our discussion has piqued interest in these differences and offered some useful suggestions on how they might be explored. The time for relatively single-minded devotion to a particular approach and classification is well past.

It is unlikely that either approach—much less any of the particular typologies—will be found overwhelmingly powerful in explaining the range of phenomena studied by scholars working in this area. It is more likely that the approaches and typologies will explain different outcomes with varying degrees of success. Some typologies may prove much more powerful than others according to the criteria we have established. Some of the typologies may fail the test of relative explanatory power, emerging as interesting and thoughtful analytical descriptions without much causal punch. Nonetheless, the two underlying approaches are likely to retain their attraction. After all, they reflect fundamental divisions in the social sciences, which have been tempered by intense debate and have withstood numerous attempts to devise and carry out "critical tests" (Barry 1970).

We are not suggesting resignation to an uncritical theoretical and analytical pluralism. The study of types of advanced industrial democratic systems has been passing through the "conversion experience" so common in the social sciences. During this phase, critiques of conventional theoretical wisdom are formulated in polar terms, with the alternative theoretical frameworks becoming mirror images of the prevailing orthodoxy (Skocpol 1977). In the turn to political economy, corporatism, interests, state, and economy have replaced pluralism, values, society, and culture (Berger 1981; for a critique, see Almond 1983).

Eventually, conversion must be followed by a systematic confrontation of the alternative approaches. A new synthesis can then be built on the results. We believe the time has come for a confrontation, and have suggested how it might be conducted. Tests of the relative explanatory power of different typologies are likely to show which are most effective in explaining a broad spectrum of outcomes. Researchers can then begin to focus attention on the most powerful concepts and variables and set aside the others.

This process of clarification will need to be followed by efforts at synthesis. Scholars must work systematically to build a more complex understanding of the processes that explain different performance outcomes in the advanced industrial democracies. Synthesis might mean combining different typologies, or it may prove more fruitful to abandon typological analysis in favor of more complex models of explanation that are built on individual variables and do not strive for simple characterizations. Empirical research that combines features of these approaches has begun to emerge (e.g., Strom 1989; Robertson 1984), and more work will undoubtedly follow.

Whichever path is taken, we can only hope that research will maintain the normative concern with democratic values that has always been at the heart of this field. The doubts and concerns about democracy in the complex, mobilized advanced industrial societies of the 1980s may be substantially different from those of the 1950s, but they are no less urgent or deserving of scholarly attention.

NOTES

We thank Peter Hall for comments on a draft of this paper.

1. Lijphart's research has made the Netherlands a critical case in explanations of political stability. For an evaluation from the perspective of Marxist political economy of Lijphart's argument with regard to the Netherlands, see Kieve 1981. Bakvis (1984) provides a balanced and insightful analysis of Lijphart, Kieve, and others.

2. Neil Beck's critique and subsequent exchange with Hibbs (Beck 1982, 1984; Hibbs 1983) raises interesting issues with regard to class-party models of policy formation.

3. We have also measured corporatism indirectly, using the centralization of the trade union movement as a proxy measure. Corporatism, however, as Almond has pointed out (Almond 1983:260), might be measured more directly as a type of bargaining process. For a more extended critique of corporatism, see Martin (1983) and Crouch's response (1983). We have followed Korpi and Shalev in defining left parties in both Figures 4 and 5 as social democratic parties and parties to their left, thus excluding the U.S. Democratic party. (See Korpi and Shalev 1980, Appendix 1.) Data on cabinet presence of left parties is drawn from *Keesing's Archives*, the *Europa Yearbook*, and Mackie and Rose (1974).

4. Olson, however, argues that encompassing organizations will be unstable in the long term, essentially because they will be captured by sectional, particularistic interests (Olson 1986; Milner 1987).

5. Two commonly used political outcomes are conspicuous by their absence: decisional efficacy and legitimacy. Eckstein suggests, in regard to the former, that efficacy should not be viewed in terms of the extent to which government outputs meet demands but rather should be seen to vary according to how well governments perform two critical tasks: budget making and the allocation of top elite roles. Although there is much merit in this approach, we were unable to collect the necessary data for the large number of systems we wish to compare.

Legitimacy has often been used in studies of performance, on the grounds that "the extent that a polity is regarded by its members as worthy of support" (Eckstein 1971:50) is a good indicator of how stable the regime is and how well it is performing. Yet, as Eckstein has acknowledged, legitimacy is extremely difficult to measure. Measures of legitimacy are bound up with broader theoretical disputes about the sources of legitimacy itself (Rogowski 1983) and, consequently, about the theoretical relationship of support to stability and performance. Because of the serious problems in measurement and interpretation, we chose not to utilize indicators of legitimacy in this chapter.

REFERENCES

Almond, Gabriel A. 1956. "Comparative Political Systems." *Journal of Politics* 18:391–409.

————. 1983. "Corporatism, Pluralism and Professional Memory." *World Politics* 35:245–60.

Almond, Gabriel, and G. Bingham Powell. 1978. *Comparative Politics*, 2d ed. Boston: Little, Brown.

Bakvis, H. 1984. "Towards a Political Economy of Consociationalism: A Commentary on Marxist Views of Pillarization in the Netherlands." *Comparative Politics* 16:315–34.

Barry, Brian. 1970. *Sociologists, Economists and Democracy*. London: Collier.

Beck, Neil. 1982. "Parties, Administration and American Macroeconomic Outcomes." *American Political Science Review* 76:83–93.

————. 1984. "Comment on Hibbs." *American Political Science Review* 78:499–502.

Berger, Suzanne, ed. 1981. *Organizing Interests in Western Europe*. London: Cambridge University Press.

Block, Fred. 1977. "The Ruling Class Does Not Rule: Notes on the Marxist Theory of the State." *Socialist Revolution* 7:5–28.

Boston, Jonathan. 1985. "Corporatist Incomes Policy, the Free-Rider Problem and the British Labour Government's Social Contract." In Alan Cawson, ed. *Organized Interests and the State: Studies in Meso-Corporatism*, pp. 65–84. Beverly Hills and London: Sage Publications.

Cameron, David R. 1978. "The Expansion of the Public Economy: A Comparative Analysis." *American Political Science Review* 72:1243–61.

————. 1979. "Economic Inequality in the Advanced Capitalist Societies: A Comparative Analysis." Paper presented at the Harvard University Center of European Studies/Center for International Affairs Seminar on Equality and the Welfare State.

————. 1985. "Social Democracy, Corporatism and Labor Quiescence." In J. Goldthorpe, ed., *Order and Conflict in Western Capitalism*. London: Oxford University Press.

Castles, Francis. 1978. *The Social Democratic Image of Society*. London: Routledge & Kegan Paul.

Castles, Francis G., ed. 1982. *The Impact of Parties, Politics and Policies in Democratic Capitalist States*. Beverly Hills and London: Sage Publications.

Cawson, Alan. 1986. *Corporatism and Political Theory*. Oxford: Basil Blackwell.

————, ed. 1985. *Organized Interests and the State: Studies in Meso-Corporatism*. Beverly Hills and London: Sage Publications.

Crouch, Colin. 1979. "The State, Capital and Liberal Democracy." In Colin Crouch, ed., *State and Economy in Contemporary Capitalism*. London: Croom Helm.

————. 1983. "Pluralism and the New Corporatism: A Rejoinder." *Political Studies* 31:452–60.

Crozier, Michel, Samuel P. Huntington, and Joji Watanuki. 1975. *The Crisis of Democracy: Report on the Governability of Democracies to the Trilateral Commission*. New York: New York University Press.

Dahl, Robert A. 1971. *Polyarchy*. New Haven and London: Yale University Press.

Dahrendorf, Ralf. 1958. *Class and Class Conflict in Industrial Society*. Stanford, CA: Stanford University Press.

Easton, David. 1965. *A Systems Analysis of Political Life*. Chicago: University of Chicago Press.

Eckstein, Harry. 1971. "The Evaluation of Political Performance: Problems and Dimensions." *Sage Professional Papers in Comparative Politics* 01-017. Beverly Hills and London: Sage Publications.

Esping-Andersen, Gosta. 1985. *Politics Against Markets*. Princeton, NJ: Princeton University Press.

Esping-Andersen, Gosta, and Walter Korpi. 1985. "Social Policy as Class Politics in Post-War Capitalism: Scandinavia, Austria and Germany." In John H. Goldthorpe, ed., *Order and Conflict in Contemporary Capitalism*, pp. 179–208. London: Oxford University Press.

Farneti, Paolo. 1973. "Introduzione." In Paolo Farneti, ed., *Il sistema politico italiano*. Bologna: Il Mulino.

Freeman, Gary P. 1986. "Migration and the Political Economy of the Welfare State." *Annals of the American Academy of Arts and Sciences* 485:51–63.

Garrett, Geoffrey, and Peter Lange. 1986. "Performance in a Hostile World: Economic Growth in Capitalist Democracies, 1974–1982." *World Politics* 33:413–35.

Golden, Miriam. 1986. "Interest Representation, Party Systems and the State. Italy in Comparative Perspective." *Comparative Politics* 18:279–302.

Goldthorpe, John, ed. 1984. *Order and Conflict in Contemporary Capitalism*. London: Oxford University Press.

Headey, Bruce. 1970. "Trade Unions and National Wages Policies." *Journal of Politics* 32:107–39.

Heisler, Martin O., ed. 1974. *Politics in Europe*. New York: David McKay.

Heisler, Martin O., and Robert O. Kvavik. 1974. "Patterns of European Politics: The 'European Polity' Model." In Heisler, *Politics in Europe*, pp. 27–89.

Hempel, Carl G. 1952. *Fundamentals of Concept Formation in Empirical Science*. International Encyclopedia of Unified Science, vol. 2, no. 7. Chicago: University of Chicago Press, 1952.

Hewitt, Christopher. 1977. "The Effect of Political Democracy and Social Democracy on Equality in Industrial Societies." *American Sociological Review* 42:450–64.

Hibbs, Douglas A., Jr. 1977. "Political Parties and Macroeconomic Policy." *American Political Science Review* 71:1467–87.

——— . 1978. "On the Political Economy of Long-Run Trends in Strike Activity." *British Journal of Political Science* 8:153–75.

——— . 1983. "Comment on Beck." *American Political Science Review* 77(2).447–51.

Hibbs, Douglas A., Jr., and Henrik Jess Madsen. 1981. "Public Reactions to the Growth of Taxation and Government Expenditure." *World Politics* 33:413–35.

Hicks, Alexander. 1988. "Social Democratic Corporatism and Economic Growth." *Journal of Politics* 50:677–704.

Hirsch, Fred, and John Goldthorpe, eds. 1978. *The Political Economy of Inflation*. London: Martin Robinson.

Hurwitz, Leon. 1973. "Contemporary Approaches to Political Stability." *Comparative Politics* 3:449–63.

Huxley, Aldous. 1940. "The New Systematics." In Julian Huxley, ed., *The New Systematics*. Oxford: Clarendon Press.

Jacek, Henry. 1986. "Pluralist and Corporatist Intermediation, Activities of Business Interest Associations and Corporate Profits. Some Evidence from Canada." *Comparative Politics* :419–38.

Jackman, Robert. 1986. "The Politics of Economic Growth in Industrial Democracies, 1974–1980: Leftist Strength of North Sea Oil." *Journal of Politics* 48:242–56.

Kaase, Max, and Alan Marsh. 1979a. "Political Action Repertory: Changes Over Time and a New Typology." In Samuel Barnes and Max Kaase, eds., *Political Action: Mass Participation in Five Western Democracies*. Beverly Hills and London: Sage Publications.

_____. 1979b. "Political Action, A Theoretical Perspective." In Samuel Barnes and Max Kaase, eds., *Political Action: Mass Participation in Five Western Democracies.* Beverly Hills and London: Sage Publications.

Katzenstein, Peter. 1983. "The Small European States in the International Economy: Economic Dependence and Corporatist Politics." In J. Ruggie, ed., *The Antinomies of Interdependence.* New York: Columbia University Press.

_____. 1985. *Small States in World Markets.* Ithaca and London: Cornell University Press.

Keeler, John T. S. 1987. *The Politics of Neo-Corporatism in France: Farmers, The State and Agricultural Policy-Making in the Fifth Republic.* New York: Oxford University Press.

Keohane, Robert O. 1984. "The World Political Economy and the Crisis of Embedded Liberalism." In John H. Goldthorpe, ed., *Order and Conflict in Contemporary Capitalism,* pp. 15–38. London: Oxford University Press.

Kieve, R. 1981. "Pillars of Sand: A Marxist Critique of Consociational Democracy in the Netherlands." *Comparative Politics* 13:313–37.

Kitschelt, Herbert. 1988. "Left-Libertarian Parties: Explaining Innovation in Competitive Party Systems." *World Politics* 40:194–234.

Korpi, Walter. 1978. *The Working Class in Welfare Capitalism.* London and Boston: Routledge & Kegan Paul.

_____. 1980. "Social Policy and Distributional Conflict in the Capitalist Democracies: A Preliminary Comparative Framework." *West European Politics* 3 (October):296–316.

_____. 1983. *The Democratic Class Struggle.* London: Routledge & Kegan Paul.

Korpi, Walter, and Michael Shalev. 1979. "Strikes, Industrial Relations and Class Conflict in Capitalist Societies." *British Journal of Sociology* 30:164–87.

_____. 1980. "Strikes, Power and Politics in the Western Nations, 1900–1976." In Maurice Zeitlin, ed., *Political Power and Social Theory,* Vol. 1.

Lakatos, Imre. 1970. "Falsification and the Methodology of Scientific Research Programmes." In Imre Lakatos and Alan Musgrave, eds., *Criticism and the Growth of Knowledge.* London and New York: Cambridge University Press.

Lange, Peter. 1980. "Crisis and Consent, Change and Compromise: Dilemmas of Italian Communism in the 1970s." In P. Lange and S. Tarrow, eds., *Italy in Transition.* London: Frank Cass.

_____. 1984. "Unions, Workers and Wage Regulation: The Rational Bases of Consent." In John H. Goldthorpe, ed., *Order and Conflict in Contemporary Capitalism,* pp. 98–123. London: Oxford University Press.

Lange, Peter, and Geoffrey Garrett. 1985. "The Politics of Growth: Strategic Interaction and Economic Performance in the Advanced Industrial Democracies." *Journal of Politics* 47:792–827.

Lash, Scott. 1985. "The End of Neo-Corporatism. The Breakdown of Centralized Bargaining in Sweden." *British Journal of Industrial Relations* 23:215–39.

Lazarsfeld, Paul F., and Allen H. Barton. 1951. "Qualitative Measurement in the Social Sciences: Classification, Typologies and Indices." In Daniel Lerner and Harold D. Lasswell, eds., *The Policy Sciences,* pp. 155–92. Stanford, CA: Stanford University Press.

Lehmbruch, Gerhard. 1974. "A Non-Competitive Pattern of Conflict Management in Liberal Democracies: The Case of Switzerland, Austria and Lebanon." In Kenneth McRae, ed., *Consociational Democracy,* pp. 90–97. Toronto: McClelland and Stewart.

_____. 1975. "Consociational Democracy in the International System." *European Journal of Political Research* 3:377–91.

Lijphart, Arend. 1968. "Typologies of Democratic Systems." *Comparative Political Studies* 1:3–44.

———. 1977. *Democracy in Plural Societies*. New Haven: Yale University Press.

Lipset, S. M. 1963. *Political Man*. New York: Doubleday Anchor.

Lorwin, Val R. 1974. "Segmented Pluralism: Ideological Cleavages and Political Cohesion in the Smaller European Democracies." In Kenneth McRae, ed., *Consociational Democracy*, pp. 33–69. Toronto: McClelland and Stewart.

Mackie, Thomas T., and Richard Rose, eds. 1974. *The International Almanac of Electoral History*. London: Macmillan.

Madsen, Henrik Jess. 1981. "Partisanship and Macroeconomic Outcomes: A Reconsideration." In Douglas A. Hibbs, Jr., and Heino Fassbender, eds., *Contemporary Political Economy*. Amsterdam and New York: North-Holland Publishing Co.

Maier, Charles S. 1977. "The Politics of Productivity: Foundations of American International Economic Policy After World War II." *International Organization* 31 (Autumn 1977):607–34.

Marin, Bernd. 1987. "From Consociationalism to Technocorporatism: The Austrian Case as a Model Generator?" In Ilija Scholten, ed., *Political Stability and Neo-Corporatism*, pp. 39–69. Beverly Hills and London: Sage Publications.

Markovits, Andrei S. 1982. "The Legacy of Liberalism and Collectivism in the Labor Movement: A Tense but Fruitful Compromise for Model Germany." In Andrei S. Markovits, ed., *The Political Economy of West Germany*, pp. 141–87. New York: Praeger.

Marks, Gary. 1986. "Neocorporatism and Incomes Policy in Western Europe and North America." *Comparative Politics* 18:279–302.

Martin, Andrew. 1975. "Is Democratic Control of Capitalist Economies Possible?" In Leon N. Lindberg, Robert Alford, Colin Crouch, Claus Offe, eds., *Stress and Contradiction in Modern Capitalism*, pp. 13–56. Lexington, MA: Lexington Books.

———. 1984. "Trade Unions in Sweden: Strategic Responses to Change and Crisis." In Peter Gourevitch et al., eds., *Unions and Economic Crisis*, pp. 190–359. London: George Allen and Unwin.

Martin, R. M. 1983. "Pluralism and the New Corporatism." *Political Studies* 31:86–102.

Masters, Marick F., and John D. Robertson. 1988. "Class Compromise in Industrial Democracies." *American Political Science Review* 82:1183–1202.

Milner, Henry. 1987. "Corporatism and the Microeconomic Foundations of Swedish Social Democracy: The Swedish Model Revisited." *Scandinavian Political Studies* 10:239–54.

Mommsen, Wolfgang J., and Hans-Gerhard Husung, eds. 1985. *The Development of Trade Unionism in Great Britain and Germany, 1880–1914*. London: George Allen and Unwin.

Offe, Claus. 1981. "The Attribution of Public Status to Interest Groups: Observations of the West German Case." In Suzanne D. Berger, ed., *Organizing Interests in Western Europe*. Cambridge and London: Cambridge University Press.

———. 1985. "New Social Movements: Challenging the Boundaries of Institutional Politics." *Social Research* 52:817–68.

Offe, Claus, and Helmut Wiesenthal. 1985 (1980). "Two Logics of Collective Action." In Claus Offe, *Disorganized Capitalism*, pp. 170–220. Cambridge, MA: MIT Press.

Olson, Mancur C. 1965. *The Logic of Collective Action*. Cambridge, MA: Harvard University Press.

———. 1982. *The Rise and Decline of Nations*. New Haven, CT: Yale University Press.

———. 1986. "An Appreciation of the Tests and Criticisms." *Scandinavian Political Studies* 9:65–80.

Panitch, Leo. 1979. "The Development of Corporatism in Liberal Democracies." In Philippe C. Schmitter and Gerhard Lehmburch, eds., *Trends Toward Corporatist Intermediation*. Beverly Hills and London: Sage Publications.

———. 1980. "Recent Theorizations of Corporatism: Reflections on a Growth Industry." *British Journal of Sociology* 31:159–87.

Pappalardo, Andriano. "Le condizioni della democrazia consociatria. Una critica logica e empirica." *Rivista Italiana de Scienza Politica* 9:367–445.

Powell, G. Bingham. 1981. "Party Systems and Political Performance: Participation, Stability and Violence in Contemporary Democracies." *American Political Science Review* 75 (December 1981).

———. 1982. *Democracies: Participation, Stability, and Violence*. Cambridge, MA: Harvard University Press.

Przeworski, Adam. 1985. *Capitalism and Social Democracy*. Cambridge: Cambridge University Press.

Przeworski, Adam, and John Sprague. 1986. *Paper Stones: A History of Electoral Socialism*. Chicago: University of Chicago Press.

Przeworski, Adam, and Henry Teune. 1970. *The Logic of Comparative Social Inquiry*. New York: Wiley-Interscience.

Przeworski, Adam, and Michael Wallerstein. 1982. "The Structure of Class Conflict in Democratic Capitalist Societies." *American Political Science Review* 76:215–38.

Regini, Marino. 1982. "Il rapporto sindacato-stato nell' Europa occidentale: Una tipologia del modello neo-corporatista." Typescript.

Robertson, John D. 1984. "Toward a Political Economic Accounting of the Endurance of Cabinet Administrations: An Empirical Assessment of Eight European Democracies." *American Journal of Political Science* 28:693–709.

Rogowski, Ronald. 1983. "Political Support for Regimes: A Theoretical Inventory and Critique." In Allan Kornberg and Harold Clarke, eds., *Political Support in Canada, The Crisis Years*. Durham, NC: Duke University Press.

Rustow, Dankwart. 1970. "Transitions to Democracy: Towards a Dynamic Model." *Comparative Politics* 2:337–63.

Sartori, Giovanni. 1966. "European Political Parties: The Case of Polarized Pluralism." In J. LaPalombara and M. Weiner, eds., *Political Parties and Political Development*. Princeton, NJ: Princeton University Press.

———. 1976. *Parties and Party Systems*. Cambridge and New York: Cambridge University Press.

Schmitter, Philippe. 1974. "Still the Century of Corporatism?" In Fredrick B. Pike and Thomas Stritch, eds., *The New Corporatism: Social-Political Structures in the Iberian World*. Notre Dame, IN: Notre Dame University Press.

———. 1981. "Interest Intermediation and Regime Governability in Contemporary Western Europe and North America." In Suzanne D. Berger, ed., *Organizing Interests in Western Europe*. Cambridge and London: Cambridge University Press.

Scholten, Ilja. 1987. *Political Stability and Neo-Corporatism*. Beverly Hills and London: Sage Publications.

Schwerin, Donald S. 1981. *Corporatism and Protest: Organizational Politics in the Norwegian Trade Unions*. Kent, OH: Kent Popular Press.

Siegfried, André. 1956. *De la IIIe à la IVe république*. Paris: Bernard Grasset.

Skocpol, Theda. 1977. "Wallerstein's World Capitalist System: A Theoretical and Historical Critique." *American Journal of Sociology* 83:1075–90.

Steiner, Jurg. 1981. "Review Article: The Consociational Theory and Beyond." *Comparative Politics* 13 (April 1981):339–53.

Stephens, John D. 1980. *The Transition From Capitalism to Socialism.* Atlantic Highlands, NJ: Humanities Press.

Strom, Kaare. 1984. "Minority Governments in Parliamentary Democracies: The Rationality of Non-Winning Cabinet Solutions." *Comparative Political Studies* 17:199–226.

———. 1989. "Party Competition and the Politics of Economic Openness." *European Journal of Political Research* 17:1–16.

Suleiman, Ezra. 1987. "State Structure and Clientelism: The French State Versus the Notaries." *British Journal of Political Science* 17:257–79.

Tarrow, Sidney. 1977. "From Cold War to Historic Compromise: Approaches to French and Italian Radicalism." In Seweryn Bialer and Sophia Sluzar, eds., *Sources of Contemporary Radicalism.* Boulder, CO: Westview Press.

Taylor, Michael, and V. M. Herman. 1971. "Party Systems and Government Stability." *APSR* 65 (March 1971):28–37.

Tilly, Charles. 1978. *From Mobilization to Revolution.* Reading, MA: Addison Wesley.

6

The Dependency Approach

TONY SMITH

Thanks to the vigor of the dependency approach, as well as others described in this book, the most important and interesting debates in the field of comparative politics are now occurring in the area of Third World development studies. Everywhere the jargon and models elaborated since the late 1950s in the United States by what may be called the "developmentalists" are being taken by storm (disintegrating, it should be noted, as much by virtue of their own exhaustion as by the force of these new ideas). In their place at conferences and in books and journals in languages the world around, a new class of paradigms established by the dependency school is coming to the fore, purporting to provide general models of development in Africa, Asia, and Latin America that explain more fully and accurately than hitherto the principal patterns of change typical of these regions.

As with any broad-based intellectual movement, debates within the dependency school are many and sharp. The clear dominance of Marxism within the literature has not prevented fierce differences over such wide-ranging matters as how to establish the identity of classes in widely disparate settings, what degree of autonomy to accord the state as a political institution charged with providing coherence in circumstances typified by rapid domestic change and extensive foreign penetration, or how to argue for typologies of stages or degrees of dependency.[1] However acute these differences, they are nonetheless overshadowed by the common allegiance of writers in this school to an approach to the study of change in the Third World whose roots go back well into the 1950s, even if it took nearly twenty years for the school to establish itself in force in the United States.

Although the term "dependency" grows out of writing on Latin America, related works dealing with Asia and Africa have until recently been more comfortable using the term "neocolonialism" to describe much the same state of affairs. Whatever the preferred nomenclature, these *dependencistas*, if we may use their Latin American name, share a common view that the force of international capitalism setting up a global division of labor has been the chief force responsible for shaping the history of the South. Capitalism—originally as mercantilism, then as free trade, later as finance

capital, and finally under the auspices of the multinational corporation—
has created a world economic system binding together the globe. The
profound changes this process has generated in every part of the world
offer a common historical experience that is at the basis of a unified
comparative model of social life in the Third World. Dependency literature
is therefore properly viewed as a subset of the so-called world system
approach, whose terms have become increasingly prominent of late in the
United States in the field of international relations.[2] As we have seen,
disputes may arise within this school over a host of matters, but on the
fundamental premise—that to understand change in the Third World or
"periphery" one must see it as a function of the power of economic imperialism
generated by the capitalist "core" of world affairs—there is no debate.

Indeed, it is the emphasis on imperialism that constitutes a recognition
on the part of many *dependencistas* themselves that their approach cannot
claim the status of a theory. For dependency literature studies the effects
of imperialism, not the nature of imperialism itself. Its focus is therefore
on the part, not on the whole—the latter alone providing the "totality" of
experience on which sound theory can be based.[3] Such basic issues as the
character of capitalist accumulation with its "anarchy of production" and
its "law of the declining rate of profit," combined with national struggles
for markets based on the pressures of "uneven development," must thus
escape the purview of the dependency approach, to fall instead into the
domain of world system analysis. As explained by Fernando Henrique
Cardoso, widely believed in the United States to be the foremost writer in
the field, "it seems senseless to search for 'laws of movement' specific to
situations that *are dependent, that is, that have their main features determined
by the phases and trend of expansion of capitalism on a world scale.*"[4]
Relying on a theory of imperialism proposed by their colleagues in world
system analysis, dependency writers content themselves with the nonetheless
difficult job of explaining the logic of capitalist expansion on the periphery.

In this undertaking, the most important conceptual tool of the dependency
school is its analysis of the dual economy. The notion of the dual economy
was itself not invented by these writers, but in their hands it has acquired
a character particular to their analysis.[5] Their basic argument is that as
capitalist penetration has occurred successively in Latin America, Asia, and
Africa under the impetus of northern imperialism, one part of the local
economy of each region has developed into a modern enclave. By virtue
of its historical origins, the basis of the modern sector is export trade, even
if subsidiary manufacturing or service sectors grow up to sustain it. Here
capital accumulates, skills are learned, and class interests are formed whose
innermost needs tie them tightly to foreign concerns. The culture of the
modern enclave may be of the Third World, but its economic and political
character make it a part of the international system. Root and branch it is
dependent.

Alongside the modern economy exists the traditional sector—whence the
term dual economy. As its name implies, the traditional order has a technology,

culture, and social institutions inherited from its past. But the traditional world is far from slumbering in a millenary torpor. Today as yesterday, the modern economy works to disintegrate traditional society, try as the latter may to preserve its integrity. Cheap manufactured goods destroy traditional artisanship; the expansion of plantation agriculture displaces large numbers of peasants, forcing them onto poorer land; elites in the traditional area invest such capital as they possess in the modern enclave, intensifying the lack of investment funds in their own sector. In short, the modern sector of the dual economy acts like a leech on the body of the traditional, ever increasing the difficulty of life there while by its very exploitation consolidating its own power. The misery of the one and the affluence of the other have a common origin.

As the foregoing account implies, economic forces do not act in a social vacuum but express themselves in class formations on the periphery. The key development is in the modern sector, where class interests form in symbiosis with the interests of international capitalism. A class alignment thus takes shape in the South wherein the power of the dominant groups derives from their role of intermediary between the international order run by imperialism and the local peoples over whom they must secure their rule. Although this collaborating class may have local concerns, its reliance on the world economic system ultimately decides its conduct. At different times or in different countries the character of these elites may vary, but their common identity lies in their dependence on the rhythms of the international economic order.

The primary intellectual debt of the dependency school is to Marxism. First, the division of labor is seen as the prime social reality, the engine of change that drives all else before it. The originality of dependency writing is to tie the dynamic of economic life on the periphery into that of the world system beyond: to see it as dependent. The dependency approach thus works on an ambitiously large canvas, linking life on the periphery to movements beyond. Second, political activity is understood to take place through social groups, or classes, differentially related around ownership of the means of production. The originality of dependency writing is to seize on the function of the collaborating class and to plot the changes in its conflicts and alliances over time. Finally, the dependency approach shares with Marxism a bias against certain other considerations. Both reject that ethnic rivalries may have a life quite their own (hence dependency's denigration of the term "tribe" in relation to groups in Africa); that the state may play a relatively autonomous and enormously significant role in the process of great historical transformations; and that in foreign affairs balance-of-power considerations are a primary calculation of leaders at critical historical junctures. To be sure, non-Marxist scholars have contributed ideas to this school: John Gallagher and Ronald Robinson with their idea of the "informal empire" of "free trade imperialism"; Gunnar Myrdal with his arguments describing how dual economies create "backwash effects" systematically disadvantaging the traditional sector; Raúl Prebisch with his work on how unequal exchange in international trade handicaps the South.[6] Such ideas are not an eclectic addition to the dependency school, however; they have been adopted because they strengthen the tools of analysis of an approach that enjoys a fundamental unity of orientation through a reliance on Marxist analysis.[7]

The principal conclusions of the dependency approach should be obvious enough. The problems of the Third World arise from the form of growth pursued by the First World; underdevelopment is the product of development. When we examine such salient features of Third World countries today as the grinding misery of the majority of the population set alongside the ostentatious affluence of the few, or the prevalence of military authoritarian governments in these regions, we must look for their origins in the momentum of capitalist-imperialist expansion.

The foregoing sketch of the dual economy was too rapid to suggest certain crucial refinements of the last several years that have added enormously to the sophistication of the dependency approach. Three relatively new conceptual qualifications are of special importance. The first is the argument that the dual economy is not actually as rigid as was once believed. Spurred on especially by the work of Fernando Henrique Cardoso, many dependency theorists have come to see abundant evidence that a genuine industrial base is being laid in parts of the South, that economies there are becoming far more advanced, diversified, and integrated than earlier writers of this persuasion had ever thought possible.[8] To be sure, both Marx and Lenin anticipated that the worldwide spread of the industrial revolution would take place under capitalist auspices.[9] But the first generation of *dependencistas* liked to talk about "growth without development" and spoke of the way the South would ever be, in their favorite cliché, the "hewers of wood and drawers of water" of the world economic system. Northern capitalism was so dominant in manufacturing and so exploitive in its trade, investment, and financial arrangements that the South seemed destined to an eternal vocation of exporting raw materials.[10] But facts are facts, and in due time dependency analysis had to face the mounting evidence that heavy industry was growing in the Third World, that the manufacturing component of exports was steadily mounting, and that internal, integrated markets were beginning to pulse with a life of their own. Indeed, statistics easily show that the vigor of economic growth in large parts of the Third World is much greater than in the North. As Peter Evans would have it, "classic dependency" is giving way to "dependent development."[11]

The second conceptual innovation made by dependency writers is their new emphasis on the crucial role of the state in this changing order of things. Whereas until the early 1970s *dependencistas* had viewed Third World politics as little more than an auxiliary function of the international economic system, during the last decade they have begun instead to insist that the growing complexity of economic and class relations locally as well as internationally calls for more assertive action on the part of the state in the South.[12] As the diversity and integration of these local economies grow, new groups arise to be controlled politically, just as some old groups must be divested of their power. In a parallel manner, foreign actors on home ground must be more closely supervised than before. Their investments must be made a part of local plans involving the creation of backward and forward production linkages, and their actions increasingly must be harmonized with more fine-tuned fiscal and employment measures. In short, the growing complexity of local economies means new demands for a competent state. In conceptual terms, the result is that the *dependencistas* now have a far richer political analysis with which to conduct their studies since the range of relevant social variables has been substantially expanded.

The first two conceptual refinements of the dependency approach prepare the ground for a third: a recognition of the diversity of Third World countries and a growing appreciation of the significance of local factors in determining the pattern of long-term development processes. Not all countries on the periphery are breaking out of their dual economies, and not all have states aggressively determined to promote domestic interests. Different natural resource endowments; preexisting lines of class or ethnic group conflict or coalition; political culture and the structure of inherited political institutions: all are acquiring a new relevance in research conducted by *dependencistas*. Stages or degrees of dependency may now be discussed as a consequence, whereas previously the approach was capable of saying little more than that a country was or was not dependent.[13]

DEPENDENCY VERSUS DEVELOPMENTALISM

During the 1970s the contest between the new dependency approach and the older developmentalist perspective seemed to be being won by the former with surprisingly little struggle. The reason for this was twofold: Developmentalism was already in a state of decline when the new paradigms of dependency made their appearance in force; and the more established school simply lacked the conceptual arms to defend itself. The causes of the moribund condition in which developmentalism found itself in the early 1970s have been discussed in Chapters 1 and 2. In essence, scholars recognized that certain key Third World problems such as poverty had escaped adequate diagnosis; that the terms by which developmentalism studied the South were frequently superficial or ethnocentric (or both); and that the field of study had in many instances compromised itself politically, as the U.S. defeat in Vietnam made particularly obvious.

The conceptual weakness of the developmentalists in facing the dependency challenge was that they lacked any articulated, clearly unified model of the political economy of Third World lands, just as they lacked any broad-based historical accounts into which to set their studies. Despite all the emphasis on "interdisciplinary studies" in the United States, the truth was that social scientists continued to live behind the restrictive boundaries of their respective narrow methodologies. Though it is surely an exaggeration to maintain, as *dependencistas* are wont, that developmentalist model building is either rigidly linear (projecting a common, converging path from less to more development) or ahistorical, developmentalism has indeed systematically discounted the importance of imperialism while separating the economic from the political domain in studies of the South.[14] Working with these conditions, and given the problems already besetting their studies of the Third World, perhaps it is no wonder that developmentalism proved unable to defend its positions against the onslaught of historians working with political economists within the parameters of Marxist methodology.

Take, for example, the book that most U.S. specialists (myself included) would agree is the finest product of the developmentalist school, Samuel Huntington's *Political Order in Changing Societies* (1968). The book has virtually no economic perspective. True, "participation" is on the upswing; "mobilization" is taking place; but the forces of the industrial revolution go quite unmentioned. Sections of the book deal with the urgency of land reform, but without a clue as to why this problem has arisen now and not a century earlier. Undeniably, the book has its merits. Its sense of political institution building is masterly in scope and nuance. But there is no recognition that the intricacies of this process occur in a world of class conflict and imperialism. Countries have self-contained histories, and political problems have political solutions.

This narrow approach to political development can be supplemented of course by reference to neoclassical economic theory, although it is remarkable how rarely this is done. From the point of view of economic developmentalism, the dual economy is only a transitory phenomenon. Ideally, the modern sector will act as a pole of development from which the industrial revolution will diffuse out to the rest of society on the periphery. Although the modern sector will initially be in league with the international system, it will invariably turn toward the local market, first for food and labor, later for intermediate manufacturing products, and finally as a source of demand for larger-scale manufacturing. Ultimately an integrated economy should form locally, still a part of the world economy producing in line with comparative advantage, but reflecting throughout the characteristics of economic modernity, including a generalized modern skill structure.[15] Where obstacles occur in this projection, they are not caused by the market, but by inadequate resource endowment; a population base that is too small or growing too rapidly; inept governments unable to oversee capital formation because of weakness or corruption or misguided notions about the merits of state planning; inherited ethnic prejudices that make the free mobility of economic factors especially difficult. In this light, the job of political development becomes more comprehensible. Its task is to engineer solutions to the obstacles to economic diffusion through the use of force, the building of consensus, or the creation of institutions that can make the process of change self-sustaining.

From a dependency perspective the problem with the diffusionist approach is its failure to see that its alleged solution to problems on the periphery—the intensification of market relations in the South—is in fact the *origin* of the difficulties there. Political instability in the Third World is caused not so much by the recalcitrance of the traditional world in the face of change as by the brutality of change inflicted on the traditional world. When peasants are dispossessed of their land and herded into urban slums; when traditional artisans find their means of livelihood destroyed; when old patterns of power that provided at least some security in the world are removed and the nuclear family is left to determine its fate as best it can, then one may indeed expect conflict. But it is modernity, not tradition, that is at the origin of the ordeal. From the dependency perspective, therefore, the authoritarian governments typical of so much of the Third World should be seen not as the inevitable response to traditional backwardness but as the unfortunate concomitant of capitalist exploitation.

Moreover, just as a collaborating class is required on the periphery to administer the penetration of these lands by international capitalism, so this latter force requires a political agency to further its interests. From a dependency perspective, the consistently counterrevolutionary character of U.S. foreign policy is thus entirely to be expected. When the power of collaborating states on the periphery proves unequal to the task, Washington aids them in repressing popular uprisings and so protects the international economic system against the challenges of socialist economic nationalism.

It should therefore be understandable that in the eyes of the *dependencistas*, developmentalists in the United States are responsible for far more than inadequate model building with respect to affairs in the Third World. This very inadequacy serves as an ideological smokescreen behind which U.S. imperialism operates. Developmentalist economists present models of the beneficient spread of the industrial revolution through the world and denounce obstacles to progress as the work of backwardness. Their colleagues in political science present institution building as an organizational technique and sanction the establishment of military governments. The separation of economics from politics is not an artificial, but rather a logical expression of the needs of advanced capitalism. The same may be said for the developmentalists' failure to credit imperialism with its proper force. In their work, the developmentalist intelligentsia of U.S. universities give the lie to all their protestations of academic freedom and integrity, revealing instead their true character as apologists for the established international division of wealth and power.

THE FUTURE OF THE DEPENDENCY SCHOOL

The analytical paradigms put forth by the dependency school represent a powerful challenge to the study of change in the Third World as it has been conceptualized in the United States over the last twenty-five years. Not only are fundamental features of the developmentalist model called sharply into question on cogent, rational grounds; the entire U.S. intellectual effort itself is put into doubt by relating its methodological blinders to the vested interests of the country wherein these typologies originated. There is therefore a moral as well as an analytical cutting edge to dependency theory that explains a good deal of the excitement that has surrounded its introduction in the United States.

The question nevertheless arises: Can the dependency approach maintain its momentum? Are its tools of analysis sufficiently flexible to generate new insights into patterns of change on the periphery while defending itself against what will probably be a mounting tide of criticism? Will it be creative enough to defend its position as the preeminent interpreter of social life in the South against rival schools and at the same time maintain its unity as an integrated set of insights based on a commonly accepted body of assumptions?

A real danger may well come from within. For as the dependency approach becomes increasingly sophisticated in its insights and broad in its applications, divergent or rival lines of analysis may adulterate the unity of view (whatever the earlier genuine differences) that characterized its literature in the 1960s and 1970s. Consider the possible fate of the three recent refinements in the dependency approach discussed above: the importance of local factors in determining the course of change in the South; the critical role of the state in development there; and the genuine gains in economic strength so apparent there over the last two decades. Couldn't these factors not persuasively be combined to suggest that a situation of dependency no longer exists (if indeed it ever did)? Looked at more closely, are these refinements not simply restatements of a version of the diffusion-developmentalist models reviewed earlier? If genuine growth is taking place, if the shape and pace of this change reflect in significant measure local economic and social circumstances, and if the state is especially responsible for how these events are occurring, one quite plausible inference would be that the ability of imperialism to make these areas dependent is declining, and that therefore the cardinal reference point of the dependency approach is fast losing its utility as a lodestar. Ironically, then, *dependencia* as a perspective may be gaining strength just as the situation that gives rise to it comes to an end, and the very sophistication of its method unwittingly points this out. To a Marxist there should be nothing paradoxical about this situation, as the doctrine teaches that ideas reflect the material world around them, usually with a time lag. Of course the judgment of history may be more severe, holding that dependency theorizing reflected only a transitory moment in the process of Third World change, and that its major contribution was not to give insight into events there but to be the ideological representation of a triumphing nationalist consciousness in these areas. To add insult to injury, it might appear in retrospect that dependency writing represented only the narrow and short-term perspective, while the diffusion-developmentalist approach proved more able to explain the course of change on the periphery over the long haul.

Intriguing as such speculation might be, the dependency approach is unlikely to run afoul for these reasons. As we have seen, dependency writing is no simple-minded affair. Its categories of analysis have already generated concepts able to pull back into line the potentially fissiparous tendencies toward apostasy sketched out above. Two of these concepts are key: the role of the multinational corporation in the South, and the repercussions on the international system of what the *dependencistas* call the semi-periphery.

The dependency approach to the role of the multinational corporation in the South invariably stresses that however much the periphery may be developing economically, the leading sectors of industry there—the "commanding heights" or the "pacesetters"—are overwhelmingly owned by Americans, Europeans, and Japanese. Moreover, as the local economy has become more integrated, it has also become far more sensitive to economic fluctuations. As a result, the international system has maintained its grip on the periphery despite the real economic change that has taken place there. And with this grip it calls the tune: a docile, cheap work force to exploit; favorable taxing regulations for private enterprise; a fiscally "responsible" state (i.e., one that does not engage in "excessive" social service expenditures)—in short, an environment to facilitate the unimpeded accumulation of profits. The paramount consequences, as already described, are the terrible poverty of a substantial portion of the population and the need for an authoritarian government to keep society in line. Industrial development on the periphery has therefore not reduced dependence but may indeed have substantially increased it.[16]

The economic modernization of the periphery has also had its effect on the international order, according to the *dependencistas,* but here again beneath the apparent change lies the more permanent continuity of imperialist control. For as countries in the South diversify and integrate their economies they may leave the periphery—but not to join the core, as neither their financial nor their technical infrastructure is autonomous enough to play a part in controlling world economic affairs. Instead, by virtue of their continued dependence these countries come to play the part in the world system played domestically by a middle class. They have little real power, but the demonstrable privileges they enjoy relative to those beneath them (and in part because of their exploitation of those less fortunate) motivate them to help keep the system operating. These "newly industrialized countries" (NICs) become junior, collaborating members of the international trading, investment, and financial system, their gains serving only to reinforce the system that binds them to its will. If in appearance the international economic system is undergoing radical change, in reality the power of capitalism and the dominance of the northern imperialist states has never been more effective.[17]

The dependency approach probably has enough internal resilience to keep its doctrine coherent despite important changes in its terms. The achievement is impressive. Dependency literature took a major step forward when it admitted evidence about change in the Third World to which it previously had been blind, then formulated new concepts to deal with the new developments, meanwhile reaffirming its primary doctrinal belief in the dependence of the periphery on the core and in the preeminence of economic affairs in determining the pattern of history. The dependency approach thus remains true to its essential political vocation: to serve as an ideological "united front" in the Leninist sense, binding Marxists together with nationalists in the Third World in their mutual resentment of imperialism and in their willingness to lay the responsibility for the many problems of their countries at the doorstep of foreign powers.

This political role of the dependency approach explains a good part of its resolve to stay united. Because *dependencistas* know that their ideas may become relevant politically to the societies they write about, they have a stake beyond companionship in a field of academic pursuit for which to maintain their common stance. In short, for both doctrinal and practical political reasons, we should expect the dependency approach to remain assertive. It will most likely not be undone, as speculated above, by its own hand.

The purpose of this chapter was to lay out the basic structure of the dependency approach to the study of the Third World. It may nonetheless be justifiable in conclusion to indicate some of the weaker parts of this perspective. One cautionary note: Piddling criticism is a waste of time. A perspective as complex and supple as *dependencia* will have no trouble explaining away as irrelevant or understandable relatively minor points about changes in the core, the periphery, or the international system, or demands that its claims be made quantifiable and so testable. Criticism would be better advised to go to the heart of the matter and to challenge on theoretical and empirical grounds the two primary assumptions of this school: that economic forces are the prime movers of history (the quintessential Marxist claim) and that it is economic forces under the impetus of imperialism that provide the fundamental point of departure for a study of change in the Third World.

Such an undertaking would be no easy affair. In essence it would entail elaborating an interpretation of change on the periphery as broad and complex as that of the dependency approach, except that the influence of local and political factors on the movement of history there would have to be shown to be at least as weighty as the foreign and economic factors proposed by the *dependencistas*. This approach could accept dependency interpretations where it seemed appropriate, even if such eclecticism is repudiated by this school itself. Establishing that the dependency approach is only a partial truth would shatter the unity of the movement intellectually.

It is the extremeness of the dependency model that provides at once its source of unity and its point of greatest vulnerability. Although the dependency perspective is a complicated set of propositions, its core claim can nonetheless be distinguished clearly. *Dependencia* asserts that the international division of labor, run under the auspices of capitalist imperialism, establishes a sector of production serving its interests in a peripheral country and oversees the formation of local class interests that can be counted on to work in harmony with the international system. (In cases where such a class alignment cannot be produced a period of direct colonial rule may be practiced, followed by decolonization and neocolonialism thereafter.)[18] Subsequently, this class, with its needs and abilities, its weaknesses and strengths, comes to control the shape of change on the periphery. It must be emphasized that for the dependency approach the preponderant or decisive strength of this class locally is central, even if no easy measurement is available. For if it can be maintained that this class in only one among many, and that indeed other factors such as the inherited political institutions and ethnic or class cleavages of a land are equally or even more significant in determining the course of events on the periphery, then the claim that a country is *dependent* would lose its essential meaning. Through the insertion of a collaborating class in the South, imperialism must dominate life there; it is not enough that this be one force among many. For if it were not dominant then the country would no longer be shaped solely, or even primarily perhaps, by the force of economic imperialism. The tie with world system analysis would snap, the claim to a unified approach to the study of the Third World would fade, the militant accusations against capitalism become more dim. Of course what one may find is that some countries at some times correspond more closely to the dependency model than do others, so that as a paradigm for analysis it clearly has its value. But the suggestion that their paradigm is only useful at times would not be acceptable to this school. Its ambition requires far more. And although this ambition is an undeniable source of strength in the dependency movement, it is likewise a weakness against which criticism may be used most devastatingly.[19]

There is no particular reason to believe that attacks against the dependency approach will stay its convictions. Like the proponents of any strong model, *dependencistas* have ways of deflecting attacks and maintaining their conceptual unity. And there are political interests to be served by such an ideology as well, nationalist and Marxist concerns that will insist on the veracity of this way of understanding the world whatever the objections. The dependency paradigm for the study of the Third World is certainly one of the foremost approaches in the comparative politics field.

The dependency approach has undoubtedly made its contribution: The question is whether it is merely a corrective or an addendum to the earlier developmentalist school, which did not talk very much about the influence of the international economy on development, or whether it can stand on its own as a full and complete explanation of development (or the lack thereof), which to me seems increasingly unlikely. Related is the question of what form of dependency theory we will use. Will it be the pragmatic dependency analysis of a Theodore Moran,[20] who realistically and without any great ideological presumptions finds that multinational corporations and foreign embassies do sometimes muck around, with highly varying degrees of intensity under different times and circumstances—most often benignly, sometimes progressively, and occasionally nefariously—in the internal affairs of other nations? Or will it be the dependency theory of the Marxian ideologues, whose approach is to use the *facts* of dependency as a convenient way to blame most of the world's problems on the United States?

We cannot answer all of these questions here, except to say that with the decline and attacks on Marxian theory and economics in the Soviet Union, China, and Eastern Europe, Western Marxists have also been thrown into a state of uncertainty. In this new, more pragmatic era, the ideologues are having a tougher time, and that will probably be reflected in the form that future dependency theory takes as well.

NOTES

1. For a discussion of debates within the dependency school see, among others, Fernando Henrique Cardoso, "The Consumption of Dependency Theory in the United States," *Latin American Research Review* 12, no. 3 (1977); Richard R. Fagen, "Studying Latin American Politics: Some Implications of a *Dependencia* Approach," *Latin American Research Review* 12, no. 3 (1977); and Ronald H. Chilcote, "A Question of Dependency," *Latin American Research Review* 13, no. 2 (1978).

2. The most influential writer in the United States on world system analysis is Immanuel Wallerstein. See his *The Modern World System: Capitalist Agriculture and the Origins of the European World Economy in the Sixteenth Century* (New York: Academic Press, 1974) and *The Modern World-System II: Mercantilism and the Consolidation of the European World-Economy, 1600–1750* (New York: Academic Press, 1980). See also the journal he edits, entitled *Review.*

3. Immanuel Wallerstein, "The Rise and Future Demise of the World Capitalist System," *Comparative Studies in Society and History* 14, no. 4 (1974).

4. Fernando Henrique Cardoso and Enzo Faletto, *Dependency and Development in Latin America* (Berkeley: University of California Press, 1979), p. xxiii.

5. For an indication of the history of the concept see Benjamin Higgins, *Economic Development: Principles, Problems, and Policies* (New York: W. W. Norton, 1979), Chaps. 12 and 14. For a comprehensive application of the theory in dependency terms see William W. Murdoch, *The Poverty of Nations: The Political Economy of Hunger and Population* (Baltimore: Johns Hopkins University Press, 1980), Chaps. 8 and 9.

6. John Gallagher and Ronald Robinson, "The Imperialism of Free Trade," *Economic History Review*, 2d ser., 6, no. 1 (1953); and Gunnar Myrdal, *Economic Theory and Underdeveloped Regions* (London: Gerald Duckworth, 1957). On Prebisch see Joseph L. Love, "Raúl Prebisch and the Origins of the Doctrine of Unequal Exchange," *Latin American Research Review* 15, no. 3 (1980); a recent essay by Prebisch is "Introducción al estudio de la crisis del capitalismo periférico," *El Trimestre Económico* 18, no. 3 (1979).

7. An interesting study would be to relate the ideas of the dependency school to publications from the Soviet Union, Eastern Europe, and Cuba. A random sampling that has come my way suggests that exchanges between these areas and *dependencistas* have been important. To my knowledge no studies of these relations have been published.

8. Fernando Henrique Cardoso, "Dependent Capitalist Development in Latin America," *New Left Review* 74 (1972); and "Associated-Dependent Development: Theoretical and Practical Implications," in Alfred Stepan, ed., *Authoritarian Brazil: Origins, Policies and Future* (New Haven, CT: Yale University Press, 1973). An early and especially strong statement on this matter is by Bill Warren, "Imperialism and Capitalist Industrialization," *New Left Review* 81 (1973).

9. For Marx, see "Letters on British Imperialism in India"; for Lenin, *Imperialism The Highest Stage of Capitalism* (1917).

10. For example, see André Gunder Frank, "Economic Dependence, Class Structure, and Underdevelopment Policy," in James D. Cockcroft et al., *Dependence and Underdevelopment: Latin America's Political Economy* (Garden City, NY: Doubleday, 1970).

11. Peter Evans, *Dependent Development: The Alliance of Multinational, State and Local Capital in Brazil* (Princeton, NJ: Princeton University Press, 1979).

12. The most important work by this school on the subject of the state has been done by Guillermo O'Donnell, *Modernization and Bureaucratic-Authoritarianism: Studies in South American Politics* (Berkeley, CA: Institute of International Studies, 1973); and "Reflections on the Patterns of Change in the Bureaucratic-Authoritarian State," *Latin American Research Review* 13, no. 1 (1978). For a volume with several essays critical of this approach, see David Collier, ed., *The New Authoritarianism in Latin America* (Princeton, NJ: Princeton University Press, 1980).

13. Cardoso and Faletto, *Dependency and Development*, Introduction and Epilogue.

14. For example, see André Gunder Frank, "Sociology of Development and Underdevelopment of Sociology," in Cockroft, *Dependence and Underdevelopment*.

15. For example, see Everett E. Hagen, *The Economics of Development*, rev. ed. (Homewood, IL: Richard D. Irwin, 1975), Part 2.

16. For example, see Evans, *Dependent Development*.

17. Although the term "semi-periphery" seems to have been coined by Immanuel Wallerstein, the earliest use of the concept of which I am aware occurs in the idea of "go-between countries" as explained in Johan Galtung, "A Structural Theory of Imperialism," *Journal of Peace Research* 8, no. 2 (1971).

18. Kwame Nkrumah, *Neo-Colonialism: The Last Stage of Imperialism* (New York: International Publishers, 1966).

19. For an attempt to de-emphasize the importance of imperialism and insist on the significance of local political factors in patterns of change on the periphery, see Tony Smith, *The Pattern of Imperialism: The United States, Great Britain, and the Late-Industrializing World Since 1815* (New York: Cambridge University Press, 1981), Chap. 2. For a more extended critique of recent refinements in the dependency model, see Tony Smith, "The Logic of Dependency Revisited," *International Organization* 35, no. 4 (1981).

20. Theodore Moran, *Multinational Corporations and the Politics of Dependence: Copper in Chile* (Princeton, NJ: Princeton University Press, 1974).

7

Toward a Nonethnocentric Theory of Development: Alternative Conceptions from the Third World

HOWARD J. WIARDA

[The Ayatullah] Khomeini has blown apart the comfortable myth that as the Third World industrializes, it will also adopt Western values.

—*Time*

A revolution of far-reaching breadth and meaning is presently sweeping the Third World, and we in the West are only partially and incompletely aware of it. This revolution carries immense implications not only for the Third World and our relations with it but also, more generally, for the social sciences and the way we comprehend and come to grips with Third World change.

We are all aware of the new social and economic forces of modernization sweeping the Third World and perhaps to a somewhat lesser extent of the political and value changes also occurring, including anti-Americanism and anti-colonialism. What has received less attention is the way these changes are now finding parallel expression in a rejection of the basic developmental models and paradigms originating in the West, both Marxian and non-Marxian varieties, and a corresponding assertion of non-Western, nonethnocentric, and indigenous ones.[1]

The ongoing Iranian Revolution may not be typical, but it is illustrative. At the popular level, awareness of the profound changes occurring in Iran has been warped and obscured by events surrounding the revolution and

An earlier version of this chapter appeared in the *Journal of Developing Areas* 17, no. (July 1983):433–52. A Senior Fellowship from the National Endowment for the Humani̶ provided research and writing assistance; the paper was written while the author w̶ Research Scholar at the Center for International Affairs, Harvard University.

131

the 1979 seizure of the hostages, by the discomfort those in the more pluralist societies of the West feel toward the Islamic fundamentalists' assertion that there is a single right way and a wrong way to do everything, and by the general "ugliness" (at least as portrayed on our television screens) of some of the revolution's leaders. Even scholars and others more sympathetic to such fundamental transformations, in Iran and elsewhere, have tended to focus on the changes occurring in their one area or country of specialization and have not analyzed the more general phenomenon or placed it in a broader, global perspective.[2] Alternatively, they have preferred to see the Iranian Revolution and the coming to power of its ayatullah as an isolated event, readily subject to ridicule and agreed-upon moral outrage and therefore not representing a serious challenge to established Western values and social science understandings.

The proposition argued here, however, is that the rejection of the Western (that is, North-West European and U.S.) model of development, in its several varieties, is now widespread throughout the Third World and that there are many new and exciting efforts on the part of intellectuals and political elites throughout these areas to assert new, indigenous models of development. Furthermore, these efforts represent serious and fundamental challenges to many cherished social science assumptions and understandings and even to the presumption of a universal social science of development. Scholars disregard such changes at the risk of both perpetuating Western malcomprehension of the Third World areas and retaining a social science of development that is parochial and ethnocentric rather than accurate and comprehensive.[3]

The Iranian Revolution, with its assertion of Islamic fundamentalism and of a distinctively Islamic social science (or model) of development, is in fact but one illustration of a far more general Third World phenomenon. There are common themes in the reexaminations presently under way by many Third World leaders: of Indian caste associations and their potential role in modernization; of African tribalism, not as a traditional institution that is necessarily dysfunctional and therefore to be discarded but as a base upon which to build new kinds of societies; of Latin American organicism, corporatism, populism, and new forms of bureaucratic-authoritarianism or of democracy; of family and interpersonal solidarities in Japan; of the overlaps of Confucian and Maoist conceptions in China. The common themes in these areas include hostility toward and often a sense of the inappropriateness of the Western developmental models in non-Western or only partially Western areas, the nationalistic and often quite original assertion of local and indigenous ones, and the questioning of some basic notions regarding the universality of the social sciences. Third World scholars and political leaders believe there are not just one or two (First and Second World capitalist and socialist, U.S. and Soviet) paths to development, but many diverse ones, and that the dichotomy drawn between traditional and modern false for societies where the blending and fusion of these is more likely the necessary or automatic replacement of the former by the latter.[4]

These themes are controversial and provocative, and not all the dimensions and issues can be dealt with here. Rather, my purpose is to present the critique Third World areas are now directing at the Western and, we often presume, "universal" developmental model; to examine the alternatives they themselves are now in the process of formulating; to assess the problems and difficulties in these alternative formulations; and to offer some conclusions regarding the issue of particularism versus universalism in the social sciences.

THE THIRD WORLD CRITIQUE
OF THE WESTERN DEVELOPMENTAL MODEL

In all frankness, much of our self-inflicted disaster has its intellectual roots in our social sciences faculties.

—West Indian economist Courtney N. Blackman
in "Science, Development, and Being Ourselves,"
Caribbean Studies Newsletter

The Third World critique of the Western model and pattern of development as inappropriate and irrelevant, or partially so, to its circumstances and conditions is widespread and growing. There has long been a powerful strain of anti-Westernism (as well as anticolonialism) among Third World intellectuals, but now that sentiment is stronger and well-nigh universal. The recent trends differ from earlier critiques of Western modernization theory in that the attacks have become far more pervasive; they are shared more generally by Third World society as a whole; they have taken on global rather than simply area- or country-specific connotations; and the criticisms are no longer solely negative but are now accompanied by an assertion of other, alternative, often indigenous approaches. Moreover the debate is no longer just a scholarly dispute between competing social science development models; rather, it has powerful policy implications as well.

One should not overstate the case. As yet, the critiques one reads are frequently as inchoate and uncertain as the concept of the Third World itself. They tend to be incomplete, fragmented, and unsystematic; long on rhetoric but short on reality; and are often as nationalistic and parochial as the Western theories they seek to replace. Yet one cannot but be impressed by the growing strength of these critiques, their increasing acceptance by Third World leaders, and the dawning realization of common themes, criticisms, and problems encountered with the Western model across diverse continents, nations, and cultural traditions.

The criticism centers, to begin with, on the bias and ethnocentrism perceived in the Western model, which makes it inapplicable to societies with quite different traditions, histories, societies, and cultural patterns.[5] For societies cast in quite different traditions from the Judeo-Christian one, lacking the sociopolitical precepts of Greece, Rome, and the Bible, without the same experiences of feudalism and capitalism, the Western model has only limited relevance.[6] Western political theory is faulted for its almost entirely European focus and its complete lack of attention to other intellectual traditions; political sociology in Emile Durkheim, Auguste Comte, Max Weber, or Talcott Parsons is shown to be based almost exclusively on the European transition from "agraria" to "industria" and its accompanying sociopolitical effects, which have proved somewhat less than universal;[7] and political economy, in both its Marxist and non-Marxist variants, is criticized for the exclusively European and hence less-than-universal origins of its major precepts: philosophical constructs derived (especially in Marx) from Germany, a conception of sociopolitical change derived chiefly from the French tradition, and an understanding of industrialization and its effects stemming chiefly from the English experience. Even our celebrated "liberal arts education" (basically Western European) has come in for criticism as constituting not an experience of universal relevance but merely the first area studies program.[8] These criticisms of the narrowness and parochialism of our major social science traditions and concepts, as grounded essentially on the singular experience of Western Europe and without appreciation of or applicability to the rest of the world, are both sweeping and, with proper qualification, persuasive.

Third World intellectuals have begun to argue secondly that the timing, sequence, and stages of development in the West may not necessarily be replicable in their own areas. Again, this argument is not new, but its sophisticated expression by so many Third World leaders is. For example, Western political sociology generally asserts, based on the European experience, that bureaucratization and urbanization accompanied and were products of industrialization; in Latin America and elsewhere, however, many Third World scholars are arguing that the phenomena of preindustrial urbanization and bureaucratization requires different kinds of analyses.[9] With regard to timing, it seems obvious that countries developing and modernizing in the late twentieth century should face different kinds of problems than those that developed in the nineteenth; because their developmental response must necessarily be different, there seems to be no necessary reason the former should merely palely and retardedly repeat the experience of the latter.[10] In terms of stages, the European experience suggests that capitalism must necessarily replace feudalism; in much of the Third World, however, feudalism in accord with the classic French case seems never to have existed,[11] capitalism exists in forms (populist, patrimonialist, etatist) that hardly existed in the West, and rather than capitalism definitely *replacing* feudalism, it seems more likely that the two will continue to exist side by side. The timing, sequences, and stages of development in most Third World nations are sufficiently different, indeed, that virtually all Western precepts require fundamental reinterpretation when applied there: the so-called demographic transition, the role of the emerging middle classes, military behavior and professionalization, the role of peasants and workers, the presumption of greater pluralism as societies develop, notions of differentiation and rationalization.[12]

Not only are the timing, sequences, and stages of Third World development likely to be quite different, but the international context is entirely altered as well. In the nineteenth century, Great Britain, Japan, and the United States were able to develop relatively autonomously; for today's Third World nations, that is no longer possible. To cite only a handful of many possible illustrations, these nations often become pawns in Cold War struggles over which they have no control; they are absolutely dependent on outside capital, technology, and markets for their products;[13] and they are part of an international community and of a web of international military, diplomatic, political, commercial, cultural, communications, and other ties from which they cannot divorce themselves. Many are entirely dependent for their continued development on external energy sources, making them victims of skyrocketing prices that have wreaked havoc with their national economies. In these and other ways it seems clear the international context of development is entirely different from that of a century to a century and a half ago.

A fourth area of difference perceived by leaders from the Third World relates to the role of traditional institutions. Western political sociology largely assumes that such traditional institutions as tribes, castes, clans, patrimonialist authority, and historic corporate units must either yield (the liberal tradition) under the impact of modernization or be overwhelmed (the revolutionary tradition) by it. Nevertheless, we have learned that in much of the Third World so-called traditional institutions have, first of all, proved remarkably resilient, persistent, and long-lasting; rather than fading or being crushed under the impact of change, they have instead proved flexible, accommodative, and adaptive, bending to the currents of modernization without necessarily being replaced by them.[14] Second, these traditional institutions have often served as filters of the modernization process, accepting what was useful and what they themselves could absorb in modernity while rejecting the rest. Third, we have learned that such traditional institutions as India's caste associations, African tribalism, and Latin American corporatism can often be transformed into agents of modernization, bridging some wrenching transitions and even serving as the base for new and more revered forms of indigenous development.[15] Indeed one of the more interesting illustrations of this process is the way a new generation of African leaders, rather than rejecting tribalism as traditional and to be discarded, as the *geist* of Western political sociology would have them do, are now reexamining tribalism's persistent presence as an indigenous, realistic, and perhaps viable base on which to construct a new kind of authentic African society.[16]

Fifth, Third World intellectuals are beginning to argue that the Eurocentrism of the major development models has skewed, biased, and distorted their own and the outside world's understanding of Third World societies, making them into something of a laughingstock, the butt of cruel, ethnic, and sometimes racial gibes. For example, the Western bias led scholars from the West and sometimes those from the Third World to overemphasize such presumably modernizing institutions as trade unions and political parties; yet in many Third World countries these institutions may not count for very much, and their absence or weakness often caused these societies to be labeled underdeveloped or dysfunctional. At the same time, institution that Western political sociology has proclaimed traditional and hence fated to disappear, such as patronage networks, clan groups, religious institutions and movements, and extended families, have been woefully understudied. This has made for immense gaps in Western knowledge of these societies, and some fundamental misinterpretations have resulted.[17]

Meanwhile, these nations actually do modernize and develop in their own terms if not always in ours—that is, through coups and barracks revolts that sometimes contribute to an expanding circulation of elites, through larger patronage and spoils systems now transferred to the national level, through assistance from abroad that is often employed not entirely inappropriately in ways other than those intended, and through elaborated corporate group, family, clan, or tribal networks. Yet the actual dynamics of change and modernization in these nations have often been made the stuff of opéra bouffe in *New York Times* headlines or *New Yorker* cartoons or have led to appalled, holier-than-thou attitudes among Westerners who would still like to remake the Third World in accordance with Judeo-Christian morality and Anglo-American legal and political precepts. As scholars and researchers, our excessive attention to some institutions that our ofttimes wishful sociology would elevate to a higher plane than they deserve, the neglect of others, and our ethnocentrism and general ignorance as to how Third World societies do in fact develop has perpetuated our woeful misunderstanding.[18] It is indeed ironic that for a long time Third World intellectuals bought, or were sold, the same essentially Western categories as the westernizers themselves had internalized, and that their understanding of their own societies therefore was often no greater than our own. That condition is now changing very rapidly.[19]

The Western development perspective has recently been subjected to an additional criticism: that it is part of the Western ideological and intellectual offensive to keep the Third World within the Western orbit.[20] In perhaps the most widespread criticism of the Western development model current in the Third World, Western modernization and development theory is seen as still another "imperialist" Cold War strategy aimed at tying Third World nations into a Western and liberal (that is, U.S.) development pattern, of keeping them within the U.S. sphere of influence, and of denying them the possibility of alternative developmental patterns. Of course, not all who fashioned the early and influential development literature had such manifest Cold War or "New Mandarin" goals in mind. Some clearly did,[21] but among other U.S. scholars the development literature was popular chiefly because it corresponded to cherished notions about the United States (that it is a liberal, democratic, pluralist, socially just, and modern nation) and to the belief that the developing nations could emulate the West if they worked hard and recast themselves in accord with the U.S. or Western model. This strategy was remarkably successful from the late 1950s, when the first development literature began to appear, until the early 1970s. Since that time, however, the development literature has been increasingly tarred with the imperialist brush and discredited throughout the Third World. A whole new generation of young Third World leaders and intellectuals no longer accepts the Western developmentalist concepts and perspectives and is searching for possible alternatives.[22]

Finally, and perhaps most harmful in terms of the long-term development of the Third World, is the damage that has been inflicted on Third World institutions because of the Western biases. "Development" is no mere intellectual construct, nor is it benignly neutral. There are consequences, often negative, in following a Western-oriented development strategy. This goes beyond the kind of damage inflicted on countries such as the Dominican Republic by Cold War rivalries and U.S. interventionism (1965), or by agencies like the International Monetary Fund, whose financial advice to Third World nations has often been unenlightened. Even more serious is the role "development" has had in undermining such viable traditional institutions as extended family networks, patronage ties, clan and tribal loyalties, corporate group linkages, churches and religious movements, historic authority relations, and the like. By eroding and often eliminating these traditional institutions before modern ones could be created, development helped destroy some of the only agencies in many Third World nations that might have enabled them to make a genuine transition to real modernity. The destruction, in the name of modernization, of these kinds of traditional institutions throughout the Third World may well be one of the most important legacies of developmentalism, and it will powerfully affect future relations between the Third World and the First. By our patronizing, ethnocentric efforts to promote development among the less-developed countries, we in the West may have inadvertently denied them the possibility of real development while at the same time erasing the very indigenous and at one time viable institutions they are now attempting, perhaps futilely and too late, to resurrect.[23]

The Third World critique of the Western development model as biased, ethnocentric, and often damaging is thus strong, sweeping, and, in its essentials, difficult to refute. Although many of the arguments are not new and though not all Third World critiques are as coherent, global, and organized as presented here, the criticisms are spreading and becoming universal, the common elements are being analyzed, and they are increasingly informed by solid facts and argument. It remains for us to examine what the Third World offers in place of the Western schema.

THE ASSERTION OF INDIGENOUS
THIRD WORLD DEVELOPMENT MODELS

The problem with us Africans is that we've not been educated to appreciate our art and culture. So many of us have been influenced by the British system of education. I went through this system here not knowing enough about my own country. It was almost as if what we natives did wasn't important enough to b studied. I knew all about British history and British art, but about Ghana and Africa nothing.

—Ghanaian art historian and intellectual Nana Apt, quoted in the *New York Times*

The purpose of this section is to provide an overview of the new development models emerging from the Third World. Space constraints rule out any detailed treatment here; this survey will provide only a hint of the new ideas, concepts, and theories.[24] Nevertheless, even this brief discussion should suffice to convey some of the main themes from each of the major areas, to show their common currents, and to begin to analyze the larger patterns. More detailed treatment is reserved for a planned book-length study.[25]

In his influential work *Beyond Marxism: Towards an Alternative Perspective*, Indian political theorist Vrajenda Raj Mehta argues that neither liberal democracy nor communism are appropriate frameworks for Indian development. He attributes their inadequacy to their unidimensional views of man and society. The liberal-democratic view that man is a consumer of utilities and producer of goods serves to legitimize a selfish, atomistic, egoistic society. Communism, he says, reduces all human dimensions to one, the economic, and transforms all human activity into one, state activity, which erodes all choice and destroys life's diversities.[26]

Mehta further argues for a multidimensional conception of man and society incorporating (1) the objective, external, rational; (2) the subjective, internal, intuitive; (3) the ethical, normative, harmonious; and (4) the spiritual and fiduciary. For the development of man's multidimensional personality, society must be structured as an "oceanic circle," an integral-pluralist system of wholes within wholes. The four social wholes of Mehta's well-organized society consist of "those devoted to the pursuit of knowledge, those who run the administration and protect the community from external aggression, those who manage the exchange of services of goods, and those who attend to manual and elementary tasks" (p. 54). Mehta claims that such an integralist-pluralist order will overcome the atomistic limitations of liberal democracy and the economic and bureaucratic collectivism of communism. The logic of "developing wholes" means that each sector of society must have autonomy or *swaraj* within an overall system of harmony and oceanic circles. Emphasizing both the autonomy of the several societal sectors and their integration within a larger whole, Mehta calls this essentially Indian-organic-corporatist system "integral pluralism." "Integral pluralism insists that the development of society has to be the development of the whole society. The whole is not one, but itself consists of various wholes, of economics and politics, ethics and religion, as also of different types of individuals. The relationship of each of them to each other is in the nature of oceanic circles" (p. 60).

Particularly interesting for our purposes are Mehta's attempts to ground ·is theory in the reality of Indian culture, history, and civilization. "Each national community," he says, "has its own law of development, its own way to fulfill itself." "The broken mosaic of Indian society," he goes on, "cannot be recreated in the image of the West—India must find its own strategy of development and nation-building suited to its own peculiar conditions" (p. 92). Instead of being dazzled by the national progress of the West and futilely trying to emulate its development model, India should define its goals and choose its means "separately in terms of its own resources and the role it wants to play on the world scene." Rejecting the thesis of a single and universal pattern of development, Mehta advocates an indigenous process of change attuned to the needs of individual societies: "A welcome process of social change in all societies is a process towards increasing self-awareness in terms of certain normatively defined goals in each case, and that the direction of the process and the definition of ends is largely defined by the society's own distinct history and way of life" (p. 104).

Mehta's theory of integral pluralism is a bold and erudite exposition of a model of indigenous development for India. Although he draws some of his ideas from the West, the specific sources of inspiration for his model are Indian: the Vedic seers, the *Mahabharata*, Rabindranath Tagore, and Gandhi. In contemporary India the model derives particular support from nationalists and from those who advocate the Gandhian model of development, which emphasizes a decentralized economy based on small industries, a reorientation of production in terms of criteria besides prosperity only, a possible decentralized defense industry, and hence a particularly Indian route to development.

Mehta believes that the form of liberal democracy derived from England, the colonial power, is inappropriate and unworkable in the Indian context. Political events in India in recent years seem to provide some though still incomplete evidence for that argument. But neither is communism in accord with India's traditions, he argues. Mehta states that the crisis in Indian politics is due to the fact that the constitution and political system are not based on what he calls the "hidden springs" or the underlying institutional and cultural heritage of Indian society. That is the cause, he writes, of the present disillusionment, institutional atrophy, spreading chaos, and the concomitant widespread desire to adopt the Gandhian model. Accordingly, the successful ruler and developer in the Indian context "will be the one who will not only have an idea of the system of international stratification and the position of the dominant powers in it, but also the one who will weave into a holistic view the fact that his society once had a glorious civilization which, due to certain structural defects and rigidities, gave way to conquerors from the outside; he will be conscious of the continuity amidst all the shifts in the historical scene, of the underlying unity amongst a panorama of immense and baffling diversities" (p. 115).

No claim is made here that Mehta's book captures the essence of contemporary Indian thinking or that it is necessarily representative of the newer currents emanating from Indian intellectuals or public opinion.[27] It is, nevertheless, illustrative of the kind of thinking and writing now beginning to emerge, and there is no doubt that its call for a nationalistic and indigenous model of development has struck an immensely responsive chord in his country. Moreover, it corresponds closely to other observed phenomena in contemporary India: the increased repudiation of English and Western influences, the rising tide of Indian nationalism, the revival of various religious movements and the corresponding criticism of Western secularism and pluralism, the justifications for authoritarian rule and for integral and harmonious development, and the reinterpretation of caste associations no longer as traditional institutions that must be destroyed but as indigenous agencies capable of modernizing and serving as transitional bridges of development. These deep-rooted trends help make Mehta's book, and the voluminous writings of numerous other scholars and popularizers, worthy of serious attention.[28]

The new and often parallel currents stirring the Islamic world have received far more popular attention than have those in India. There can be no doubt that a major religious revival is sweeping the world of Islam,[29] but Western understanding of the forces at work has been obscured, biased, and retarded by events in Iran and by general Western hostility. It is relatively easy in the Iranian case to express appalled indignation at the summary trials and executions, the brutal treatment of the U.S. hostages, and the sometimes wild fulminations of an aging ayatullah; but by so doing students may miss some of the deeper, permanent, and more important aspects of the changes under way.[30]

Two major features of the Islamic revival command special attention here. Both also occur in the Indian case. One is the criticism of the Western models, either liberal or communist, as inappropriate and undesirable in the Islamic context. The widespread sentiment in favor of rejecting Western values and the Western developmental model has been obscured in the popular media by their focusing only on the sometimes ludicrous comments of Iran's religious leaders that the Western model is sinful and satanic. This makes it easy to satirize and dismiss what is, in fact, a widespread and serious criticism that, coming from other Islamic mouths and pens—in, for instance, Saudi Arabia and Pakistan—is quite realistic and telling. The Islamic argument is that the excessive individualism of the liberal model and the excessive statism of the communist one are both inappropriate in the Islamic context: They violate its customs and traditions by importing a system without strong indigenous roots, and they are positively damaging to the Islamic world's own preferred values and institutions.[31]

The second aspect, complementary to the first, is the effort by the Iranians and others, once the Western influences were excised or repudiated, to reconstruct society and polity on the bases of indigenous Islamic concepts and institutions. Once more, what is in fact a serious process has frequently been ridiculed in the media, where only the comic-opera and most brutal aspects have received attention. But surely the efforts to reforge the links between state and society that had been largely destroyed by the shah, to lay stress on the family, the local community, a corporate group life and

solidarity, and on a leader who provides both direction and moral values—
in contrast to the alienation and mass society that are among the more
visible results of the Western pattern of development—are serious and
therefore must command our attention. Important too are the efforts at
religious revival and the attempts to reconstruct law, society, and behavior
in accordance with religious and moral principles, to rejoin politics and
ethics in ways that in the West have been abandoned since Machiavelli.
Rather than reject such developments out of hand—which further postpones
understanding of them—Westerners must begin to take Islamic society on
its own terms, not from the point of view of automatic rejection or a haughty
sense of superiority, but with empathy and understanding. Among the more
fascinating products of this Islamic revival are both a set of new, indigenous
institutions and a distinctive Islamic social science of development to go
with it.[32]

In Africa the institution around which the discussion revolves is tribalism.
Tribalism is one of those traditional institutions, like India's caste associations
or Islamic fundamentalism, that was supposed to decline or disappear as
modernization went forward. The belief that tribalism was destined for the
dustbins of history was so deeply ingrained that African leaders themselves
often felt ashamed of their own background and origins. Tribalism was
repressed and denied and the nation-state or the single-party mass-mobilizing
system was elevated to an artificial importance.[33] When tribalism refused
to die, it was rebaptized under the rubric of ethnicity and ethnic conflict,
which somehow made it seem more modern.

There are still Westerners and Africans alike who deny the existence of
tribalism or seek to stamp it out, but among other Africans there is a new
and refreshing realism about tribalism, even some interesting—albeit not
as yet overly successful—efforts to reconstruct African society using tribalism
as a base. These include new variations on the federal principle, new forms
of consociationalism, a corporately based communalism in Tanzania, or the
African authenticity of Zaire. Whatever the precise name and form, these
newer approaches to tribalism are both more realistic and more interesting
than the past denial of or wishful thinking about it.

At a minimum, the tribe often gives people what little they have in rural
Africa: a patch of land for their huts and maize, leadership, order, and
coherence. The tribe often has its own police force, which offers a measure
of security. In some countries without effective national welfare or social
security, tribal authority and tradition help provide for the old and sick.
Tribal ties and solidarities in the cities also help provide jobs, patronage,
and positions within the army or bureaucracy. Parties and interest associations
are often organized along tribal lines. In the absence of strong states and
national political structures, the tribe may be an effective intermediary
association providing services and brokering relations between the individual,
family, or clan and the national government. Tribalism may weaken over
time, but it surely will not disappear, and there is a growing and realistic
recognition on the part of African leaders that tribalism is part of Africa

Many will find this new realism refreshing and see the effort to refashion African polities and social structures in accordance with its own indigenous traditions exciting and innovative.[34]

The case of Latin America is somewhat different since it is an area that we think of as already Western.[35] Properly qualified (taking into account Latin America's large indigenous populations, the periodic efforts to resurrect and glorify its Indian past, and the efforts of nations such as Mexico to ground their nationalism in part upon their mestizo heritage—the new "cosmic race"), this assertion is valid. One must also remember, however, that Latin America is an offshoot or historical fragment of a special time and place in the West, Iberia circa 1500,[36] whose own conformity to the Western model has been and in many ways still is somewhat less than total.[37] With this in mind, Latin America may be looked on as something of a mixed case, Western and Third World at the same time.

In various writings I have wrestled with the issue of where and in what ways Latin America conforms to the Western pattern and where it diverges.[38] In the context of this discussion, however, what is striking are the remarkable parallels between some of the newer currents in Latin America and in other Third World areas. First, there is widespread nationalistic rejection of the U.S.-favored route to development, a rejection that has even stronger historical roots than in other Third World areas and that found expression as early as the nineteenth century in fears and hostility toward the "colossus of the north" and in widespread acceptance of the arguments of José E. Rodó, who contrasted the spiritualism, Catholicism, personalism, and humanism of Latin America (Ariel) with the crassness, materialism, secularism, pragmatism, and utilitarianism of the United States (Caliban).[39]

The reverse side of this coin is the effort to identify what is distinctive in Latin America's own past and present and to determine whether these characteristics can be used to erect a separate Latin American political sociology of development. Such a formulation would emphasize Latin America's persistent corporatism and organic statism, its neomercantilist and state-capitalist economic structures, its personalism and kinship patterns, its Catholicism and the institutions and behavioral patterns of Catholic political culture, its patrimonialism and unabashed patriarchalism, its patron-client networks now extended to the national political level, its distinctive patterns and arenas of state-society relations, and its historical relations of dependency (particularly in recent times) vis-à-vis the United States.[40] There are, as we shall see in the next section, problems with these formulations, not the least of which is that not all Latin Americans accept them or wish to accept them, still preferring to see themselves in terms of and to cast their lot with the Western model. Nevertheless, the parallels with other Third World areas are striking, and the attempts by Latin Americans to fashion their own indigenous model and social science of development deserve our attention.

Analogous developments in other areas also merit serious study, though only passing mention can be made of them here. In China, for example, the combination of Marxist and Confucian elements in Mao's thought provided not only a new and fascinating synthesis but also some of the key ingredients in the distinctively Chinese model of development.[41] Japan has achieved phenomenal economic growth rates by borrowing, copying, or synthesizing the technology and organizational models of the West and adapting these to historic and preferred Japanese forms, structures, and ways of doing things.[42] In Poland and elsewhere in Eastern Europe, Marxism is being adapted to local institutions such as Catholicism and nationalism. In the Soviet Union there is of course a Marxist socialist state, but no one would disagree it is also a *Russian* Marxist state (however ambiguous and open to disagreement may be its precise meaning).[43] Finally, in Western Europe itself, which originally inspired the Western model, there is both a new questioning of what the Western model consists of and whether even the nations of Western Europe conform to it, as well as a rethinking of whether that Western model is in fact applicable to the rest of the world.[44]

These various national and regional traditions need to be examined in greater detail and the arguments more fully amplified. What seems clear even from this brief survey, however, is that there is a growing rejection of the Western model as irrelevant and inappropriate in areas and nations where the traditions and institutions are quite different and that there exists a growing search for indigenous, national institutions and models, based on local traditions instead of those imported from or imposed by the West. These trends seem now to transcend national and cultural boundaries.

PROBLEM AREAS AND DILEMMAS

The notion of a bright new world made up of young emerging nations is a fairy tale.

—V. S. Naipaul, *Among the Believers*

The idea of a native, indigenous model and social science of development, reflecting and deeply rooted in local practices and institutions rather than imported and surface ones, is enormously attractive. Social scientists need to analyze this rather than merely celebrate it, however, and when that is done numerous problems arise.

First, the search for indigenous models of development may prove to be more romantic and nostalgic than realistic.[45] In some areas and nations (several of the Central American countries, for example), indigenous institutions may well prove weak or nonexistent, incapable of serving as the base for national development. They may, as with the Western model, reflect the preferences of intellectuals rather than those of the general population—or they may reflect a nostalgic longing for a past that cannot be revived. Such indigenous institutions may have been destroyed in whole or in part by the colonial powers or discredited by the earlier generation of Western-oriented local elites. There may be no institutional foundation of indigenous institutions and practices on which to build and hence, for many Third

World nations, no light at the end of the development tunnel. The Western model has not worked well, but an indigenous one will not work either if it reflects the politics of romance and nostalgia rather than the politics of reality.[46]

Second, there are class, partisan, and other biases often implicit in a political strategy that seeks to fashion a model of development based upon indigenous institutions. Such a strategy could serve to defend the status quo or to restore the status quo ante, both nationally and internationally. It could justify an existing class, caste, leadership group, or clan remaining in power. It may be manipulated for partisan or personal advantage. For example, in Francisco Franco's efforts to restore and maintain traditional Spanish institutions and practices, it was clear that only his rather narrow and particular interpretation of what that special tradition was would be allowed and that other currents and possibilities within that tradition would be suppressed.[47]

Third, the actual practice of regimes that have followed an indigenous development strategy has not produced very many successes. Even on its own terms, it is hard to call the Iranian Revolution, so far, a success. The Mexican Revolution that was once trumpeted as providing an indigenous third way is acknowledged to have sold out, run its course, or died.[48] There has been a lot of talk about African authenticity in recent years, but in countries such as Togo or Zaire the application of the concept has served mainly to shore up corrupt and despotic regimes. Even in Tanzania, which has been widely cited as an example of a serious attempt to build an original African development model, there are immense difficulties accompanying this experiment and a notable lack of enthusiasm on the part of both the peasants who are presumably its prime beneficiaries and the government officials charged with implementing it.[49]

Fourth, in the present world, indigenous developmental models may no longer be possible. The time when a nation could maintain itself in isolation and develop on its own terms may well have passed. All of the Third World is now affected by what Lucian Pye once called the "world culture"—not only styles in dress and music (largely Western) but in social and political systems as well.[50] Third World countries are also caught up in what Immanuel Wallerstein called the "world system"—factors such as trade patterns, economic dependency relationships, world market prices, oil requirements, and so on, which have major effects on them but over which they have no control.[51] Additionally, whether one speaks of Afghanistan, El Salvador, or numerous other Third World nations, Cold War and other international political conflicts make them pawns in the global arena and often profoundly affect their internal development as well. All these conditions make it virtually impossible that the outside world would not impinge on any effort at indigenous development, if not destroying it then certainly requiring compromise in numerous areas.[52]

Fifth, not all indigenous elites and intellectuals wish to follow a native path. For them, traditional and indigenous institutions are not necessarily symbols of pride and nationalism. They may see them as signs of back-wardness and underdevelopment, or have mixed feelings that breed confusion, irresolution, and lack of direction. By no means are all African leaders convinced that tribalism can become a new basis of political organization; hence in Kenya and elsewhere concerted efforts are under way not to build it up but to snuff tribalism out. Indian intellectuals, especially from the lower castes, are not yet ready to accept arguments concerning the modernizing role the castes may play. Not all Iranian intellectuals accept the virtues of a theocratic state led by the ayatullah or, even if they are believers in Islamic fundamentalism, agree on what precise institutional form that should take.

Latin America is an especially interesting area in this regard, for while most of its intellectuals share varying degrees of antipathy to the United States model and the U.S.-favored development route and want to have a hand in fashioning a nationalistic and Latin American one, they are also terribly uncomfortable with the implications of that position. That new route would imply acceptance of a political system built in some degree upon the principles of corporatism, hierarchy, authoritarianism, and organic-statism—none of which are popular or fashionable in the more democratic nations and salons of the modern world, into which Latin America and its intellectuals, historically plagued by a sense of inferiority and backwardness, also wish to be accepted. Hence they have ambivalent feelings regarding indigenous models and prefer theories of dependency or international strat-ification that conveniently and more comfortably place the blame on external instead of internal forces.[53]

In the last decade Latin America has made some remarkable transitions to democracy. It appears to have repudiated its authoritarian past and embarked on a democratic course, to the applause of the outside world and most Latin Americans. At last they seem to have "made it" into the modern, Western, democratic camp. But often forgotten in this euphoria is both how fragile democracy remains there and how strongly even its new democratic institutions are still infused by the traditional institutions of organicism, corporation, and patrimonialism. Latin America may have made a transition to democracy, but its practice remains more Rousseauean than Lockean. Few Latin American analysts have come to grips with this reality, that the transition is still incomplete and that what we are witnessing is not a complete triumph of Westernism but rather a partial blending of modern democratic with more traditional and historical features.[54]

Sixth and finally, emphasis must be placed on the sheer diversity of Third World nations and areas and hence the immense difficulties of achieving a consensus on any development strategy, indigenous or otherwise. At some levels of analysis, Latin America (and Iberia) may be thought of as part of a single culture area, but it must also be kept in mind that Paraguay is quite different from Argentina, Brazil and Peru from Chile, Nicaragua from Mexico—and all are at different levels of development. Hence different strategies and models of modernization, even if they could be conceptualized within certain common parameters, would have to be designed for each country of the area.[55] In the Islamic world the same qualifications would have to be introduced; it obviously also makes a major difference if we are talking of the Sunni, Shiite, or other traditions and combinations of them.[56] A similar case exists in Africa: Some observers feel that Islam is the only organized cultural and ideological force capable of offering a coherent and continent-wide alternative to the heretofore dominant Western model. This point of view, however, ignores the still-strong Christian and Western influences, the fact that only a small minority of African states are essentially Muslim (that is, at least 75 percent Islamic), the continuing influence of traditional beliefs, and in some parts of Africa, the lack of a strong cultural identity of any sort. All of these factors would have to be taken into account in creating an indigenous model, or models, of development. Nor should one underestimate the sheer confusion, uncertainty, and chaos surrounding these issues in many Third World nations. In the Third World as a whole and in its component geographic regions and distinct cultural areas, there is too much diversity to be subsumed under any single theory or set of concepts.

CONCLUSION: TOWARD A NONETHNOCENTRIC THEORY OF DEVELOPMENT

The aspiration for something different, better, more truly indigenous than Western systems of development and yet as socially and materially effective is palpable everywhere. "Our own way" is the persistent theme; but it is far more often advanced as a creed than as a plan.

—Flora Lewis, *New York Times*

In numerous areas, the West and the Western model of development intimately associated with its earlier progress seem to be in decline. Western Europe suffers from various malaises of uncertain and often obscure origins; the economies of the Western nations have experienced severe recessions; U.S. institutions have not always worked well in recent years; NATO and the Western Alliance are in disarray; and the global system of U.S. hegemony and dominance is being challenged. With this Spenglerian "Decline of the West"[57] has come a new questioning of and challenge to the development model that was a part of the nearly 500-year-long Western era of domination. It is not just the model itself that is now being challenged, however, but the larger, preeminently Western, and for that reason parochial and ethnocentric, philosophical and intellectual tradition that went with it. What many Westerners assumed to be a universal set of norms and processes by which societies developed and modernized—with the West as presumed leader and model—has now been demonstrated to be parochial and ethnocentric.

With the decline of Western hegemony and the pretension to universalism of the intellectual constructs that are part and parcel of it, and concomitant with the rise and new assertiveness of various non-Western and Third World areas, have come demands for local, indigenous models of development. The critique of the Western model as particularistic, parochial, Eurocentric, considerably less than universal, and powerfully biased, as not only perpetuating misunderstanding regarding these areas but also wreaking downright harm upon them, seems devastating, persuasive, and perhaps unchallengeable.

The Western model still survives, of course, and it goes through ups and downs of popularity; but now along with the Western model there have grown up various indigenous ones often overlapping, coexisting, and comingling with it. In some few cases the indigenous model has supplanted the Western one.

The Reagan era of the 1980s gave an enormous impetus to the Western model. On the one hand, the formula of democracy and free markets appears to have "worked," to have buried all its competitors, and has proved enormously attractive. At the same time, the influence of materialism, consumerism, and Western culture in general has just been overwhelming. For most Third World countries the issue is not whether they can isolate themselves from the West and keep out its influences; they cannot. The only issue is whether they can still choose selectively from the outside influences, filter them, blend them with local ways, and at the same time fashion institutions and interpretations that combine Western and indigenous models. Western influences are ubiquitous, but they must still be adapted to non-Western practices.

These issues would seem to represent the next great frontier in the social sciences.[58] Shorn of its romantic and nostalgic aspects, unfettered by the class or partisan biases that sometimes surround it, incorporating both national currents and international ones, taking account of practical realities and not just intellectual constructs, cognizant of both the mixed sentiments of local elites and the diversities of the societies studied—or at least recognizing these when they do occur—the notion of a nonethnocentric theory of development is now on the front burner. The study of such local, indigenous, native cultural traditions and models, Samuel P. Huntington has said, may well be the wave of the future for the social sciences.[59]

Scholars need now for the first time to begin to take non-Western areas and their ofttimes peculiar institutions seriously, in their own context and traditions rather than from the slanted perspective of the Western social sciences. They need to reexamine virtually all of the Western social science notions of development. A serious mistake made by Western scholars, for example, is to assume that as people become modernized and educated, they also, automatically, become westernized. In much of the Middle East, for instance, urbanization and the growth of a literate middle class are prime causes in the growth of interest in Islam. The examples could easily be multiplied. Scholars should see local indigenous institutions not necessarily as dysfunctional or doomed but frequently as viable and necessary, as filters and winnowers of the modernization process, as agencies of transition between traditional and modern, and as a means for reconciling and blending the global with the indigenous, the nationalist with the international. This undertaking implies both greater empathy on our part and greater modesty in terms of the claims made for the universalism of the Western examples.

The implications of coming to grips with indigenous institutions and nonethnocentric theories and concepts of development are enormous.[60] Three major areas of impact may be noted here. The first has to do with the Third World and non-Western nations themselves: their efforts to overcome historical inferiority complexes, their reconceived possibilities for development, the newfound importance of their traditional institutions, the rediscovery of many complex routes to development, their new sense of pride and accomplishment and so on. It will take some time before the Third World is able to articulate and mold these diverse concepts into realistic development models, and the translation of concepts like authenticity into concrete political institutions, educational policies, and health programs is liable to take even longer. Nevertheless, we cannot doubt the reality or growth of such new interpretations, perspectives, and syntheses—as between Marxism and an indigenous development tradition, for example, or in the form of a homegrown type of democracy, or as an updated and modernized Islam.

Second, the arguments presented here have immense implications for the social sciences. Not only must we reexamine a host of essentially Western social science assumptions but we must also be prepared to accept an Islamic social science of development, an African social science of development, a Latin American social science of development—and to strike some new balances between what is particular in the development process and what does in fact conform to more universal patterns. In exploring such indigenous models, scholars will need to fashion a dynamic theory of change as well as examine a variety of normative orientations;[61] we will need also to distinguish between a theory of development that comes from many sources *and* different theories of development for different regions. In the process the rather tired, even moribund, study of development itself, in all its dimensions, is likely to be revived.

Third, there are major implications for policy. In the past three decades not only have virtually all U.S. intellectual concepts and models with regard to developing nations been based upon the Western experience, but virtually all U.S. assistance programs, developmental recommendations, and foreign policy presumptions have been grounded on these same conceptual tools.[62] The approach suggested here is likely to upset many cherished social science notions and, if considered seriously, will necessitate a fundamental set of foreign policy reconsiderations as well.

NOTES

1. P. T. Bauer, *Dissent on Development* (Cambridge, MA: Harvard University Press, 1976); David E. Schmitt, ed., *Dynamics of the Third World* (Cambridge, MA: Winthrop, 1974); Frank Tachau, ed., *The Developing Nations: What Path to Modernization?* (New

York: Dodd, Mead, 1972); W. A. Beling and G. O. Totten, eds., *The Developing Nations: Quest for a Model* (New York: Van Nostrand, 1970); Robert E. Gamer, *The Developing Nations* (Boston: Allyn and Bacon, 1976); Lyman Tower Sargent, *Contemporary Political Ideologies* (Homewood, IL: Dorsey, 1981); Paul E. Sigmund, ed., *The Ideologies of the Developing Nations* (New York: Praeger, 1972); and John Kenneth Galbraith, *The Voice of the Poor* (Cambridge, MA: Harvard University Press, 1982).

2. For example, Edward Said, *Orientalism* (New York: Pantheon, 1978); Howard J. Wiarda, ed., *Politics and Social Change in Latin America: The Distinct Tradition*, 2d ed. rev. (Amherst: University of Massachusetts Press, 1982).

3. These arguments are expanded in Howard J. Wiarda, "The Ethnocentrism of the Social Sciences: Implications for Research and Policy," *Review of Politics* 42 (April 1981):163–97; also Wiarda, *Ethnocentrism in Foreign Policy: Can We Understand the Third World?* (Washington, DC: American Enterprise Institute for Public Policy Research, 1985).

4. For some parallel arguments see Reinhard Bendix, "Tradition and Modernity Reconsidered," *Comparative Studies in Society and History* 9 (April 1967):292–346, reprinted in his *Embattled Reason* (New York: Oxford University Press, 1970); also Joseph R. Gusfield, "Tradition and Modernity: Misplaced Polarities in the Study of Social Change," *American Journal of Sociology* 72 (January 1967):351–62.

5. This and other criticisms will not be new to many students of political development. What is new is the widespread articulation of such views within the Third World. Moreover, this critique of the Western model needs to be presented as a prelude to the discussion of indigenous models that follows. For some earlier critiques of the Western development model see Wiarda, "Ethnocentrism"; Bendix, "Tradition and Modernity"; Dean C. Tipps, "Modernization Theory and the Comparative Studies of Society: A Critical Perspective," *Comparative Studies of Society and History* 15 (March 1973):199–226; and C. D. Hah and J. Schneider, "A Critique of Current Theories of Political Development and Modernization," *Social Research* 35 (Spring 1968):130–58. See also the statements on the different meanings of democracy by Costa Rican President Luis Alberto Monge and Nigerian President Alhaji Shehu Shagari at the Conference on Free Elections, Department of State, Washington, DC, 4–6 November 1982; also R. William Liddle, "Comparative Political Science and the Third World," mimeographed (Columbus: Ohio State University, Department of Political Science).

6. An excellent treatment of these themes is Claudio Veliz, *The Centralist Tradition in Latin America* (Princeton, NJ: Princeton University Press, 1980); also Clifford Geertz, *Negara: The Theatre State in Nineteenth Century Bali* (Princeton, NJ: Princeton University Press, 1980), in which he shows that the culture and the theater are the substance, not just superstructure.

7. Especially relevant is the general critique of the Western sociological bias in T. O. Wilkinson's "Family Structure and Industrialization in Japan," *American Sociological Review* 27 (October 1962):678–82; also Alberto Guerreiro Ramos, "Modernization: Toward a Possibility Model," in *Developing Nations*, ed. Beling and Totten, pp. 21–59; and Gusfield, "Tradition and Modernity."

8. William P. Glade, "Problems of Research in Latin American Studies," in *New Directions in Language and Area Studies* (Milwaukee: University of Wisconsin at Milwaukee for the Consortium of Latin American Studies Programs, 1979), pp. 81–101.

9. Veliz, *The Centralist Tradition.*

10. For a general statement, Leonard S. Binder et al., eds., *Crises and Sequences in Political Development* (Princeton, NJ: Princeton University Press, 1971).

11. See the classic statement by Marc Bloch, *Feudal Society* (Chicago: University of Chicago Press, 1961).

12. Daniel Bell, *The Coming of Post-Industrial Society* (New York: Basic Books, 1973). On 26 May 1981, in a personal conversation, Professor Bell asserted that by a quite different route he had also "come to similar conclusions regarding the inadequacies of many social science concepts since they derive almost exclusively from a particular Western tradition." Much of the new social science literature emanating from Latin America since the 1960s makes many of the same arguments.

13. The dependency literature is extensive; among the best statements is Fernando Henrique Cardoso and Enzo Faletto, *Dependency and Development in Latin America* (Berkeley: University of California Press, 1978).

14. For a general discussion, S. N. Eisenstadt, "Post-Traditional Societies and the Continuity and Reconstruction of Tradition," *Daedalus* 102 (Winter 1973):1–27; and also by Eisenstadt, *Modernization: Protest and Change* (Englewood Cliffs, NJ: Prentice-Hall, 1966).

15. Lloyd I. Rudolph and Susanne Hoeber Rudolph, *The Modernity of Tradition* (Chicago: University of Chicago Press, 1967).

16. The case of Tanzania is especially interesting in this regard.

17. The arguments are detailed in Wiarda, "Ethnocentrism."

18. A more complete discussion with regard to one region is in Howard J. Wiarda, ed., *The Continuing Struggle for Democracy in Latin America* (Boulder, CO: Westview Press, 1980).

19. G.A.D. Soares, "Latin American Studies in the United States," *Latin American Research Review* 11 (1976); and Howard J. Wiarda, "Latin American Intellectuals and the 'Myth' of Underdevelopment" (Presentation made at the Seventh National Meeting of the Latin American Studies Association, Houston, 2–5 November 1977), in Wiarda, *Corporatism and National Development in Latin America* (Boulder, CO: Westview Press, 1981), pp. 236–38.

20. Susanne J. Bodenheimer, *The Ideology of Developmentalism: The American Paradigm-Surrogate for Latin American Studies* (Beverly Hills, CA: Sage Publications, 1971); Teresa Hayter, *Aid as Imperialism* (Baltimore, MD: Penguin, 1971); Ronald H. Chilcote, *Theories of Comparative Politics: The Search for a Paradigm* (Boulder, CO: Westview Press, 1981); Hah and Schneider, "Critique."

21. In our Harvard faculty Seminar, several of whose members were part of the original and highly influential SSRC Committee on Comparative Politics, it was striking to note in the occasional Seminar remarks by these members how strongly the anticommunist ideology of that time pervaded the SSRC Committee's assumptions. One of our Seminar members, himself part of the original SSRC Committee, flatly stated that the purpose of this group was to formulate a noncommunist theory of change and thus to provide a non-Marxist alternative for the developing nations.

22. Selig S. Harrison, *The Widening Gulf: Asian Nationalism and American Policy* (New York: Free Press, 1978). My critique of the development paradigm is contained in "Is Latin America Democratic and Does It Want to Be? The Crisis and Quest of Democracy in the Hemisphere," in Wiarda, *The Continuing Struggle*, pp. 3–24.

23. Samuel P. Huntington, *Political Order in Changing Societies* (New Haven, CT: Yale University Press, 1968); and Wiarda, "Ethnocentrism."

24. See also Sigmund, *Ideologies.* Especially striking are the differences between the old and new editions of this study, and the differences in Sigmund's own thinking as contained in his introductions.

25. Tentatively entitled *Third World Conceptions of Development*, also growing out of the Harvard seminar on "New Directions in Comparative Politics."

26. Vrajenda Raj Mehta, *Beyond Marxism: Towards an Alternative Perspective* (New Delhi: Manohar Publications, 1978), p. 12. I am grateful to my colleague Thomas Pantham for bringing this work and the debate that swirls about it to my attention. Subsequent page references to Mehta will be in parentheses in the text. A parallel volume from Latin America is José Arico, *Marx e a America Latina* (Rio de Janeiro: Paz e Terra, 1982).

27. For a critique see Thomas Pantham, "Integral Pluralism: A Political Theory for India?" *India Quarterly* (July–December 1980):396–405.

28. For another outstanding Indian contribution to the theory of development see Rajni Kothari, *Footsteps into the Future* (New York: Free Press, 1975).

29. G. H. Jansen, *Militant Islam* (New York: Harper & Row, 1980), as well as the special series by Sir Willie Morris in the *Christian Science Monitor*, August–September 1980, and that by Flora Lewis in *New York Times*, December 1979.

30. An especially good statement is by Harvard anthropologist Mary Catherine Bateson, "Iran's Misunderstood Revolution," *New York Times*, 20 February 1979, p. 14.

31. Jansen, *Militant Islam*; Said, *Orientalism*; Barry Rubin, *Paved with Good Intentions* (New York: Oxford University Press, 1980); Shahrough Akhavi, *Religion and Politics in Contemporary Iran* (Albany: State University of New York Press, 1980); Ali Masalehdan, "Values and Political Development in Iran" (Ph.D. diss., University of Massachusetts at Amherst, 1981); and Michael Fischer, *Iran: From Religious Dispute to Revolution* (Cambridge, MA: Harvard University Press, 1980). See also the discussion led by Fischer on "Iran: Is It an Example of Populist Neo-Traditionalism?" Joint Seminar on Political Development (JOSPOD), Cambridge, MA, Minutes of the Meeting of 15 October 1980.

32. Anwar Syed, *Pakistan: Islam, Politics and National Solidarity* (New York: Praeger, 1982). The implications of Syed's discussion are considerably broader than the case he discusses. See also Inayatullah, *Transfer of Western Development Model to Asia and Its Impact* (Kuala Lumpur: Asian Center for Development Administration, 1975).

33. David Apter, *Ghana in Transition* (New York: Atheneum, 1967); and Ruth Schachter Morgenthau, "Single Party Systems in West Africa," *American Political Science Review* 55 (June 1961) have both helped to popularize (and, to a degree, romanticize) the notion of the viability of African single party systems. Henry L. Bretton, *Power and Politics in Africa* (Chicago: Aldine, 1973) helped to explode those myths.

34. My understanding of these currents in Africa has been enriched by various exchanges with and the seminar presentations of Africanist Naomi Chazan, a colleague in both Jerusalem and Cambridge; and by the writings of Swiss sociologist Pierre Pradervand, *Family Planning Programmes in Africa* (Paris: Organization for Economic Cooperation and Development, 1970) and "Africa—The Fragile Giant," a series of articles in the *Christian Science Monitor*, December 1980. See also Crawford Young, *The Politics of Cultural Pluralism* (Madison: University of Wisconsin Press, 1976).

35. For a partial and inconclusive exchange on this theme see the comments of Susan Bourque, Samuel P. Huntington, Merilee Grindle, Brian Smith, and me in a JOSPOD seminar on "Neo-Traditionalism in Latin America," in Minutes of the Meeting of 19 November 1980.

36. Louis Hartz et al., *The Founding of New Societies* (New York: Harcourt, Brace, 1964).

37. Howard J. Wiarda, "Spain and Portugal," in *Western European Party Systems*, ed. Peter Merkl (New York: Free Press, 1980), pp. 298–328; and Wiarda, "Does Europe Still Stop at the Pyrenees, or Does Latin America Begin There? Iberia, Latin

America, and the Second Enlargement of the European Community," in *The Impact of an Enlarged European Community on Latin America*, ed. Georges D. Landau and G. Harvey Summ (forthcoming); also published under the same title as Occasional Paper no. 2 (Washington: American Enterprise Institute for Public Policy Research, January 1982).

38. Wiarda, *Politics and Social Change; Corporatism and Development; The Continuing Struggle*; and "Toward a Framework for the Study of Political Change in the Iberic-Latin Tradition: The Corporative Model," *World Politics* 25 (January 1973):206–35.

39. José E. Rodó, *Ariel* (Montevideo: Dornaleche y Reyes, 1900); an English translation by F. J. Stimson was published under the same title (Boston: Houghton Mifflin, 1922).

40. Among others, Veliz, *The Centralist Tradition*; Glen Dealy, *The Public Man: An Interpretation of Latin America and Other Catholic Countries* (Amherst: University of Massachusetts Press, 1977); Leopoldo Zea, *The Latin American Mind* (Norman: University of Oklahoma Press, 1963); Octavio Paz, *The Labyrinth of Solitude* (New York: Grove Press, 1961); Richard M. Morse, "The Heritage of Latin America," in Hartz, *The Founding*.

41. H. G. Creel, *Chinese Thought: From Confucius to Mao Tse-tung* (Chicago: University of Chicago Press, 1963); Stuart H. Schram, *The Political Thought of Mao Tse-tung* (New York: Praeger, 1976).

42. T. O. Wilkinson, *The Urbanization of Japanese Labor* (Amherst: University of Massachusetts Press, 1965); Ezra F. Vogel, *Japan as No. 1* (Cambridge: Harvard University Press, 1979); and Peter Berger, "Secularity—West and East" (Paper presented at the American Enterprise Institute Public Policy Week, Washington, DC, 6–9 December 1982).

43. For example, Stanley Rothman and George W. Breslauer, *Soviet Politics and Society* (St. Paul, MN: West, 1978); Archie Brown and Jack Gray, eds., *Political Culture and Political Change in Communist States* (New York: Holmes and Meier, 1978); Jerry F. Hough and Merle Fainsod, *How the Soviet Union Is Governed* (Cambridge, MA: Harvard University Press, 1979).

44. See, for instance, Raymond Grew, ed., *Crises of Political Development in Europe and the United States* (Princeton, NJ: Princeton University Press, 1978); and Charles Tilly, ed., *The Formation of Nation States in Western Europe* (Princeton, NJ: Princeton University Press, 1975).

45. This is one of the criticisms leveled in Pantham, "Integral Pluralism?" against Mehta's *Beyond Marxism*.

46. Pradervand, "Africa."

47. Pantham, "Integral Pluralism" and "Political Culture, Political Structure, and Underdevelopment in India," *Indian Journal of Political Science* 41 (September 1980):432–56; also Wiarda, *Corporatism and National Development*.

48. Susan Eckstein, *The Poverty of Revolution: The State and the Urban Poor in Mexico* (Princeton, NJ: Princeton University Press, 1977); Kenneth F. Johnson, *Mexican Democracy: A Critical View* (Boston: Allyn and Bacon, 1971); Octavio Paz, *The Other Mexico* (New York: Grove Press, 1972).

49. Pradervand, "Africa."

50. Lucian Pye, *Aspects of Political Development* (Boston: Little, Brown, 1966).

51. Immanuel Wallerstein, *The Modern World-System* (New York: Academic Press, 1976).

52. Unless of course a nation is willing to withdraw entirely and consciously into isolation, but as Cambodia illustrates, that strategy may not work very well either.

53. These issues are addressed in the introduction to the Portuguese language version of Wiarda, *Corporatism and National Development*, published as *O modelo corporativo na América Latina e a Latinoamericanização dos Estados Unidos* (Rio de Janeiro: Ed. Vozes, 1983). For an example of such ambivalence see Norbert Lechner, ed., *Estado y política en América Latina* (Mexico City: Siglo Veintiuno Editores, 1981); also Carlos Franco, *Del Marxismo Eurocentrico al Marxismo Latino-americano* (Lima: Centro de Estudios para el Desarrollo y la Participacion, 1981).

54. Howard J. Wiarda, *The Democratic Revolution in Latin America: History, Politics, and U.S. Policy* (New York: Holmes and Meier, A Twentieth Century Fund Book, 1990).

55. For a country-by-country analysis combined with a common set of theoretical concepts see Howard J. Wiarda and Harvey F. Kline, *Latin American Politics and Development*, 3rd ed. (Boulder, CO: Westview Press, 1990).

56. Masalehdan, *Values and Political Development in Iran*.

57. Oswald Spengler, *The Decline of the West* (New York: Knopf, 1932); and much recent literature.

58. See the research agenda set forth in Howard J. Wiarda, ed., *Third World Conceptions of Development*, forthcoming. See also Chapter 1 in this book.

59. In a personal conversation with the author, December 1979.

60. The research perspectives suggested here and the implications of these as set forth in the concluding paragraphs are explored in greater detail in Wiarda, "Ethnocentrism"; *Politics and Social Change; The Continuing Struggle for Democracy*; and *Corporatism and National Development*.

61. I have attempted to formulate such a theory in "Toward a Framework for the Study of Political Change in the Iberic-Latin Tradition," and in *Corporatism and National Development*.

62. For example, U.S. community development, family planning, agrarian reform, military assistance, labor, economic development, and numerous other foreign aid programs have all been based on the "Western" (i.e., U.S. and Western European) model, which is one key reason, I would argue, that few of them have worked or produced the anticipated consequences. On this see Robert A. Packenham, *Liberal America and the Third World: Political Development Ideas in Foreign Aid and Social Science* (Princeton, NJ: Princeton University Press, 1973); Howard J. Wiarda, "At the Root of the Problem: Conceptual Failures in U.S.–Central American Relations," in Robert S. Leiken, ed., *Central America: Anatomy of Conflict* (New York: Pergamon Press, 1984), pp. 259–78; and Wiarda, "Ethnocentrism and Third World Development," *Society* 24 (September–October 1987):55–64.

8

Alternative Approaches to Comparative Politics

RONALD H. CHILCOTE

The lack of coherent direction or any common understanding as to the appropriate content and theory of comparative politics is probably related to the general dissatisfaction that pervades the discipline of political science itself. It is not surprising that academics and students alike seek alternative approaches as they attempt to define what the study of politics is about. Other disciplines, notably anthropology, economics, history, and sociology, have turned to radical thought in an attempt to define and modify their endeavor. Though the results of this effort are uneven in terms of scholarship, there is no question that radical thought has left its imprint. In contrast, political science has lagged in the development of radical thought, although the Caucus for a New Political Science and its journal, *New Political Science*, represent a movement in that direction. Within political science in general and comparative politics in particular, however, some alternative contributions are identifiable.

In the search for an alternative comparative politics, several assumptions can be suggested. First, it should be emphasized that theory and clear conceptualization are the essence of inquiry. In contrast, the discipline struggles with a legacy of a comparative approach that is largely descriptive and configurative, focused on studies of individual countries or institutions. Comparative politics also comprises more than the study of government, especially U.S. government, which influences the values and premises about what and how we should study politics. The discipline of comparative politics in the United States has been shaped in large measure by a perspective that embraces the idea of democracy, idealized as a pluralistic polity and based on capitalism as a foundation of material life. Finally, if a paradigm dominates thinking in the field, we should examine its origins and evolution.[1]

As a point of departure, it is useful to recognize that much thinking about the nature of comparative inquiry emanates from nineteenth-century thought and debate. The ideas of Max Weber and Karl Marx are particularly significant. For example, Marx interpreted the structure of the state as monolithic and tied to the interests of the ruling class, whereas Weber saw that structure as sanctioning a plurality of interests. Marx viewed all forms of dominance under the capitalist state as illegitimate; Weber identified legitimate forms of dominance. Marx advocated the abolition of the state and its classes, whereas Weber envisaged the enhancement of the state through the legitimation of its activities. Marx understood changes in the state and the ruling class as reflections of historical materialism and of the conflictual interplay of social relations and forces of production that have characterized various epochs. Weber, in contrast, concerned himself with the resolution of conflict through the rationalization of the bureaucratic order, for he saw European capitalism as promoting a highly rationalized and therefore stable form of society. Though both men examined the use of force or violence, Marx viewed the state as nothing but a subtle instrument of coercion to suppress the lower strata, and Weber offered a narrower explanation that combined state force and violence with legitimacy.

Contemporary comparative politics is influenced by these and other thinkers. However, since about 1953, the field has shaped and refined its paradigm, largely following the positivistic and Weberian methodology of social science. The Social Science Research Council's Committee on Comparative Politics organized the field around four traditional areas: system; culture; development; and elites. During the early 1950s David Easton introduced the concept of system to politics, together with a vocabulary of inputs and outputs, demands and supports, and feedback. Partially influenced by Easton but also by group theory and the work of functionalist anthropologists and sociologists, Gabriel Almond first presented a typology of political systems and later set forth categories of structures and functions that related to all national systems. Within this framework Almond also introduced a cultural dimension to comparative politics. With Sidney Verba he applied the concept of civic culture to a study of five nations and formulated a typology of political cultures. With the emergence of many new states in the Third World, Almond and others directed their attention to backward areas and to questions of development in the world. Finally, sometime during the middle 1960s, interest turned to the study of elites.[2]

However defined, the dominant paradigm in contemporary comparative politics relates to these four areas, and criticism of them helps clarify the need for alternative approaches and methodology, including Marxist approaches. Marxists, of course, do not subscribe to the mainstream concerns, but relate to them through constructive criticism.

THE POLITICAL ECONOMY APPROACH

Given this state of the field, what are our options? I believe that as scholars we should seek a perspective that understands politics in a historical context and views political phenomena holistically, within a theoretical framework. In particular, it is useful to relate comparative and international politics to political economy, in the classical ways provided by Adam Smith, David Ricardo, and Marx and along the lines of contemporary radical political economy. Indeed, a reformulation of comparative politics as political economy, with attention to state and class at the national level and to such phenomena as imperialism and dependency at the international level, might lead us in a promising direction.

Methodologically, political economy should be understood in both its Marxist and non-Marxist traditions. The political lines of thinking in political and social science today are understood in terms of past thinking. For example, John Locke related labor to private property and wealth and favored individual effort to satisfy human needs. Smith formulated a labor theory of value by bringing together the themes of commodity, capital and value, and simple and complex labor. He identified laws of the market that explain the drive of individual self-interest in competitive situations. Ricardo offered refinements of political economy, advocating the accumulation of capital as the basis for economic expansion. He believed that governments should not intervene in the economy and that at the international level a division of labor and free trade policies would benefit all nations. There were also utopians like Henri Saint-Simon, who leaned toward socialism. Marx transcended the ideas of the utopians and the classical liberals to set forth a theory of surplus value and an explanation for class struggle.

From these thinkers some guidelines can be suggested for the study of political economy. Pedagogically, mainstream ideas might be distinguished from radical ideas, and conservative and liberal notions differentiated from Marxist thought. Theoretically, Marxist thought may be considered holistic, broad in range, unified, and interdisciplinary, in contrast to the ahistorical, compartmentalized, and often narrow parameters of mainstream thinking. This use of Marxism is intended to be open and flexible, for Marx himself considered Marxism unfinished and subject to change in accordance with practical experience. Methodologically, dialectics may serve as a method in the search for understanding. Marx combined dialectics with a materialist view of history, whereas Hegel delineated a mystical and idealistic dialectics as a rigid system. The Marxist usage serves not as a precise formula, but as a means for looking at the interconnection of problems to all of society; as a dynamic, not static, way of examining issues; and as a way to identify opposing forces, their relationship and conflict. Conceptually, political economy focuses on the relationship of an economic base and a political superstructure.

> The totality of these relations of production constitutes the economic structure of society, the real foundation, on which arises a legal and political superstructure and to which correspond definite forms of social consciousness. The mode of production of material life conditions the general process of social, political, and intellectual life. It is not the consciousness of men that determines their existence but their social existence that determines their consciousness.[3]

Thus attention should be directed, on one hand, to such concepts as the mode of production (the mix of productive forces and relations of production among people in society); forces of production (the productive capacity, including plant and machinery, technology, and labor skill); relations of production (the division of labor that puts productive forces in motion); and the means of production (the tools, land, buildings, and machinery with which workers produce material goods for themselves and others). On the other hand, one must consider the state (the legal forms and instruments, such as police and standing army, that maintain class rule); class (large groups of people distinguished by their relation to the means of production, division of labor, share of wealth, and position); and ideology (false consciousness related to legal, political, religious, and philosophical forms).

These considerations help in assessing work on state and class. Since Aristotle and Plato the study of politics has focused on the idea of the state. David Easton once wrote that political science was a discipline in search of an identity, and he acknowledged a debt to Marx for differentiating between state and society: "In part, political science would emerge as a discipline separate from the other social sciences because of the impetus Marx had given to the idea of the difference between state and society, an idea virtually unheard of before his time."[4] Specialists of comparative politics focused on the state until, in despair, they abandoned the concept during the late 1950s and replaced it with the system.

Coincidentally, Easton popularized the idea of system in political science. He attempted to interpret for political science the mainstream thought of his times, but was unable to develop any significant theory in spite of considerable effort.[5] Casting aside past attention to legal and formal institutions and focusing on the political system rather than the state, he sought a grand theory that would transcend middle-range efforts to study parties and pressure groups. Easton was influenced by organic or physiological assumptions, and he believed that social and political behavior was governed by processes similar to those in natural sciences.[6] It has also been suggested that Easton's notion of allocation resembled "theories of income distribution and the allocation of resources in economics, and particularly neoclassical theory since there, too, the emphasis is upon the economy as a distributive process or system."[7] Furthermore, there may be a similarity to the classical economic model of Adam Smith: "The Eastonian model and the traditional economic approach share not only the notions of system and input-output but those of scarcity, allocation, competition, maximization, homeostatic equilibrium, functional interdependence, self-regulation, goal-seeking, and feedback."[8] However, some critics found the thought of Easton to be outside the limits of classical liberalism and political economy, especially with his emphasis on diffuse support and system persistence.[9]

It is also clear that Easton's work was not much concerned with structural analysis, even though his work occasionally refers to A. R. Radcliffe-Brown, Bronislaw Malinowski, Robert Merton, and Marion Levy of the structural-functional school. Easton was instead interested in the interdisciplinary tradition of understanding the "whole" system rather than only its parts. However, Gabriel Almond, influenced by Easton, also pushed for the application of system to politics and the abandonment of the state concept.

In 1956 he offered a simple typology of national political systems.[10] Together with other comparative political scientists, Almond later set forth a structural-functional model for the comparative study of political systems. His formulation was spawned by some of the same influences that affected Easton, but it turned from grand theory to middle-range analysis, and it gave direction to comparative politics in the ensuing decades. Especially important was the substitution of the phrase *political system* for *state* and an emphasis on interacting units of the system, somewhat in the tradition of Weber and Talcott Parsons.

The obscuring of concepts such as the state concerned younger radical scholars within the discipline. These concerns were recognized by Easton, who, in his 1969 presidential address to the American Political Science Association,[11] identified the postbehavioral revolution of the late 1960s with value premises, issues, and actions related to the reshaping of society to meet the needs of its people. Easton is not a radical, but as a theorist he appreciates alternative tendencies within the discipline.

Recently, Easton reviewed some Marxist work on the theory of the state, contrasting it to his own contributions to systems theory.[12] He noted that the concept of the state in contemporary social science had been revived not only in Marxist work, in particular the theory of Nicos Poulantzas, but also by scholars interested in studying strong authority, economic liberalism, and policy analysis. Yet Easton continues to express concern about the conceptual imprecision of a term such as the state. Acknowledging that the renewed interest in the state has represented "a necessary challenge to the ideological presupposition of conventional social research," Easton nevertheless urged Marxists to abandon the state as a concept: "The central perspective of Marxism in its many forms depends less on the notion of the state than on that of modes of production, class struggle, and 'contradictions.'" He believed that Nicos Poulantzas had made a valiant effort to resurrect the term, although his theory was obscure and theoretically complex; one must question its theoretical adequacy and its operational potential for empirical and theoretical research. While "the state . . . laid siege to the political system," Easton hoped for "more rigorous analysis."

Easton's own formulation has not necessarily led to a more rigorous political science. Furthermore, although Easton is correct in emphasizing mode of production and class struggle as central orienting concepts of Marxist analysis, he errs in setting the state and its apparatuses aside, disregarding Marx's suggestion of a dialectical relationship between the state and the economic base of society. Recently, political scientists who use Marxist methodology have shown considerable interest in the study of state and class.

TOWARD A THEORY OF STATE AND CLASS

Contemporary Marxist political economy has addressed questions of the state and system in two ways. First, there was an effort to view the system as capitalist. Marx's functionalism was premised on the contributions major institutions make to capitalist society to ensure that profit maximization becomes a major activity and the state becomes the managing force of the bourgeoisie. Al Szymanski emphasized dialectics and functionalism, drawing upon Marx and Engels. Dialectical functionalism, he believed, implies moving back and forth between abstractness and concreteness, between theory and reality. He argued that although phenomena may be interdependent, they also have internal contradictions. Under capitalism, for example, the greater accumulation of goods in society may result in an expanded proletariat and struggle against those who control the means of production. This emphasizes the possibility of change, the consequence of opposing forces within a given system.[13] Using this approach, some Marxists analyze racism, education, family, military, and the state in functional terms.

Most Marxists, however, envisage the system as the state and draw upon the thought of Hegel, Marx, Engels, and Lenin for various conceptions of state and class. Various perspectives appear in the literature.

The pluralist conception of the state emanates from classical elitist theory of democracy and from the proposition that in every society a minority makes the major decisions. In developing this idea, which originated with Plato, two Italian political sociologists, Vilfredo Pareto and Gaetano Mosca, were particularly influential at the turn of the century. Pareto not only distinguished between elites and nonelites but also suggested the idea of a circulation of elites, in which one elite replaces another as aristocracies decay or regenerate. There might also be mobility from a nonelite stratum to an elite stratum or governing class of people who rule directly or indirectly.[14] Mosca used terms such as political class, ruling class, and governing class, and also recognized the possibility that the composition of a ruling class may change with the rise of new interests and groups. If a ruling class is deposed, another organized minority within the masses would assume the functions of the ruling class.[15] Such ideas contributed to the pluralist view of state and class, as did James Madison's vision in the *Federalist Papers* that the U.S. democratic order is characterized by multiple diverse interests and a wide dispersion of power. During the early 1960s Robert Dahl and other political scientists were especially effective in moving students toward pluralist studies of power in the United States.[16]

Although these ideas still dominate the mainstream of political science, Dahl shifted ground in the late 1970s, arguing that pluralism "is no longer limited to Western bourgeois thought." He suggested that socialist economies can also be highly decentralized and pluralistic: for example, Yugoslavia after 1950, Czechoslovakia in early 1968, and Portugal immediately after the 1974 coup.[17] The ideas of democratic socialism or socialist democracy, of course, have been especially popular in Europe since the turn of the century. However, several issues should be considered. For example, given the inclination of most U.S. social scientists to favor pluralism, with its emphasis on resolution and consensus, can they incorporate an analysis that accounts for contradictions and conflict in class society? Can they focus seriously on class struggle, without idealizing the notion of a classless society that is sometimes implied in the pluralist stance? These are important questions, for class distinctions should persist under either capitalism or socialism for some time.

Another view of state and class draws upon the early Marx who contended with Hegel, especially with the proposition that the distinction between the state and the institutions of civil or private society could be overcome. Marx argued that the state is the organization the bourgeoisie adopts to protect its property and interests. Marx's "critical" assessment of Hegel aimed to expose the ideology or "false consciousness" that accompanies the capitalist era. Marx explored the meaning of consciousness and the alienation of the worker in his early writings. These ideas thus served as the basis for the Hegelian-Marxist tradition, the thought of Georg Lukacs, and the representatives of the Frankfurt school, including Theodor Adorno and Herbert Marcuse, as well as contemporary philosopher Jürgen Habermas. Habermas showed that the class struggle assumes the form of ideological delusion, implying that the struggle is unrecognizable by capitalists and workers alike. Habermas is concerned primarily with the consciousness of classes and with avoiding mechanistic treatments of the relationship of base to superstructure.[18]

In still another conception of the state, inherent in the writing of G. William Domhoff and in the more explicitly Marxist stance of Ralph Miliband, the capitalist ruling class uses the state as an instrument for dominating society. This instrumentalism derives from the *Communist Manifesto*, in which Marx and Engels asserted that "the modern state is but a committee for managing the common affairs of the whole bourgeoisie."[19]

Domhoff emphasized this idea of ruling class manipulation of the state by linking members of the upper class to control of the corporate economy and affirming that life in the United States is dominated by a relatively unified corporate elite. He attempted to demonstrate empirically the existence of an interacting national power structure, through contingency, reputational, positional, and network analysis. This theory limited itself to showing ties among persons who occupy important positions, and tended to view class in static, one-dimensional terms rather than as a dynamic dialectical relationship involving more than a single class.[20]

Ralph Miliband, in *State in Capitalist Society*, agreed that the ruling class in capitalist society holds power and uses the state as an instrument of domination, but he moved away from simply positioning influential people into a monolithic economic power structure. He focused on the "whole" bourgeoisie, examining its separate parts and autonomy as well as the proposition that the state may act in the interests of capitalists, but not always at their command.[21]

The structuralist view of state and class differs from instrumentalism, even though Miliband tries to bridge the gap between them. French structuralist Nicos Poulantzas argued that the direct involvement of members of the ruling class does not necessarily account for actions of the state: "the capitalist state best serves the interests of the capitalist class only when the members of this class do not participate in the state apparatus."[22] Poulantzas believed that the structures of society determine the functions of state rather than influential people. He related the functions of the capitalist state to the impact of the state on the capitalist and working classes, suggesting that the state functions in several ways to reproduce the capitalist society as a whole. The state tends to obscure the division of classes, and attempts to represent the "unity" of the masses as if a class struggle could not exist. To demonstrate that the state is not simply the instrument of the ruling class, Poulantzas shows how the state tolerates the organization of political parties so that internal contradiction and fractionalization result in struggles within the working class and disunity within the bourgeoisie, so that the bourgeoisie is unable to rise as a united class to a position of hegemony. Thus the state stands above the special interests of individual capitalists and capitalist class fractions.[23]

The origins and influences of structuralist thought are found in the early texts of anthropologist Claude Lévi-Strauss, Italian Marxist Antonio Gramsci, and French Marxist Louis Althusser. Although the work of Lévi-Strauss is not Marxist, it has been incorporated into Marxism because, as noted by Jonathan Friedman, "they both attempt to explain reality in terms of what are conceived of as fundamental underlying relations."[24] Maurice Godelier believed that Marx initiated structuralism, for Marx offered a scientific understanding of the capitalist system by discovering "the internal structures hidden behind its visible functioning."[25] Gramsci's notes on the state emphasize hegemony, or the dominance of some social group or class in power. He observed that crises in the hegemony of the ruling class occur when it fails in some political task.[26] Althusser was partially influenced by Gramsci, but he drew his ideas primarily from the "mature" or later writings of Marx. In an essay on the state and class Althusser sketched what he believed to be Marx's representation of the structure of every society, an infrastructure (or economic base) of productive forces and relations of production and a superstructure of politico-legal and ideological character. He conceived of the state as a repressive apparatus of bureaucracy, police, courts, prisons, and army that allows the ruling class to dominate and exploit the working class. The state intervenes in times of crisis and shields the bourgeoisie and its allies in the class struggle against the proletariat.[27]

TOWARD A THEORY
OF DEVELOPMENT AND UNDERDEVELOPMENT

Along with the movement toward studying theories of state and class, there has been considerable interest in the prolific literature of development and underdevelopment. The mainstream of comparative politics has concerned itself with questions of political development, usually conceived in terms of political democracy; development and nationalism; and modernization.[28] In addition, the mainstream appears to have incorporated much of the literature on underdevelopment, dependency, and to a lesser extent, imperialism. Because these themes are usually considered "radical," I offer a brief critical summary of them and then turn to a discussion of new alternatives.[29]

Traditionally, the idea of development was associated with the possibility of development in the less-developed nations. The assumption was that the diffusion of capital and technology would resolve the problems of poverty and hunger everywhere. This assumption has been challenged by many writers, perhaps most conspicuously by André Gunder Frank in his work on Latin America and later by Walter Rodney, who focused on Africa in a similar way.[30]

The ideas of Frank are probably better known in U.S. social science than those of Rodney. Frank emphasized commercial monopoly rather than feudalism to explain how the dominant national and regional metropolises exploit and appropriate surplus from their dependent satellites. The idea of surplus was drawn from Paul Baran;[31] the dichotomy of metropolis and satellite assumes that capitalism on a world scale is responsible for the underdevelopment of peripheral nations. These ideas influenced Immanuel Wallerstein to elaborate the theory of world system in his interpretive history of the origins and evolution of capitalism in Europe.[32]

The literature is replete with terminology that deals with these themes. Argentine economist Raúl Prebisch was one of the first to divide the world into a center and a periphery and, under the Economic Commission for Latin America (ECLA), to study the problem of underdevelopment and offer reformist solutions. This tradition was carried on by others associated with ECLA, including Brazilian economist Celso Furtado, Chilean economist Osvaldo Sunkel, and Brazilian political sociologist Fernando Henrique Cardoso. Furtado examined inequalities in Brazil throughout historical periods.[33] Sunkel assumed that underdevelopment was part of the process of international capitalist development and believed that inequalities could be corrected by structural transformations.[34] Cardoso advanced the thesis that dependent capitalist development has become a new form of monopolistic expansion in the Third World: Within dependent capitalist situations, development can benefit classes associated with international capital, such as the local agrarian, commercial, financial, and industrial bourgeoisie.[35] Mexican political sociologist Pablo González Casanova suggested a national solution to the problem of internal colonialism; internal colonialism, he argued, is found within nations where a metropolis dominates the isolated peripheral communities, deforming the indigenous economy and exploiting relations of production.[36]

This reformist tradition contrasts with a more radical line of thinking on development and underdevelopment, found originally in the thought of Brazilian economic historian Caio Prado Junior, Argentine economic historian Sergio Bagú, and Argentine political scientist Silvio Frondizi. Bagú and Prado focused on colonialism and dependency; Frondizi looked at two types of imperialism, British and U.S., in assessing the impact of capitalism upon dependent societies.[37] These writers argued that capitalism, not feudalism, had prevailed since colonial times and that the national bourgeoisie in their countries was unable to fulfill its historical role of bringing about autonomous capitalism. This position led them to favor revolutionary rather than reformist solutions to underdevelopment.

More refined versions of this line were set forth by two Brazilian social scientists, Theotonio dos Santos and Ruy Mauro Marini. Dos Santos wrote of several types of dependency: colonial dependency, based on a monopoly of trade by European nations over their colonies; financial-industrial dependency, which was consolidated at the end of the nineteenth century under the domination of capital in the hegemonic centers; and the new dependency, represented by the investments of multinational corporations after the Second World War. Dos Santos attempted to show that the relationship of dependent countries to dominant ones cannot be altered without a change in internal structure and external relations. Additionally, the structure of dependency tends to deepen, resulting in underdevelopment in dependent countries: "The unequal and combined character of capitalist development at the international level is reproduced internally in an acute form. . . . the industrial and technological structure responds more closely to the interests of the multinational corporations than to internal needs."[38] Marini advocated the theory of subimperialism. He characterized Brazilian capitalism as superexploitative, with rapid capital accumulation benefiting the owners of the means of production. Given small internal consumption and a decline in surplus after the 1964 coup, the military regime implemented its subimperialist model by exploiting mass consumption and penetrating foreign markets. Brazilian expansion necessitated the combination of interests of the state, bourgeoisie, and the multinationals.[39]

A host of other writers have pursued some of these lines of thought. Arghiri Emmanuel, for example, has stressed inequalities in international exchange and markets.[40] Samir Amin emphasized unequal development because the periphery, given its integration within the world market, is without the economic means to challenge foreign monopolies. Underdevelopment is thus accentuated, growth is blocked in the periphery, and autonomous development is impossible. The capitalist mode of production tends to become exclusive in the center but not in the periphery, where other modes may be evident.[41] The uneven and combined features of development, stressed by Dos Santos and others, are drawn from the writings of Leon Trotsky but emphasized in analysis by Ernest Mandel and Michael Lowy.[42]

Criticism of all these theories is prolific. A major problem is the inclination to label dependency a theory, when in fact there is no unified theory. Students would profit by applying the dependency idea to situations, as suggested by Cardoso, or to describe relationships and conditions between countries in the world international political economy. There is also a tendency to emphasize underconsumption as the consequence of imperialism and the need of industrialized nations to seek new markets abroad to take up the slack for production at home. A frequent complaint is that studies of underdevelopment focus on relations of market rather than production and consequently ignore class conflict and struggle. Few practical solutions for underdevelopment are offered. Finally, there are serious questions on the compatibility of underdevelopment and dependency to a theory of Marxism.[43]

Given the debate on the old and new ideas of development and underdevelopment, whither the future? The evidence suggests that although mainstream comparative politics has embraced many of these ideas, alternative approaches are also appearing. The work of Frank and Wallerstein on the world system, an extension of earlier efforts, is quite popular and has stimulated theorists to reassess the historical development of capitalism, especially in the European experience. However, two other theories are receiving attention: internationalization of capital and modes and articulation of modes of production.

INTERNATIONALIZATION OF CAPITAL

A French political economist, Christian Palloix, has elaborated a theory of the internationalization of capital. He has attempted to apply the methodology and categories of Marx's *Capital* to the movement of capital and class struggle on an international level. He is concerned with such themes as international valorization, modes of international accumulation of capital, and the internationalization of the productive and financial system.[44] He does not focus on exploitation in the periphery, but on exploitation in the process of production on a world scale; this emphasis differentiates his approach from most writers who have attempted to explain underdevelopment in the Third World.[45]

Henrik Secher Marcussen and Jens Erik Torp have also argued that new forms of internationalization of capital have appeared since the European crisis caused by the rise of petroleum prices in 1973. They show that capital has been directed from Europe to the periphery in the search for new investments and markets, allowing for national capital accumulation within some countries while others continue to suffer from the blocked development described by the dependency school. "We have reached the conclusion that dynamic elements exist in the changing historical conditions for capital accumulation in Western countries, particularly the economic crisis since 1973, and that these elements are responsible for the creation of new reproductive structures in parts of the Periphery which may very well break with the 'blocked development' situation."[46] Marcussen and Torp apply their thesis that national accumulation of capital is possible in some parts of the periphery. They analyze the impact of French capital in the Ivory Coast and attempt to demonstrate that this country can transcend blocked development.

Other works that follow this line are Stephen Hymer's early studies on the multinational corporation in terms of international capital movements[47] and the writing of the late Bill Warren. Warren was one of the early critics of underdevelopmentalism, and his work emphasized the progressive aspects of capitalism in the periphery. He argued that imperialism has been a progressive force capable of promoting industrialization and economic growth, even in backward areas.[48]

MODES AND ARTICULATION OF MODES OF PRODUCTION

In the 1980s, the search for a theory of development has turned to the study of modes of production. Marx was primarily interested in the capitalist mode, but he referred frequently to precapitalist modes of production. His ideas stimulated debate as to the nature of society. Maurice Dobb and Paul Sweezy debated on feudalism and capitalism,[49] for example, and Sweezy and Charles Bettelheim debated the nature of the transition to socialism.[50] The work of French structuralists, especially in economic anthropology, deserves particular attention. The French Marxists use the language and methodology of Louis Althusser and Etienne Balibar, particularly the concept of articulation of modes of production; articulation implies the combining of different modes of production as well as a dialectical relationship between the economic base and the political superstructure of a society. Another French thinker, Pierre-Philippe Rey, explicitly uses this terminology in his focus on modes of production. He argues that both old and new modes are evident in any transition. He believes that capitalism will eventually destroy all relations of exploitation that characterize precapitalist modes of production. Thus, he denies the view that dependent capitalism in the periphery operates as its own mode of production with its own laws of motion.[51]

Many of the theories of underdevelopment and dependency emanated from Latin America. The attention to modes of production was a response to such theories, and some of the most interesting empirical work on modes of production also comes from Latin America. The work of Mexicans Domenico Sindico and Roger Bartra, Peruvian Rodrigo Montoya, and Bolivians Gustavo Rodrigues O. and Antonio Rojas is representative.[52]

This review of alternative theories has surveyed some of the ideas and literature relating to state and class as well as development and underdevelopment. The recent work and new directions share a common concern— that class analysis be used in research and study and that we continue our search for a theory of class struggle. The effort to develop a theory of dependency was a response to the failure of imperialism to explain the impact of international capitalism upon the class structure of underdeveloped nations, yet the dependency literature continued to neglect class analysis. Both the internationalization of capital and the modes of production approaches claim to meet this deficiency. Curiously, some scholars interested in the theory of state and class conclude that analysis should focus on class struggle.[53] Likewise, both critics and supporters of the dependency approach insist on class analysis.[54]

166

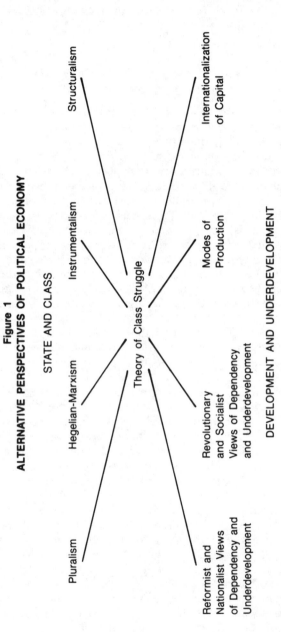

Figure 1
ALTERNATIVE PERSPECTIVES OF POLITICAL ECONOMY

STATE AND CLASS

Pluralism   Hegelian-Marxism   Instrumentalism   Structuralism

Theory of Class Struggle

Reformist and
Nationalist Views
of Dependency and
Underdevelopment

Revolutionary
and Socialist
Views of Dependency
and Underdevelopment

Modes of
Production

Internationalization
of Capital

DEVELOPMENT AND UNDERDEVELOPMENT

Having reviewed a variety of ideas, discussing both strengths and weaknesses, I suggest the need for a theory of class struggle, as emphasized in Figure 1—an attempt to delineate the many threads in the literature. It is clear that the task ahead in the search for alternative theories must take into account questions of both politics and economics, and recognize that the study of real situations must include a more profound understanding of capitalism and socialism in the contemporary world.

NOTES

1. I have examined the roots of comparative politics in Ronald H. Chilcote, *Theories of Comparative Politics: The Search for a Paradigm* (Boulder, CO: Westview Press, 1981), Chapter 3.

2. These trends and the relevant sources are fully elaborated in Chilcote, *Theories of Comparative Politics:* see especially Chaps. 1, 5, 6, 7, and 8.

3. Karl Marx, in the preface to his "Contribution to the Critique of Political Economy," pp. 425–426 in Karl Marx, *Early Writings* (New York: Vintage Books, 1975).

4. David Easton, "Political Science," in *International Encyclopedia of the Social Sciences* (New York: Macmillan Co. and Free Press, 1968), vol. 12, p. 295.

5. See David Easton, *The Political System: An Inquiry into the State of Political Science* (New York: Alfred A. Knopf, 1953) and "An Approach to the Analysis of Political Systems," *World Politics* 9 (April 1957):383–400. In these writings he set forth some concepts and a general model for analysis of the political system. Later, he attempted to refine his model, in David Easton, *A Framework for Political Analysis* (Englewood Cliffs, NJ: Prentice-Hall, 1965) and *A Systems Analysis of Political Life* (New York: John Wiley & Sons, 1965).

6. Colin Campbell, "Current Models of the Political System: An Intellective-Purposive View," *Comparative Political Studies* 4 (April 1971):26. See also John D. Astin, "Easton I and Easton II," *Western Political Quarterly* 25 (December 1972):726–737.

7. William C. Mitchell, "Politics as the Allocation of Values: A Critique," *Ethics* 71 (January 1961):79.

8. J. S. Sorzano, "David Easton and the Invisible Hand," *American Political Science Review* 69 (March 1975):91–106.

9. For example, Thomas J. Lewis, "Parsons' and David Easton's Analysis of the Support System," *Canadian Journal of Political Science* 7 (December 1974):672–686.

10. Gabriel A. Almond, "Comparative Political Systems," *Journal of Politics* 18 (August 1956):391–409.

11. David Easton, "The New Revolution in Political Science," *American Political Science Review* 63 (December 1969):1051–1061.

12. David Easton, "The Political System Besieged by the State," *Political Theory* 9 (August 1981):303–325.

13. Szymanski argued that functionalism has been and continues to be used in conservative ways, but when interpreted dialectically, it "is a fundamental part of Marxist methodology, and a very powerful tool for the advance of social science." See Al Szymanski, "Malinowski, Marx, and Functionalism," *Insurgent Sociologist* 2 (Summer 1972):35–43.

14. See Vilfredo Pareto, *Sociological Writings*, selected and introduced by S. E. Finer (New York: Praeger, 1966).

15. See Gaetano Mosca, *The Ruling Class: Elementi de Scienza Politica*, edited and revised with an introduction by Arthur Livingston (New York: McGraw-Hill, 1939).

16. See Robert A. Dahl, *Who Governs? Democracy and Power in an American City* (New Haven, CT: Yale University Press, 1961) and *Polyarchy, Participation, and Opposition* (New Haven, CT: Yale University Press, 1971).

17. Robert A. Dahl, "Pluralism Revisited," *Comparative Politics* 10 (January 1978):191–203.

18. Tony Flood, "Jürgen Habermas's Critique of Marxism," *Science and Society* 41 (Winter 1977–1978):448–464.

19. Karl Marx and Friedrich Engels, "The Manifesto of the Communist Party," pp. 35–65 in vol. 1, *Selected Works in Two Volumes* (Moscow: Foreign Language Publishing House, 1958), quote on p. 36.

20. See, for example, G. William Domhoff, *The Higher Circles: The Governing Class in America* (New York: Vintage Books, 1970).

21. Ralph Miliband, "Theories of the State and the Capitalist State," *New Left Review* 82 (November–December 1973):85; also see his *The State in Capitalist Society: An Analysis of the Western System of Power* (New York: Basic Books, 1969).

22. Nicos Poulantzas, "The Problem of the Capitalist State," *New Left Review* 58 (November–December 1969):74.

23. This position is elaborated in Nicos Poulantzas, *Political Power and Social Classes* (London: New Left Books and Sheed and Ward, 1973).

24. Jonathan Friedman, "Marxism, Structuralism, and Vulgar Materialism," *Man* 9 (September 1974):453.

25. Maurice Godelier, "Structure and Contradiction in Capital," in Robin Blackburn, ed., *Ideology in Social Science* (New York: Vintage Books, 1973), p. 336.

26. See especially Antonio Gramsci, *Selections from the Prison Notebooks of Antonio Gramsci* (London: Lawrence and Wishart, 1971).

27. Louis Althusser, "Ideology and the Ideological State Apparatuses (Notes Towards an Investigation)," pp. 121–173 in his *Lenin and Philosophy and Other Essays* (London: New Left Books, 1971).

28. An example of work on political development is Lucian Pye, *Aspects of Political Development* (Boston: Little, Brown, 1966). Karl Deutsch's *Nationalism and Social Communication* (New York: Technology Press of MIT and John Wiley & Sons, 1953) is representative of works on nationalism and development; examples of attention to modernization include David E. Apter, *The Politics of Modernization* (Chicago: University of Chicago Press, 1965), and Samuel P. Huntington, *Political Order in Changing Societies* (New Haven, CT: Yale University Press, 1968).

29. I have more fully discussed theories of development and underdevelopment in Chilcote, *Theories of Comparative Politics*, Chapter 7, pp. 271–346, and in *Theories of Development and Underdevelopment* (Boulder, CO: Westview Press, 1984).

30. André Gunder Frank, *Capitalism and Underdevelopment in Latin America* (New York: Monthly Review Press, 1967); and Walter Rodney, *How Europe Underdeveloped Africa* (London and Dar es Salaam: Bogle-l'Ouverture and Tanzania Publishing House, 1972).

31. Paul Baran, *The Political Economy of Growth* (New York: Monthly Review Press, 1957).

32. Immanuel Wallerstein, *The Modern World System: Capitalist Agriculture and the Origins of the European World Economy in the Sixteenth Century* (New York: Academic Press, 1974), the first of a four-volume series.

33. Celso Furtado, *Economic Growth of Brazil: A Survey from Colonial to Modern Times* (Berkeley: University of California Press, 1963).

34. Osvaldo Sunkel, "Big Business and 'Dependencia,'" *Foreign Affairs* 50 (April 1972):517–531.

35. Fernando Henrique Cardoso, "Dependency and Development in Latin America," *New Left Review* 74 (July–August 1972):83–95, and "Associated-Dependent Development: Theoretical and Practical Implications," pp. 142–176 in Alfred Stepan, ed., *Authoritarian Brazil: Origins, Policies, and Future* (New Haven, CT: Yale University Press, 1973).

36. Pablo González Casanova, *Sociología de la explotación*, 2d ed. (Mexico City: Siglo Veintiuno, 1978).

37. Sergio Bagú, *Economia de la Sociedad Colonial: Ensayo de Historia Comparada de América Latina* (Buenos Aires: Librería "El Ateneo," 1949); and Silvio Frondizi, *La integración mundial, última etapa del capitalismo (Respuesta a una crítica)* (Buenos Aires, 1947 and 1954).

38. Theotonio dos Santos, "The Structure of Dependence," *American Economic Review* 60 (May 1970):234–235.

39. Ruy Mauro Marini, *Subdesarrollo y revolución* (Mexico City: Siglo Veintiuno, 1969).

40. Arghiri Emmanuel, *Unequal Exchange: A Study of the Imperialism of Trade* (New York: Monthly Review Press, 1972).

41. Samir Amin, *Unequal Development* (New York: Monthly Review Press, 1976).

42. See, for example, Ernest Mandel, *Late Capitalism* (London: New Left Books, 1975); and Michael Lowy, *The Politics of Combined and Uneven Development: The Theory of Permanent Revolution* (London: New Left Books, 1981).

43. These and other criticisms are brought out in Ronald H. Chilcote, ed., *Dependency and Marxism: Toward a Resolution of the Debate* (Boulder, CO: Westview Press, 1982).

44. See Christian Palloix, *L'Internalisation du Capital* (Paris: François Maspero, 1975).

45. Christian Palloix, "The Self-Expression of Capital on a World Scale," *Review of Radical Political Economics* 9 (Summer 1977):1–28, including an introductory note by Robert B. Cohen.

46. Henrik Secher Marcussen and Jens Erik Torp, *Internationalization of Capital: Prospects for the Third World, A Reexamination of Dependency Theory* (London: Zed Press, 1982), p. 10.

47. Stephen Hymer, "The Internationalization of Capital," *Journal of Economic Issues* 6, no. 1 (1972):91–111.

48. Bill Warren, *Imperialism: Pioneer of Capitalism* (London: New Left Books, 1980).

49. In Rodney Hilton, ed., *The Transition from Feudalism to Capitalism* (London: New Left Books, 1976).

50. Paul M. Sweezy and Charles Bettelheim, *On the Transition to Socialism* (New York: Monthly Review Press, 1971).

51. Pierre-Philippe Rey, *Les alliances de classes* (Paris: François Maspero, 1973).

52. Their work is published in English in the journal *Latin American Perspectives*—see vol. 7, no. 27 (Fall 1980), for example. Richard Harris reviews the influence of French structuralism in "The Influence of Marxist Structuralism on the Intellectual Left in Latin America," *Insurgent Sociologist* 9 (Summer 1979):62–72.

53. Gosta Esping-Andersen, Rodger Friedland, and Erik Olin Wright, "Modes of Class Struggle and the Capitalist State," *Kapitalistate* 4–5 (Summer 1976):186–220.

54. See Dale L. Johnson, "Economism and Determinism in Dependency Theory," pp. 108–117, and James Petras, "Dependency and World System Theory: A Critique and New Directions," pp. 148–155 in Chilcote, *Dependency and Marxism*.

9

Public Policy and Administration in Comparative Perspective

LAWRENCE S. GRAHAM

Over the last decade the study of public policy has come of age. Although policy analysis has a long and distinguished history in political science, especially in studies of U.S. politics, it is only relatively recently that this approach has achieved the status of an integrating concept sufficiently broad within the discipline to span the diverse fields into which political science has become divided. For more than a decade now a public policy perspective has been central to the analysis of issues lying at the core of the U.S. political process.[1] Quietly but no less clearly, it has also come to serve as the catalyst for reestablishing communication between academic political science and practitioner-oriented public administration. As a consequence, today no serious analyst of public policy can neglect the importance of implementation as an integral part of the policy process, any more than a faculty member in a well-developed public affairs program can overlook the saliency of politics in preparing students for careers in the public service.[2]

In comparative politics the signs of this shift in focus are not nearly as clear as they are in the analysis of U.S. governmental institutions and political behavior. Yet they are present nonetheless. Accordingly, when Guy Peters introduced his survey of recent works on comparative policy in 1981 for the *Policy Studies Review* he opened his remarks on a somewhat apologetic note.

> Although it is commonly regarded as an esoteric field, comparative public policy actually has a huge and growing literature. It is fair to say that there is a dearth of truly comparative analysis, in which the same theoretical and analytical approaches are applied to data from different cultures. There is,

Revised version of "Intergovernmental Relations in Comparative Context" (Paper presented at the annual American Political Science Association meeting, Chicago, 1–4 September 1983).

however, an immense body of material for everyone's theoretical mill in the body of case studies and single country analyses. What we as Americans may regard as foreign and hence "comparative" policy others regard as domestic, and consequently have both an intimate knowledge of the political system and its policies as well as a more direct interest in the consequence of the policy.[3]

By the mid-1980s several notable shifts had occurred in comparative public policy that heightened its salience in cross-national research. These shifts have given comparative politics a whole new impetus, the first since the "new comparative politics" of the 1960s and the works of Gabriel Almond and others in his generation became the generally accepted way of examining politics cross-nationally. This literature in comparative public policy can be characterized as containing four basic elements: concern with process; awareness of the complexity of public policy, and the corresponding need to focus new research on different policy sectors; the move toward more truly comparative cross-national work, incorporating a more rigorous definition of policy arenas and specifying a more limited number of relevant country cases; and the reintegration of administration into the study of politics, through a rediscovery of the centrality of the state and the significance of the governmental apparatus as a critical variable in cross-national work.[4]

What has been missing from most of this literature to date is the very perspective Almond had emphasized in 1958 as lacking in the existing literature on comparative government: a perspective on the developing countries. This chapter seeks to fill that gap.

TOWARD A POLICY PERSPECTIVE ON THE THIRD WORLD

Since 1945 most discussions of development have centered around two commonly accepted criteria: economic differences and ideological distinctions. According to the one, countries are divided into rich and poor nations on the basis of such factors as per capita income, gross national product, and aggregate social and demographic characteristics. The latter separates capitalist from socialist societies by distinguishing free-market, mixed economies from command-oriented, centrally planned economies, and isolates countries representing variants of state socialism from those characterized by greater or lesser degrees of political pluralism. These divisions have to some extent been modified over the last several decades by the appearance of scholarship on authoritarianism in the nonsocialist world and by experimentation with market socialism in the Eastern European countries. But in public administration the models and constructs employed still maintain the dichotomy between administration in the developed and developing worlds and public management in socialist as opposed to nonsocialist societies.

This study endeavors to transcend these divisions by summarizing new field research conducted on the semi-periphery and periphery of the developed world—in southern Europe and Latin America—rather than by reviewing a scant literature, which would only restate the conclusion reached by Peters in the above quote.[5] It seeks to analyze in a wider comparative context the diverse roles of the state in the economies and polities of late modernizing countries, focusing on older national societies—those whose modernization endeavors predate World War II—rather than on more recently created states. Most of these countries are located in southern Europe and Latin America, although the fit is far from perfect. Exceptions that quickly come to mind are Thailand and Turkey; Albania, Paraguay, and Haiti are cases that fall outside the chosen set.

With these exceptions noted, then, there is a body of experience with modernization and development throughout southern Europe, Mexico, and South America that extends across a considerable period of time and dates largely from the latter part of the nineteenth century. Argentinians and Mexicans, Romanians and Italians are all quick to explain to outsiders that, despite current economic difficulties and obstacles to further economic growth and diversification, theirs are very old national societies whose quality of life separates them from the Third World. Their developmental experience differs substantially from that of the North Atlantic nations, whose accelerated economic growth during the latter part of the nineteenth century swept them across the threshold into becoming fully developed industrial societies. Although the southern European and Latin American states did achieve a great deal of progress in the three primary eras of economic and political change that have shaped the modern world—the 1890s, the 1920s, and the 1960s—they remain apart. Paralleling modern urban and industrial centers comparable to those of the richer nations are sizable underdeveloped regions where conditions of life and opportunities for economic growth and development are on a par with those of the poor nations. Whether their experience since 1945 has been shaped by state socialism or state capitalism, these conditions remain much the same, despite sustained periods of impressive economic growth. Regions whose economic modernization had begun by the 1890s now have standards of living and economic productivity comparable to the rest of the industrial world. Other regions remain poor, despite the investment of public funds in urban centers in those areas designed to stimulate economic growth and thereby ameliorate the conditions of underdevelopment. These are areas of emigration where skilled labor is scarce, zones of hardship frequented by natural disasters.

Having selected a manageable number of cases from this range of countries that includes a diversity of polities and economies, my goal was to examine their common experience with development-oriented programs conducted under state auspices. My core research question centered on isolating similarities and differences in the administration of development programs in these countries across a fifteen-year time period. For this I needed to select a topic in the comparative study of public policy and administration specific enough to produce concrete results on the role of the state in economic development, yet broad enough to generate comparative data that might be utilized in other settings to identify the problems involved in implementing development-oriented programs.

The core cases selected for comparative study are Mexico, Portugal, and Romania. These three countries share a long-standing experience with political and administrative centralism transcending any one particular regime, a revolutionary breakthrough in the recent past that removed power groups occupying crucial roles in the preceding economy and polity, and experimentation with decentralization strategies. They represent the three major subregions within the area defined as southern Europe and Latin America (i.e., the European Mediterranean world and its cultural extensions into the Americas):[6] Mexico is the Latin American case; Portugal, the southwestern European case; and Romania, the southeastern European one.

Despite these commonalities, there are also important differences. Each has a decidedly different regime. Mexico is a dominant single-party authoritarian system; Portugal, a multiparty competitive regime; and Romania was for a long time an orthodox Marxist-Leninist state.

Because discussion of decentralization strategies, political as well as administrative, is closely linked to alternative patterns of state power, I added two other cases to the study, providing additional contextual data important to the comparative analysis of the implementation of development-oriented programs. These are the only two countries in southern Europe and Latin America where there has been meaningful experimentation with federalism, political as well as administrative: Yugoslavia and Brazil.

RESEARCH DESIGN

Within this range of countries my subject of research has been intergovernmental management experience. As conceptualized comparatively, assessing intergovernmental management experience involves identifying the particular nexus that has developed across time between regional and local authorities and specifying the relationship between center (political and administrative organizations and officials in the national government) and periphery (regional and community-based public organizations and officials). For the purposes of this study, development-oriented programs were defined as those linked to the implementation of a government's industrialization policy, expansion in agricultural productivity, and urban development policy (water supply, sewerage, public transportation, housing, streets, electrification, education, and social services). In all five cases, each dimension received comparable attention. However, I conducted intensive field research, centered around a common semistructured interview guide and elite in-depth interviewing, for only three of the countries: Mexico, Portugal, and Romania. For Brazil and Yugoslavia, my sources were extensive library documents, research in the host country, language sources, and informal elite in-depth interviewing. As it was, the logistics of locating research funding, arranging leave time, developing local contacts, establishing within-country institutional sponsorship, acquiring relevant system-wide knowledge of each country, and developing the necessary language skills consumed more than a decade of on-again, off-again field research.[7]

In Mexico, Portugal, and Romania, the existing subnational governmental demarcations suggested comparable units of analysis for the study of intergovernmental relations. In each, three units were selected from within historic, well-defined regions broader than current political demarcations. In Mexico these were states; in Portugal, districts; and in Romania, *judete* or counties (the translation Romanians prefer). Although the original research design prescribed the selection of major subnational units belonging to the periphery rather than to the center, in Romania central government controls over social science research precluded the selection of field research sites according to strictly academic criteria. Michoacan (with its capital in Morelia, just south of the Guadalajara–Mexico City axis), Oaxaca (in the far southwest, where city and state bear the same name), and Tabasco (on the Caribbean coast, where Villahermosa's status as a regional center in a limited territorial area makes it virtually synonymous with the state) constituted the Mexican cases. In Portugal they were Braga in the north (in the Minho region), Viseu in the center (in Beira Alta), and Evora in the south (in the Alentejo). In each case, city and district bore the same name, as was true for the subnational units selected in Romania—Cluj in the region of Transylvania (to the west), Buzau in Oltenia (in the southeastern quadrant of the country), and Iasi in Moldavia (to the northeast).

These very different field settings made it impossible to interview in the same number of communities in each country, and variations in territory, population size, and distribution of urban centers precluded selecting the same number of units or interviewees. The greatest extremes were in Mexico where Oaxaca had by far the largest number of *municipios* (570) and Tabasco the smallest (18). There also the goal of interviewing local authorities in each major subregional population center was the most difficult to realize, due to terrain and distance in the former and access in the latter. Despite this disparity at the community level, the regimes of all three countries conceptualized the municipio in similar terms—as the modern day equivalent of the *municipium* with its incorporation of surrounding rural areas as part of the city's prescribed jurisdiction. For details concerning the number of communities included and interviews completed see Table 1.

To understand the data base on which the following findings and conclusions are based, a number of further explanations are warranted. First, the actual number of communities included in the Romanian panel is 20, although 24 local authorities in executive positions were interviewed. In the largest communities—such as the regional governments—collective leadership practices made it important to include the first vice-president, who was the official charged primarily with administrative oversight responsibilities. In medium-size and smaller communities, despite collective leadership principles, effective local decisionmaking authority and administrative control was vested in a single individual, the *primar*.

Second, the larger size of the Mexican sample for regional authorities reflects the two tiers of authorities at this level: field representatives of central ministries and other national-level public organizations (54 in this

Table 1   INTERVIEW PANELS

	Local Authorities	Regional Authorities	National Authorities[a]
Mexico	18	81	10
Portugal	25	36	13
Romania	24 (20)[b]	21	5

[a]In contrast to the semistructured interviewing used for local and regional authorities, these were exploratory interviews.

[b]The number of communities and number of local authorities coincide in Mexico and Portugal, but in Romania 24 local authorities were interviewed and 20 communities were visited during this phase of the project.

sample) and state government officials (27). Although scholars and observers of the Mexican scene generally agree that Mexican federalism does not have much meaningful content and that this governmental system should be considered another instance of marked centralism, public bureaucracy (that is, the myriad of ministries, departments, commissions, and enterprises identified with the state) follows the federalist principle. From the standpoint of program implementation, the Mexican case is accordingly best defined as an instance of political centralism combined with administrative federalism. In the other cases, unitary state organization coincides with political and administrative centralism. Besides these differences, the Mexican sample is also larger because of the plethora of individual public organizations at the regional level. In all three countries and all nine subnational units, I interviewed the heads of all offices involved in industry and commerce, agriculture, and urban services.

Third, in Romania considerable negotiation with governmental authorities in Bucharest was necessary to obtain permission to interview regional and local authorities. As a result, I included Cluj and Iasi (major regional centers second only to the industrial city of Brasov) and excluded the peripheral regions.

Fourth, all three cases required considerable additional exploratory interviewing and background library work before more structured work could begin. In each it soon became apparent that greater in-depth knowledge of these governmental systems would have to be established prior to beginning more focused field work. These exploratory interviews number 78 and are distinct from those reported in Table 1. They are not listed in tabular form because they are drawn from disparate population groups. My objective here was to explore the bureaucratic arena and the surrounding political system in each country. The core questions concerned the functions of the governmental units the interviewees represented, their responsibilities, their intragovernmental linkages, and the extent to which they participated in the making and implementing of development policy. I also used these interviews to evaluate the political structure within which I would need to operate. Lastly, I experimented with alternative data-gathering techniques.

In Lisbon, exploratory interviewing focused on developing a Portuguese-language version of the rice-production questionnaire which Richard Gable et al. had arrived at as the vehicle most appropriate for their research in Asia. After much time spent first blocking in the policy environment and then obtaining permission and sponsorship for the pre-tests and full interviews through a staff unit in the Ministry of Corporations, I abandoned that instrument as simply unfeasible in the intensely politicized and regulated environment I was working within. In Mexico, exploratory interviews were the fewest because I knew that system the best and only needed new, more up-to-date information on current bureaucratic structures. In Romania my efforts centered on the problem of how to obtain comparable data and how to work through their escort-interpreter system. By the time I had completed this exploratory work and learned how to operate in that research environment, I had acquired sufficient knowledge of Romanian to ask my own questions and record the answers without the benefit of an interpreter—although I continued to use my escorts to check for accuracy.

In the Portuguese case I conducted 43 exploratory interviews with pre-1974 Lisbon-based governmental authorities. In Mexico, 6 additional state officials (including 2 governors) and 5 local authorities were included. In Romania, this work involved contacting 13 judete officials and 11 local authorities. The majority of the Romanian officials were interviewed during a short-term preliminary trip; the remainder, during a second exploratory field trip. These later interviews focused on developing an appropriate phraseology in Romanian and clarifying what would be necessary in order to conduct my own interviewing, but they also produced useful information and established familiarity with prevailing governmental practices and procedures.

Combined, the semistructured and exploratory interviews total 311. Excluded from this total are interviews with other knowledgeable and strategically well-located individuals (academics, business executives, military officers, and diplomatic personnel), all of whom were of considerable assistance in assessing the wider political and economic context within which program implementation occurred. Also excluded are 1972 Portuguese government personnel employed at the time in Angola and Mozambique. What makes the 311 interviews hang together as a set, as opposed to the others, is their common concern with the same basic research questions about how public administration operated in a spatial setting. Even in the exploratory interviews I used specific groups of questions prepared in advance, phrased in terms of the objects and subjects of research defined above, and directed at territorial administration.

PROJECT CONCEPTUALIZATION

A cross-national review of the literature on territorial administration identified three models for organizing public services at the subnational level: functional field systems, integrated prefectural systems, and unintegrated prefectural systems.[8]

Functional Field Systems

Functional field systems imply extensive decentralization. Whatever the form of the state (unitary as in British practice, federalist as in the United States, or confederal as in post-Tito Yugoslavia), functional field systems entail the dispersal of administrative power and the organization of distinct field services according to the needs of individual organizations. Some involve quite extensive field operations, with branch offices located in major cities. State and local organizations complement national-based public organizations. In both the United States and Brazil, public organizations have proliferated at the state and national level; in Yugoslavia, national-level public organizations have been reduced to such core national responsibilities as defense, foreign relations, and finance, while the majority of public services have been transferred to regional territorial units (the republics) and self-governing local units (communes). In the United States and Brazil, one is consequently faced with a bewildering number of state and national public entities, and in Yugoslavia, governance of the major cities has produced enormously complex local bureaucracies. Over time these local units of governance, which involve much more than a single community-based organization, have taken on the character of self-contained communities with a well-defined consciousness of collective self-interest that continually frustrates party and republican officials. Whatever the particular mix of national, regional, and local organizations, coordination of public policy and coherency in program administration by sector becomes enormously difficult to achieve in functional field systems.

Integrated Prefectural Systems

The opposite of functional field systems is integrated prefectural systems. Long considered obsolete in the West, they have reappeared in the administrative systems of Eastern Europe and the Soviet Union since World War II. The original model (nineteenth-century France) placed the responsibility for coordination and control of political and administrative activities at the subnational level in the hands of the prefect. Considered the representatives of the state in the provinces, these prefects answered directly to the Minister of Interior. They also exercised extensive controls over the actions of other public officials belonging to the field services of the central ministries. Of the cases included in this study, prewar Romania and overseas Portugal (Portugal's colonial possessions before independence) followed this model most closely. Elsewhere, as industrialization proceeded, the expansion of state activities and growing complexity in individual public services led to the decline of such field systems. Or, in instances where the state failed to develop a coherent model for territorial administration—continental Portugal prior to 1974 and many of the Latin American states—prefect-governors often had extensive political powers but little effective influence over the operation of the field services of central ministries.

The twin necessities of control and development in the Eastern bloc countries have produced a socialist equivalent of the integrated prefectural model. In central and southeastern Europe the principle of collective leadership has replaced the practice of individual decisionmaking and local Communist party officials have provided the control and coordination function. (Poland is an exceptional case, where the absence of system legitimacy has dictated the vesting of executive authority in single individuals in political administration to maintain subnational control.) However, the socialist bloc countries do not use this terminology, as prefectural systems are identified with state forms replaced in the transition from capitalism to socialism. Furthermore, there are some notable differences among the integrated prefectural systems of Eastern Europe. Formal separation between state and party officials is the rule; the concentration of political and management functions in the same group of individuals, as in Nicolae Ceausescu's Romania, is exceptional. Even then, the coincidence between state administration and party is rarely complete. Regional and local-level party first secretaries always serve as presidents of the corresponding administrative councils. But below them, dual office holding is not particularly common in other leadership roles in party and state administration executive committees.

Unintegrated Prefectural Systems

The unintegrated prefectural model constitutes a third alternative. In this model, a prefect or governor is charged with order-maintaining and police functions and is given responsibility for supervising local governments, especially at election time and whenever local authorities are unable to resolve their needs at the community level. These regional authorities do not as a rule become involved in the normal operations of the field services of central ministries and other national offices with branches in the region. Except when there is the need to coordinate a particular set of activities— the development of a system of roads, the creation of basic urban services for a community lacking them, dam construction and related projects in irrigation and electrification—each regional office is primarily responsible for coordinating the activities of community-based delegations and responding to its central office in the capital. Except for their use of existing subregional political demarcations as the basis for organizing field operations, public management activities in these cases are quite similar to those of functional field systems. They resemble integrated prefectural systems in the role ascribed to the governor, who is the maximum political authority in the district. The governor supervises the operations of technical field services when the need arises.

Mexico and post-1974 Portugal fall into this category. The pre-1974 Portuguese system of field administration was never very well organized; it functioned effectively only for the more developed public organizations, such as the national employment service and state security organizations. The political imperative to control local politics disappeared with the 1974 revolution and the subsequent democratic regime.

Mexico rationalized its system of field administration and moved toward an integrated prefectural system between 1969 and 1979. In 1969, for example, river commissions still exercised a great deal of autonomy and determined their own administrative districts largely on the basis of physical and human geographic criteria. By 1979, these commissions had lost their political clout and economic resources, and virtually all other effective public organizations with field services were conforming to state jurisdictional lines. Second, the increase in tensions at the local level in various parts of the country—either through the emergence of parties capable of competing with the government's own Institutional Revolutionary Party (PRI) or through public protest or guerrilla activity—had brought about a corresponding increase in the power of the governor. The 1979 Oaxaca governor was a military officer. Those familiar with the history of modern Mexico might object that this has always been the case, but what was different in 1979 was the rationalization of state authority and the ability of the Office of the President to mobilize and withhold financial and human resources within political districts according to the situation at hand. Third, the introduction of concepts promoting integral sectoral development within the states (during the López-Portillo administration) had strengthened the primacy of state governors. Despite the rhetoric of decentralization, federal subsidies and grants-in-aid increased the ability of the state's chief executive to intervene in the bureaucratic arena and to get programs moving without confronting the bottlenecks and rigidities characteristic of classic integrated prefectural systems.

PROPOSITIONS FOR ORGANIZING CROSS-CULTURAL DATA

In every governmental system one encounters frequent debate over the proper mix between central control and policy coordination, on the one hand, and organizational autonomy, defined in functional and area terms, on the other. Since World War II, reliance on the state in both mixed economy and socialist countries has caused tremendous growth in the number, the size, and the complexity of public organizations. This has inspired numerous experiments with alternative centralization/decentralization mixes. Yugoslavia reduced bureaucratization by devolving as many administrative functions as possible to the local level; Brazil tried to reduce the size of the state sector by limiting the number of public enterprises; Mexico rationalized its state structures and coordinated functions at the national and regional level. The dynamic in Portugal and Romania has been a bit different. In the former, the rapid transition from an authoritarian to a democratic regime produced a hybrid system in which the central ministries were left intact while local political autonomy was insured. In Romania Stalinist controls have precluded anything other than a rigid, hierarchically defined system.

Despite these differences, in all five countries analysis of development policy involves literally thousands of individual programs and organizations, and in actuality no significant progress has been made in any of them in reducing the size and complexity of the state sector as coordination and control concerns have reemerged.

For the purposes of this project, development policy was defined as including three policy subsets: industrialization policy, agricultural development policy, and urban development policy. Rather than examine policy formation, I focused on policy implementation, on how governmental authorities have converted general statements on development into specific sets of programs. The dependent variable, or object of study in this instance, was defined as changes in development policy across time. Development policy was defined as the allocation of economic resources by government to accomplish publicly announced program objectives. Change in development policy was measured for the three types of programs outlined above across the fifteen-year period from 1966 to 1981. Differences in development policy performance were conceptualized as a consequence of three primary variables—the state's economic and political structure, its administrative organization, and the role expectations of government bureaucrats—and a series of nonspecifiable secondary variables. The state's economic and human resources and external political and economic forces were considered intervening variables.

All three independent variables were handled as composites of specific sets of indicators. The state's political and economic structure was understood to mean current practices in the allocation of goods and services, the status accorded to individuals and groups within the state, the devices adopted for the transmission of information, compliance mechanisms, and authority patterns. Administrative organization involved those public organizations and their subnational units responsible for the implementation of development policy at the regional level. Role expectations of government bureaucrats (those persons responsible for implementing development programs) derived from four factors: ideology, societal norms, organizational values, and reference group identity. The nonspecifiable secondary variables influencing development policy were uncovered as the research project advanced; these were factors unique to the individual country cases. Economic and human resources referred to public monies and to the specialized labor available to the state for development purposes. External political and economic forces included those factors beyond state control that limit its capacity for autonomous action and impinge on development policy.

The wealth of data collected in accounting for circumstances unique to each of these cases was sufficiently complex to require separate analysis in a series of monographic studies. The earliest was a study of Mexican state government (1971), the second, an analysis of politics and administration in Romania (1982), followed by two studies of Portuguese administration—an overview of the Portuguese administrative system and an examination of public services from below.[9]

Research Design

The social sciences commonly distinguish among exploratory, descriptive, and hypothesis-testing research designs. For this particular project I used an exploratory format, for several reasons. First, systematic research on public organizations in a comparative, cross-national context is at best limited—if one includes case studies of individual organizations and research on policy sectors such as public housing or public health—or nonexistent—if one considers only truly cross-national research that analyzes the interaction between public policy and public bureaucracy. Second, as an outsider, my research on administrative behavior in the public sector was limited by the very nature of public organizations themselves. It required sensitivity to the character of the dominant political regimes—post-Stalinist, single-party authoritarian in Romania; noncommunist, single-party authoritarian in Mexico; and unstable, multiparty polyarchical in Portugal. Because my objective was to gain greater familiarity with development policy in these three older, developing states than had hitherto been possible, an exploratory research design appeared to be the most appropriate strategy. Once field research in Romania was completed, I realized the Yugoslav experience really could not be excluded, and after I had added this sole instance of federalism under state socialism, my earlier research in Brazil and continued political systems analysis of that country made it theoretically interesting to include the Brazilian case as well.[10]

Central Hypothesis

The core question around which my central hypothesis was built was directed specifically at Mexican, Portuguese, and Romanian development experience. What resources had been allocated by these governments for socioeconomic development from 1966 through 1981, and how? Development policy was defined as including not only industrialization programs designed to stimulate economic growth and to provide for greater employment opportunities, but also programs to increase agricultural output (measured in terms of quantity and quality) and expand urban services (water, electricity, sanitation, transportation, education, and housing).

Beyond this central research question, which focused on first-order policy changes, several second-order questions warranted attention.[11] What were the determinants of development policy? Who were the major groups involved in development policymaking and implementation? What has been the impact of government decisions? Did feedback mechanisms develop? A third set of research questions concerned implementation. Who benefited from the allocation of public resources? What factors intervened to reshape policy as it moved through implementation? What changes, if any, occurred in development policy between 1966 and 1981?

Methodology

Recognizing that field research must be adapted to meet local conditions, I used only nonobtrusive methods. These ranged from documents, books, and periodicals research in local libraries, archives, and special collections to exploratory and semistructured interviewing.

Because the accessibility of government officials in public organizations was linked to prior clearance, the project was designed so that concrete results could be produced even if systematic interviewing in all three countries might not always be possible. In Romania a strictly structured questionnaire, parallel to that utilized in Mexico and Portugal, proved impossible. But despite the need to submit questions for prior approval and the practice of collective interviews—in which the interviewee was always monitored and I nearly always had an escort—the same basic categories were used, and I was careful to ask questions that would produce comparable results with research under way in Mexico and Portugal. This strategy of limited anticipated results paid off the most where I least expected it to be necessary, because of the very positive initial signs I had received—in Yugoslavia.

Of the five countries, Yugoslavia was by far the most closed and the most tightly controlled at the local level for my kind of research. Fred Riggs's admonition about the divergence between form and reality in the developing world carried the most weight in Yugoslavia. There the forms prescribe local participation, local self-government, and local self-management, but behind these elaborate rituals and image building lay the reality of a tightly controlled, closed, and rigid bureaucratized system that has lost its capacity to innovate and to deal effectively with the problems facing it. Whereas in the past the party was always the cement that held the system together, increasingly in post-Tito Yugoslavia the only national institution capable of transcending the nationalities question that has continued to plague the Yugoslav federation is the military.

Complementing these approaches was participant observation through prolonged residence in a limited number of research sites (Morelia in Mexico, metropolitan Lisbon in Portugal, Bucharest in Romania, and Zagreb in Yugoslavia). I employed this technique at several levels, ranging from the use of existing services to specific interactions with professionals and academics in the host country. My practice was to keep a log of encounters with local bureaucracies and bureaucrats.[12]

At the same time, as noted in Table 1, I interviewed selected members of bureaucratic elites as an integral part of the project. Previous experience in public administration work and research in Latin America and southern Europe had convinced me that such people are more readily accessible than is often assumed, and they can provide important data. In this aspect of my research, the rigor that is stressed so often in research design and questionnaire formation in the social sciences, especially in political science work on the United States and Western Europe, was sacrificed in the interest of talking with as many people and in as many different contexts as possible. In Eastern Europe, where formal interviewing is at times very difficult to arrange, this more journalistic approach reaped untold dividends in helping me understand the societies I was living in. When access to local authorities was closed off, I used the time to focus instead on current political and economic dynamics. Then, when focused interviewing was possible, I found this approach particularly adaptable to the changing field environments I had to confront and a rich source of new data.

Although many researchers reject the elite in-depth interview as imprecise and excessively subjective for accurate data collection, in dealing with influential government officials in authoritarian regimes the more rigorous techniques developed in survey research and structured questionnaires are simply not appropriate. When I did experiment with structured questionnaires in authoritarian, pre-1974 Portugal and authoritarian, post-Tito Yugoslavia, it made even the most routine questioning extremely difficult and at times impossible. My conclusion is that the elite in-depth interview can and does provide insight more readily into the internal workings of public policy in cross-cultural contexts. Furthermore, if the interview guide is fully developed and pretested beforehand to insure maximum data reliability, it can provide useful and systematic comparative data. Interviewing according to these standards in Mexico, Portugal (in authoritarian and nonauthoritarian periods), and Romania produced a common body of data relevant to the questions formulated at the outset.

FINDINGS

The results of this comparative, cross-national research project on inter-governmental relations are fivefold. First, the major subnational political demarcation—be it state, county, district, or republic—provided a much more effective unit of analysis for assessing center-periphery dynamics and analyzing the implementation of programs in comparative context than the community did. Second, comparison of specific sets of policies suggested that whether a system was unitary or federal was far more important in accounting for differences in program implementation than individual political regime variations. On this axis one set of policy responses was common to Mexico, Portugal, and Romania; another reflected the Yugoslav and Brazilian experience. Third, analysis of the interaction between regional and local authorities provided an effective way of attacking the policymaking/imple-mentation nexus and gaining new insights into political power and economic relations at the national level. Fourth, in all five cases, despite the wide range of policy choices pursued since World War II, marked regional disparities persist and unbalanced development remains. Fifth, analysis of the field administration construct utilized in each case proved to be by far the most effective way of getting at the centralization/decentralization mix in these countries.

Significance of the Subnational Unit

Once research was completed in all five countries, the decision to focus on political regions (as defined by existing state demarcations) was reassessed

Did each country's intermediate territorial division constitute a more viable unit of analysis than the community for cross-national comparison at the subnational level? In general terms, the answer was yes, but with an important qualification. In Mexico, Romania, and Brazil, local communities did not constitute meaningful subsystems insofar as linkage politics and administration were concerned, but their larger political units—the state and the judet—did. It was to regional political centers in these larger units that economic resources were allocated and political authority delegated. Officials at these regional levels conducted the primary negotiations with local authorities. In contrast, in Portugal and Yugoslavia, although district and republic were much more viable units to work with than local communities, it was difficult to isolate meaningful subsystems linking together regional governmental authorities and community leaders in a way comparable with Mexican, Romanian, and Brazilian experience. Why these differences?

In both Romania and Mexico local government today is more an appendage of regional government than an autonomous subsystem. Although legal descriptions of the national state in both countries emphasize the status of the community as a distinct political unit, the realities of political power and the distribution of economic resources allow little if any effective local autonomy. Each system has its own ideology and rationale, which on the surface make these two countries quite different. Mexico is a mixed economy country with a federal form of government. There constitutional guarantees accord the municipality the status of a sovereign, free, and self-governing entity. Romania is a socialist state with a unitary form of government. The 1968 reforms not only decentralized authority (by ostensibly abandoning the Soviet model for territorial administration and recreating a more traditional form of subnational governance) but emphasized planning as a two-way process (extending upward and downward, linking together communities, regional centers, and the national capital). However, once one moves beyond the formal legal system, both Romania and Mexico are highly centralized states in which great value is placed on control and coordination functions by regional government over local authorities. The systems differ only in degree.

Territorial administration in Romania may be classified as an integrated prefectural government, in which judet party organization and the judet people's council frequently overlap. At the executive level, dual office holding in the party's judet committee and the state's executive committee is common, and prevailing practice is to make the judet first secretary the president of the executive committee and the people's council as well.

Mexico has a more rationalized and disciplined field system, which has moved the country in the direction of an integrated prefectural system. Although the primacy of the governor in state politics has long been an established fact, under López Portillo administrative reforms increased the governor's role in administrative matters through the development of a system of grants-in-aid programs (known as Convenios Unicos de Coordinación—CUC, Programas Integrales de Desarrollo Regional—PIDER, and Comites de Promoción del Desarrollo—COPRODE). Initially classified as an unintegrated prefectural system, Mexican practice approximated more closely the Romanian experience, especially in those states where CUC, PIDER, and COPRODE agreements predominated and where the concern in the center with control over local-level politics was acute—either because of atrophy in the local PRI organization and the rise of strong alternative parties or in response to a revival of organized rural violence.

The Brazilian case differs from Mexican and Romanian experience in that, despite centralized military rule from 1964 to 1985, it continues as one of the rare instances in the developing world of a functioning federal system. Post-1964 Brazil is similar to pre-1964 Brazil at the subnational level in that state political and administrative organizations have real meaning as distinct subsystems only in the more developed regions of the country. In many parts of the northeast, functional federalism has always been more a myth than a reality because of the long-standing dependency of state and local government on central government subsidies. Thus, although the center-periphery dynamic in Brazil is different from that encountered in Mexico and Romania, the state does function as a subsystem from the standpoint of linkage politics, and it provides a way of determining networks of influence and power relationships within the diverse organs of the federal and state government.

In neither Portugal nor Yugoslavia did existing political demarcations at the regional level coincide with meaningful subsystems. For comparative purposes Portugal's experience is the most instructive. At the beginning of the 1960s, in one of his early papers in comparative administration, James Fesler compared and contrasted functional and prefectural field systems of administration. Fesler pointed out that in moving outside the Anglo-American world, one must abandon the concept of field administration as an area primarily of routine administrative concerns and understand that elsewhere such systems are closely tied to politics at the subnational level. In his analysis of prefectural systems he emphasized the primacy of political over administrative functions because of the determination of the center to exercise effective control over the periphery.[13]

In the Portuguese case, official state forms dominant before 1974 prescribed an integrated prefectural system under the district governor system. However, actual implementation of the system never really occurred in continental Portugal. Once vested in the hands of the civil governor, political control over localities never expanded in any coherent way to include administrative services. Some central ministries maintained field offices; others did not. Throughout the history of the New State, no single coherent system of field administration ever emerged; when field services were provided they followed essentially ad hoc criteria. But overseas, in the more developed parts of Angola and Mozambique—where the government was most sensitive t guerrilla incursions—district governors functioned much as their nineteen century counterparts had in France, with ample powers over administra as well as political affairs within their districts. With the coming of the revolution, independence for the colonies, and the consolidation of a democratic regime in mainland Portugal, district governors overseas disappeared, while on the Continent civil governors ceased to have any real function.

Today Portugal's "prefect-governors" continue as representatives of the Lisbon government in the districts, but the field services follow their own individual organizational dynamics, and local governments constitute the real force in subnational politics. Administrative services are bargained for and there is intense competition for central government subsidies. Interviews with twenty-five mayors in the fall of 1981—a sample that included half the municipalities in each of three representative districts—revealed that the dominant criterion determining which communities received central government support was political party allegiance. The basic issue was whether or not the community had voted for the government in power, but when actual funds allocation was examined further it became clear that only those community councils identified with the dominant party in the ruling Democratic Alliance (AD), the PSD—the centrist Social Democrats—reported access to credits and transfers from the central government beyond what the law had provided. Mayors identified with other parties in the AD (independents, CDS—the rightist Social Democratic Center—and PPM—the Popular Monarchists) did not fare much better than the opposition (Socialist or Communist mayors).[14]

Yugoslav experience constitutes the deviant case not only for this five-country study but also for the southern European and Latin American region as a whole. Yugoslavia has a federation of six republics and two autonomous regions based on distinct national communities, in which all basic administrative services devolve to the local level (except for a core group of activities linked to the maintenance of national government). In this context, the republics are larger, more diverse, and more restricted in number than the subnational units of any other country in the region. They compare with Italy's regional governments, functioning since 1972; the regions of the Azores and the Madeira Islands, granted autonomous status under Portugal's 1976 and 1982 constitutions; and recent experimentation in Spain with autonomy for Catalonia and the Basque country. Yet in Italy, Spain, and Portugal, a dominant national community forms a core state that is missing in the Yugoslav federation, even though historically Serbia has been and continues to be the dominant nationality forming and maintaining the Yugoslav state.

Within Yugoslavia's republics there is no effective integrating political and administrative unit between community and republican government. The political districts (zajednice opcina) that do exist have little if any significance. The devolution of responsibility for public services has progressed to such a point in Zagreb, for example, that there is no longer a single metropolitan government for the city but ten separate municipal governments (opcine), of which the centar constitutes only a very small part even of the "old city" (Zagreb's original urban nucleus). The government of greater

Zagreb is made more complex by the fact that two additional opcine in the Zagreb district (*zajednica*) also belong in the urban region defined as Zagreb. The general picture becomes even more complicated when one considers that the basic units in Yugoslav politics and administration are groups of working people and citizens organized into different sets of public organizations: working organizations per se (enterprises), which are grouped together in communities of associated labor; self-managing communities of interest for social security, health, research activity, and education and culture; local government proper, termed local communities; and sociopolitical organizations that are responsible for mass mobilization under state socialism. The theory of the system emphasizes the involvement of citizens at the grass-roots level in all aspects of state and society. But now that the system has become institutionalized and routinized, it is in actual practice a fragmented, stalemated, bureaucratized society, with declining popular participation. The tremendously complex system of competing organizations based in the communities, each jealous of its jurisdiction, is difficult for anyone—even party officials—to transcend.

In all five countries, whether or not the political regions coincided with the existence of a coherent subsystem, they all constituted an effective unit of analysis for comparing cross-nationally the interaction of national, regional, and local authorities.

Unitary Versus Federal

What were the primary determinants of the variations encountered in territorial administration and center-periphery relations? They were (1) degree of concentration of political and administrative authority and (2) the centralization/decentralization mix in field administration systems. Within the five cases studied it was impossible to separate questions of program autonomy and choice of field system from political values identified with the larger governmental system. Explaining these differences required a comprehensive view of the state in which political and administrative organizations were seen as integral parts of the same governmental process. It was not a case of one system being more politicized than another, but simply a question of different policy choices reflecting the degree of concentration of political and administrative authority. In this regard, access to regional and local authorities depended on the responsiveness of these regional and local authorities to citizen groups operating within their own immediate policy environment and the degree to which these authorities had to consult with higher levels of government to resolve programmatic needs in areas under their jurisdiction. Within the five cases, the factor with the greatest amount of explanatory power was subsystem autonomy—whether the system was unitary or federal.

The most notable contrast was in Portugal, where basically the same executive-level bureaucratic officials—those overseeing central government-funded public services at the regional level—served under two very different regimes. The difference in their behavior, in decisionmaking patterns, a in the dynamics affecting center-periphery relations derived from the replacement of an authoritarian regime—closed to those outside accepted ruling circles and rigidly controlled from the center—with a democratic regime, in which local government authorities were directly accountable to local electorates and no longer dependent on district authorities. The altered behavior of mayors after the change of system showed great uniformity. Whether right or left in political affiliation, all became equally concerned with responsiveness to their immediate constituencies and with the provision of basic public services in rural and urban areas alike.

In contrast, Romanian bureaucratic behavior in areas involving the administration of basic public services was the least likely to be responsive to the local community. It reflected instead the directives issued by higher levels of government. Grass-roots organizations put much larger numbers of citizens in immediate and direct contact with the state, but mass mobilization was not necessarily linked to meaningful participation in government.

Table 2 suggests one way of organizing this body of governmental experience in comparative perspective. This table, which is in essence classificatory, is designed to represent visually the complexities encountered in examining intergovernmental management experience in the administration of development programs in five countries across a fifteen-year span. My primary conclusion here is that greater emphasis should be placed on the integrity of the modern state and on the administrative and political dimensions of intergovernmental relations. Understanding the interrelationships among governmental institutions and authorities horizontally and vertically is essential to the analysis of public policy (when the contemporary state is viewed from below) in unitary as well as federal systems of government and in centralized as well as decentralized instances of governmental authority. The intergovernmental relations construct has been identified primarily with federal systems, especially that of the United States, yet in all five cases a complex set of intergovernmental relations and multiple levels of decision-making were clearly involved in all aspects of implementation of development-oriented programs.

When the administration of development-oriented field programs was disaggregated into distinct policy arenas—industrialization policy, urban development policy, and agricultural policy—distinct mixes of political and administrative authority emerged. In Mexico, Portugal, and Romania, industrialization policy was uniformly a consequence of central government decisions. In Portugal, I found not a single instance of involvement by district and local governmental authorities in any significant discussion concerning industrialization, commerce, or even routine business operations for that matter, such as new plant location, expansion of existing facilities, or contract negotiations. In Romania and Mexico, such decisions were also a central government function, involving a constellation of central government rganizations. Where industrialization had already become well established regional centers, regional authorities were able to bargain more effectively

Table 2 VARIATIONS IN THE ADMINISTRATION OF DEVELOPMENT-ORIENTED PROGRAMS

Concentration of Governmental Authority	System of Field Administration			
	Functional		Prefectural	
	Local-level Admin. Units	Regionally Based Admin. Units	Unintegrated Field Admin.	Integrated Field Admin.
Decentralized polit. and admin. authority	Late-1960s Yugoslavia		Post-1974 Portugal	
Regionally based polit. & admin. authority	Yugoslavia after 1971	Pre-1964 Brazil		
Political centralism & admin. federalism		Post-1964 Brazil	Pre-1976 Mexico	Post-1976 Mexico
Centralized polit. & admin. authority			Pre-1974 Portugal	Ceausescu's Romania

with the national government. Such negotiations by local officials and managers of local industries with central government authorities gave regional and local authorities considerable weight in obtaining additional governmental resources, thereby triggering additional economic growth and diversification in their regions.

Though the patterns of state organization differed considerably in Romania and Mexico, in both the underdeveloped regions were dependent on central government resources and decisionmaking while the developed regions enjoyed relative autonomy. Falling within the developed-region category were Brasov in Romania (where I interviewed judet and municipal officials during a January 1977 exploratory field trip) and Monterrey in Mexico (researched through analysis of the business conglomerate known as the Alfa Group and the role played by leading local industrialists during the Luis Echeverria government). The decisionmaking pattern encountered in Iasi in Romania and Tabasco in Mexico was also similar. Both are under-developed regions undergoing marked socioeconomic change. In the former, the primary stimulus was the commitment of the Ceausescu government to the economic modernization of Iasi, a region considered to be part of the irreducible core of the Romanian state. In Tabasco, the development of petroleum and gas resources in the Reforma area (just across the state line in Chiapas) and the development of port facilities and corresponding economic expansion in Villahermosa (the governmental, market, and residential center for the region) has produced accelerated patterns of socioeconomic change. In each instance, however, the policies designed to channel economic growth, to handle socioeconomic change, and to provide technical and material support were all determined by the central government.

In contrast, urban development policy was the policy arena in which regional governmental authorities were likely to exercise the greatest amount of influence and discretion. In Braga, Viseu, and Evora in Portugal; in Cluj, Iasi, and Buzau in Romania; and in Morelia, Oaxaca, and Villahermosa in Mexico, decisions related to the improvement of public services in the regional capital involved regional governmental authorities primarily and municipal authorities in the city proper only secondarily. In all cases but one, routine urban services (water and wastewater services, garbage collection and street cleaning, regulation of the local public market, public transportation) were the province of municipal authorities, but anything related to major capital investments required the support and assistance of regional governmental authorities. The one instance of disarticulation of interests between municipal and district authorities was in Evora, Portugal, where the opposition APU alliance was in the majority and the mayor was a member of the Portuguese Communist party (PCP). There, as in the case of Uruapan (a regional Mexican commercial and population center analyzed in my 1971 monograph), ·hen the city was captured by the opposition National Action Party (PAN) the late 1960s, the city was largely bypassed in questions concerning ·tal improvements. In Evora, decisions affecting its economic well-being ·handled by resident governmental and political personalities identified with the national regime, in collaboration with regional and central government authorities There was little or no consultation with municipal authorities.

In each of the five countries, agricultural policy depended on a set of dynamics removed from the control of the officials charged with responsibility for implementing such programs. Of the three policy arenas, policy change and innovation was least likely to occur in agricultural policy. In all five cases, questions of agricultural policy were intimately related to questions of regime, ideology, and previous historical commitments of the national government. Likewise, governmental offices involved in agricultural policy were the most responsive to central government directives and the most likely to operate independently of other regional authorities. In both Romania and Mexico there was a pattern of dual subordination, but it was clearly the national links that were the most important. In Romania, few central ministries had their own field services. The principle of debureaucratization had led to the establishment of parallel regional services under the control of regional authorities, and technical responsibilities were vested in the central ministry while executive oversight was concentrated in the hands of regional authorities (national-regional dual subordination). In Mexico and Portugal, the pattern of dual subordination accentuated an older and more traditional pattern in which central government field services exercised a great deal of autonomy in attending to their more technical and routine responsibilities.

The same three policy areas—industrialization, urban development, and agriculture—were also examined in Yugoslavia and Brazil to see if functional federalism produced notably different patterns. On first inspection—prior to undertaking new research on Brazil—it appeared that these patterns were not notably different. But once I acquired new data from the Brazilian states and subjected my research on the Republic of Croatia, within the Yugoslav federation, to the same scrutiny applied to Portugal, Romania, and Mexico, I came to the opposite conclusion.[15] The primary difference between the two sets of experiences is in the complexity of intergovernmental relations and the autonomy accorded to regional authorities. Both Brazil and Yugoslavia have three tiers of political and administrative authorities, with regional and local officials exercising influence nearly as great as the national government in the arenas ascribed to their jurisdiction. Although the content of regional autonomy differs from the classic cases of federalism (United States, Canada, Australia), it is no less meaningful, even though Yugoslavia and Brazil have pronounced authoritarian political practices.

Brazil differs from Yugoslavia primarily in terms of the greater weight given to the private sector and the variation in the degree of autonom enjoyed by individual states. In Brazil the capacity of state governments function autonomously is derived from the strength of the regional econo (as, for example, in the state of São Paulo) or the effectiveness of re elites in extracting resources from the national government (such a case with the state of Bahia). There the economic and political available to regional elites are distributed unequally and many of the smaller, less well developed states are outright dependencies of the federal government.

Yugoslavia differs from Brazil, first of all, in that its republics are identified with distinct cultural and historical groupings among the South Slavs. An additional cause is the regime's commitment to decentralization. The complex system of governance emergent in post-Tito Yugoslavia is also the consequence of self-contained bureaucracies within the republics, organized around units of production, particular sets of public services, and numerous economic entities making independent judgments on marketing, pricing, and investment.

Regional/Local Interaction

The third finding of this comparative project is that the pattern of interaction established in all political systems between regional and local authorities is a crucial component of the policy process, especially insofar as implementation practices are concerned. In all five cases the crucial component was how regional and local officials fulfilled brokerage roles. Even when regional officials had lost oversight powers over local authorities (post-1974 Portugal) and municipal officials belonging to an opposition party had directly challenged the ruling coalition (Mexico), role expectations centered around how well officials had handled their brokerage functions.

It is important to note that in Portugal and Mexico, electoral victory by an opposition party at the local level did not necessarily provoke a breakdown in brokerage activities. It was only when an opposition party belonged to the category of antisystem forces that normal patterns for negotiating external community resources were ruptured—for example, with the PCP in Portugal and PAN in Mexico. In contrast, victory by the Socialist party (PS) in Portugal in local elections did not noticeably alter the situation for a local mayor and his council anymore than did victory by one of the minority parties in the ruling alliance, the CDS or the PPM. In Mexico, by the same token, coalition councils formed by the PRI with small leftist parties in several Oaxaca communities did not affect brokerage patterns until irreconcilable conflicts emerged in one of them (Juchitan de Zaragoza).

Elsewhere, prevailing patterns of influence and power were centered around routinized brokerage activities. The effectiveness of a judet first vice-president (the figure in Romanian regional executive committees charged with overseeing administrative activities) was linked to his capacity to influence others in the judet executive committee and in the central government regarding the desirability of this or that action. When available public funds were limited, especially in less-developed regions that were more dependent on national government subsidies and transfers, interpersonal ᴿ ations and the ability to influence national policymakers was crucial. In ᴵ ico, one can speak of the brokerage functions of municipal presidents ᴼ overnors alike. In Portugal, civil governors exercised similar supervisory ᴼ kerage functions before 1974, but this ended with the consolidation ᴼ ocratic regime after 1976.

The patterns encountered in Brazil and Yugoslavia were similar to those found in Mexico, Portugal, and Romania. On first inspection Brazilian practice most closely approximated the experience of Mexico, but the size and complexity of Brazilian government at the state level added an element not found in Mexico. Both countries had experienced tremendous growth in autonomous agencies, institutes, and commissions outside the traditional ministerial core of the national government, but Mexican state governments did not begin to approach the bureaucratic development that Brazilian state governments had undergone in this fifteen-year period, especially in the more developed region of the country (the Center-South).

Yugoslav practice differed in the emphasis placed on debureaucratization at the national level and the shifting of public service responsibilities to individual republics and communities, but there too the size and complexity of each republic's government introduced a second tier of authorities and actions not present in Romania, Mexico, or Portugal. The brokerage function of the president of the Communal Assembly (the political executive) and the president of the Executive Council (the administrative executive in charge of local administration) involved negotiations with a much larger number of local groups and institutions than was the case in the other four countries. The channels of access and linkages between local communities and republican institutions centered in regional capitals were also more numerous.

Uneven Development

From the standpoint of the wider comparative intent of this project, the most interesting finding in researching, in traveling, and in interviewing throughout these countries was the way in which long-standing patterns of unbalanced development have been reinforced, not resolved, in all five cases—despite the wide range of developmental strategies pursued since the Second World War. Italy has been the harbinger of developmental outcome for all five—be they mixed or socialist economies, authoritarian or nonauthoritarian regimes. Within the range of countries embraced by southern Europe and Latin America, Italy is the most developed; that is to say, the furthest advanced in developing uniform market structures throughout its national territory and in building an industrialized society with a commercialized and productive agriculture. This is far from the deviant case role so often ascribed to Italy by Europeanists comparing Italian politics, economics, and society with patterns established in northwestern Europe. All five countries studied here reflected the same juxtaposition of development and underdevelopment. The patterns of growth are proceeding apace in the already more developed regions, while the underdeveloped areas have remained underdeveloped despite growth in these regions' urban cente and much change in political, social, and economic institutions over last half-century. In Romania, centralized state planning and commit to balanced economic growth through reallocation of resources to ta underdeveloped regions has not substantially lessened the devel contrasts. This is not to belittle the very real economic progress m

World War II, for Romania is certainly not the underdeveloped agrarian state it was before the war. But the same may be said of any of the other states included in this study and within this region at large.

In Yugoslavia, development strategies since 1948 have rejected the Stalinist model in favor of self-management and self-government concepts. To replace central economic planning and directives, an elaborate scheme was developed whereby republican and federal funds and transfers would provide the working capital to transform underdeveloped regions. Yet Yugoslavia entered the 1980s—with its problems of worldwide inflation, irregular energy supply, and a slowdown of economic growth rates—with its own great regional disparities intact. In Yugoslavia, economic differences are compounded by cultural differences; the areas that are least Western, where Islamic and Turkish influence remain strongest, are also the least developed. In contrast, the most Western region of the country, Slovenia—the republic adjacent to Austria and Italy, which was an integral part of the developed areas of Austria under the Dual Monarchy—has socioeconomic characteristics comparable to the industrialized regions of Europe.

Analyzing the Centralization/Decentralization Mix

The fifth finding concerns patterns of field administration and the centralization/decentralization mix. The review of the literature conducted during the research design stage and later expanded by in-country research (through consulting source material in the language of each society) identified essentially three models for field administration. But once the information for all five cases was compared systematically and individual case-study work on Mexico, Romania, and Portugal was successfully completed, this categorization of field administration systems required adjustment. As noted in Table 2, the variations encountered dictated a distinction between type of field system on one axis and different mixes of political and administrative authority on another.

The distinction between integrated and unintegrated prefectural systems served to organize data collected in Mexico, Portugal, and Romania, but a single functional model failed to account for the variation encountered in Brazil and Yugoslavia. In the former, central ministries maintained an elaborate field administration apparatus organized on a regional basis according to each organization's needs. Parallel to these was a variety of governmental agencies staffed by individual state governments—similar to the U.S. system. In the latter, federal and republican agencies had few if any field offices. Virtually all client-centered services were administered through community-based organizations, while republican and federal-level administrative activity was restricted essentially to supervisory and coordination responsibilities—except for a few core functions (defense and foreign relations) that remained the exclusive prerogative of the national government. At the local level, there were essentially two sets of grass-roots organizations: local services per se, housed in the offices of the local government, social services regulated through what are known as self-managing communities of interest. Coordination theoretically occurred through an elaborate delegate and assembly system, which followed a progressively narrower base of representation as one moved upward from neighborhood or work unit to community to republic to federation. With policy guidelines being developed at the national and republican levels through assemblies, commissions, and committees, responsibility for implementation was vested primarily in community-based organizations, in which individual citizen representation and collective decisionmaking were maximized.

Distinct from these issues of territorial organization were questions concerning the concentration of governmental authority. This concept became essential to distinguish among the very different administrative patterns encountered in pre-1964 and post-1964 Brazil and in pre-1974 and post-1974 Portugal.

In Yugoslavia, a distinction must be drawn between administration through self-regulating, community-based organizations and through stringent political controls. Much has been written about the authoritarian responses to what is known as the Croatian spring of 1971 and the crackdown imposed by Tito over the movement toward a more open society in Croatia. But little if anything has been written about the significance of this return to authoritarian practices for day-to-day administration, the negative impact it had on problem-solving and policy experimentation during the 1970s, or the stasis it has produced as this system of government has moved into the 1980s. The current stalemate results in part from the consensus required on all major issues of a political, social, and economic nature now that Tito is dead. In the past, what made Tito's Yugoslavia a federation was the cement that he and the party, the League of Communists of Yugoslavia (LCY), provided for the system, offsetting and balancing the powers granted to the republics. The collective management principle that went into effect with his demise and the obligation that all levels of government follow the model set by the example of the national collegial executive has reduced the historic role of the party. Although Serbs have always constituted the dominant element in the party and the military, increasingly the military alone is the most effective federal or national institution and the major force holding together the Yugoslav state. The party, in contrast, reflects the stalemate so visible in the external governmental system.

This last point provides the conclusion to this chapter, with its overview of data collected over the last decade on public administration in Latin America and southern Europe, through attention to five country case studies. To explain variations in administrative behavior among them required returning to the larger political context within which they operated and developing an integral view of the state. The sum of these experiences has been to heighten my understanding of politics, although my original goa was to increase my knowledge of administrative problems linked to d velopment issues in a cross-cultural context. In a world in which so m of public policy is made and determined within bureaucratic organs o state, this analysis of public organizations has led to a reencounte politics. Authoritarianism under capitalism as well as socialism has indeed produced a new administrative state that warrants comparative analysis in a way that defies existing divisions between East and West and transcends current ideological differences. For, regardless of ideological content and variations in political theory, it is unrestrained bureaucracy that has always been and remains the source of the destruction of democracy.

NOTES

1. Although this literature is extensive, in my estimation the most useful recent text providing an overview of the policy approach in general political science, with full reference to the increased methodological sophistication in this field, is Stuart S. Nagel's *Public Policy: Goals, Means, and Methods* (New York: St. Martin's Press, 1984).

2. Most reference lists of the implementation literature begin with Jeffrey L. Pressman and Aaron Wildavsky's *Implementation* (Berkeley: University of California Press, 1973). However, for the beginning student, the best place to start is with a book that sums up the state of our knowledge in this field, before taking on the monographic literature. An excellent overview of this literature is to be found in Robert T. Nakamura and Frank Smallwood, *The Politics of Policy Implementation* (New York: St. Martin's Press, 1980).

3. B. Guy Peters, "Comparative Public Policy," *Policy Studies Review* 1 (August 1981):183–197.

4. Representative source material summarizing these developments and illustrating this shift in comparative politics include Richard Rose, "Comparing Public Policy: An Overview," *European Journal of Political Research* 1 (1973):67–94; David R. Cameron and Richard I. Hofferbert, "The Impact of Federalism on Education Finance: A Comparative Analysis," *European Journal of Political Research* 2 (1974):225–258; Hugh Heclo, "Frontiers of Social Policy in Europe and America," *Policy Sciences* 6 (1975):403–421; T. Alexander Smith, *The Comparative Public Policy: The Politics of Social Choice in Europe and America* (New York: St. Martin's Press, 1975). For a very good overview of bureaucratic politics in comparative perspective and why questions of administration are central to cross-national work on the state, consult B. Guy Peters, *The Politics of Bureaucracy*, 2d ed. (New York: Longman, 1984).

5. When dealing with the southern European states, Allan Williams makes the observation that one is speaking more correctly of a "semi-peripheral area." This concept will be used here but with one important modification: It will be expanded to include as equally relevant to this discussion the socialist states of southeastern Europe. Williams, in contrast, limits his discussion to Greece, Italy, Spain, and Portugal. See Allan Williams, ed., *Southern Europe Transformed: Political and Economic Change in Greece, Italy, Portugal, and Spain* (London: Harper & Row, 1984), especially his introductory chapter, pp. 1–26.

6. For those interested in the rationale for grouping together the southern European and Latin American states for purposes of comparing their experiences with modernization and development, see the discussion in Lawrence S. Graham, *Romania: A Developing Socialist State* (Boulder, CO: Westview Press, 1982), pp. xi–xv, 7–10, and the wider theoretical framework provided by Fernand Braudel, *The Mediterranean and Mediterranean World in the Age of Philip II* (New York: Harper & Row, 1973), 13–43, 53–66, 75–78, 160–170, 231–246 (vol. 1); 757–776, 826–827, 1238–1244).

7. I began the project with fluency already established in Spanish and Portuguese, but in the process had to acquire a working knowledge of French, Italian, Romanian, and the Croatian variant of Serbo-Croat. In working through the relevant literature in these six languages plus English and interviewing governmental authorities in each of them, I ran into one of the classic problems Giovanni Sartori alluded to in "Concept Misformation in Comparative Politics," *American Political Science Review* 64,4 (December 1970):1033–1053. Whereas the term "intergovernmental relations" developed in studies of U.S. federalism is the accepted term for the field of public administration, in a comparative, cross-national context readers unfamiliar with this terminology in writings on U.S. politics and bureaucracy may find my use of it confusing. Throughout this chapter "intergovernmental relations" refers to relations among distinct levels of government (national, regional, and local) and not to relations between distinct nation-states and their respective governments.

8. This review is summarized in Lawrence S. Graham, "Centralization versus Decentralization Dilemmas in the Administration of Public Services," *International Review of Administrative Sciences* 3 (1980):219–232.

9. All by Lawrence S. Graham: *Mexican State Government: A Prefectural System in Action* (Austin: Institute of Public Affairs, University of Texas, 1971); *Romania*; "Bureaucratic Politics and the Problem of Reform in the State Apparatus," in *In Search of Modern Portugal: The Revolution and Its Consequences*, ed. Lawrence S. Graham and Douglas L. Wheeler (Madison: University of Wisconsin Press, 1983); and "O Estado Português visto a partir de baixo," *Análise Social* 18, no. 72-74 (April–December 1982):959–974.

10. With the ending of its twenty-year-old authoritarian regime in sight, I undertook new research on Brazil in 1983–1984, which included a field component in summer 1984. The results of that research are reported in two articles, "The Revival of Brazilian Federalism," in *Latin America and Caribbean Contemporary Record*, ed. Jack W. Hopkins, vol. 3 (1983–1984) (New York: Holmes and Meier, 1985), pp. 207–218, and "The Role of the States in the Brazilian Federation," in *Subnational Politics in the 1980s: Organization, Reorganization, and Economic Development*, eds. Louis A. Picard and Raphael Zariski (New York: Praeger, 1987). A book-length study summing up the results of the long-term research project and reassessing their import for the analysis of the state and public policy in the Latin American context is available as *The State and Policy Delivery in the Latin American Vortex* (New York: Hoover Institution Series, Praeger, forthcoming).

11. This distinction among first-order, second-order, and third-order development questions is adapted from John D. Montgomery, *Technology and Civic Life: Making and Implementing Development Decisions* (Cambridge, MA: MIT Press, 1974).

12. This information is contained in "Portugal: The Bureaucracy of Empire," *LADAC Occasional Papers* (Austin: Institute of Latin American Studies, University of Texas, 1973), my two end-of-grant reports filed with the National Academy of Sciences for research in Romania (1977–1978) and Yugoslavia (1981), and Chapter 4, "Policy Outcomes in a Quasi-Federal Republic: The Case of Mexico," in *The State and Policy Outcomes in the Latin American Vortex* (New York: Hoover Institution Series, Praeger, forthcoming). Between the time the first draft of this manuscript was completed (1984) and the final study was submitted and accepted for publication (1989), an additional Mexican state was added. This was the state of Nuevo León, with i capital city of Monterrey, where field research was conducted during the summer 1987. Other new fieldwork involved in the final study includes research in B· summer 1984; Portugal, summer 1984 and spring 1987; Colombia, summer and Nicaragua, summer 1986.

13. James W. Fesler, "The Political Role of Field Administration," in *Papers in Comparative Public Administration*, ed. Ferrell Heady and Sybil L. Stokes (Ann Arbor: Institute of Public Administration, University of Michigan, 1962), pp. 117–143.

14. The breakdown of these data, percentages, and overall assessment of the Portuguese case is contained in "O Estado Português," pp. 959–976. This article is the revised version of a paper prepared for the colloquium "A Formação de Portugal Contemporânea: 1900–1980," Lisbon, 2–5 December 1981.

15. Detailed analysis of Brazilian and Yugoslav experience along these lines is available in Lawrence S. Graham, "Yugoslav and Brazilian Experience with Federalism," *Technical Paper*, no. 41 (Austin: Institute of Latin American Studies, University of Texas, 1984).

10

Bureaucratic-Authoritarianism, Transitions to Democracy, and the Political-Culture Dimension

JOHN D. MARTZ

At one juncture in his monumental intellectual synthesis of the so-called modern world system, Immanuel Wallerstein enunciated an eloquent denigration of disciplinary separations within the social sciences. Among many other things, he declared that

> when one studies a social system, the classical lines of division within social science are meaningless. . . . They make a certain limited sense if the focus of one's study is organizations. They make none at all if the focus is the study of social systems, but for a unidisciplinary approach.[1]

The point is important, although the debate is scarcely new or fresh. Whatever the Circean seductiveness of this position, students of comparative politics as a practical matter customarily find their collective analytical capacities sorely tried by the need to incorporate widely, even wildly, disparate political systems, to say nothing of the need to integrate insights and expertise from several disciplines. Among the complicating divisions of the past quarter-century have been those that distinguish analysts of the Third World from scholars who concentrate on the Western industrializing states.

This has created countless problems, at least a few of which are alluded to in later passages. But the tendency within comparative politics to erect sturdy if often artificial barriers is being progressively eroded both by political events and intellectual perspectives. Recent developments have drawn upon direct experience throughout the world. The apparent authoritarian impulse of the 1970s has given way to a wave of democratic transitions, heartening to all those who value such systems. Whatever one's ideological proclivities the fact remains that such changes—from the Philippines to Argentina ar~ incorporating such intermediate if incomplete and qualified cases as Sou

Korea and Pakistan—demand systematic and concerted attention. For comparativists, the obvious task is that of undertaking an explanation of such transitions.

Approaches to understanding social change, regime stability, and their manifest permutations have customarily shared two broad characteristics. First, they tend to mount strong attacks on previous theorizing, out of which new ideas then germinate. In addition, their exclusivistic claims to new insights scarcely obscure the fact that a cumulative process is operative. Consequently, approaches coming under fire from new intellectual perspectives will at the same time make their own contribution to subsequent theorizing. In this chapter three heuristically important conceptual patternings are reviewed: bureaucratic-authoritarian (B-A) models, the variegated forms of transition to democracy, and a renaissance of the culturalist perspective. The character and utility of such explanatory models will necessarily and properly constitute our major preoccupation.

THE BUREAUCRATIC-AUTHORITARIAN IMPULSE

By the close of the 1960s and the opening of the next decade, heightened intellectual ferment among comparativists intersected with political events to stimulate new conceptual trends. A malaise concerning modernization theory and liberal developmentalism had spread, increasingly attacked and challenged by dependency theory. Where major spokespeople of the former current were in most cases from the United States, *dependencia* originated with Latin American scholars and was subsequently buttressed by other Third World intellectuals. This reinforced the symbiosis between scholarship and politics, with many party-based liberal democracies in Latin America having deteriorated or been replaced by proliferating military regimes. Events encouraged the observation that existing theoretical frameworks "were inadequate to analyze the important role of the state in Latin America or to deal with the complex process by which the interactions between the state and organized societal groupings have been structured and restructured over time."[2] Attention was drawn especially to the Southern Cone, where modernizing authoritarian regimes characterized by delayed dependent development took hold. One by-product was the 1973 publication of Guillermo O'Donnell's highly influential *Modernization and Bureaucratic-Authoritarianism.*[3]

Accepting many premises of dependency literature and its major theorists, he presented a thoughtfully sophisticated study of the trend toward authoritarianism in Latin America. An examination of Brazil and, especially, Argentina emphasized "dependent capitalist development." As economies moved beyond import substitution to deepening industrialization, conditions promoted the control or elimination of populist forces through a repressive state apparatus. The developmental process would thereafter be stimulated essentially through the work of a technocratic elite operating in tandem with the armed forces. The installation of these authoritarian governments, brief, assured the adoption of harsh actions against democratic sectors to curb their participatory role in politics. These new systems would be geared to centralized control of public policy. For O'Donnell, it was a logical supposition that the modernization process in developing areas naturally led to authoritarianism. In contemporary South America, therefore, "the higher and lower levels of modernization are associated with nondemocratic political systems, while political democracies are found at the intermediate levels of modernization."[4]

At the outset, it was the Argentine and Brazilian experiences that led O'Donnell to argue that, contrary to earlier theories, economic progress would encourage neither democracy nor revolution but rather military-dominated bureaucratic-authoritarianism. In due course he extended the analytic net to suggest the heuristic potential in adopting bureaucratic-authoritarianism for such states as Mexico, Spain, and Greece. B-A features were anticipated as likely political characteristics in such countries as South Korea, Indonesia, and the Philippines.[5] Such speculation, on which O'Donnell exercised self-restraint, nonetheless encouraged others to overgeneralize. This tendency eventually exacerbated growing discontent with the B-A perspective, especially as the authoritarian regimes of the 1970s were in most cases supplanted by elected governments in the 1980s. Consequently, it has become far from uncommon to encounter assessments of the O'Donnell position in which it is described as relevant "only to a limited number of cases and for only a very limited period of time, and therefore . . . of little help in generating broad-gauged theory."[6]

Before bureaucratic-authoritarian theorizing became a small-scale cottage industry, O'Donnell and a thoughtful band of comparativists had fortuitously examined the original formulation empirically in *The New Authoritarianism*.[7] This proved an instructive and insightful demonstration of the relative strengths and weaknesses of B-A theory. A host of Latin and North American scholars strongly questioned and in some instances rejected the "industrial deepening" economic explanation of authoritarianism. David Collier in particular offered a polite but sharp critique in his summary chapter. In the process of separating out major components of bureaucratic-authoritarianism, he questioned the important B-A contention that the crisis of import substitution had been a basic explanatory variable powerfully promoting authoritarianism in the late 1960s and thereafter. Furthermore, writing for a volume that appeared in 1979, he saw that more competitive regimes were likely to replace authoritarian governments in the near future. Consequently, research would be required to dissect such democratic restorations. It would also be essential

> to consider the possibility that . . . a restoration of democracy would be part of a long-term cycle of authoritarianism and democracy within the region and that attempts to understand the prospects for democratization should be linked to attempts to explain this long-term cycle of change.[8]

O'Donnell himself proceeded to reformulate and refine his conceptu- ization, often in a continuing dialogue with both critics and advocates included alternative models of the authoritarian impulse.[9] An especially constructive exchange revolved about the 1982 critique by Karen L. Remmer and Gilbert W. Merkx. They summarized perhaps better than any other reviewers the strengths and concomitant problems found in O'Donnell's theoretical contributions to the literature. First, he had begun by concentrating with singular effectiveness on the rise of redefined authoritarianism while devoting limited attention to the subsequent consolidation of bureaucratic-authoritarianism. Second, he had proceeded by extending his conceptualization to nations far beyond the Southern Cone. Yet, as they saw it, his description of B-A phases seemed to generalize from the Brazilian experience, which they argued was insufficient for broad generalization. Ultimately, they held, an understanding of bureaucratic-authoritarianism demanded "more systematic and empirically grounded comparisons among cases and consideration of a broader range of explanations of postcoup developments."[10]

O'Donnell's response, which illuminated many issues without resolving them, nonetheless sharpened insights into the dynamics of the bureaucratic-authoritarian impulse.[11] Moreover, his own personal theorizing progressed with increasingly incisive exploration of political reality in his native Argentina. A prime example was O'Donnell's exhaustive examination of the regime in Buenos Aires during 1966–1973, where the subtleties of his analyses were directed at the nation's political elite.[12] Without question, his characterization of bureaucratic-authoritarian regimes had vividly encapsulated the level of terror and torture that became an all-too-familiar, institutionalized feature. In terms of broader comparativist concerns, however, this literature was hard-pressed to surmount its theoretical limitations. For O'Donnell, there was an eventual abandonment of the seductive but unproductive effort to theorize generally about the state. As a result, bureaucratic-authoritarianism came to be viewed as descriptive of a type of regime rather than a type of state.[13]

In the end, students of Third World regimes beyond the boundaries of the Southern Cone were destined to consider bureaucratic-authoritarianism critically and at length. However, it was evident that the conditions and circumstances found in many individual cases significantly diluted the conceptual value of B-A theory. It had tended to overgeneralize from a limited number of specific cases. As Jorge Domínguez put it, the rise of authoritarian regimes from the late 1960s in Latin America had constituted a reflection of political instability, not the fundamental emergence of new regimes. Furthermore, a "herd effect" had driven scholars to untrammeled conceptual exaggeration.[14] Among the more perspicacious assessments, delivered during the heyday of B-A theoretical popularity, was Douglas Chalmers's skepticism about the true universality of its applicability. In his words,

The enduring quality of Latin American politics in this century may not be particular form of regime, but rather the fact of change and the quality of ▪litics in any regime which has only a short history and the prospect of a brief future. It is always possible that the cycles of varied types of regimes have come to an end.[15]

The bureaucratic-authoritarian impulse, in short, had benefited from the increasingly apparent problems in applying modernization theory; from the course of political events in Latin America; and as a consequence of O'Donnell's dense reasoning and scholarly theorizing. Although this perspective was too subtle to suggest a unidimensional explanation, the emphasis on the economic variable was undeniable. In time, even as O'Donnell refined and reshaped his own thinking, the B-A concept attracted critics who questioned its relevance beyond a limited number of nations, who were confounded by efforts to apply its features in the stage of regime consolidation, and who sought to document in analytic terms the progressive demise of authoritarian regimes. This in turn powerfully nudged comparativists away from discussions of democratic breakdown, refocusing their attention on the dismaying array of newly democratizing nations progressively emerging throughout the Third World.

TRANSITIONS TO DEMOCRACY

Following publication of their ambitious *Breakdown of Democratic Regimes,* Juan Linz and Alfred Stepan called for a new research agenda. High priority, they argued, "should now be given to the analysis of the conditions that lead to the breakdown of authoritarian regimes, to the process of transition from authoritarian to democratic regimes, and especially to the political dynamics of the consolidation of postauthoritarian democracies."[16] Within a short time, this advice was being strongly underlined by changing political realities. It was not surprising, as James Malloy remarked, that scholarly attention "shifted from the military overthrow of civilian regimes and Latin American authoritarianism toward the prospects and processes of redemocratization."[17] Two major collaborative efforts—one of which is not yet complete—have marked the democratization thrust of comparativists.

The first, a seven-year project organized by the Latin American Program of the Woodrow Wilson Center, involved three editors and nearly two dozen contributors in producing the massive *Transitions from Authoritarian Rule: Prospects for Democracy* (1986).[18] The second project is focusing on democracy in developing countries, with individual chapters for twenty-six nations presented in separate volumes on Asia, Africa, and Latin America. The broad overview will be published in a fourth installment under the subtitle "Persistence, Failure, and Renewal."[19] Originating with a December 1985 conference funded largely by the National Endowment for Democracy, this undertaking in conjunction with the Wilson project helps to illustrate both the strengths and weaknesses that have characterized the study of democracy and democratic transitions.

For works of this genre, the initial question relates to authors' definition of democracy; the absence of any clear consensus is scarcely surprising. the case of *Democracy in Developing Countries,* the coeditors—Larry Diame

Linz, and Seymour Martin Lipset—proffer their unqualified declaration that
political democracy is a concept well worth valuing and studying as an end
in itself. Consequently, they are willing "to state quite clearly here our bias
for democracy as a system of government."[20] In the process, they also deny
that economic and social rights are more important than civil and political
liberties. Indeed, they avowedly restrict their use of the term "democracy"
to the political realm, separate from the economic and social system. A
distinctive aspect of their approach is the insistence that issues of social
and economic democracy be separated from questions of government structure.

> Otherwise, the definitional criteria of democracy will be broadened and the
> empirical reality narrowed to a degree that may make study of the phenomena
> very difficult. In addition, unless the economic and social dimensions are kept
> conceptually distinct from the political, there is no way to analyze how variation
> on the political dimension is related to variation on the others.[21]

Diamond and colleagues further underline their concerns by identifying
three essential, preeminently political conditions for their study of democracy:
competition, participation, and civil/political liberties. In all of this they
embrace not only political democracy but also the concept of stability as a
critical dependent variable. This requires examination of the persistence of
democratic and other regimes over time, especially through times of conflict.
Their definitional narrowing of emphasis to the political dimension stands
in contrast to the investigators for the Wilson study, who were inclined to
examine democracy through different optics. Despite an insistence on their
pro-democratic normative leanings, these editors left a powerful impression
that in their hearts they believed the ideal form of governance might be
rather different. In the closing paragraph of the entire work, for example,
O'Donnell and Philippe Schmitter hinted as much in contending that political
democracy is the product less of unity and consensus than of stalemate.

> Transition toward democracy is by no means a linear or a rational process.
> There is simply too much uncertainty about capabilities and too much suspicion
> about intentions for that. Only once the transition has passed . . . can one
> expect political democracy to induce a more reliable awareness of convergent
> interests.[22]

Most of the contributors shared the editors' relative malaise with liberal
democracy, evidently preferring the quest for a highly participatory form of
social and economic democracy. Among the results is a preoccupation with
transitions rather than with political democracy per se, which reflects the
challenge to the bureaucratic-authoritarian paradigm as its representative
regimes began to drop from the scene, shattering the aura of inevitability.
Such political changes emanated "from the very presence of democracy in
countries once thought doomed to endless authoritarianism as a byproduct
the political dynamics of peripheral capitalism."[23] As Daniel Levine

observed, *Transitions* consistently presented a distinction between political liberalization and a broader definition of democratization that also encompassed social equity and economic justice.

The diverse definitional perspectives found respectively in *Transitions* and *Democracy in Developing Countries* are instructive in epitomizing classic debates on democracy. As I wrote elsewhere, the roots of the Greek derivation *demokratia* provide the bases for contemporary debate over which the two overarching traditions eternally compete.[24] The more restrictive version, which Diamond and associates espouse, places emphasis on institutionalization. In an earlier discussion, Alexander Wilde used the following language:

> "Democracy" can be defined in more restricted, procedural terms as those rules that allow (although they do not necessarily bring about) genuine competition for authoritative political roles. No effective political office should be excluded from such competition, nor should opposition be suppressed by force. More specifically, such rules would include freedom of speech, press, and assembly, and the provision of regular institutional mechanisms for obtaining consent and permitting change of political personnel (normally, elections).[25]

The more all-inclusive definition, which constitutes the operative base for the Wilson study, drives its proponents toward an implicit championing of social change. Coming from a belief that critical theory should produce an altering of injustice and oppression, they are inevitably dissatisfied with practical institutional arrangements that emphasize accommodation and compromise. Negotiations among elites become undemocratic, whereas the legitimacy of elite-mass linkages are ignored or undervalued. Levine is sharp in charging that the editors of *Transitions* not only "pay little heed to democracy as a coherent political system" but "are unhappy with the outcomes democracies produce, and consistently look beyond existing or likely democracies to better alternatives—presumably some form of socialism."[26]

It should be noted that by no means all of the contributors shared the views of the editors. Furthermore, the editors' outlook was scarcely an anomaly in the literature. In a three-country study drawing upon the democracies of Colombia, Costa Rica, and Venezuela, for instance, John Peeler holds that liberal democracy masks an elitist concentration of power and that popular participation is illusory. He sees structural accommodation between elites as strengthening immobilism and shielding the socioeconomic status quo.[27] This view, at the same time, stands in contrast to that of the editors of *Democracy in Developing Countries*, who cite the 1980s as a time for the development of "a renewed and deeper appreciation for the democratic institutions that, with all their procedural messiness and sluggishness, nevertheless protect the integrity of the person and the freedoms of conscience and expression."[28] As a result, notwithstanding the cynicism over political democracy earlier engendered by bureaucratic-authoritarian regimes, the collapse of such dictatorships—including those in southern Europe in the 1970s—"along with the revalorization of political democracy as an en itself . . . has now refocused the attention of the scholarly world on the conditions for liberal democracy."[29]

The scholarly impulse concerning regime transition was further demonstrated by two compendia edited respectively by Malloy and Mitchell A. Seligson and by Enrique A. Baloyra. The former concentrated on the Southern Cone, the Andes, and Central America. Seligson reflected a positive attitude toward liberal democracy, rejecting the old conventional wisdom about the "natural" authoritarianism of Latin America, whereas his coeditor emphasized at greater length the theoretical challenge of emergent democracy to bureaucratic-authoritarianism.

> Latin America's recent experiences with authoritarianism demonstrate that the argument for the existence of a powerful cultural predisposition to authoritarianism is quite wrong. At most, authoritarian propensities exist alongside equally powerful predilections for some mode of competitive politics in a constitutional framework.[30]

Malloy saw the country studies as leading toward two observations. First, the wide diversity precludes the development of broad models or theories of democratic governance; and, second, the linkage between recurring economic issues and regime shifts is not deterministic. Thus, scholars should concentrate on issues, problems, and trends with which the political actors must contend. In brief, there is no better approach for studying what may well be "the best and worst of times for democracy in Latin America," with its future "far from certain."[31]

In *Comparing New Democracies*,[32] the southern European experience as well as that of selected South American nations is presented in order to study both the transition to and consolidation of "new democracies." Baloyra describes democracy in political rather than social and economic terms. This he differentiates from the process of democratization, which involves implementation of the agenda of political transition on behalf of democracy. His introduction provides a rigorous application of terminology—fortunately elaborated in a separate glossary—designed to sketch a model for the comparative and diachronic analyses of transition. The impact is heuristically subtle, although simultaneously revealing theoretical problems that this stream of literature has yet to resolve.

In the meantime, a modest rise in election studies has accompanied studies of transitional processes, among other things providing a partial antidote to the relative denigration of elections and political parties that was especially striking in *Transitions*. The best of these is the volume edited by John Booth and Seligson, which examines the contemporary Central American experience.[33] Booth provides a definitional framework in which democracy, though predominantly institutional and political, is extended beyond the narrow and electorally oriented position of the pluralist-elitist school.[34] He views the concept as *"participation by the mass of people in a community in its governance (making and carrying out decisions)."*[35] Rather than being a constant, democracy stands as a variable, with participatory dimensions bespeaking the relative character of democracy in any given system. As identified by Cohen, these embrace breadth (type and extent of participation), range (array of issues on which the public exercises decisions), and depth (efficacy and autonomy of popular participation).[36]

Booth then proceeds to link the issue of regime consolidation with the character of elections themselves. Whether or not the electoral process contributes a democratizing effect in systemic consolidation remains an empirical question.[37] At the least, the electoral theme aids in the understanding of democracy as well as the initial stage of redemocratization. This is welcome, for the genre of transitions to democracy is theoretically diffuse, creating major difficulties in constructing a true theoretical framework for analysis. Contrasting ideological assumptions and a diversity of definitions complicate matters. In addition, the literature has not yet directed close attention to the role of participatory mass protest against authoritarian regimes, although important examples can be readily cited. Perhaps the illustration par excellence is that of "people power" in the Philippines. Whatever the character of regime consolidation under Corazon Aquino's government, the popular wrath that forced Ferdinand Marcos's retreat and resignation constitutes a fascinating element in the study of transitions to democracy.

In South Korea the role of mass protests has also helped to bring about certain systemic reforms as well as a change of leadership. The ouster of Jean-Claude Duvalier in Haiti, though it failed to produce a major shift in regime type, nonetheless provides an additional case that can lend understanding to the dynamics of transitions. Contemporary events in Chile will also be instructive as a prolonged authoritarian era draws toward a close. Ongoing changes in Eastern Europe further emphasize both the diversity and the theoretical richness of changes in the direction of democracy. Comparativists' attention, enhanced by their renewed preoccupation with the fundamentals of democracy, is now being engaged not only in studying presumably less stable developing nations, but in probing the modern democracies. The work of Mattei Dogan and eminent collaborators in rigorously comparing pluralist democracies is an outstanding sample of the theoretical sophistication that can be employed.[38] This further underlines the universality of comparativists' concerns. It also highlights a shared preoccupation with the explanation of differences; the quest for such differentiation lies at the heart of theories of political culture.

THE POLITICAL-CULTURE DIMENSION

A concern with political culture was conspicuous among comparativists in the decade of the 1960s. Their way had been paved by the earlier work of anthropologists, sociologists, and even psychologists. In describing the orthodox conceptualization of culture, Ronald Chilcote reported that as early as 1952 Alfred Kroeber and Clyde Kluckhohn were able to review no fewer than 160 interpretations.[39] The work of Edward A. Shils was influenti both through his writings[40] and in his role as chairman of the Comparative Study of New Nations, which began work in 1959–1960 with a grant from the Carnegie Corporation. Daniel Bell and Clifford Geertz were also prominent in putting forward cultural factors as decisive elements in the shaping of development.[41] The concept of political culture was generally linked to nations, thus representing in part a resurrection of hoary discussions of national character. For comparativists, it was applied at the outset almost exclusively to what would later be called the Third World.

Moreover, in the late 1950s and early 1960s, this revolved principally about the study of newly independent states, which basically meant Asia and Africa. As Shils argued, they were not unique phenomena. Indeed, they revealed "marked affinities with all states, and above all with the undeveloped states of their own continents and Latin America. But they have enough that is unique to them and common to them to justify our decision to put them at the center of our attention."[42] In due course the cultural dichotomy was transformed into distinctions between the so-called Western and non-Western states. As early as 1955 a contribution to the *American Political Science Review* had dealt explicitly with non-Western countries,[43] and three years later Lucian W. Pye identified seventeen distinctive characteristics of the non-Western political process.[44] Despite the heuristic insight of such works, other comparativists, including the present author, raised questions about the breadth of such theoretical generalizations.[45]

Cultural dimensions were incorporated into more empirically oriented research, most notably the seminal work of Gabriel Almond and Sidney Verba.[46] Covering five nations, their *Civic Culture* probed public opinion as related to the political symbols and beliefs that provided the backdrop for political action. It sought to establish the connection between political attitudes and regime type. The authors constructed a typology that attempted to delineate respective parochial, subject, and participant characteristics. This dramatically innovative undertaking was inevitably accompanied by serious flaws.[47] For those who criticized the work for allegedly idealizing an Anglo-American model of politics, a response was offered by the work of Third World country specialists. The prime example was Pye and Verba's compendium, *Political Culture and Political Development.*[48] Yet comparativists increasingly challenged the cultural approach as being classificatory and static. There was a feeling that the typologies raised up were inadequate for scientific explanation. Even the respected Asian specialist Robert E. Ward, in his 1973 presidential address to the American Political Science Association, conceded that scholars had sometimes been too swift to accompany their explanations with the justification that differences were cultural. To be sure, at the same time he sturdily refused to deny the impact of cultural influences.[49]

For a full two decades, the concept of political culture continued to animate debate among political scientists. As a pair of French scholars aptly put it, "Rarely has a concept been so frequently used and so often contended. The choice of the word 'culture' denotes the concept's derivation and emphasizes how comparativists have followed a road opened by anthropology, sociology, and psychology."[50] Yet for a time there was an inclination to disregard or to cast aside the cultural dimension as both unscientific and substantively irrelevant, notwithstanding its intellectually intriguing character. This mirrored a natural if too facile rejection of a presumed fad whose time had passed, but at the same time underlay legitimate grounds for doubts over the analytic significance of the cultural dimension. From a neo-Marxist posture, there were arguments that orthodox political culture lacked explanatory power. In the view of one thoughtful critic, neither were the related concerns over political socialization and communications sufficiently germane. For Chilcote, therefore, "Studies are classificatory and descriptive rather than analytical. Political culture is conceived of in ideal form as a civic culture. Change is incremental and gradual. Rather than being independent of the political system, political culture instead depends on the system."[51]

Differing intellectual perspectives shared the sense that there were analytic and scientific weaknesses embodied in the prevailing application of cultural elements. In an essay from the 1980s that was by no means hostile to the cultural dimension, Samuel Huntington succinctly reviewed its scientific problematics. He properly saw the concept as "a tricky one" because it was simultaneously easy and unsatisfying to use. "It is easy (and also dangerous) to use because it is, in some sense, a residual category. If no other causes can plausibly explain significant differences between societies, it is inviting to attribute them to culture."[52] In addition, Huntington saw the concept of culture as frustrating for the social scientist, running counter to the proclivity to generalize. Yet he joined a host of other analysts who had concluded that the comparative study of political culture had moved far beyond the "national character" studies of earlier years. Recognition of renewed conceptual vitality was accurately summarized by Howard Wiarda in the following terms:

> In research project after research project over the past three decades focused on the developing nations, traditional political culture and institutions have proved to be remarkably long-lived and persistent. Rather than being swept aside by the tides of history, or consigned to history's ashcans, these institutions—whether in Asia, the Middle East, Africa, or Latin America—have repeatedly shown themselves to be flexible and accommodative, most often bending to change rather than being overwhelmed by it.[53]

Indications of a renaissance in political-culture studies need not imply deterministic explanation but rather a recognition that it constitutes a valuable perspective. Three separate pieces have been published in the *American Political Science Review* recently; interestingly, none of the authors is regarded as a Third World specialist. Aaron Wildavsky addressed cultural issues in his APSA presidential address, drawing largely on the U.S. political experience in arguing that political preferences were rooted in political culture. In recommending the study of political culture, Wildavsky argued that constituted a powerful conceptual construct.

Appraising the consequences of living lives of hierarchical subordination or of the purely voluntary association of egalitarian liberation or the self-regulation of individualistic cultures, at different times, on different continents, with different technologies, languages, and customs would be a remarkably productive research program. So would comparing cultures rather than countries or, put precisely, comparing countries by contrasting their combinations of cultures.[54]

The Wildavsky address and article sparked an illuminating exchange with David D. Laitin in a subsequent issue of *APSR*.[55] There were sharp differences of opinion, including a debate over the alleged Janus-faced character of culture. The richness of the dialogue did not obscure both scholars' advocacy of research in political culture. Each had incorporated his notion of the concept into recent or forthcoming books.[56] The next *APSR* presented a thoughtful statement by Harry Eckstein. He sought to counter the influential criticisms of earlier years that had insisted that political-culture theory was inadequate in its treatment of political change. For Eckstein, only two viable approaches to political theory and explanation have been proffered in the past third of a century to replace traditional formal-legalism: the culturalist and the rationalist. He sought to establish for the former a theoretical expectation of change to accompany earlier assumptions of continuity. A painstaking elaboration led to his closing declaration that a cogent and powerful theory of political change could be derived from culturalist premises. Although it was true that the theories of political culture had "not heretofore met the challenge of developing a general theory of change; . . . neither have others."[57]

For Ronald Inglehart, who closely studies Western Europe, the cultural dimension was both durable and heuristically valuable. In yet another *APSR* piece, he departed from many longtime critics of *The Civic Culture* in lauding what he saw as a major advance from earlier imprecise and literarily impressionistic studies. Denying that the cultural perspective was either static or ethnocentrically Anglo-Saxon in character, Inglehart drew extensively on Western European survey data for his analysis. He termed rational choice models useful for short-term fluctuations but intrinsically inadequate without cross-national cultural elements. Persuaded that cultural differences were durable, he wrote that such factors "have an important bearing on the durability of democracy, which seems to result from a complex interplay of economical, cultural, and institutional factors. To neglect any of these components may compromise its survival."[58] Thus, overall life satisfaction and the perceived level of economic development become important correlates of interpersonal trust. Inglehart's empirical research strongly supported the contention that political culture constituted an intervening variable that was logically linked both to economic development and to modern mass-based democracy.

Interest in political culture was similarly reflected in an empirically grounded study of public support for democracy in Korea. The authors employed public opinion data to test Douglas and Wildavsky's theory of culture, concluding that their findings showed that levels of public support in Korea were dependent more on culture than on socioeconomic and demographic characteristics. Consequently, they argued that the Douglas-Wildavsky typology of culture "can serve as a meaningful framework for integrating a variety of political and nonpolitical orientations that have been found in prior research to promote democratic development."[59]

The increasing appearance of such articles in major disciplinary journals bespeaks the vitality of the culturalist renewal. There have been other indications as well. For instance, the Center for International Affairs at Harvard organized a faculty political culture seminar. In addition, an important publisher for works in the developing areas committed itself to a new series on Political Cultures. Edited by none other than Wildavsky, the series is intended to broadly describe people sharing values, beliefs, and preferences on political and social life. The series stresses its openness to a variety of approaches yet identifies a set of common concerns: "what values are shared, what sorts of social relations are preferred, what kinds of beliefs are involved, and what the political implications of these values, beliefs, and relations are."

From Wildavsky to Inglehart and beyond, there seems to be a serious commitment to wrestle in one fashion or another with the cultural dimension. Lucian Pye, a recent APSA president, has again published on China, employing an explicit cultural emphasis.[60] For that matter, the effects of East Asian economic miracles may well produce renewed culturally related research, as Wiarda has noted.[61] There is also reviving interest in Latin America after some years of relative inactivity. Seligson has recently given multiple explanations for past regional unenthusiasm, although perhaps diluting his case by unduly narrowing his focus. In harking back to *The Civic Culture* and insisting that "political culture is invariably quantitative in nature and therefore reflects the mainstream of the positivist, empirical paradigm of North American social science,"[62] he seemingly equates cultural investigation with survey research. Furthermore, although it is certainly true that such projects may well require a large investment of human and financial resources, it is also possible to exaggerate logistical difficulties.[63] In addition, field research abroad—especially in the developing world—is rarely easy or inexpensive, whether or not attitudinal studies are involved.[64]

Any contemporary reassessment of comparative politics must now embrace political culture as an important dimension, even granting undeniable problems. For Dogan and Dominique Pelassy, the concept of political culture has aged like good wine. It reflects the political beliefs and values prevailing in a nation at a given point in time. "Because it filters perception, determines attitudes, and influences modalities of participation, culture is a major component of the political game."[65] Huntington is also persuaded of the relevance of culture in explaining differing developmental patterns, which he further sees as an important means of improving links between area specialists and comparativists with developmental concerns. And more importantly, such an approach becomes nearly indispensable for those wishing to explain the extent to which different countries have made different progress toward achieving the goals of development. "Culture and its impact on development cry out for systematic and empirical comparative and longitudinal study by the scholars of political development."[66]

Exponents of Wallerstein's world system, operating with quite different assumptions, have also shared in the reinvigorization of cultural factors. Criticizing modernization theorists for overlooking the multiplicity of historical and cultural characteristics in Third World analyses, they have insisted that to conceive of development and change simply as a natural process "is to ignore that it is fundamentally a historical process with cultural and political as well as economic components."[67] Once again, it seems undeniable that both disciplinary and regional scholars are introducing or reincorporating political culture into their comparative analyses of societies and politics. Without for a moment reifying the heuristic potential of the cultural dimension, it can no longer be marginalized as irrelevant or useless.

To repeat my earlier point, which I share with Wiarda, political culture is in no sense a sole explanatory variable, nor should it be. At the same time, it cannot be undervalued or ignored. Whatever the region of the world, historic cultural and intellectual traditions cannot be gainsaid. I noted elsewhere that those who elaborate presumably "modern" analytic constructs "without taking account of the legacy of past patterns of thought will but encourage generalizations and theoretical frameworks that become often incomplete or distorted reflections of reality."[68] I was speaking of Latin America, as was Wiarda in observing that the region must come to grips with the reality of cultural continuity.[69] In the broader context, however, the least that could be said was that the cultural dimension emphatically and incontrovertibly demanded—and was receiving—serious intellectual attention.[70]

CONCLUSIONS

The intellectual ferment among comparativists over the last decade has been pronounced. Theoretical sophistication has grown, research has been stimulated, and scholarly productivity has increased. The effort to link empirical studies to broader trends in comparative politics has become self-conscious, and in many instances heuristically significant. At the same time, there has been a gradual if sometimes grudging admission that no single approach in itself can adequately pave the royal road to understanding. It has become evident to many, for example, that recurring economic variables do not possess predictive power as regards regime change. "Rather, economic issues have mainly posed problems to be solved while limiting the options for their solution."[71] Consequently, if some found economic explanations disturbingly wanting, this was not to deny weaknesses with both institutional and cultural perspectives.

At the same time, it was noteworthy that the two latter dimensions had not received extensive attention for some years. Only toward the close of the 1980s had scholarly interest, whether for industrialized or developing nations, revived. An obvious observation at this juncture is the potential utility of broader eclecticism and more synthetic theorizing. It leads in turn to a recognition of the value in linking economic, institutional, and cultural factors. The prospect of less reductionist explanation, erected on multivariate sociopolitical analysis, may well provide a level of scientific insight currently absent from theoretical efforts to dissect contemporary political reality. As always, intellectual agility and audacity will be central to the quest for genuine analytic comparison.

NOTES

1. Immanuel Wallerstein, *The Modern World System: Capitalist Agriculture and the Origins of the European World Economy in the Sixteenth Century* (New York: Academic Press, 1974), p. 11.

2. James M. Malloy, "Preface," in Malloy, ed., *Authoritarianism and Corporatism in Latin America* (Pittsburgh, PA: University of Pittsburgh Press, 1977), p. ix.

3. Guillermo A. O'Donnell, *Modernization and Bureaucratic-Authoritarianism: Studies in South American Politics* (Berkeley: Institute of International Studies, University of California, 1973).

4. Ibid., p. 51.

5. Guillermo A. O'Donnell, "Reflections on the Patterns of Change in the Bureaucratic-Authoritarian State," *Latin American Research Review* 13 (1978):1, especially 27–31.

6. Mitchell A. Seligson, "Political Culture and Democratization in Latin America," in James M. Malloy and Eduardo Gamarra, eds., *Latin American and Caribbean Contemporary Record*, vol. 7, 1987–1988 (New York: Holmes and Meier, 1990). My thanks to Dr. Seligson for sharing with me a prepublication copy of his paper.

7. David Collier, ed., *The New Authoritarianism in Latin America* (Princeton, NJ: Princeton University Press, 1979).

8. David Collier, "The Bureaucratic-Authoritarian Model: Synthesis and Priorities for Future Research," in ibid., p. 394.

9. In addition to his 1978 restatement and elaboration in *Latin American Research Review*, see Guillermo O'Donnell's contribution to the Collier-edited compendium, "Tensions in the Bureaucratic-Authoritarian State and the Question of Democracy," pp. 285–319.

10. Karen L. Remmer and Gilbert W. Merkx, "Bureaucratic-Authoritarianism Revisited," *Latin American Research Review* 17, 2 (1982):35.

11. Guillermo A. O'Donnell, "Reply to Remmer and Merkx," *Latin American Research Review* 17, 2 (1982):41–51.

12. Guillermo A. O'Donnell, *1966–1973: El estado burocratico autoritaria; triunfos, derrotas y crisis* (Buenos Aires: Editorial de Belgrano, 1982).

13. See the recent discussion in David Lehmann, "A Latin American Political Scientist: Guillermo O'Donnell," *Latin American Research Review* 24, 2 (1989):187–200.

14. For a broader, regionally based discussion, see Jorge I. Domínguez, "Political Change: Central America, South America, and the Caribbean," in Myron Weiner and Samuel P. Huntington, eds., *Understanding Political Development* (Boston: Little, Brown, 1987), pp. 65–101.

15. Douglas A. Chalmers, "The Politicized State in Latin America," in Malloy, ed., *Authoritarianism and Corporatism*, p. 23.

16. Juan J. Linz and Alfred Stepan, eds., *The Breakdown of Democratic Regimes* (Baltimore, MD: Johns Hopkins University Press, 1978), p. xii.

17. James M. Malloy, "The Politics of Transition in Latin America," in James M. Malloy and Mitchell A. Seligson, eds., *Authoritarians and Democrats: Regime Transition in Latin America* (Pittsburgh, PA: University of Pittsburgh Press, 1987), pp. 235–236.

18. Guillermo O'Donnell, Philippe C. Schmitter, and Laurence Whitehead, eds., *Transitions from Authoritarian Rule: Prospects for Democracy* (Baltimore, MD: Johns Hopkins University Press, 1986).

19. Larry Diamond, Juan J. Linz, and Seymour Martin Lipset, eds., *Democracy in Developing Countries* (Boulder, CO: Lynne Rienner, 1988–1989).

20. See the Preface in ibid., pp. xxiii–xxiv.

21. Ibid., p. xvi.

22. O'Donnell et al., *Transitions*, vol. 4, p. 72.

23. Daniel H. Levine, "Paradigm Lost: Dependence to Democracy," *World Politics* 50,3 (April 1988):379. Levine's analysis is both perceptive and provocative; it merits thoughtful attention by all who are concerned with this area of inquiry.

24. John D. Martz, "Democracy and the Imposition of Values: Definitions and Diplomacy," in John D. Martz and Lars Schoultz, eds., *Latin America, the United States, and the Inter-American System* (Boulder, CO: Westview Press, 1980), pp. 145ff. The general renewal of interest in modern democracy and its theoretical foundations has been notable. Five recent works have been discussed by three reviewers under the rubric "The Meaning of Democracy" in the *American Political Science Review* 83, 2 (June 1989):603–610.

25. Alexander W. Wilde, "Conversations Among Gentlemen: Oligarchical Democracy in Colombia," in Linz and Stepan, *Breakdown*, p. 29.

26. Levine, "Paradigm Lost," p. 393. Another critical review with somewhat different emphases is Jorge Nef, "The Trend toward Democratization and Redemocratization in Latin America: Shadow and Substance," *Latin American Research Review* 23, 3 (1988):131–154. He finds the volume to have fallen short of its intellectual promise, demonstrating among other qualities "an unequivocal sense of haste" (ibid., p. 149).

27. John Peeler, *Latin American Democracies* (Chapel Hill: University of North Carolina Press, 1985).

28. Diamond, Linz, and Lipset, "Preface," in *Democracy in Developing Countries,* p. x.

29. Ibid., p. xiii.

30. Malloy, "The Politics of Transition," in *Authoritarians and Democrats,* p. 246. For a comparable theoretical argument that goes further to argue the coexistence of three intellectual and cultural streams in Latin American political experience, see John D. Martz and David J. Myers, "Understanding Latin American Politics: Analytic Models and Intellectual Tradition," *Polity* 16, 2 (Winter 1983):214–242.

31. Malloy, "The Politics of Transition," p. 257.

32. Enrique A. Baloyra, ed., *Comparing New Democracies: Transition and Consolidation in Mediterranean Europe and the Southern Cone* (Boulder, CO: Westview Press, 1987), p. 303. Baloyra credits William C. Smith, along with Morlino, for the definitional treatment of democratization proffered in his book.

33. John A. Booth and Mitchell A. Seligson, eds., *Elections and Democracy in Central America* (Chapel Hill: University of North Carolina Press, 1989).

34. Booth cites the definitional problems centering on the North American tendency to equate democracy with elections. With such eminent figures as Joseph Schumpeter and Robert Dahl having established the electorally oriented pluralist-elitist conception,

it was not until the writings of such critics as Peter Bachrach and Carol Pateman that mainstream political science was challenged to rethink the true meaning of classical democracy.

35. John A. Booth, "Elections and Democracy in Central America: A Framework for Analysis," in Booth, *Elections and Democracy*, p. 11. The emphasis is his.

36. Carl Cohen, *Democracy* (New York: Free Press, 1971), pp. 8–37.

37. Another anthology of this type was the collection of papers produced by a 1985 conference on "Recent Electoral Changes in the Americas." A number of individual elections between 1980 and 1985 were examined, but theorizing was largely absent, as individual chapters traced in mechanistic fashion the institutional unfolding and interplay of traditional political variables in analyzing electoral results and party changes. A number were very well informed, but those seeking theoretical insight could find it only through indirection. In published form the papers are found in Paul W. Drake and Eduardo Silva, eds., *Elections and Democratization in Latin America, 1980–85* (San Diego: Center for Iberian and Latin American Studies, University of California, 1986).

38. Mattei Dogan, ed., *Comparing Pluralist Democracies: Strains on Legitimacy* (Boulder, CO: Westview Press, 1988).

39. See the thorough and informative overview of Ronald H. Chilcote, *Theories of Comparative Politics: The Search for a Paradigm* (Boulder, CO: Westview Press, 1981), pp. 218ff.

40. A characteristic work was Edward Shils, "Mass Society and Its Culture," in Norman Jacobs, ed., *Culture for the Millions* (New York: Van Nostrand, 1961), pp. 1–27.

41. See especially Daniel Bell, *The Cultural Contradictions of Capitalism* (New York: Basic Books, 1976); and Clifford Geertz, *The Interpretation of Cultures* (New York: Basic Books, 1973).

42. Edward A. Shils, "On the Comparative Study of the New States," in Clifford Geertz, ed., *Old Societies and New States: The Quest for Modernity in Asia and Africa* (New York: Free Press of Glencoe, 1963), p. 5.

43. George McT. Kahin, Guy J. Pauker, and Lucian W. Pye, "Comparative Politics of Non-Western Countries," *American Political Science Review* 49, 4 (December 1955).

44. Lucian W. Pye, "The Non-Western Political Process," *Journal of Politics* 20, 3 (August 1958):468–486.

45. John D. Martz, "The Place of Latin America in the Study of Comparative Politics," *Journal of Politics* 28, 1 (February 1966):57–81.

46. Gabriel A. Almond and Sidney Verba, *The Civic Culture: Political Attitudes and Democracy in Five Nations* (Princeton, NJ: Princeton University Press, 1963).

47. A stimulating reevaluation of the entire project two decades after the survey research was conducted is Gabriel Almond and Sidney Verba, eds., *The Civic Culture Revisited* (Boston: Little, Brown, 1980).

48. Lucian W. Pye and Sidney Verba, eds., *Political Culture and Political Development* (Princeton, NJ: Princeton University Press, 1965).

49. Robert E. Ward, "Culture and the Comparative Study of Politics, or The Constipated Dialectic," *American Political Science Review* 68, 1 (March 1974):190–201.

50. Mattei Dogan and Dominique Pelassy, *How to Compare Nations: Strategies in Comparative Politics* (Chatham, NJ: Chatham House, 1983), p. 58.

51. Chilcote, *Theories of Comparative Politics*, p. 250.

52. Samuel P. Huntington, "The Goals of Development," in Weiner and Huntington, *Understanding Political Development*, pp. 22–23.

53. Howard J. Wiarda, "Political Culture and National Development." Paper prepared for the special issue entitled "Culture in Development: New Perspectives," *The Fletcher Forum: A Journal of Studies in International Affairs* 13 (Summer 1989):194.

54. Aaron Wildavsky, "Choosing Preferences by Constructing Institutions: A Cultural Theory of Preference Formation," *American Political Science Review* 81, 1 (March 1987):18. In his notes Wildavsky also refers to his unpublished 1985 manuscript entitled "A World of Differences: The Public Philosophies and Political Behaviors of Rival American Cultures."

55. David D. Laitin and Aaron Wildavsky, "Political Culture and Political Preferences," *American Political Science Review* 82, 2 (June 1988):589–597.

56. Laitin was the author of a study of the Yorubas entitled *Hegemony and Culture* (Chicago: University of Chicago Press, 1986). Wildavsky made reference to his forthcoming work with Michael Thompson, *The Foundations of Cultural Theory.*

57. Harry Eckstein, "A Culturalist Theory of Political Change," *American Political Science Review* 82, 3 (September 1988):801. Of particular note is Eckstein's appendix on culture, which sets forth his own axiomatic definition and use of the concept on pp. 801–803.

58. Ronald Inglehart, "The Renaissance of Political Culture," *American Political Science Review* 82, 4 (December 1988):1229. He is also author of *Culture Change in Advanced Industrial Society* (Princeton, NJ: Princeton University Press, forthcoming), described by Richard I. Hofferbert as a work that "at last draws political values from the splendid isolation enforced artificially upon them by past scholars," thereby setting the agenda of comparative social research for the years ahead.

59. Doh Chul Shin, Myung Chey, and Kwang-Woong Kim, "Cultural Origins of Public Support for Democracy in Korea: An Empirical Test of the Douglas-Wildavsky Theory of Culture," *Comparative Political Studies* 22, 2 (July 1989):235. The work on which they focus their theoretical attention is Mary Douglas and Aaron Wildavsky, *Risk and Culture* (Berkeley: University of California Press, 1982).

60. Lucian W. Pye, *The Mandarin and the Cadre: China's Political Cultures* (Ann Arbor: Center for Chinese Studies, University of Michigan, 1988). He also probed politico-cultural linkages in his *Asian Power and Politics: The Cultural Dimensions of Authority* (Cambridge, MA: Harvard University Press, 1985).

61. Wiarda makes the observation on pp. 200–201 of "Political Culture and National Development" that economic development in the two regions displays sharp contrasts, despite similar structural features. He writes that culture could well be the missing explanatory variable.

62. Seligson's "Political Culture and Democratization," forthcoming in vol. 7 of *Latin American and Caribbean Contemporary Record,* is quoted here from manuscript page 11.

63. Among the largest in Latin America over the past two decades was the National Science Foundation–funded support for John D. Martz and Enrique A. Baloyra's investigation of Venezuelan democracy and political attitudes. Its resultant wealth of hard empirical data was completed by institutional links made available to investigators from both Venezuela and the United States. Smaller-scale undertakings are not unimaginable for young scholars, although Seligson is certainly correct in noting that both practical and psychological barriers exist.

Of the several publications resulting from the Venezuelan project, the most empirically data-rich is Enrique A. Baloyra and John D. Martz, *Political Attitudes in Venezuela: Societal Cleavages and Political Opinion* (Austin: University of Texas Press, 1979).

64. For a practical discussion of problems of field research that extends far beyond those of survey research, see John D. Martz, "The Conduct of Social Research in

Latin America: A Personal View of Problems in Open and Closed Societies," *Studies in Comparative International Development* 24, 1 (Spring 1989):47–65.

65. Dogan and Pelassy, *How to Compare Nations,* p. 58.

66. Huntington, "The Goals of Development," p. 28.

67. Terry R. Kandal and Michael T. Martin, "Introduction," in Michael T. Martin and Terry R. Kandal, eds., *Studies of Development and Change in the Modern World* (New York: Oxford University Press, 1989), p. 7.

68. John D. Martz and David J. Myers, "Understanding Latin American Politics: Analytic Models and Intellectual Traditions," *Polity* 16, 2 (Winter 1983):215.

69. Wiarda, "Political Culture and National Development," pp. 202–203.

70. Among the most recent examples of the culturalist renaissance is Susan and Peter Calvert, *Argentina: Political Culture and Instability* (Pittsburgh, PA: University of Pittsburgh Press, 1989). The authors analyze a large sampling of survey data in probing what is described as Argentina's mixed heritage of Iberian and European cultures.

71. See Malloy's discussion in *Authoritarians and Democrats,* pp. 237–244.

PART THREE

Conclusion

11

Toward the Future:
Old and New Directions
in Comparative Politics

HOWARD J. WIARDA

In looking back over the past thirty or forty years in comparative politics, it is striking how closely the dominant models and concepts in the field are related to actual events and the broad currents sweeping the world of nations, to attitudinal and opinion changes in the United States (where most, but by no means all, of the comparative politics literature is written), and to intellectual and methodological innovations within the political science discipline. It is not that comparative politics exactly follows the headlines (although at times it may do that, too) with their almost daily and often fickle flights from one dramatic crisis or area to the next; but it does tend to reflect the long-term trends in public and elite opinion that help determine which geographic or issue areas, or which intellectual approach, are to receive priority. Such fluctuations in our thinking, attention, and values have also affected the field of comparative politics and its changing emphases, research priorities, and conceptual perspectives over the past several decades.

The purpose of this concluding chapter is in broad terms to review these developments and interrelations in comparative politics; to show how comparative politics developed from its earlier formal-legal approach to a more vigorous, dynamic, and genuinely comparative discipline; to trace the rise of the dominant political development approach and its later decline; to analyze the approaches that supplanted it as well as the fragmentation of the field; and to assess the current condition of the field—its liveliness, its pluralism of approaches, and the competition among rival viewpoints, including now a revived political development approach. In all of these

Parts of this chapter were earlier published in a quite different version as "Rethinking Political Development," *Studies in Comparative International Development* 24 (Fall 1989):65–82; and as "Political Development Reconsidered" in Dankwart A. Rustow and Kenneth Paul Erickson, eds., *Comparative Political Dynamics* (New York: Harper Collins, 1991).

considerations we seek to show how the field interacts with and is part of a larger national, international, cultural, and political environment. For as American (and maybe global) politics and policymaking became increasingly divided, fragmented, and in some disarray in the 1970s, comparative politics seemed to follow these same trends. But as many world economic and political trends seemed, at least in some countries, to turn upward again in the 1980s, comparative politics also became more energetic, with a lively research agenda and a wide diversity of research approaches. Ultimately we need to answer the question whether this new ferment, lack of unity, or (its reverse side) vigorous competition among approaches is a pathetic sign for the future of the field or an indication of its health and vitality.

OLD AND NEW IN COMPARATIVE POLITICS

Traditional comparative politics is universally thought to have been dominated by a parochial (in its almost exclusively European focus), static, descriptive, monographic, and formal-legalistic approach that has now been discredited. Actually, some of the scholars against whom these charges were directed—Taylor Cole, Carl Friedrich, John Herz, Herman Finer, Karl Loewenstein, and others—wrote some very good studies in the 1940s and 1950s, studies that are still well worth reading.[1] But a new generation of scholars then rising to the fore was impatient with the old approach, caught up with new ideas and methodologies, and wished to go off in new directions. They wanted to emphasize the more dynamic, informal, change-oriented, and process aspects of comparative politics: political parties, interest groups, public opinion, decisionmaking. That was the message of the Social Science Research Council/Committee on Comparative Politics (SSRC/CCP) meetings and studies in the 1950s and of Roy Macridis's tub-thumping, flag-waving, and very influential little book published in 1955.[2] Then, as apparently in every age, a new group of scholars with new perceptions hoped to "make it" in the profession, over the backs, to an extent, of their elders.

The new generation of scholars wished to concentrate on the dynamics of change and to examine the multifaceted aspects of politics, not just the formal and legal features. They had been influenced, in varying degrees, by structural-functionalism, the new influences of sociology in political science, the systems approach, the focus on interest groups and other informal actors, and the new trend toward a more systematic and behavioral methodology in the discipline. Their approach, which soon became the dominant one in comparative politics, corresponded to other changes that we might call global. For our purposes, the most important of these global changes were the emerging Cold War in the 1940s and 1950s and the sudden emergence of a large number of new nations onto the world's stage in the late 1950s and early 1960s.

The interrelations among these three events—a more dynamic comparative politics, the Cold War, and the new or emerging nations—have yet to be analyzed adequately, in my view.[3] Some U.S. officials, and doubtless a few scholars as well, saw the fashioning of a body of literature dealing with the developing nations as a means by which U.S. foreign policy could control and dominate these countries for Cold War purposes—that is, to deny them to the Soviet Union and to keep them within the U.S. orbit. Other scholars saw the constructs of development theory as a purely intellectual approach, a way of understanding and probably of encouraging development, but not a means of manipulation. Still others—the majority, most likely—saw some (perhaps varying degrees of) interrelations between U.S. Cold War strategies and a theory to analyze and help shape the politics of the developing nations, but saw no incompatibility between the two, thought of them as complementary, or thought both goals were worth pursuing at once. We still need, in short, a good study showing the interrelations between changes in comparative politics, especially the new focus on the developing nations, and the political context of the 1950s in which so many of the major shifts in the field took place.

There are other lacunae in our knowledge dating from this period—gaps, overlooked research areas, and social science biases that have also affected the study of comparative politics. For example, the horrors and excesses of fascism were such that they led us to dismiss, ignore, and often misunderstand such regimes as those of Francisco Franco in Spain and Antonio de Oliveira Salazar in Portugal, whose systems were closer to Catholic organicism and corporatism than to fascism. Because of its association with fascism in the interwar period, the study of corporatism was largely neglected in the post–World War II period, thus depriving us of a major research tool to place in perspective the Iberian and various Latin American and other countries, and perpetuating many misconceptions about these nations. Only in the 1970s did corporatism come back as a major research focus after some twenty-five years of its neglect.

Another influence in the field related to the particular generational time period in which so many of its leading scholars grew up. The major shaping events included the market crash of 1929–1930 and the world depression that followed, the Weimar Republic in Germany and its degeneration into fascism, the breakdown of democratic regimes in Eastern and southern Europe, the Nazi regime and its horrors and depravities, Stalin's bloody purges and Soviet totalitarianism, the expansion of the Soviet empire into Eastern Europe, the Chinese revolution and its bloody upheavals. These events led to a revulsion from extremist regimes and ideologies that also had an impact on comparative politics. Radical regimes of both left and right had perforce to be resisted in favor of a middle way that often protected the status quo. The models used in comparative politics during this period also eschewed more radical solutions and opted for middle-class, middle-of-the-road regimes that often bore a striking resemblance to that of the United States. Many radical scholars accused comparative politics of following a conservative research agenda.

As comparative politics turned in the 1950s from the developed to the developing nations, many of these same biases reappeared in new forms.

In the models that were used, the developing nations were pictured as egalitarian, socially just, based on achievement criteria, pluralistic, democratic, and so on. These are all marvelous criteria, and they happen to correspond closely to my own preferred and political values. They also correspond closely to a vision of what we would like to believe the United States is or stands for. The trouble is that few of these values have much to do with the actual situation in most developing countries or even with their realistic prospects for the future. Essentially, they represent an idealized version of the United States transferred to the developing nations, where the model simply does not fit. Little thought was given in the development literature to the fact that the model might not be applicable in the emerging nations, that it might not even be wanted there, or that the developing nations might have indigenous institutions that they wished to base their development on and that might be worth salvaging. We have since seen that the attractive idea of various indigenous models of development has not worked out very well in practice either, but that should still not lead us entirely to ignore Third World institutions in favor of a theory imported from and often imposed by the West.

Quite a number of these biases and presuppositions in the field emerged from the fact of U.S. power and hegemony in the world during this period, not just politically and militarily but also in terms of the dominance of U.S. social science constructs. The United States had emerged from World War II as the globe's great superpower. Both its economy and its political system seemed superior; furthermore, the U.S. example appeared to offer lessons from which others might learn, to provide a model to emulate. Given these conditions, it is probably no accident that the prevailing social science models of the time derived mainly from the U.S. experience, that the development literature was almost exclusively a U.S. creation, and that the United States took strenuous efforts to export its model to other nations. This effort was both a conscious plan (on the part of some officials and scholars) and a by-product of the U.S. position as the world's most powerful and, seemingly, successful nation.

It also stemmed from a pervasive sense of noblesse oblige and idealism. The overwhelming majority of Americans wished not to exploit the rest of the world but to bring to it what we in the United States enjoyed—whether the rest of the world desired precisely the same values and institutions or not. The era of American superiority and hegemony after World War II corresponded almost exactly with the dominance of the comparative politics paradigms here discussed. The years from 1945 to 1965 have been called "the American decades," and they were indeed that, not just in an economic and security sense but in the social sciences as well. To use only a slight exaggeration, the "pax Americana" reigned not just in the global diplomatic, security, and financial spheres but in the comparative politics field as well.

It would seem logical to assume that as the U.S. model became increasingly tarnished in the late 1960s and throughout the 1970s, and as the United States' international place and power in the world were simultaneously diminished, the comparative politics models based so heavily on them would also come under increased challenge. The world did indeed change after the mid-1960s, and so did comparative politics. In the aftermath of Vietnam, Watergate, increased domestic economic problems, racial and social tensions, and a relatively declining position in terms of the power of the U.S. economy, the United States became a more chastened nation, no longer so convinced of the superiority of its institutions and its ability to export them. Its position as *the* dominant superpower was similarly challenged. Hence, as the United States lost to a degree its hegemonic position as a nation and world power, so did the prevailing social science and comparative politics paradigms that had reigned for twenty years. As the world changed and the place of the United States in it, the comparative politics field also seemed to flounder, to lose its unity and its assumptions of global applicability, as a variety of new approaches, discussed in successive chapters in this book, were put forward and challenged the old approach.

But by the 1990s the world has turned again. The United States still has its problems, and its economic position in the world is not so secure as it could be. On the other hand, with the decline of the Soviet Union, the triumph of the democracy idea among the world's ideologies,[4] the renewal of American strength and self-confidence, and the apparent absence for the foreseeable future of any serious challengers, the United States still—and again—remains the dominant power in the world. Some analysts have written that this position of hegemony is so secure and without challenges at present that it is likely to last well into the twenty-first century.[5] We cannot, of course, assess the accuracy of that statement here except to say that, if the past is a useful guide to the future, such hegemony is certain to have an impact also on comparative politics and on the models and interpretations that the field uses.

Comparative politics has thus gone from a traditional, formal-legal approach to one emphasizing informal political aspects. It also went from an emphasis on European politics to one (discussed more fully below) that focused on the developing nations. In all these sea changes in the field, the approaches used in comparative politics were, sometimes loosely and sometimes closely, linked to global changes, not the least of which was and remains the relative power and position of the United States in the world.

THE TRIUMPH OF THE
POLITICAL DEVELOPMENT APPROACH

By the 1960s the political development approach had emerged as the dominant one in comparative politics. Some scholars continued to labor in the vineyards of the more traditional institutional approaches and others continued to write first-rate books on Western Europe. But the developing nations were clearly where the action was, particularly with the election of John F. Kennedy, the creation of the Peace Corps and the U.S. Agency for International Development (AID), which sought to *bring* development to the emerging nations and not just study it, as well as the new university programs and fellowships aimed at channeling some of our best young students into Third World development studies.[6]

Considerable variation existed among the several leading writers and approaches to development—differences that have been blurred in our memories over the years or that have been purposely subordinated to the goal of lumping all "developmentalists" together for the sake of more easily criticizing or discrediting them. First, there are the disciplinary differences: the more deterministic approaches of economists such as W. W. Rostow[7] or Robert Heilbroner,[8] for example; the sociological—but sometimes also deterministic—studies of Karl Deutsch,[9] Marion Levy,[10] or Seymour Lipset;[11] and the generally more nuanced, subtle, and multifaceted political science approaches of David Apter,[12] Lucian Pye,[13] Dankwart Rustow,[14] Myron Weiner,[15] and others.

Among the political scientists, considerable and important differences also existed. Not all the political scientists, for example, shared Gabriel Almond's attachment to structural-functionalism or to Talcott Parsons's pattern variable. Quite a number of area specialists, in addition, borrowed selectively from the Almond framework in *The Politics of the Developing Areas,* adapting it to their own regions and never entirely accepting the model in its entirety. Other scholars focused on development and modernization from their own vantage points and presented alternatives to the Almondian perspective.[16]

Nor should one assume the developmentalist model was fixed or entirely static over time. Almond himself continued to modify and amplify his views.[17] The Cambridge-area scholars who were members of the Joint (Harvard-MIT) Seminar on Political Development (JOSPOD) continued to explore new development-focused topics every year for over twenty-five years and to develop new concepts and refine old ones in the process.[18] Other scholars who were members of the original SSRC/CCP group similarly continued to refine their analyses. Still others were like Guy Pauker, who began the study of developing nations as a committed Parsonian but, after spending an extensive research period in Indonesia, came back convinced that the Parsons framework was not useful. Samuel P. Huntington, late in the 1960s,[19] was similarly critical of earlier approaches but remained committed to a developmentalist perspective.

What is required, then, is a considerable disaggregation, sorting out, and reevaluation of the earlier developmentalist approach. There is a rich body of literature "out there" that deserves to be read and considered anew. It is not a monolithic "school," nor were its principal advocates all of one mind on this issue. Rather, right from the beginning there were diverse views and approaches and a wealth of sophisticated scholarship and ideas. Far too often the developmentalist approach has been dismissed with a blanket condemnation. Its key figures have all been lumped together in one amorphous category. Although it is true that certain of its intellectual thrusts seem in retrospect to have taken us in some wrong directions, this early focus on the developing areas yielded a wealth of insights and a vast literature. It is a shame this literature is now sometimes dismissed so easily; the abundance of information and theory still found in this approach make it a marvelously fertile ground for the student of developing nations.

The second related point to remember is that the strong criticisms of development theory were not necessarily applicable to the whole body of thought and research. That has been the practical result (that is, criticism of one particular study was often applied to the literature as a whole); but in fact some of the critique is, in my view, misplaced. The criticisms usually have been leveled against the most vulnerable of the developmentalist writings (for example, those of Rostow), those that are the easiest to turn into straw men and knock down. But it may be that these are, in some of their particulars, not always representative of the more sophisticated writings in the developmentalist approach. By attacking the weakest links in the chain, critics have sought to demolish the developmentalist approach as a whole. But the field is far too rich, varied, nuanced, and diverse for us at this stage to dismiss (or smear) an entire body of work because a few of its spokespersons went too far, claimed too much, said some things that can easily be reproached, or exaggerated the universality of their model. Given the overkill to which the developmentalist approach was subjected early on, it should not be surprising, therefore, to find renewed efforts currently to try to salvage the model or to extract from it those features that remain useful.

CRITICISMS OF THE
DEVELOPMENTALIST APPROACH

During most of the 1960s the developmentalist approach was the dominant one in comparative politics. Although other comparative politics scholars continued to write in different genres and from other points of view, the political development paradigm became the prevailing one. Political development seemed at the time to be the most intellectually stimulating approach; that was where the money was, in the form of research grants and opportunities; that was where the most prestigious publication outlets (*World Politics*, Princeton University Press) were; and because development had also been accepted as a major goal of U.S. foreign policy toward the Third World, that was also the route through which the opportunity to influence policy lay.

Eventually the criticisms of development and the developmentalist approach began to build.[20] They came from diverse directions; ultimately their cumulative impact was devastating—so much so that today's students, though acquainted with the criticisms, hardly know the original literature at all, no longer read it, and tend to treat it (if at all) dismissively in one brief session in their seminars—if that! As we have already provided, in Chapters 1 and 7, an extensive critique, here we offer only a summary of the main points— and add a few others.

First, the political development literature is called biased and ethnocentric, derived from the Western experience of development and, therefore, of doubtful applicability in the Third World, whose culture and history are entirely different.[21]

Second, it has been agreed that the timing, sequences, and stages of development à la Rostow that the West experienced cannot be replicated in today's developing nations.[22]

Third, the international context of development of today's emerging nations, characterized by both dependence on and complex interdependence with other nations and blocs, is quite different from the early, nineteenth-century stages of development in the West, where relative isolation from the outside world and autonomous development were still prevalent.[23]

Fourth, the critics argue, the political development literature often misrepresented the role of traditional institutions, condemning them to the ashcans of history when, in fact, many traditional institutions have proved both flexible and viable.[24]

Fifth, within the developing nations the sense is strong that the early political development literature raised false expectations and created unrealistic goals for these societies to achieve by underestimating the difficulties of development, understating development's wrenching traumas, and forcing on unprepared nations the creation of ephemeral Western institutions that only paved the way for coups, bloodshed, and national breakdowns.[25]

Sixth, the logic, methodology, and main concepts of the development literature—the structural-functional approach, the pattern variables, the implied dichotomy between traditional and modern, and the problem of comparing "apples" (Asia), "oranges" (Africa), and "pears" (Latin America) whose cultures and histories were, in fact, so different that there was little basis for comparison—were said to be wrong or inappropriate.

A seventh criticism was that political development was part of a Cold War strategy by the United States to keep the Third World depressed and "in chains." No evidence was ever presented in support of this dubious proposition; in fact, even if development was in part connected with a U.S. foreign policy strategy, the goal was to help these nations grow economically, not to hold them back. The reality is that the foremost advocates of development believed that Third World modernization and U.S. foreign policy goals were eminently compatible and could both be advanced at the same time.[26]

Eighth, the political development perspective has been accused of wreaking downright harm on the developing nations by denigrating and undermining local and "traditional" institutions (patronage networks, family and clan groups, religious institutions) before the modern ones had a chance to grow, and thus leaving many emerging nations with neither traditional nor modern institutions but rather an institutional vacuum.[27]

One final criticism of the development approach needs to be made, and that involves not so much the developing nations per se as the political relations of the dominant SSRC/CCP group with their fellow scholars. There were early rivalries for leadership within the political development movement as well as resentments on the part of some SSRC/CCP members against the leadership; and some of these rivalries and the bitterness engendered are still alive and strongly felt by the participants over thirty years later. More important from the point of view of the receptivity of the political development approach was that the SSRC/CCP group that dominated the field for at least a decade failed sufficiently to broaden its base, bring in adequate numbers of new members, and incorporate the concepts and research findings of very many comparativists besides themselves. Year after year as the SSRC/CCP volumes came out over the decade of the 1960s, they had mostly the same editors and contributors. Very little fresh blood or new, fresh ideas were introduced, which stimulated deep resentment among many other scholars of the developing areas who also had important and worthwhile things to say. Later, quite a number of them would become severe critics of the developmentalist approach.

These criticisms of the literature and approach of political development were powerful and quite devastating. Eventually, by the end of the 1960s, not only were these criticisms widespread but some new scholarly and contextual factors were operating as well. So many case studies of the developing nations had by now been written in which the developmentalist approach was found wanting in various ways that eventually the assumptions of the approach itself were questioned. In 1968 Huntington weighed in with his powerfully written critique. The Vietnam War was another blow, for in some quarters the war was pictured as a disastrous consequence of heavy-handed U.S. involvement in another nation's development. Some of the early writers on development were viewed as supporters of the war effort or even its "architects."

A generational factor was also involved: The political development literature was largely fashioned by one generation of scholars, and by the end of the 1960s that generation began to be supplanted by a new generation who were critical of their forebears or simply had other ideas. Fad and fashion were also involved: Political development was a product of the hopeful and optimistic 1950s and early 1960s, of the perhaps excess enthusiasms of the Kennedy administration, of the Alliance for Progress, and of the "Camelot" character of that period. But by the late 1960s and early 1970s, with Vietnam, Watergate, and other traumas, that era, that fashion, and that body of literature had already come and gone. By then a number of new approaches—dependency theory, corporatism, bureaucratic-authoritarianism, political economy, a revived Marxism—had come to the fore or reemerged. The analysis now turns to these newer approaches.

NEW AND ALTERNATIVE APPROACHES

The decline in the consensus undergirding the political development approach brought a variety of other approaches to the fore. In part, these changes were due to logical or methodological flaws in the developmentalist approach itself; in part, as we have seen, they were due to broader changes within the larger society. One is tempted even to draw parallels between the decline of the developmentalist approach after the 1960s and the decline of the American societal and foreign policy consensus, and to relate the fragmentation and multiple approaches in comparative politics in the 1970s to increasing divisions, even fragmentation, in American society as a whole. It may be that such cosmic conclusions are too large to reach at the present time, but they may be worth speculating about.

What were, specifically, the major global changes of this period that also impacted the study of and approaches used in comparative politics? Only some of the broadest global trends will be noted, along with a brief comment on their influence on the field:

1. The United States by the 1970s had lost its position of overwhelming superiority and hegemony in the world and could no longer so easily impose its superiority—military, economic, or political—on the rest of the world. With this reality of a more diverse and pluralistic world came also a greater diversity of approaches in the social sciences and a series of challenges to the prevailing U.S.-based social science paradigms.

2. Along with a certain decline of the United States came a new assertiveness and expression of nationalism on the part of the Third World, manifest not just in the United Nations and other international bodies but also in the social sciences. The new Third World assertiveness was reflected in the frequently expressed claim that, though economically they were "less developed," in the social, political, or moral spheres they were not necessarily "backward" or "primitive" but only *different*. Instead of viewing their own traditional institutions as "dysfunctional" or deserving of consignment to the dustbins of history, Third World scholars and political leaders were more inclined to see them as *functional within their own context*, worthy of serious study, and perhaps useful as the basis for a new and indigenous route to development. With considerable justification, in addition, such "historic nations" as India, Egypt, or Iran began to emphasize the viability of their own traditional institutions and cultures, a number of which have been in existence for longer than our own, which evoke in these nations strong feelings of national pride, and which might be quite rational and functional in non-Western terms. Other Third World nations and areas similarly became more assertive in putting forward *their own* ways of doing things.

3. Along with the relative decline in the U.S. international position, and of the frequent assertion of the superiority of U.S. political institutions and its developmental model, came a strong challenge to the dominant approach in comparative politics. The older paradigm had stressed stability, moderate democratic development, and manageable change. But in the aftermath of Vietnam and Watergate, along with severe strains in many U.S. political and social institutions came a new questioning of and sometimes radical challenge to the prevailing mores and beliefs.

4. Research interests shifted. The comparative politics of the 1960s concentrated on "inputs"—public opinion, interest organizations, and political parties. Moreover, the focus was almost exclusively on political variables to the exclusion of economic ones. This meant that little attention was paid

to the actual processes of decisionmaking or to what came "out" of the political system in the form of public policies and their impact on the population. But the successive oil shocks of the 1970s, the worldwide economic recession that followed, and the growing realization of the facts of global economic interdependence made it imperative that scholars also study political economy.

5. The communist model declined. Neither in the Soviet Union, China, Eastern Europe, Angola, Ethiopia, Cuba, or Nicaragua is the Marxist-Leninist model working very well. Both economically and politically, the regimes based on Marxist-Leninist principles are proving unattractive. It is democracy, human rights, and Western culture (including blue jeans and Coca-Cola, as well as freedom and greater opportunities) that people worldwide have come to prefer. These trends have now led back in comparative politics to a reemphasis on political development and Western models, and to somewhat greater skepticism not only of Marxism-Leninism but also of indigenous routes to development.

There are undoubtedly other reasons besides those mentioned here for the changes in comparative politics in recent decades and the growing plurality of approaches and models in the field. We have sought to highlight some of the main "global" reasons, not with the idea of having exhausted what is a complex subject, but chiefly as a way of showing the interrelations between the intellectual directions of comparative politics and the broader societal and political milieu in which the field's dominant approaches have been planted, taken root, and grown—and have by now been transformed or supplanted by newer shoots.

By the mid-1970s, in any case, the dominant political development approach in comparative politics had been attacked, discredited, and was no longer in such widespread use. A variety of new theories and approaches had emerged to take its place. The decline of the older consensus in the field need not necessarily be lamented, for, as we have seen, there are major problems with the political development approach. In addition, the new approaches have, for the most part, made important contributions to the field. The trouble is, as with development theory, that there are useful and not-so-useful, sophisticated as well as vulgar, versions of all these approaches that need to be sorted out. Furthermore, by the end of the 1980s many of these newer approaches, like political development before, have in turn run their course and begun to be replaced. By what, we must eventually ask; and what, therefore, is the future of the field?

Dependency Theory

Dependency theory grew directly out of dissatisfaction with the developmentalist approach in the 1960s, and specifically out of the criticism that development theory ignored international "dependency" variables, such as international market forces over which the Third World had little control, the manipulation of those markets by the developed nations at the expense of the poorer countries, the role of multinational corporations in the Third

World, and the machinations of U.S. embassies abroad.[28] Although it need not necessarily be that way, dependency theory was closely identified with a radical, usually Marxian critique of U.S. society and the U.S. role internationally.

There are, of course, dependency relations in the world, growing mainly out of asymmetries of size and power among nations, as well as complex relations of interdependence; and all of us understand that U.S. embassies (as well as many others) and various transnational actors (churches, lobbies of various sorts, as well as the multinational corporations) do sometimes get involved—usually for good but not always so—in the internal affairs of other nations. The trick in utilizing dependency theory is to distinguish between those analysts who use the approach pragmatically to shed light on the role of international actors operating within the borders of Third World nations or otherwise shaping their destinies[29] and those who wish to use the theory as an ideological weapon, usually from a Marxist or Marxist-Leninist perspective, to flagellate the United States.[30] A sophisticated dependency theory can be a useful tool of analysis to investigate those international forces that development theory largely ignored, but the more ideological version of *dependencia* should be viewed as more a political than a scholarly instrument.

Corporatism

The corporatist approach similarly arose out of discontent with development theory and was meant to shed light on those political phenomena—labor relations, social policy, state-society relations, interest group interactions, bureaucratization, and centralized decisionmaking—that the other main approaches generally touched on only peripherally. Two schools of thought within the corporatist approach emerged early on: One viewed corporatism as an ideology or a general pattern of political cognition, like liberalism or Marxism, that seemed to have had an especially strong influence (but not exclusively so) on the Catholic countries of southern and eastern Europe between the two world wars, and on Latin America and continuing in Iberia in the post–World War II period.[31] A second school took corporatism as a general model of the political system, without particular regional or culture-area affinities, implying a structure of state dominance, control, and structuring of interest group activity, including most particularly the *incorporation* of interest groups into the regulatory armature of the modern state apparatus.[32] These differing perspectives on corporatism should not be seen as contradictory or incompatible; indeed, the two perspectives ought to be seen as complementary, to be utilized in tandem with each other rather than as polarized opposites.[33]

Corporatism has by now been found to be present, in different forms, in virtually all political regimes. Its very ubiquitousness, however, has somewhat diminished its attractiveness as a new frontier in the discipline and its utility as an explanatory device. If everyone and everything is corporatist, how can this approach be used to compare and contrast countries, which is what comparative politics is all about? The answer is that different countries have different forms, types, and systems of corporatism, thus enabling us to point out the general aspects of the corporatism phenomenon but also to differentiate between countries. The result is that the corporatist approach has experienced a different fate than dependency theory: Corporatism is seldom controversial anymore, it is found almost universally, its usefulness as an explanatory device (a necessary but not a sufficient one) has been widely recognized, and most scholars—once the excitement of this new approach had worn down—have accepted the approach and gone on to other things. Because of its widespread acceptance in the comparative politics field, corporatism is no longer the subject of intense controversy (as is, still, dependency theory); rather, corporatism has become somewhat less exciting precisely because it is widely accepted.

Political Economy

The early writings on political development largely ignored political economy variables. In part, that was because in the 1950s, when the political development approach was first formulated, the lines between the social science disciplines were sharper than is true today; interdisciplinary work was less appreciated; the autonomy of political variables was widely assumed in the field; and most scholars simply took for granted that political scientists did their work while economists would do theirs. Hence, there was not thought to be a great need for explicitly political economy analysis. In part, also, the absence of a focus on political economy stemmed from the fact that the earliest studies of development had been done by economists (Hagen,[34] Rostow) and sociologists (Lipset), and political scientists wished to stake out their own independent claim within the broadening field of development studies. In addition, it seems likely that, given that the political development approach was first formulated in part to provide an alternative to Marxian appeals in the developing world,[35] a conscious effort was made to stay away from political economy explanations that could too easily be confused with Marxism.

And, like dependency theory, that is still sometimes the problem with the political economy approach. In subtle, sophisticated hands, it can be an exceedingly useful and insightful approach.[36] That has generally been the orientation of the scholars who edit and write for *International Organization*. In less sophisticated hands, or among those who wish consciously to use it that way, the political economy approach has a tendency to tail off into a Marxian explanation with, again, greatly varying levels of refinement or vulgarity.

Indigenous Theories

The idea of a homegrown, locally devised model of development for the Third World, or for the various parts of it, is undoubtedly an enormously attractive one. But in practice, since its apostles sounded the clarion call in the 1970s, the plan and hope of indigenously based theory and institutions have not worked out very well.

Joseph Mobutu's idea of African "authenticity" in Zaire degenerated into "just another" corrupt dictatorship. The often noble and innovative political experiments that began elsewhere in Africa in the 1960s have, sadly, often similarly degenerated into some bloody military regimes. In Latin America, where corporatism and organic-statism were once seen as a possible basis for an indigenous theory of development, those ideas have been rejected in favor of massive support for democracy and representative government. It is hard to say that China, with its new emphasis on capitalism, is following an "indigenous" route to development; or even, with its 1989 political crackdown, that China represents a model of anything attractive. Nor is Iran, which has gone about as far as any country (except perhaps Cambodia) to reject Western ways and erect its own alternative Islamic model, a particularly captivating example. One would be hard-pressed, indeed, to find a *single* Third World country that has successfully implemented a homegrown plan of development.

Instead, what has happened is that, for good (mainly) and ill (sometimes), the Western model of culture, politics, and economics has triumphed overwhelmingly. Some intellectuals may still prefer indigenous and often exotic forms, but the vast mass of the people in the developing world have made it very clear what they want: Western music, dress, and tastes; Western-style democracy and freedom; and Western capitalism and consumerism. In the process, the idea of an indigenous model of development for all or each of the developing areas has been largely abandoned. At best, what might be hoped for is a blend that combines what is still useful and viable among native institutions with a selected or filtered set of imports from the West. We return to this theme later in the discussion.

Bureaucratic-Authoritarianism

Bureaucratic-authoritarianism arose out of the self-same disillusionment with the developmentalist approach as did dependency theory and the corporatist approach. It was particularly aimed at explaining the rash of military coups that occurred in Latin America in the 1960s and 1970s. That same wave of coups in both Africa and Latin America had also helped undermine the developmentalist approach by suggesting rather emphatically that all good things (economic growth, social modernization, and political development or democracy), contrary to the theory of development, did *not* go together. The term *bureaucratic*-authoritarian was used by this school of thought to distinguish the newer, more institutionalized types of military rule in such countries as Argentina, Brazil, or Peru from the older, more personalistic or *caudillo*-dominated military regimes of the past.[37]

Bureaucratic-authoritarianism is a good term, for in fact the newer Latin American authoritarian regimes were more bureaucratic, less personalistic, more institutionalized, more "modern" than those in the past. The trouble was that this useful contribution was accompanied by an attempt to explain the B-A phenomenon through a convoluted argument that pointed to the crisis of Latin America's growth strategy of import substitution as *the* cause of bureaucratic-authoritarianism, and thus shaded off into a kind of economic determinism that the evidence could not sustain. Among other fallacies of reasoning, the question was asked: If Latin America's crisis of import substitution was responsible for the rise of dictatorship in the 1960s, how could a similar crisis of import substitution in the late 1970s and early 1980s be used to explain Latin America's transition to democracy?[38] You cannot have it both ways: Either the crisis of import substitution causes the rise of dictatorship or it causes the rise of democracy, but it surely cannot cause both. Other factors must be involved. Hence, like so many of the approaches examined here, B-A marked a significant contribution, but it needed to be shorn of its ideological baggage and the cautionary flag again waved that a useful but still partial explanation should not be elevated to the status of a single and all-encompassing one.

Marxism

There are few scholars who do not find the Marxian paradigm of use in providing a rough map, a broad-gauged explanation for the transition from feudalism to capitalism. That is what has made the Marxian explanation popular intellectually in the developing nations, for that is often the kind of transition through which they are presently going. The trouble comes (1) when the Marxian categories are applied too literally, for recent scholarship has shown that many other factors besides the Marxian class-based ones are involved in the transition away from feudalism to some form of modernity; (2) when it is used to explain the transition from capitalism to the next stage, on which Marx was neither clear nor accurate; (3) when the Marxian categories are applied to specific groups where they do not fit very well (for example, in explaining the political behavior of such critical institutions as religious bodies or armed forces); and (4) when it is used as a rigidly ideological formula rather than a flexible tool of analysis.[39]

In addition, the socialist countries have found that Marxism is not a particularly useful guide in providing for an efficient and productive economy; their intellectuals have abandoned Marxism almost to a person;[40] and many developing nations—once enamored of the Marxist model—are no longer so strongly attracted to it. In the present era Marxism and especially Marxism-Leninism appear to be valued as a formula for gaining, consolidating, and hanging onto power, but not as a way to achieve either political freedom or economic development.[41]

Political Culture

The study of political culture flourished in the 1960s,[42] and then went into a decline. Now it is being revived. Political culture studies focus on the basic values, beliefs, and psychological ways of behaving in different countries and culture areas. The argument is that values and beliefs are important factors in telling us how people behave and their orientations toward the political system. Political culture, when systematically based on survey data or careful historical analysis, is much preferable to the old-fashioned "national character" studies that involved dangerous stereotyping.

But political culture was attacked on several fronts. Marxists saw it as just part of the superstructure determined by underlying class configurations and not an independent variable in its own right. Some continued to be offended by the national characterizations that political culture studies often led to. Still others were worried about its looseness as a concept and the tendency to use political culture as a catchall category to explain factors that could not be accounted for in other ways. The argument over what explains development in East Asia and elsewhere—culture or structural factors—went on endlessly.

Recently political culture has enjoyed a renaissance.[43] Culture *is* important as a political explanation—along with other factors such as class relations, political institutions, or the play of international forces. Many political phenomena cannot be explained without understanding the cultural context in which they take place. In careful hands political culture can be an important explanatory device. It is doubtful that political behavior in Latin America, Asia, Africa, the Islamic world, and elsewhere can be understood without comprehending such political-cultural variables as the role of religion, the legal context, values, ideologies, and psychology. No one claims that political culture is the only variable in understanding other political systems; rather that in conjunction with other factors political culture can be a useful explanatory tool.

State-Society Relations
and Public Policy Analysis

Both the focus on state-society relations and the comparative study of public policy have added significantly to our knowledge as well as to our conceptual armature. Each of these newer approaches arose in partial reaction to the earlier political development approach, and it is not coincidental that they emerged in the mid-1970s. The political development approach had placed heavy emphasis on public opinion, interest groups, political parties, and the like, but it had not devoted equal attention to the role of the state or to governing institutions. In part, the political development approach reflected in this regard the prevailing American interest group model of liberalism, which saw the state chiefly as a neutral referee in the larger interest group struggle. The state-society focus sought to correct this oversight by showing how the state, often acting autonomously, has major influence on class structure and the interest group struggle as well as being influenced by them. The state-society focus helped bring the state back in as an independent variable, in contrast to the neutral referee image of interest group theory or the "part of the superstructure" idea of Marxism. Moreover, the focus on state-*society* relations provided a dynamic element to this approach, enabling us to see how the relations between the state and its component societal units—armies, churches, universities, trade unions, and so on—could change over time.

The comparative public policy focus, which also emerged in the mid-1970s, similarly stemmed in part from a dissatisfaction with the earlier political development approach's focus on inputs. Not only did the public policy approach wish to emphasize bureaucratic and state decisionmaking and the "output," or policy side, of the political system, but it also argued that these public policies had a feedback effect on public opinion and on the interest group competition that went "into" the political system. Public policy analysis thus closed the political process circle, from inputs, to decisionmaking, to public policy, to feedback, and hence again to inputs. The public policy focus also spoke to the demand in the Third World as well as already industrialized nations that government not only be reflective of society on the input side but that it also *deliver* in the way of effective programs and services.

Both the state-society and the public policy approaches have now found their way into the broader comparative politics field.

* * *

Many of these newer approaches have provided useful contributions to comparative politics. Quite a number—state-society relations, corporatism, political economy, public policy—have by now been successfully integrated into the broader field. The dependency approach, bureaucratic-authoritarianism, and the idea of indigenous models of change have also made their contributions but remain more controversial. It should be remembered, however, that *all* these theories, by themselves, provide only partial explanations, not complete ones; and that they, too, like the political development approach in earlier decades, have gone through a virtual life cycle of birth, growth, flourishing, acceptability or co-optation within the field, and then usually a gradual decline or fading away. That is a natural and not necessarily an unhealthy process for any intellectual field. But now we have to face a new phenomenon: a revival and reinvigoration of the political development approach. Political development is once again taking its place as one of the leading approaches in comparative politics. Given what has been said before, we need to know how and why that is occurring, as well as the larger implications of these newer trends for the field.

POLITICAL DEVELOPMENT REVIVED

In the early 1960s, when there was tremendous hope for democratic development in the Third World, it was widely assumed that democracy, development, peace, and security would be closely related. Intellectual justifications for such correlations were provided in the development literature of that period, particularly in the writings of Rostow,[44] Lipset,[45] Deutsch,[46] Daniel Lerner,[47] and others. Using his famous aeronautical metaphor, Rostow demonstrated that—based on the European and U.S. experiences—as countries develop economically, they also tend to become more middle-class, pluralistic, democratic, stable, prosperous, and peaceful. Lipset and Deutsch, in path-breaking articles about that same time, showed the close correlations among literacy, social mobilization, economic development, and democracy; Lerner similarly focused on the interrelations among education, development, and democracy. An obvious foreign policy lesson also followed from this research: If the United States can help the developing nations to be more literate, pluralistic, affluent, and middle-class, they will consequently become more democratic and more able to resist the appeals of communism.

But correlations do not imply causal relationships, and in Africa and Latin America during the 1960s a wave of military coups swept the civilian democratic governments out of power. Greater literacy and accelerated social mobilization did not lead to democracy and stability but to upheaval and repression. The middle class proved to be not a bastion of stability and democracy but deeply divided and often very conservative, goading the military to seize power from the civilian democrats. By the mid-1970s none of the correlations that the development literature posited were correlating very well: Development had inched forward, but democracy had collapsed; in Latin America seventeen of the twenty-one nations were under military or quasi-military rule; the developmentalist assumptions and literature were in a shambles; and the new post-developmentalist interpretations—dependency theory, corporatism, Marxist explanations, bureaucratic-authoritarianism—were in their heyday.[48]

But since the late 1970s nations as diverse as South Korea, the Philippines, and the Republic of China (Taiwan) have embarked on some remarkable transitions to democracy. In Latin America the figures cited for the authoritarianism of the mid-1970s have been reversed: now, seventeen of the twenty-one countries and over 90 percent of the population are governed democratically or are en route to democracy. Even the People's Republic of China, the Soviet Union, and some countries of Eastern Europe have taken some steps toward greater openness and, in some cases, even pluralism. This impressive movement toward democracy in so short a period is remarkable. Not only has this given rise to a whole new approach and body of literature (called "transitions to democracy")[49] in comparative politics, but it also forces us to reconsider and maybe resurrect the developmentalist approach. Suddenly, the correlations suggested by developmentalism between development, democracy, stability, moderation in politics, and so on are again correlating very well. At least six factors are at work here demanding our attention and forcing us to rethink the developmentalist approach.

What Works in Development

By this time we have over thirty years' experience with development. Our discussions about development, therefore, no longer need to be entirely at the conceptual and theoretical level, as they were to a large extent in the 1960s, when the developing nations had just begun to emerge onto the world scene. With the proper qualifications, we now *know* what works in development. We no longer have just theories but actual experience. We have a three-decade-long track record, we have abundant case histories, and we have sophisticated comparative studies. We are now able to be fairly confident about what is likely to be a successful development strategy and what an unsuccessful one. Overwhelmingly, the evidence now points to the conclusion that what works in development is democracy, stability, pluralism, representative government, a judicious blend of state regulation and open market economies, social modernization, and peaceful, moderate change[50]— all the elements that Almond, Rostow, Lipset, et al. suggested several decades ago as being necessary for development.

A World Political Culture in Favor of Democracy

The concept of a "world political culture," first articulated by Lucian Pye,[51] is and always will be imprecise and difficult for empirical verification. Nevertheless, there can be no doubt that in the past decade a remarkable global transformation has occurred. In Asia, Latin America, and perhaps even in the communist countries, the sentiment in favor of democracy is now overwhelming. Democracy has proven to be the only form of political regime that works; democracy now enjoys world legitimacy, as no other political regime does. Public opinion surveys in Latin America indicate that over 90 percent of the population in country after country favors democratic, representative government. Not "neodemocracy" or "relative democracy" or "tutelary democracy" but *democracy*—without adjectives. At the same time *glasnost* and *perestroika* may have ushered in one of the most fundamental transformations of the late twentieth century: political opening and somewhat greater democracy within communist regimes. A host of authoritarian regimes in Mediterranean Europe, East Asia, and Latin America have similarly been swept from power. Though the measures are sometimes inexact and though the term needs to be defined with precision, few of us can doubt that a revolution of profound dimensions, in favor of democracy, has begun to sweep the world.[52]

U.S. Foreign Policy

Most of the recent transitions to democracy have been the products of indigenous forces and only secondarily of external ones. Nevertheless, in some countries at key times a U.S. policy in favor of democracy has been critical—either in keeping a threatened democracy alive or in nudging a regime toward democracy. A democracy/human rights agenda has been pursued by the United States, both for strong (albeit on-again, off-again) moral and humanitarian reasons and because it is our history as a nation to push for an ethical foreign policy, *and* for strong practical reasons: It is in our interests to do so. That is, democratic regimes tend to be more stable, tend not to get involved in wars, do not interfere in their neighbors' internal affairs, and in general cause far fewer problems for U.S. foreign policy. The United States' most recent campaign for democracy and human rights began under President Jimmy Carter and continued in altered form under President Ronald Reagan. Carter emphasized human rights and helped begin the process, whereas Reagan gave it a broader democracy focus and stressed that global human rights tend to flow from American strength, not American weakness. By this point, democracy and human rights have acquired a consensus of bipartisan support, and it is inconceivable that any future U.S. administration could have a successful foreign policy without these components.[53]

The Unattractiveness of Other Models

Further strengthening democracy has been that the main alternatives to it—and the models helping to justify them—have proved to be so unattractive. No one wants to live under corporatism anymore—neither in Iberia nor in Latin America, where corporatism had in the past been powerful and where the corporatist model had sometimes been proffered as an alternative to democracy and to Marxism-Leninism. Nor does anyone want anymore to live under bureaucratic-authoritarianism, with its repression, widespread violations of human rights, and disastrous social and political programs. Nor are Cuba, Ethiopia, or the Soviet Union—the Marxist-Leninist regimes— any longer viewed as viable and appealing models, either politically or economically. The demise or discrediting of these alternative regimes and the corresponding unattractiveness of the models that go with them, together with the resurgence of democracy, have given rise to the sentiment that maybe the democracy/developmentalist paradigm has a great deal to recommend it after all.[54]

Changed Political Attitudes
in the United States

After Vietnam, Watergate, the relative decline of the United States in the 1970s, and President Carter's idea that the United States was afflicted by "malaise," the sense was strong in the United States that we had little to offer the world. Both our real position in the world and our self-confidence at home had been eroded by events abroad and in our own country. But during the 1980s, as the economy recovered and then flourished, American self-confidence began to recover. Millions of people from all over the world clamored to enter the United States. Contrary to some of the earlier "ethnocentrism" literature, the sense grew—in contrast to the 1970s—that maybe the United States was not such a bad place after all (at least as compared with most others) and still had a great deal to offer the rest of the world. There are many criticisms that may be raised against it, but Allan Bloom's book[55]—and probably those of Paul Johnson[56] and even Tom Clancy[57]—which emphasized the democratizing and civilizing values in the Western cultural tradition and pointedly suggested, in contrast to much of the prevailing cultural relativism, that some cultures (the Western one) are, in fact, more democratic, more humane, and more civilized than others (let us say, the Iranian one) undoubtedly struck a responsive chord. These cultural forces also helped give a new impetus to the resurrection of development theory.

Development in the Short Run
—and in the Long

The democratization, development, and modernization that have occurred in many Third World areas in the past decade force us to reassess the Lipsetonian and Rostowian theories previously discussed in the light of these new circumstances. Lipset, Rostow, and the entire developmentalist school were thoroughly discredited in the 1960s and 1970s—and often for good reasons, as outlined in earlier parts of this book. They and their followers, as well as many U.S. government officials, tended to portray the relationship between development and democracy in ways that proved far too simple, positing a causative relationship that was not borne out by the facts, basing their theories of development too heavily on the Western experience, and thus for a long time helping lead development theory and the policies that flowed from it astray.

But we now need to face the fact that, if Lipset, Rostow, and the developmentalist approach were incorrect in their models and forecasts for the short run, they may still prove to have been correct in the long run. That is, although there is no necessary, automatic, or exactly causative relationship between development and democracy—as some of the early development literature suggested—there are tendencies, correlations, and long-term relationships among these factors that cannot be ignored. It is necessary, therefore, the editor believes, to begin a serious reexamination of the earlier development literature to see what should be saved and what jettisoned. We will likely find that there is more worth saving than ten years ago would have seemed likely.[58]

We learned during the 1960s, for example, that—contrary to what developmentalism posited—there was no necessary correlation between democracy and the size of the middle class, because in many countries it was the middle class that plotted to overthrow democracy. But then in the 1980s the middle class led the opposition to military authoritarianism and is now convinced, having tried other formulas, that democracy is much to be preferred. The Latin American continent, in addition, is about 70 percent urban now as compared with 30 percent forty years ago; and so urbanization now correlates nicely with both development and democracy, as the earlier literature suggested. Employing other indices yields further correlations: The armed forces are now more professionalized and more middle-class than thirty years ago, and also more in favor of democracy. Literacy is now far greater, and so is the spread of democracy. Economic development over the past three decades has generally gone forward, industrialization has accelerated, and affluence is generally greater—and so is the desire for democracy. All these indicators of development *and* democracy that did not correlate very well in the 1960s now seem to be correlating very well indeed.[59]

These strong correlations raise the distinct possibility that whereas Lipset, Rostow, and others were too optimistic about development and democracy in the short run, in the longer term their correlations (and the predictions that flowed from them) may yet prove to be accurate. One decade (the 1960s) was simply too short a period for the propositions of the developmentalist approach to be tested adequately. Moreover, the more sophisticated theories of development had recognized all along that these were long-term processes, that the transitional phase was almost certain to be chaotic, and that there were bound to be many setbacks on the road to development. But over the course of three decades now, we have a longer time period to observe; we have considerable experience with development; and the earlier assumptions and correlations of the development approach have begun to look better and better.

The socioeconomic base for democracy in Asia and Latin America is bigger, more solid, and more promising now than it was in the 1960s. The middle class is larger; there is far greater affluence; bureaucracies are better trained and more experienced with development; the associational and institutional life has grown and become better consolidated; literacy is far higher; vast social changes have occurred, leading to greater pluralism; the military is better educated and more professional; per capita income is higher; more citizens are better educated; the private sectors are larger and more active; and so on.[60]

These fundamental social and economic changes may well mean that the current openings to democracy in much of the developing world may prove more than just cyclical, popular now but subject, when the next crisis comes, to a new round of coups. When civil society was weak and development was just beginning for many countries in the 1960s, an authoritarian regime might have seemed to some a possible alternative; but as development and pluralism have gone forward in more recent decades, a new wave of military takeovers seems increasingly unlikely—at least in the better institutionalized and more viable of the developing countries. It may be that the developmental changes of the past thirty years have been sufficiently profound that many countries can look forward to a stabler future based on development and democracy. And the processes involved seem to oblige us to reconsider the main premises of the development approach in a new and more positive light.

THE "ISLANDS OF THEORY" APPROACH

The field of comparative politics has become more and more fragmented since the 1960s. There is no one approach that dominates the field, nor is there an approved body of theoretical knowledge on which all or even most scholars can agree. With the earlier decline and discrediting of the developmentalist approach, the field had lost its earlier unity. Perhaps this was a reflection of the increasing fragmentation within the larger political science discipline, perhaps of increasing fragmentation within the United

States more generally. Whatever the ultimate answers to those questions, it is evident that what now exist in comparative politics are separate subsections within the field, each with its own research agenda, its own theories, its own apostles, and its own work and studies. Usually only limited efforts are made to connect these discrete subsections of the field to each other. We have, in short, various "islands" of research work and theory, often with few efforts to connect them and almost no central or overarching structure or theory that would provide unity to the field as a whole.

Some scholars, particularly senior scholars whose intellectual roots reach back into the 1930s and whose orientation helped shape the emerging comparative politics field of the post–World War II period, are understandably concerned by the challenges to the older approaches launched in recent decades and by what they see as an increased and possibly destructive fragmentation of the field. They see their ideas and contributions being questioned and sometimes rejected, then replaced by what to them seem vague and often uncongenial theories. They believe their earlier writings have sometimes been misrepresented by the critics. It should be said that a number of the senior scholars in the field have adapted to and accepted the newer currents, even incorporating their more useful aspects into their own work. But some others have seen no reason to adapt and a few have turned bitter and resentful toward both the new approaches and their proponents. The debate within the field has sometimes been heated.

The thrust of this book, however, has been in another direction. It seems to us unlikely that any time in the near future the unity that reigned in the 1960s in the comparative politics field as a whole will be restored. Nor are we at all certain, given the rich diversity of approaches that we now have, that such unity is desirable. The unity that centered on the political development approach in the 1960s contributed valuable new insights and approaches but also led students of comparative politics down some wrong trails and blinded us to phenomena and alternative approaches that did not seem to fit comfortably within the development paradigm. There were other social and political phenomena that developmentalism failed adequately to explain and that required alternative kinds of explanations.

We have tried in this book to be neither overly laudatory nor overly critical of the older, dominant schools in comparative politics but to strike a judicious balance. We have sought to weigh and assess both the valuable insights and contributions of these older approaches *and* their biases, presumptions, and oversights. Different chapters have addressed the useful and the not-so-useful in these approaches, at the same time placing them in historical perspective and providing a "sociology of knowledge" that helps explain how and why these approaches emerged when they did, why they later came under challenge and attack, and why some have survived or been revived and others not. Most of the scholars who contributed to this book were, in fact, brought up with the older focus and with the categories of the development literature, and many still employ the helpful insights of these approaches. Others, in large part as a result of their extensive field experience in Third World areas, have gone on to adopt the newer concepts and categories. Still others attempt to bridge the several approaches.

The newer approaches have also gone through a certain life cycle, however. Some have largely run their course and been exhausted; others have been accepted within the mainstreams of the field. In still other cases, events occurring in the outside world have affected the approach we use. For example, we are no longer in an era of bureaucratic-authoritarianism or of attraction to corporatist solutions but in a period of vast social and political changes, of profound international transformations, and, in several regions, of quite remarkable transitions to democracy. These changes have not only forced some of the approaches analyzed here to the sidelines but have also made the older developmentalist approach look better and deserving of a second consideration. Shorn of its ethnocentrism, its biases, and its blindnesses, the developmentalist approach, we have rediscovered, contains a rich body of sophisticated literature and a storehouse of theory, insight, and case studies from which we can still—and again—profitably learn. The developmentalist approach is unlikely to recapture the central place in the field that it enjoyed in the 1960s—too much has changed in the interim, and so have we and the field—but it can certainly retake its place as one of the half dozen or so major approaches.

The lesson is that the field of comparative politics is constantly in flux; approaches advance and retreat and sometimes advance again, corresponding both to intellectual trends and to changes in the world of nations with which students in the field must grapple. Such changes are natural, and they demand flexibility and adaptation of students in comparative politics. We need not be so attached to one approach that we remain blindly tied to it even after changing realities oblige us to utilize other approaches.

Although in this book we have often found fault with the older, more traditional approaches in comparative politics, we have also tried not to give too great a stress to the newer approaches or to accept them uncritically. Indeed, some of our contributors have condemned the new approaches about which they have written. Other authors have shown how the newer approaches have built upon, and would not have been possible without, the more traditional perspectives of the 1950s and 1960s. Seeing continuities and overlaps between the older and newer approaches, not dichotomous or either-or choices, most of our authors are quite pragmatic and eclectic in these matters, often borrowing from several approaches in their own research work and combining and reconciling them. Another valuable suggestion is Sidney Verba's injunction offered earlier in this book that one might appropriately look more at what students of comparative politics have actually done and produced in their research, as much as the grand theories, philosophical premises, and stated rationalizations for doing what they did.

Our perspective, then, is to see the new diversity in the field, as well as the periodic ascendance and decline of the different approaches, as normal, customary, and healthy for comparative politics and not a cause for handwringing. Any approach in any field, and particularly in the social sciences, that over time becomes the dominant one has a tendency also to become stale and ossified, unable to absorb new findings and ideas. That is precisely what happened to some of the older approaches in comparative politics. Hence, what we have tried to do is to take cognizance of the major contributions these earlier approaches made, while recognizing they do not represent any final truth, and at the same time accommodating to and using the insights of the newer approaches where they are useful and relevant. We tend to agree with Abraham Kaplan that these should be pragmatic choices and not ideological ones.[61]

A price is, of course, exacted for such eclecticism. The field tends to lose its unity and some of its coherence. It is sometimes upsetting to beginning students who may want greater coherence and a body of "revealed truth" that comparative politics is not able to provide. On balance, however, we believe the field has not been destroyed nor its deathknell sounded by the pluralism of approaches but, in fact, broadened, deepened, and enriched by the newer approaches.

Stanley Hoffmann in our Harvard Seminar initially suggested the "islands of theory" concept. He argued cogently and convincingly that, because the comparative politics field had lost its earlier unity, those active in the field should now accept this fact realistically rather than simply lamenting it or wishing it away. That is, we should recognize that there is no longer a single, overarching paradigm on which all or even most students in the field can agree. Rather, what we now have are various "islands of theory" appropriate for the several, quasi-self-contained parts of the field—political culture studies, political socialization studies, political party studies, interest group studies, political economy studies, voting behavior studies, public policy studies, government performance and effectiveness studies, and the like.

Given this diversity in the field, what now is to be done? What should be the task of those who work in comparative politics? The Harvard Seminar suggested four main lines of approach:

1. Recognize and come to grips realistically with the absence any longer of a single, all-encompassing principle or theory on which the field could be based and on which all or even most scholars could agree.
2. Continue working in each subfield on specific research projects that to individual scholars seem worthwhile and interesting.
3. Develop, clarify, and elaborate the various islands of theory (development, corporatism, political economy, state-society relations, public policy, dependency, and others) that enlighten and provide useful guidelines for research in these various subfields. Build theory at middle-range levels. Such assessments should include the rise, decline, or rise again of these several approaches and the implications of such changes for the field as a whole.
4. Meanwhile, seek to build bridges between and among these various islands of research as a way, tentatively and conditionally, of beginning

to reforge the elements of a larger integrating theory, one based on reality and careful investigation and not on the sometimes false or romantic concepts of the past.

The erecting of such bridges is in the final analysis what theory building and conceptualization should consist of in any field. One of our seminar members later elaborated on Hoffmann's "bridges among the islands of theory" metaphor by defining the task as "constructing causeways among the archipelagos."

Whatever the precise image used, we see such bridge building as the next major step forward in comparative politics—every bit as intellectually exciting as the earlier efforts to forge a single unity within the field. For instance, we can foresee a great deal of insight and useful information coming out of the efforts to combine the new focus on state-society relations with comparative public policy analysis.[62] As scholars, we would like to see more sophisticated analyses of the relationship between class structure, the "world system" of markets and economic dominance, and comparative political development—in short, to build international political economy variables back into the developmentalist approach. We are intrigued by the application of dependency theory to socialist as well as capitalist economies.[63] We would also like to see the older vision of a universal social science of development tested against the newer arguments for development models at the geographic or culture area level. Political culture needs to be refactored into our comparative politics analyses;[64] and we would love to see a theoretical reconciliation of the development literature, corporatism, and dependency analysis.[65] One can envision other potential combinations and fusions.

To us that makes comparative politics an exciting research frontier, really a whole series of new research frontiers. Some of that excitement has been captured in the various contributions to this book. We hope it is contagious.

NOTES

1. Taylor Cole, *European Political Systems* (New York: Knopf, 1953); Carl Friedrich, *Constitutional Government and Democracy* (Boston: Ginn, 1941); Herman Finer, *The Theory and Practice of Modern Government* (New York: Holt, 1949); John Herz and Gwendolen Carter, *Major Foreign Powers* (New York: Harcourt, Brace, Jovanovich, numerous editions); Karl Loewenstein, *Political Power and the Governmental Process* (Chicago: University of Chicago Press, 1957).

2. Roy Macridis, *The Study of Comparative Government* (New York: Random House, 1955).

3. A useful but still incomplete effort is Irene I. Gendzier, *Managing Political Change: Social Scientists and the Third World* (Boulder, CO: Westview Press, 1985).

4. Francis Fukuyama, "The End of History?" *National Interest* 16 (Summer 1989).

5. Edward Kolodziej, "Introduction," in Kolodziej and Roger Kanet, eds., *The Cold War as Cooperation* (New York: Routledge, forthcoming).

6. For some reflections on the "political culture" in which political development studies began and flourished, see Gabriel A. Almond, *Political Development: Essays in Heuristic Theory* (Boston: Little, Brown, 1970), Introduction.

7. *The Stages of Economic Growth: A Non-Communist Manifesto* (Cambridge: Cambridge University Press, 1960).

8. Robert Heilbroner, *The Great Ascent* (New York: Harper & Row, 1963).

9. Karl W. Deutsch, "Social Mobilization and Political Development," *American Political Science Review* 55 (September 1961):493–514.

10. Marion Levy, *The Structure of Society* (Princeton, NJ: Princeton University Press, 1952).

11. Seymour Martin Lipset, "Some Social Requisites of Democracy: Economic Development and Political Legitimacy," *American Political Science Review* 53 (March 1959):69–105.

12. David E. Apter, *The Politics of Modernization* (Chicago: University of Chicago Press, 1965).

13. Lucian W. Pye, *Aspects of Political Development* (Boston: Little, Brown, 1966).

14. Dankwart Rustow, *World of Nations: Problems of Political Modernization* (Washington, DC: Brookings Institution, 1967).

15. Myron Weiner, ed., *Modernization* (New York: Basic Books, 1966).

16. For example, J. Fred Riggs, *Administration in Developing Countries: The Theory of Prismatic Society* (Boston: Houghton Mifflin, 1964).

17. Gabriel A. Almond and G. Bingham Powell, Jr., *Comparative Politics: A Developmental Approach* (Boston: Little, Brown, 1966); Almond, ed., *Comparative Politics Today* (Boston: Little, Brown, 1974); Almond and Powell, *Comparative Politics: Systems, Processes, and Policy.* 2d ed. (Boston: Little, Brown, 1978).

18. Myron Weiner and Samuel P. Huntington, eds., *Understanding Political Development* (Boston: Little, Brown, 1987).

19. Samuel P. Huntington, *Political Order in Changing Societies* (New Haven, CT: Yale University Press, 1968).

20. See, among others, Sidney Verba, "Some Dilemmas in Comparative Research," *World Politics* 20 (October 1967):111–127; Mark Kesselman, "Order or Movement: The Literature of Political Development as Ideology," *World Politics* 26 (October 1973):139–153, Philip H. Melanson and Lauriston R. King, "Theory in Comparative Politics: A Critical Appraisal," *Comparative Political Studies* 4 (July 1971):205–231; Geoffrey K. Roberts, "Comparative Politics Today," *Government and Opposition* 7 (Winter 1972):38–55; Sally A. Merrill, "On the Logic of Comparative Analysis," *Comparative Political Studies* 3 (January 1971):489–500; Robert T. Hold and John E. Turner, "Crises and Sequences in Collective Theory Development," *American Political Science Review* 69 (September 1975):979–995; R. S. Milne, "The Overdeveloped Study of Political Development," *Canadian Journal of Political Science* 5 (December 1972):560–568; Philip Coulter, "Political Development and Political Theory: Methodological and Technological Problems in the Comparative Study of Political Development," *Polity* 5 (Winter 1972):233–242; Ignacy Sachs, "The Logic of Development," *International Social Science Journal* 24, 1 (1972):37–43.

21. A. H. Somjee, *Parallels and Actuals of Political Development* (London: Macmillan, 1986); Howard J. Wiarda, *Ethnocentrism in Foreign Policy: Can We Understand the Third World?* (Washington, DC: American Enterprise Institute for Public Policy Research, 1985).

22. Reinhard Bendix, "Tradition and Modernity Reconsidered," *Comparative Studies in Society and History* 9 (April 1967):292–346; S. N. Eisenstadt, *Post-Traditional Societies* (New York: Norton, 1974).

23. Fernando Henrique Cardoso and Enzo Faletto, *Dependency and Development in Latin America* (Berkeley: University of California Press, 1978).

24. See Lloyd I. Rudolph and Susanne Hoeber Rudolph, *The Modernity of Tradition* (Chicago: University of Chicago Press, 1967).

25. Somjee, *Parallels*; Wiarda, *Ethnocentrism*.

26. Max M. Millikan and W. W. Rostow, *A Proposal: Key to an Effective Foreign Policy* (New York: Harper, 1957); Gendzier, *Managing Political Change.*

27. Huntington, *Political Order*; A. H. Somjee, *Political Capacity in Developing Societies* (New York: St. Martin's, 1982).

28. Cardoso and Faletto, *Dependency and Development.*

29. Among the better examples would be Theodore H. Moran, *Multinational Corporations and the Politics of Dependence* (Princeton, NJ: Princeton University Press, 1974).

30. See André Gunder Frank, *Capitalism and Underdevelopment in Latin America* (New York: Monthly Review Press, 1967).

31. Charles W. Anderson, review in *American Political Science Review* (December 1978):1478; also Howard J. Wiarda, "Toward a Framework for the Study of Political Change in the Iberic-Latin Tradition: The Corporative Model," *World Politics* 25 (January 1973):206–235.

32. Philippe C. Schmitter, "Still the Century of Corporatism?" *The Review of Politics* 36 (January 1974):85–131.

33. Howard J. Wiarda, *Corporatism and National Development in Latin America* (Boulder, CO: Westview Press, 1981).

34. Everett Hagen, *On the Theory of Social Change: How Economic Growth Begins* (Homewood, IL: Dorsey, 1962).

35. Millikan and Rostow, *A Proposal*; Gendzier, *Managing Political Change.*

36. David Cameron, "The Expansion of the Public Economy: A Comparative Analysis," *American Political Science Review* 72 (December 1978):1243–1261; Douglas A. Hibbs and Heino Fassbender, eds., *Contemporary Political Economy* (Amsterdam and New York: North-Holland Publishing, 1961).

37. Guillermo O'Donnell, *Modernization and Bureaucratic-Authoritarianism: Studies in South American Politics* (Berkeley: Institute of International Studies, University of California, 1973).

38. David Collier, *The New Authoritarianism in Latin America* (Princeton, NJ: Princeton University Press, 1979).

39. Among the better approaches is Ronald Chilcote, *Theories of Comparative Politics: The Search for a Paradigm* (Boulder, CO: Westview Press, 1981).

40. Vladimir Tismaneanu, *The Crisis of Marxist Ideology in Eastern Europe* (London: Routledge, 1988).

41. W. Raymond Duncan, "Ideology and Nationalism in Attracting Third World Leaders to Communism: Trends and Issues in the Late Twentieth Century," *World Affairs* 151 (Fall 1989):105–116.

42. Lucian W. Pye and Sidney Verba, eds., *Political Culture and Political Development* (Princeton, NJ: Princeton University Press, 1965); Gabriel A. Almond and Sidney Verba, eds., *The Civic Culture* (Princeton, NJ: Princeton University Press, 1963); and Howard J. Wiarda, ed., *Politics and Social Change in Latin America*. 3d ed. (Boulder, CO: Westview Press, 1991).

43. Gabriel A. Almond and Sidney Verba, eds., *The Civic Culture Revisited* (Boston: Little, Brown, 1980); Harry Eckstein, "A Culturalist Theory of Social Change," *American Political Science Review* 82 (September 1988):789–904; Aaron Wildavsky, "Choosing Preferences by Constructing Institutions: A Cultural Theory of Preference Formation," *American Political Science Review* 81 (March 1987); and Ronald Inglehart, "The Renaissance of Political Culture," *American Political Science Review* 82 (December

1988):1203–1230. See also the special issue "Culture in Development: New Perspectives," *Fletcher Forum of World Affairs*, 13 (Summer 1989).

44. Rostow, *Stages*.

45. Lipset, "Social Requisites."

46. Deutsch, "Social Mobilization."

47. Daniel Lerner, *The Passing of Traditional Society* (Glencoe, IL: Free Press, 1958).

48. Howard J. Wiarda, ed., *The Continuing Struggle for Democracy in Latin America* (Boulder, CO: Westview Press, 1979).

49. Enrique Baloyra, ed., *Comparing New Democracies* (Boulder, CO: Westview Press, 1987); Guillermo O'Donnell, Philippe C. Schmitter, and Laurence Whitehead, eds., *Transitions from Authoritarian Rule* (Baltimore: Johns Hopkins University Press, 1986); and Larry Diamond, Juan Linz, and S. M. Lipset, eds., *Democracy in Developing Countries* (Boulder, CO: Lynne Rienner, 1988).

50. See Peter Berger, *The Capitalist Revolution* (New York: Basic Books, 1986); also Howard J. Wiarda, *The Relations Between Democracy, Development, and Security: Implications for Policy* (New York: Global Economic Action Institute, 1988); and Nigel Harris, *The End of the Third World* (London: Penguin Books, 1986).

51. Pye, *Aspects of Political Development*.

52. See especially Diamond, Linz, and Lipset, *Democracy*.

53. Howard J. Wiarda, *The Democratic Revolution in Latin America: History, Politics, and U.S. Policy* (New York: Holmes and Meier, A Twentieth Century Fund Book, 1990).

54. For a discussion of the discrediting and demise of the older, more radical left- and right-wing models in Latin America, see Howard J. Wiarda, *Latin America at the Crossroads: Debt, Development, and the Future* (Boulder, CO: Westview Press for the Inter-American Development Bank, 1987).

55. Allan Bloom, *The Closing of the American Mind: How Higher Education Has Failed Democracy and Impoverished the Souls of Today's Students* (New York: Simon and Schuster, 1987).

56. Paul Johnson, *Modern Times: The World from the Twenties to the Eighties* (New York: Harper & Row, 1983).

57. Tom Clancy, *The Hunt for Red October* (New York: Berkley, 1985); *Red Storm Rising* (New York: Berkley, 1987); *Patriot Games* (New York: Putnam, 1987); *The Cardinal of the Kremlin* (New York: Berkley, 1989).

58. Ronald Scheman, ed., *The Alliance for Progress: A Retrospective* (New York: Praeger, 1988); also Howard J. Wiarda, "Development and Democracy: Their Relationship to Peace and Security." Paper presented at the conference on "Regional Cooperation for Development and the Peaceful Settlement of Disputes in Latin America," International Peace Academy and the Peruvian Center for International Studies, Lima, October 27–29, 1986.

59. The outstanding study is Diamond, Linz, and Lipset, eds., *Democracy in Developing Countries*.

60. The most substantial report is Department of State, *Democracy in Latin America: The Promise and The Challenge* (Washington, DC: Bureau of Public Affairs, Department of State, Special Report no. 158 [March 1987]).

61. Abraham Kaplan, "Systems Theory and Political Science," *Social Research* 35 (July 1968):30–47.

62. Alfred Stepan, *State and Society* (Princeton, NJ: Princeton University Press, 1978); Howard J. Wiarda, "State-Society Relations and Public Policy in Latin America." Paper presented at the Center for International Affairs, Harvard University, April 15, 1980.

63. Robert Packenham, "Capitalist Dependency and Socialist Dependency: The Case of Cuba." Paper presented at the Annual Meeting of the American Political Science Association, New Orleans, August 29–September 1, 1985.

64. Ronald Inglehart, "The Renaissance of Political Culture," *American Political Science Review* 82 (December 1988):1203–1230.

65. An excellent effort at synthesis is John D. Martz and David J. Myers, "Understanding Latin American Politics: Analytical Models and Intellectual Traditions," *Polity* 16 (Winter 1983):214–241.

Select Bibliography

COMPILED BY JANINE T. PERFIT
AND HOWARD J. WIARDA

Akhavi, Shahrough. *Religion and Politics in Contemporary Iran*. Albany: State University of New York Press, 1980.

Almond, Gabriel A. *The Appeals of Communism*. Princeton, N.J.: Princeton University Press, 1954.

_____. "Comparative Political Systems." *Journal of Politics* 18 (August 1956):391–409.

_____. "A Comparative Study of Interest Groups and the Political Process." *American Political Science Review* 52 (March 1958):270–282.

_____. "Corporatism, Pluralism and Professional Memory." *World Politics* 35 (1983):245–260.

_____. *Political Development: Essays in Heuristic Theory*. Boston: Little, Brown, 1970.

Almond, Gabriel A., and G. Bingham Powell, Jr. *Comparative Politics: Systems, Processes, and Policy*. 2d ed. Boston: Little, Brown, 1978.

Almond, Gabriel A., et al. "A Suggested Research Strategy in Western European Government and Politics." *American Political Science Review* 49 (December 1955):1042–1049.

Almond, Gabriel A., and James S. Coleman, eds. *The Politics of the Developing Areas*. Princeton, N.J.: Princeton University Press, 1960.

Almond, Gabriel A., and Sidney Verba, eds. *The Civic Culture Revisited*. Boston: Little, Brown, 1980.

Almond, Gabriel A., et al., eds. *Comparative Politics Today: A World View*. Boston: Little, Brown, 1980.

Amin, Samir. *Unequal Development*. New York: Monthly Review Press, 1976.

Anderson, Charles W. "Political Design and the Representation of Interests." In P. Schmitter and G. Lehmbruch, eds., *Trends Toward Corporatist Intermediation*, pp. 271–298. Beverly Hills, Calif.: Sage, 1979.

Apter, David. *Ghana in Transition*. New York: Atheneum, 1967.

_____. *The Gold Coast in Transition*. Princeton, N.J.: Princeton University Press, 1955.

_____. *The Politics of Modernization*. Chicago: University of Chicago Press, 1965.

Arendt, Hannah. *The Origins of Totalitarianism*. New York: Harcourt, Brace, Jovanovich, 1951.

Astin, John D. "Easton I and Easton II." *Western Political Quarterly* 25 (December 1972):726–737.

Baldwin, David A. "Power Analysis and World Politics: New Trends Versus Old Tendencies." *World Politics* 31 (January 1979):162–163.

Baloyra, Enrique, ed. *Comparing New Democracies*. Boulder, Colo.: Westview Press, 1987.

Baran, Paul A. *The Political Economy of Growth*. New York: Monthly Review Press, 1957.

Barringer, Herbert R., et al., eds. *Social Change in Developing Areas*. Cambridge, Mass.: Schenkman Publishing Co., 1966.

Barry, Brian. *Sociologists, Economists and Democracy*. London: Collier, 1970.

Bauer, P. T. *Dissent on Development*. Cambridge, Mass.: Harvard University Press, 1976.

Beer, Samuel H. *Modern Political Development*. New York: Random House, 1974.

Beer, Samuel H., et al. *Patterns of Government: The Major Political Systems of Europe*, 3d ed. New York: Random House, 1972.

Beling, W. A., and G. O. Totten. *The Developing Nations: Quest for a Model*. New York: Van Nostrand, 1970.

Bell, Daniel. *The Coming of Post-Industrial Society*. New York: Basic Books, 1973.

Bendix, Reinhard. "Tradition and Modernity Reconsidered." *Comparative Studies in Society and History* 9 (April 1967):292–346.

Berger, Suzanne, and Michael J. Piore. *Dualism and Discontinuity in Industrial Societies*. New York: Cambridge University Press, 1980.

Berger, Suzanne, ed. *Organizing Interests in Western Europe*. New York: Cambridge University Press, 1981.

Binder, Leonard, James S. Coleman, Joseph LaPalombara, Lucian Pye, Sidney Verba, and Myron Weiner, eds. *Crisis and Sequences in Political Development*. Princeton, N.J.: Princeton University Press, 1971.

Binedijk, Hans, ed. *Authoritarian Regimes in Transition*. Washington, D.C.: Foreign Service Institute, Department of State, 1987.

Black, C. E. *The Dynamics of Modernization: A Study in Comparative History*. New York: Harper and Row, 1968.

Bloch, Marc. *Feudal Society*. Chicago: University of Chicago Press, 1961.

Block, Fred. "The Ruling Class Does Not Rule: Notes on the Marxist Theory of the State." *Socialist Revolution* 7 (1977):5.

Blondel, Jean. *Comparing Political Systems*. New York: Praeger, 1972.

Bodenheimer, Susanne J. *The Ideology of Developmentalism: The American Paradigm-Surrogate for Latin American Studies*. Beverly Hills, Calif.: Sage, 1971.

Bowen, R. *German Theories of the Corporative State*. New York: Whittlesey, 1947.

Braudel, Fernand. *The Mediterranean and the Mediterranean World in the Age of Philip II*. New York: Harper and Row, 1973.

Braveboy-Wagner, Jacqueline A. *Interpreting the Third World*. New York: Praeger, 1986.

Bretton, Henry L. *Power and Politics in Africa*. Chicago: Aldine, 1973.

Brown, Archie, and Jack Gray, eds. *Political Culture and Political Change in Communist States*. New York: Holmes and Meier, 1978.

Bryce, Lord James. *The American Commonwealth*, 2 vols. Folcroft: Folcroft Library Editions, 1978 reprint of 1891 edition.

Brzezinski, Zbigniew. *Between Two Ages: America's Role in the Technetronic Era*. New York: Penguin Books, 1976.

Cameron, David R. "The Expansion of the Public Economy: A Comparative Analysis." *American Political Science Review* 72 (December 1978):1243–1261.

_____ . "Social Democracy, Corporatism and Labor Quiescence." In J. Goldthorpe, ed., *Order and Conflict in Contemporary Capitalism*. London: Oxford University Press, 1984.

Campbell, Colin. "Current Models of the Political System: An Intellective-Purposive View." *Comparative Political Studies* 4 (April 1971):26.

Cantori, Louis J., and Andrew H. Ziegler, Jr., eds. *Comparative Politics in the Post-Behavioral Era.* Boulder, Colo.: Lynne Rienner, 1988.

Cardoso, Fernando Henrique. "Associated-Dependent Development: Theoretical and Practical Implications." In Alfred Stepan, ed., *Authoritarian Brazil: Origins, Policies, and Future,* pp. 142–176. New Haven, Conn.: Yale University Press, 1973.

Cardoso, Fernando Henrique, and Enzo Faletto. *Dependency and Development in Latin America.* Berkeley: University of California Press, 1979.

Castles, Francis. *The Social Democratic Image of Society.* London: Routledge & Kegan Paul, 1978.

Charlton, Roger. *Comparative Government.* London: Longman, 1986.

Chenery, Hollis, et al. *Industrialization and Growth: A Comparative Study.* New York: Oxford University Press, 1986.

Chilcote, Ronald H. *Theories of Comparative Politics: The Search for a Paradigm.* Boulder, Colo.: Westview Press, 1981.

Chilcote, Ronald H., ed. *Dependency and Marxism: Toward a Resolution of the Debate.* Boulder, Colo.: Westview Press, 1982.

Coleman, James S., ed. *Education and Political Development.* Princeton, N.J.: Princeton University Press, 1965.

Collier, David, ed. *The New Authoritarianism in Latin America.* Princeton, N.J.: Princeton University Press, 1979.

Committee on Comparative Politics. *A Report on the Activities of the Committee, 1954–70.* New York: Social Science Research Council, 1971. Mimeo.

Comparative Politics, especially vol. 1, no. 1, for some thorough surveys of the field.

Coulter, Philip. "Political Development and Political Theory: Methodological and Technological Problems in the Comparative Study of Political Development." *Polity* 5 (Winter 1972):233–242.

_____ . *Social Mobilization and Liberal Democracy.* Lexington, Mass.: Lexington Books, 1975.

Creel, H. G. *Chinese Thought: From Confucius to Mao Tse-tung.* Chicago: University of Chicago Press, 1963.

Dahl, Robert A. "Pluralism Revisited." *Comparative Politics* 10 (January 1978):191–203.

_____ . *Polyarchy, Participation, and Opposition.* New Haven, Conn.: Yale University Press, 1971.

_____ . *Who Governs? Democracy and Power in an American City.* New Haven, Conn.: Yale University Press, 1961.

Dahrendorf, Ralf. *Class and Class Conflict in Industrial Society.* Stanford, Calif.: Stanford University Press, 1958.

Dealy, Glen. *The Public Man: An Interpretation of Latin America and Other Catholic Countries.* Amherst: University of Massachusetts Press, 1977.

Dennon, A. R. "Political Science and Political Development." *Science and Society* 33 (Summer–Fall 1969):285–298.

Deutsch, Karl. *Nationalism and Social Communication.* New York: Technology Press of MIT and John Wiley & Sons, 1953.

_____ . *The Nerves of Government: Models of Political Communications and Control.* London: Free Press, 1963.

_____ . "Social Mobilization and Political Development." *American Political Science Review* 55 (September 1961):493–514.

Deutsch, Karl, et al. *Comparative Government: Politics of Industrialized and Developing Nations.* Boston: Houghton Mifflin, 1981.

Deutsch, Karl, and William J. Foltz, eds. *Nation Building.* New York: Aldine, 1963.

Diamond, Larry, Juan J. Linz, and Seymour Martin Lipset, eds. *Democracy in Developing Countries.* Boulder, Colo.: Lynn Rienner, 1988–1989.

Dodd, Clement H. "Political Development: The End of an Era." *Government and Opposition* 8 (Summer 1973):367–374.

Dogan, Mattei, ed. *Comparing Pluralist Democracies: Strains on Legitimacy.* Boulder, Colo.: Westview Press, 1988.

Dogan, Mattei, and Dominique Pelassy. *How to Compare Nations: Strategies in Comparative Politics.* Chatham, N.J.: Chatham House Pubs., 1984.

Domhoff, G. William. *The Higher Circles: The Governing Class in America.* New York: Vintage Books, 1970.

Dos Santos, Theotonio. "The Structure of Dependence." *American Economic Review* 60 (May 1970):234–235.

Downs, Anthony. *An Economic Theory of Democracy.* New York: Harper and Row, 1965.

Easton, David. "An Approach to the Study of Political Systems." *World Politics* 9 (April 1957):383–400.

———. *A Framework for Political Analysis.* Englewood Cliffs, N.J.: Prentice-Hall, 1965.

———. "The New Revolution in Political Science." *American Political Science Review* 63 (December 1969):1051–1061.

———. "Political Science." In *International Encyclopedia of the Social Sciences* 12, p. 295. New York: Macmillan Company and Free Press, 1968.

———. *The Political System: An Inquiry into the State of Political Science.* New York: Alfred A. Knopf, 1953.

———. "The Political System Besieged by the State." *Political Theory* 9 (August 1981):303–325.

———. *A Systems Analysis of Political Life.* New York: John Wiley & Sons, 1965.

Eckstein, Harry. "A Culturalist Theory of Political Change." *American Political Science Review* 82 (September 1988).

———. "The Evaluation of Political Performance: Problems and Dimensions." *Sage Professional Papers in Comparative Politics,* 1971, pp. 1–17.

Eckstein, Harry, and David E. Apter, eds. *Comparative Politics: A Reader.* New York: Free Press, 1963.

Eckstein, Susan. *The Poverty of Revolution: The State and the Urban Poor in Mexico.* Princeton, N.J.: Princeton University Press, 1977.

Ehrmann, Henry W., ed. *Interest Groups on Four Continents.* Pittsburgh, Pa.: University of Pittsburgh Press, 1958.

Eisenstadt, S. N. *Modernization: Protest and Change.* Englewood Cliffs, N.J.: Prentice-Hall, 1966.

———. *Post-Traditional Societies.* New York: Norton, 1974.

———. "Post-Traditional Societies and the Continuity and Reconstruction of Tradition." *Daedalus* 102 (Winter 1973):1–27.

Elbow, M. H. *French Corporative Theory: 1789–1948.* New York: Columbia University Press, 1953.

Esping-Andersen, Gosta, Rodger Friedland, and Erik Olin Wright. "Modes of Class Struggle and the Capitalist State." *Kapitalistate* 4-5 (Summer 1976):186–220.

Field, George L. *Comparative Political Development: The Precedent of the West.* Ithaca, N.Y.: Cornell University Press, 1967.

Finer, Herman. *The Theory and Practice of Modern Government.* New York: Holt, 1949.

Finkle, J. L., and R. W. Gable. *Political Development and Social Change*. 2d ed. New York: John Wiley & Sons, 1971.

Fischer, Michael. *Iran: From Religious Dispute to Revolution*. Cambridge, Mass.: Harvard University Press, 1980.

The Fletcher Forum of World Affairs 13 (Summer 1989). "Culture in Development: New Perspectives."

Frank, André Gunder. *Capitalism and Underdevelopment in Latin America*. Rev. ed. New York: Monthly Review Press, 1969.

Fried, Robert C. *Comparative Political Institutions*. New York: Macmillan, 1966.

Friedrich, Carl J. *Constitutional Government and Democracy*. Boston: Ginn and Company, 1941.

Furtado, Celso. *Economic Growth of Brazil: A Survey from Colonial to Modern Times*. Berkeley: University of California Press, 1963.

Gamer, Robert E. *The Developing Nations*. Boston: Allyn and Bacon, 1976.

Geertz, Clifford. *Negara: The Theatre-State in Nineteenth Century Bali*. Princeton, N.J.: Princeton University Press, 1980.

Glade, William P. "Problems of Research in Latin American Studies." In *New Directions in Language and Area Studies*, pp. 81–101. Milwaukee: University of Wisconsin at Milwaukee for the Consortium of Latin American Studies Programs, 1979.

González Casanova, Pablo. *Sociología de la Explotación*. 2d ed. Mexico City: Siglo Veintiuno, 1978.

Graham, Lawrence S. "Centralization Versus Decentralization Dilemmas in the Administration of Public Services." *International Review of Administrative Sciences* 3 (1980):219–232.

———. *Mexican State Government: A Prefectural System in Action*. Austin: Institute of Public Affairs, University of Texas, 1971.

———. *Romania: A Developing Socialist State*. Boulder, Colo.: Westview Press, 1982.

Graham, Lawrence S., and Douglas L. Wheeler, eds. *In Search of Modern Portugal: The Revolution and Its Consequences*. Madison: University of Wisconsin Press, 1983.

Gramsci, Antonio. *Selections from the Prison Notebooks of Antonio Gramsci*. London: Lawrence and Wishart, 1971.

Grew, Raymond, ed. *Crises of Political Development in Europe and the United States*. Princeton, N.J.: Princeton University Press, 1978.

Groth, Alexander J., et al. *Contemporary Politics: Europe*. Boston: Little, Brown, 1976.

Hah, C. D., and J. Schneider. "A Critique of Current Studies of Political Development and Modernization." *Social Research* 35 (Spring 1968):130–158.

Harris, Nigel. *The End of the Third World: Newly Industrializing Countries and the Decline of an Ideology*. Harmondsworth, Middlesex: Penguin, 1986.

Hartz, Louis, et al. *The Founding of New Societies*. New York: Harcourt, Brace, 1964.

Hayter, Teresa. *Aid as Imperialism*. Baltimore: Penguin, 1971.

Heady, Ferrel, and Sybil L. Stokes, eds. *Papers in Comparative Public Administration*. Ann Arbor, Mich.: Institute of Public Administration, University of Michigan, 1962.

Heeger, Gerald A. *The Politics of Underdevelopment*. New York: St. Martin's Press, 1974.

Heidenheimer, Arnold J., et al. *Comparative Public Policy: Policies of Social Choice in Europe and America*. New York: St. Martin's Press, 1975.

Heisler, Martin O., ed. *Politics in Europe: Structures and Processes in Some Postindustrial Democracies*. New York: David McKay Co., 1974.

Hewitt, Christopher. "The Effect of Political Democracy and Social Democracy on Equality in Industrial Societies." *American Sociological Review* 42 (1977):450–464.

Hibbs, Douglas A., Jr. "Political Parties and Macroeconomic Policy." *American Political Science Review* 71 (December 1977):1467–1487.

Hibbs, Douglas A., Jr., and Heino Fassbender, eds. *Contemporary Political Economy.* Amsterdam and New York: North-Holland Publishing Company, 1961.

Hilton, Rodney, ed. *The Transition from Feudalism to Capitalism.* London: New Left Books, 1976.

Hoffmann, Stanley, and Pashalis Kitromilides, eds. *Culture and Society in Contemporary Europe.* Boston: Allen and Unwin, 1981.

Holt, Robert T., and John E. Turner. "Crises and Sequences in Collective Theory Development." *American Political Science Review* 69 (September 1975):979–995.

Holt, Robert T., and John E. Turner, eds. *The Methodology of Comparative Research.* New York: Free Press, 1970.

Horowitz, Irving L. *Three Worlds of Development: The Theory and Practice of International Stratification.* 2d ed. New York: Oxford University Press, 1972.

Hough, Jerry F., and Merle Fainsod. *How the Soviet Union Is Governed.* Cambridge, Mass.: Harvard University Press, 1979.

Hughes, H. Stuart. *The Sea Change: The Migration of Social Thought, 1930–65.* New York: McGraw-Hill, 1977.

Hunter, Robert, and John Rielly. *Development Today: A New Look at U.S. Relations with the Poor Countries.* New York: Praeger, 1972.

Huntington, Samuel P. *Political Order in Changing Societies.* New Haven, Conn.: Yale University Press, 1968.

Huntington, Samuel P., and Clement H. Moore, eds. *Authoritarian Politics in Modern Society: The Dynamics of Established One-Party Systems.* New York: Basic Books, 1970.

Huntington, Samuel P., and Joan M. Nelson. *No Easy Choice: Political Participation in Developing Countries.* Cambridge, Mass.: Harvard University Press, 1976.

Hurwitz, Leon. "Contemporary Approaches to Political Stability." *Comparative Politics* 3 (1973):449–463.

Hymer, Stephen. "The Internationalization of Capital." *Journal of Economic Issues* 6, 1 (1972):91–111.

Ilchman, Warren F., and Norman T. Uphoff. *The Political Economy of Change.* Berkeley: University of California Press, 1969.

Inglehart, Ronald. *Cultural Change in Advanced Industrial Society.* Princeton, N.J.: Princeton University Press, 1990.

_____. "The Renaissance of Political Culture." *American Political Science Review* 82 (December 1988).

Jansen, G. H. *Militant Islam.* New York: Harper and Row, 1980.

Jervis, Robert. "Political Decision Making: Recent Contributions." *Political Psychology,* Summer 1980, pp. 86–101.

Kaplan, Abraham. "Systems Theory and Political Science." *Social Research* 35 (July 1968):30–47.

Katzenstein, Peter. "The Small European States in the International Economy: Economic Dependence and Corporatist Politics." In J. Ruggie, ed., *The Antinomies of Interdependence.* New York: Columbia University Press, 1983.

Kautsky, John H. *Communism and the Politics of Development.* New York: John Wiley & Sons, 1968.

_____. *Political Change in Underdeveloped Countries: Nationalism and Communism.* New York: John Wiley & Sons, 1962.

Kesselman, Mark. "Order or Movement: The Literature of Political Development as Ideology." *World Politics* 26 (October 1973):139–153.

Korpi, Walter. *The Democratic Class Struggle*. London: Routledge & Kegan Paul, 1983.

———. "Social Policy and Distributional Conflict in the Capitalist Democracies: A Preliminary Comparative Framework." *West European Politics* 3 (October 1980).

———. *The Working Class in Welfare Capitalism*. London and Boston: Routledge & Kegan Paul, 1978.

Kothari, Rajni. *Footsteps into the Future*. New York: Free Press, 1975.

Krasner, Stephen D. "Domestic Constraints on International Economic Leverage." In Klaus Knorr and Frank N. Trager, eds., *Economic Issues and National Security*. Kansas City: Regents Press of Kansas, 1977.

Lange, Peter. "Crisis and Consent, Change and Compromise: Dilemmas of Italian Communism in the 1970s." In P. Lange and S. Tarrow, eds., *Italy in Transition*. London: Frank Cass, 1980.

LaPalombara, Joseph, ed. *Bureaucracy and Political Development*. Princeton, N.J.: Princeton University Press, 1963.

LaPalombara, Joseph, and Myron Weiner, eds. *Political Parties and Political Development*. Princeton, N.J.: Princeton University Press, 1966.

Lazarsfeld, Paul F., and Allen H. Barton. "Qualitative Measurement in the Social Sciences: Classification, Typologies and Indices." In Daniel Lerner and Harold D. Lasswell, eds., *The Policy Sciences*, pp. 155–192. Stanford, Calif.: Stanford University Press, 1981.

Lerner, Daniel. *The Passing of Traditional Society*. New York: Free Press, 1958.

Leys, Colin, ed. *Politics and Change in Developing Countries: Studies in the Theory and Practice of Development*. Charlotte, N.C.: UNI Publications, 1969.

Lijphart, Arend. *Democracy in Plural Societies*. New Haven, Conn.: Yale University Press, 1977.

———. "Typologies of Democratic Systems." *Comparative Political Studies* 1 (April 1968):3–44.

Lipset, Seymour Martin. *Political Man: The Social Bases of Politics*. New York: Doubleday-Anchor, 1959.

———. "Some Social Requisites of Democracy: Economic Democracy and Political Legitimacy." *American Political Science Review* 53 (March 1959):69–105.

Lipton, Michael. *Why Poor People Stay Poor: Urban Bias in World Development*. Cambridge, Mass.: Harvard University Press, 1977.

Lowenstein, Karl. *Political Power and the Governmental Process*. Chicago: University of Chicago Press, 1957.

Lowy, Michael. *The Politics of Combined and Uneven Development: The Theory of Permanent Revolution*. London: New Left Books, 1981.

McLennan, Barbara N. *Comparative Political Systems: Political Processes in Developed and Developing States*. North Scituate, Mass.: Duxbury Press, 1975.

McRae, Kenneth, ed. *Consociational Democracy*. Toronto: McClelland and Stewart, 1974.

Macridis, Roy. *Modern Political Regimes: Patterns and Institutions*. Boston: Little, Brown, 1986.

———. *The Study of Comparative Government*. New York: Random House, 1955.

Macridis, Roy C., and Roy Cox. "Research in Comparative Politics." *American Political Science Review* 47 (September 1953):641–675.

Macridis, Roy C., ed. *Modern Political Systems: Europe*. New York: Prentice-Hall, 1978.

Macridis, Roy C., and Bernard E. Brown, eds. *Comparative Politics: Notes and Readings*. 6th ed. Homewood, Ill.: Dorsey Press, 1986.

Malloy, James, ed. *Authoritarianism and Corporatism in Latin America*. Pittsburgh, Pa.: University of Pittsburgh Press, 1977.

Mandel, Ernest. *Late Capitalism*. London: New Left Books, 1975.

Maniruzzaman, Talukder. *Military Withdrawal from Politics: A Comparative Study*. Cambridge, Mass.: Ballinger, 1987.

Manoilescu, M. *Le siècle du corporatisme*. Paris, 1936.

Marcussen, Henrik, and Jens Erik Torp. *Internationalization of Capital: Prospects for the Third World, a Reexamination of Dependency Theory*. London: Zed Press, 1982.

Martin, R. M. "Pluralism and the New Corporatism." *Political Studies* 31 (1983):86–102.

Martz, John D., and David J. Myers. "Understanding Latin American Politics: Analytical Models and Intellectual Traditions." *Polity* 16 (Winter 1983):214–241.

Masalehdan, Ali. *Values and Political Development in Iran*. Ph.D. diss., University of Massachusetts at Amherst, 1981.

Mayer, Lawrence. *Comparative Political Inquiry*. Homewood, Ill.: Dorsey Press, 1972.

Mehta, Vrajenda Raj. *Beyond Marxism: Towards an Alternative Perspective*. New Delhi: Manohar Publications, 1978.

Melanson, Philip H., and Lauriston R. King. "Theory in Comparative Politics: A Critical Appraisal." *Comparative Political Studies* 4 (July 1971):205–231.

Merkl, Peter H. *Modern Comparative Politics*. 2d ed. New York: Holt, Rinehart and Winston, 1977.

Merkl, Peter H., ed. *Western European Party Systems: Trends and Prospects*. New York: Free Press, 1980.

Merrill, Sally A. "On the Logic of Comparative Analysis." *Comparative Political Studies* 3 (January 1971):489–500.

Metzger, Walter, et al. *The Cultural Migration: The European Scholar in America*. New York: Arno Press, 1977.

Migdal, Joel. *Strong Societies and Weak States*. Princeton, N.J.: Princeton University Press, 1986.

Miliband, Ralph. *The State in Capitalist Society: An Analysis of the Western System of Power*. New York: Basic Books, 1969.

Miller, John D. *Politics of the Third World*. New York: Oxford University Press, 1967.

Millikan, Max F., and Donald L. Blackmer, eds. *Emerging Nations: Their Growth and United States Policy*. Boston: Little, Brown, 1967.

Milne, R. S. "The Overdeveloped Study of Political Development." *Canadian Journal of Political Science* 5 (December 1972):560–568.

Montgomery, John D. *Technology and Civic Life: Making and Implementing Development Decisions*. Cambridge, Mass.: MIT Press, 1974.

Moore, Barrington, Jr. *The Social Origins of Dictatorship and Democracy: Lord and Peasant in the Making of Modern World*. Boston: Beacon Press, 1966.

Moran, Theodore H. *Multinational Corporations and the Politics of Dependence*. Cambridge, Mass.: Center for International Affairs, Harvard University, 1975.

Morgenthau, Ruth Schachter. "Single Party Systems in West Africa." *American Political Science Review*, June 1961.

Morse, Richard. "The Heritage of Latin America." In L. Hartz, ed., *The Founding of New Societies*. New York: Harcourt, Brace and World, 1964.

Neumann, Franz. *Behemoth: The Structure and Practice of National Socialism*. New York: Oxford University Press, 1944.

O'Donnell, Guillermo, Philippe C. Schmitter, and Laurence Whitehead, eds. *Transitions from Authoritarian Rule*. Baltimore: Johns Hopkins University Press, 1986.

Organski, Kenneth. *The Stages of Political Development*. New York: Alfred A. Knopf, 1965.

Packenham, Robert. *Liberal America and the Third World: Political Development Ideas in Foreign Aid and Social Science.* Princeton, N.J.: Princeton University Press, 1973.

Palloix, Christian. *L'Internalisation du Capital.* Paris: François Maspero, 1975.

Palmer, Monte. *Dilemmas of Political Development.* Itasca, Ill.: Peacock Publishers, 1989.

Palmer, Monte, ed. *Human Factor in Political Development.* Waltham, Mass.: Xerox College Publishing, 1970.

Panitch, Leo. "Recent Theorizations of Corporatism: Reflections on a Growth Industry." *British Journal of Sociology* 31 (1980):159–187.

Pantham, Thomas. "Integral Pluralism: A Political Theory for India?" *India Quarterly* (July–December 1980):396–405.

Parsons, Talcott. *The Social System.* Glencoe, Ill.: Free Press, 1951.

Parsons, Talcott, and Edward A. Shils, eds. *Toward a General Theory of Action.* Cambridge, Mass.: Harvard University Press, 1951.

Paz, Octavio. *The Labyrinth of Solitude.* New York: Grove Press, 1961.

Pike, Fredrick B., and Thomas Stritch, eds. *The New Corporatism: Social-Political Structures in the Iberian World.* Notre Dame, Ind.: University of Notre Dame Press, 1974.

Poulantzas, Nicos. *Political Power and Social Classes.* London: New Left Books and Sheed and Ward, 1973.

————. "The Problem of the Capitalist State." *New Left Review* 58 (November–December 1969):74.

Powell, G. Bingham, Jr. *Contemporary Democracies: Participation, Stability, and Violence.* Cambridge, Mass.: Harvard University Press, 1982.

Przeworski, Adam, and Harry Teune. *Logic of Comparative Social Inquiry.* New York: John Wiley & Sons, 1970.

Pye, Lucian W. *Asian Power and Politics: The Cultural Dimensions of Authority.* Cambridge, Mass.: Harvard University Press, 1985.

————. *Aspects of Political Development.* Boston: Little, Brown, 1966.

————. *Guerrilla Communism in Malaya: Its Social and Political Meaning.* Princeton, N.J.: Princeton University Press, 1956.

Pye, Lucian W., ed. *Communications and Political Development.* Princeton, N.J.: Princeton University Press, 1963.

Pye, Lucian W., and Sidney Verba, eds. *Political Culture and Political Development.* Princeton, N.J.: Princeton University Press, 1965.

Rey, Pierre-Philippe. *Les Alliances de Classes.* Paris: François Maspero, 1973.

Riggs, Fred W. *Administration in Developing Countries.* New York: Holmes and Meier, 1964.

Roberts, Geoffrey K. "Comparative Politics Today." *Government and Opposition* 7 (Winter 1972):38–55.

Rodney, Walter. *How Europe Underdeveloped Africa.* London and Dar es Salaam: Bogle-l'Ouverture and Tanzania Publishing House, 1972.

Rodó, José E. *Ariel*, trans. F. J. Stimson. Boston: Houghton Mifflin, 1922.

Rostow, W. W. *The Stages of Economic Growth.* New York: Cambridge University Press, 1960.

Rothman, Stanley, and George W. Breslauer. *Soviet Politics and Society.* St. Paul, Minn.: West, 1978.

Rubin, Barry. *Paved with Good Intentions.* New York: Oxford University Press, 1980.

Rudolph, Lloyd I., and Suzanne Rudolph. *The Modernity of Tradition.* Chicago: University of Chicago Press, 1967.

Rustow, Dankwart. "Transitions to Democracy: Towards a Dynamic Model." *Comparative Politics* 2 (1970):337–363.

———. *World of Nations: Problems of Political Modernization.* Washington, D.C.: Brookings Institution, 1967.

Rustow, Dankwart, and Kenneth F. Erickson, eds. *Comparative Political Dynamics.* New York: Harper Collins, 1990.

Sachs, Ignacy. "The Logic of Development." *International Social Science Journal* 24, 1 (1972):37–43.

Said, Edward. *Orientalism.* New York: Pantheon, 1978.

Sargent, Lyman Tower. *Contemporary Political Ideologies.* Homewood, Ill.: Dorsey, 1981.

Sartori, Giovanni. *Parties and Party Systems: A Framework for Analysis.* Vol. 1. Cambridge and New York: Cambridge University Press, 1976.

Schmitt, David E., ed. *Dynamics of the Third World.* Cambridge, Mass.: Winthrop, 1974.

Schmitter, Philippe. "Paths to Political Development in Latin America." In D. Chalmers, ed., *Changing Latin America.* New York: Academy of Political Science, 1972.

———. "Still the Century of Corporatism?" In Fredrick Pike and Thomas Stritch, eds., *The New Corporatism,* pp. 93–94. Notre Dame, Ind.: University of Notre Dame Press, 1974.

Schmitter, Philippe C., and Gerhard Lehmbruch, eds. *Trends Toward Corporatist Intermediation.* Beverly Hills, Calif.: Sage Publications, 1979.

Schram, Stuart H. *The Political Thought of Mao Tse-tung.* New York: Praeger, 1976.

Seaton, S. Lee, and Henry J. M. Claessen, eds. *Political Anthropology: The State of the Art.* The Hague: Mouton, 1979.

Shils, Edward. *Center and Periphery.* Chicago: University of Chicago Press, 1975.

———. *Political Development in the New States.* Paris: Mouton, 1966.

Sigmund, Paul E., ed. *The Ideologies of the Developing Nations.* New York: Praeger, 1972.

Silvert, Kalman. "The Costs of Anti-Nationalism: Argentina." In *The Conflict Society.* New York: American Universities Field Staff, 1966.

Skillings, H. Gordon. *Communism National and International: Eastern Europe After Stalin.* Toronto: University of Toronto Press, 1964.

Skocpol, Theda. *States and Social Revolutions: A Comparative Analysis of France, Russia, and China.* New York: Cambridge University Press, 1979.

———. "Wallerstein's World Capitalist System: A Theoretical and Historical Critique." *American Journal of Sociology* 83 (1977):1075–1090.

Smith, T. Alexander. *The Comparative Policy Process.* Santa Barbara, Calif.: ABC-Clio, 1975.

Soares, G.A.D. "Latin American Studies in the United States." *Latin American Research Review* 11 (1976).

Somjee, A. H. *Parallels and Actuals of Political Development.* London: Macmillan, 1986.

———. *Political Capacity in Developing Societies.* New York: St. Martin's Press, 1982.

Sorzano, J. S. "David Easton and the Invisible Hand." *American Political Science Review* 69 (March 1975):91–106.

Spengler, Oswald. *The Decline of the West.* New York: Alfred A. Knopf, 1932.

"The State." *Daedalus,* Fall 1979.

Stepan, Alfred. *State and Society: Peru in Comparative Perspective.* Princeton, N.J.: Princeton University Press, 1978.

Sunkel, Osvaldo. "Big Business and 'Dependencia.'" *Foreign Affairs* 50 (April 1972):517–531.

Sutton, F. X. "Social Theory and Comparative Politics." Prepared for the SSRC/CCP in 1955 and published in Harry Eckstein and David E. Apter, eds., *Comparative Politics*, pp. 67–81. New York: Free Press, 1963.

Sweezy, Paul M., and Charles Bettelheim. *On the Transition to Socialism.* New York: Monthly Review Press, 1971.

Szymanski, Al. "Malinowski, Marx, and Functionalism." *Insurgent Sociologist* 2 (Summer 1972):35–43.

Tachau, Frank, ed. *The Developing Nations: What Path to Modernization?* New York: Dodd, Mead, 1972.

Tilly, Charles, ed. *The Formation of the National States in Western Europe.* Princeton, N.J.: Princeton University Press, 1975.

Tipps, Dean C. "Modernization Theory and the Comparative Studies of Society: A Critical Perspective." *Comparative Studies of Society and History* 15 (March 1973):199–226.

Tocqueville, Alexis de. *Democracy in America*, 2 vols. Edited by Bradley Phillips. New York: Alfred A. Knopf, 1944.

Truman, David B. *The Governmental Process: Political Interests and Public Opinion.* New York: Alfred A. Knopf, 1951.

Véliz, Claudio. *The Centralist Tradition in Latin America.* Princeton, N.J.: Princeton University Press, 1980.

Verba, Sidney. "Some Dilemmas in Comparative Research." *World Politics* 20 (October 1967):111–127.

Vogel, Ezra F. *Japan as No. 1.* Cambridge, Mass.: Harvard University Press, 1979.

Wallerstein, Immanuel. *The Modern World System I: Capitalist Agriculture and the Origins of the European World Economy in the 16th Century.* New York: Academic Press, 1974.

————. *The Modern World System II: Mercantilism and the Consolidation of the European World Economy, 1600–1750.* New York: Academic Press, 1980.

Ward, Robert E., and Dankwart A. Rustow, eds. *Political Modernization in Japan and Turkey.* Princeton, N.J.: Princeton University Press, 1964.

Warren, Bill. *Imperialism: Pioneer of Capitalism.* London: New Left Books, 1980.

Weiner, Myron, ed. *Modernization: The Dynamics of Growth.* New York: Basic Books, 1966.

Weiner, Myron, and Samuel P. Huntington, eds. *Understanding Political Development.* Boston: Little, Brown, 1987.

Welch, Claude E., Jr., ed. *Political Modernization: A Reader in Comparative Political Change.* 2d ed. Belmont, Calif.: Duxbury Press, 1971.

Wesson, Robert. *Communism and Communist Systems.* Englewood Cliffs, N.J.: Prentice-Hall, 1978.

Wiarda, Howard J. *The Continuing Struggle for Democracy in Latin America.* Boulder, Colo.: Westview Press, 1980.

————. *Corporatism and Development: The Portuguese Experience.* Amherst: University of Massachusetts Press, 1977.

————. *Corporatism and National Development in Latin America.* Boulder, Colo.: Westview Press, 1981.

————. *The Democratic Revolution in Latin America: History, Politics, and U.S. Policy.* New York: Holmes and Meier, A Twentieth Century Fund Book, 1990.

————. *Ethnocentrism in Foreign Policy: Can We Understand the Third World?* Washington, D.C.: American Enterprise Institute for Public Policy Research, 1985.

————. "The Latin Americanization of the United States." *New Scholar* 7 (1979):51–85.

———. "Toward a Framework for the Study of Political Change in the Iberic-Latin Tradition: The Corporative Model." *World Politics* 25 (January 1973):206–235.

Wiarda, Howard J., et al. *The Relations Between Democracy, Development, and Security: Implications for Policy.* New York: Global Economic Action Institute, 1988.

Wiarda, Howard J., ed. *Politics and Social Change in Latin America: The Distinct Tradition.* Boulder, Colo.: Westview Press, 3d ed., 1991.

Wiarda, Howard J., and Harvey F. Kline, eds. *Latin American Politics and Development.* Boston: Houghton Mifflin, 1979. 3d ed. Boulder, Colo.: Westview Press, 1990.

Wilkinson, T. O. "Family Structure and Industrialization in Japan." *American Sociological Review* 27 (October 1962):678–682.

———. *The Urbanization of Japanese Labor.* Amherst: University of Massachusetts Press, 1965.

Winch, Peter. *The Idea of a Social Science and Its Relation to Philosophy.* Atlantic Highlands, N.J.: Humanities Press, 1970.

Young, Crawford. *The Politics of Cultural Pluralism.* Madison: University of Wisconsin Press, 1976.

Zea, Leopoldo. *The Latin American Mind.* Norman: University of Oklahoma Press, 1963.

About the Book

Theories of comparative politics have splintered at an accelerated pace since the initial publication of this respected text. The revised edition has been updated to confront such theoretical developments in comparative politics as the emerging importance of the state-society approach, the wide acceptance of the corporatist approach, and the decline of Marxist and dependency theories.

A new chapter by John Martz heralds the renaissance of the political culture model and explicates the difficulties with bureaucratic-authoritarianism. Particularly relevant today in light of recent world events is Martz's discussion of transitions to democracy. A new conclusion by the editor, Howard Wiarda, ties the volume into a cohesive whole and reevaluates the significance of development theory.

For the upper-level undergraduate and graduate student, the revised edition of *New Directions in Comparative Politics* provides new and classic essays on the most important theoretical and methodological concerns of the field. The volume's authoritative bibliography has been expanded and updated to include the most recent literature.

About the Editor
and Contributors

Howard J. Wiarda is Professor of Political Science and Comparative Labor Relations at the University of Massachusetts at Amherst. He is an Associate of the Center for International Affairs, Harvard University; Adjunct Scholar at the American Enterprise Institute (AEI) in Washington, D.C.; and Associate of the Foreign Policy Research Institute in Philadelphia. He has been a Visiting Scholar at Harvard, Visiting Professor at MIT and George Washington University, and Course Chairperson at the Foreign Service Institute of the Department of State. Professor Wiarda was the Chair of the Latin American Studies Program at the University of Massachusetts; editor of the journal *Polity*; a Resident Scholar and Director of the Center for Hemispheric Studies at AEI; Lead Consultant to the National Bipartisan Commission on Central America; and, by appointment of the president of the United States, a member of the White House Task Force on Project Economic Justice. Dr. Wiarda's extensive publications on Latin America, southern Europe, the Third World, and U.S. foreign policy include *The Democratic Revolution in Latin America* (1990); *Foreign Policy Without Illusion* (1990); *Latin American Politics and Development* (Westview, 3d ed., 1990; with Harvey F. Kline); *The Transition to Democracy in Spain and Portugal* (1989; with Iêda Siqueira Wiarda); *Democracy, Development, and Security* (1988); *The Politics of External Influence in the Dominican Republic* (1988; with Michael J. Kryzanek); *Finding Our Way? Toward Maturity in U.S.–Latin American Relations* (1987); *The Iberian-Latin American Connection* (Westview, 1987); *Latin America at the Crossroads* (Westview, 1987); *The Communist Challenge in the Caribbean and Central America* (1987); *Ethnocentrism in Foreign Policy: Can We Understand the Third World?* (1985); *Corporation and National Development in Latin America* (Westview, 1981); and *Corporation and Development: The Portuguese Experience* (1977).

Douglas A. Chalmers is Professor and Chair in the Political Science Department at Columbia University. He has written on a variety of theories and problems in European and Latin American politics, authored *The Social Democratic Party of Germany: From Working Class Movement to Modern Political Party* (1964), and edited *Changing Latin America: New Interpretations of Its Politics and Society* (1972). His work, "Why Power Contenders Choose Liberalization," *International Studies Quarterly* (March 1982, with Craig Robinson), concerns Latin American regime changes.

Ronald H. Chilcote is Professor of Political Science at the University of California at Riverside. He has written extensively in the field of comparative politics, concentrating especially on Brazil, Portugal, and Lusophone Africa. Dr. Chilcote is the author of *Theories of Comparative Politics: The Search for a Paradigm* (Westview, 1981), *Dependency and Marxism: Toward a Resolution of the Debate* (Westview, 1982), and

Theories of Development and Underdevelopment (Westview, 1984). His *Power and the Ruling Classes in Northeast Brazil* will be published in 1990.

Lawrence S. Graham is Professor of Government at the University of Texas at Austin. He has published extensively in the areas of comparative bureaucracy (civil and military) and development policy. His books include studies of public policy and civil service reform in Brazil, the state and policy outcomes in Latin America, and the policy process in Portugal, Yugoslavia, and Romania.

Peter Lange is Professor of Political Science at Duke University. He has written extensively on the relationship of trade unions, politics, and economic performance in the advanced industrial democracies, as well as on Italian politics and the Italian Communist Party. Among his publications are *Unions, Change and Crisis* (1982, with George Ross and Maurizio Vannicelli), and *Union Democracy and Liberal Corporatism: Exit, Voice and Wage Regulation in Postwar Europe* (1984), and *State, Market and Social Regulation: New Perspectives on Italy* (1989, edited with Marino Regini).

John D. Martz is Professor of Political Science at Pennsylvania State University. The most recent of his many books is the edited *United States Policy in Latin America: A Quarter Century of Crisis and Challenge, 1961–1986* (University of Nebraska Press). He is the editor of *Studies in Comparative International Development.*

Hudson Meadwell is Assistant Professor of Political Science at McGill University. His research interests include ethnic nationalism and social movements and rational choice applications in comparative politics. His publications include articles in the *British Journal of Political Science, Comparative Politics, Comparative Political Studies,* and *Archives européennes de sociologie.* He has also completed a book-length manuscript entitled *Nationalism and Rationality: Ethnic Collective Action in Brittany.*

Joel S. Migdal is professor and chairman of the International Studies Program in the Henry M. Jackson School of International Studies at the University of Washington. He recently published *Strong Societies and Weak States* (1988), which deals with the interaction of states and societies in the Third World. He has also published several other well-known books including *Peasants, Politics, and Revolution* (1974) and *Palestinian Society and Politics* (1980). Dr. Migdal is currently working on a manuscript outlining the historical development of the Palestinians, which will be published by The Free Press.

Tony Smith is Professor of Political Science at Tufts University. He has published three books on Western imperialism. His most recent book is *Thinking Like a Communist: State and Legitimacy in the Soviet Union, China, and Cuba* (1987).

Sidney Verba is Carl H. Pforzheimer University Professor at Harvard. He has written extensively in comparative and American politics. Books he has authored or coauthored include: *Small Groups and Political Behavior* (1961); *The Civic Culture* (1963); *Participation in America* (1972); *Participation and Political Equality* (1978); *The Changing American Voter* (1976); *Injury to Insult* (1979); *Equality in America* (1985); and *Elites and the Idea of Equality* (1987).

Index

Philippines, 201, 207, 238
PIDER. *See* Programas Integrales de Desarrollo Regional
Plato, 11, 158, 159
Pluralism, 10, 17, 21, 73, 94, 97, 99, 110, 171, 238, 239, 242
  compared to corporatism, 59–60, 61–62, 64, 65, 75, 77, 78
  and consensus, 83, 159
Poland, 143, 178
Police, 53, 54, 141
Policy Studies Review, 170
Political anthropology, 36
Political culture, 25, 36, 87, 155, 207–212, 235–236, 239, 246
Political Culture and Political Development (Pye & Verba), 208
Political development, 18, 19, 25, 225–229, 237–242, 243
Political Development: Essays in Heuristic Theory (Almond), 38
Political economy, 21, 25, 36, 38, 40, 108, 110, 155–158, 163, 166(fig.), 231, 233, 246
  international, 109
  methodology, 156
  outcomes, 107–109
  and Third World, 134
  typologies, 86–87, 93–99, 96(fig.)
Political Man: The Social Bases of Politics (Lipset), 16, 35
Political movements, 87
Political Order in Changing Societies (Huntington), 7, 123
Political outcomes, 106–109
Political participation, 38
Political parties, 19, 33, 94–95, 135, 161, 230, 236
  extremist, 92–93
  ideology, 90, 91, 92
  left, 96
  social democratic, 100–101
  and social groups, 92, 103
  and trade unions, 101
  typologies for party systems, 89–91, 90(fig.), 93(fig.)
Political power, 87, 101
Political science, 11–12, 15, 27–28(n14), 33, 124, 154, 157, 221, 242
  fields, 3, 32
Political society, 63
Political sociology, 13, 36, 40, 134, 142
Politics of the Developing Areas, The (Almond & Coleman), 14, 16, 17, 29(n34), 35, 38, 226
Polyarchy, 85
Popular Monarchists (PPM) (Portugal), 186
Populist policies, 77. *See also* Latin America, populism
Portugal, 65, 67, 159, 173, 175(table), 176, 178, 180, 181, 182, 183, 189(table), 190, 194, 223
  bureaucracy, 179
  center-periphery relations, 187–188
  colonies, 176, 177, 185–186
  Communist party (PCP), 190, 192
  development policy, 188
  Socialist party (PS), 192
  subnational governmental units, 174, 184, 185–186
Poulantzas, Nicos, 158, 160–161
Poverty, 122, 126
Powell, G. Bingham, 91–93
PPM. *See* Popular Monarchists
Prado Junior, Caio, 162
Prebisch, Raúl, 120–121, 162
Prefectural systems, 177–179, 184, 185, 189(table), 194
PRI. *See* Institutional Revolutionary Party
Prices, 101, 164. *See also* Inflation
Princeton University Press, 227
Profit maximization, 159
Programas Integrales de Desarrollo Regional (PIDER) (Mexico), 185
Property rights, 51
Przeworski, Adam, 37, 101

PS. *See* Portugal, Socialist party
PSD. *See* Social Democrats
Psychology, 207, 209
Public choice theory, 23
Public opinion, 37, 210, 221, 230, 236, 237, 239
Public policy analysis, 23, 25, 38, 70, 170–171, 236, 237, 246
  implementation literature, 196(n2)
  methodology, 172, 173–176, 180–183
  subnational governmental units, 174, 183–187
  Third World, 171–173
Pye, Lucian W., 4, 7, 14, 35, 144, 208, 211, 226, 239

Quantitative methods, 37

Radcliffe-Brown, A. R., 157
Rationalization, 100, 134, 155
Reagan, Ronald, 24, 147, 240
Recent Electoral Changes in the Americas (1985 conference), 215(n37)
Relations of production, 156
Remmer, Karen L., 202
Repression, 75
Republic of China, 238
Research grants, 227
"Research in Comparative Politics" (SSRC), 15
Resource utilization, 69
Rey, Pierre-Philippe, 165
Ricardo, David, 155, 156
Riggs, Fred, 182
Riots, 92, 107
Robinson, Ronald, 120
Rodney, Walter, 162
Rodó, José E., 142
Rodrigues O., Gustavo, 165
Rojas, Antonio, 165
Romania, 172, 173, 175(table), 176, 177, 178, 179, 180, 182, 183, 190, 194
  bureaucracy, 188, 191
  centralization, 184, 193
  development policy, 188, 189(table)
  subnational governmental units, 174, 184, 192
Rostow, W. W., 7, 14, 16, 17, 35, 226, 227, 228, 233, 237–238, 241, 242
Rural sector, 55. *See also* Agriculture
Rustow, Dankwart, 226

Saint-Simon, Henri, 156
Salazar, Antonio de Oliveira, 67, 223
São Paulo state (Brazil), 191
Sartori, Giovanni, 89–91, 92
Saudi Arabia, 140
Scandinavia, 35
Schmitter, Philippe C., 38, 61, 62, 63, 72–73, 74, 76, 95, 101, 204
Schumpeter, Joseph, 214(n34)
Seligson, Mitchell A., 206, 211
Semi-periphery, 126, 130(n17), 171, 196(n5). *See also* Center-periphery relations
Serbia/Serbs, 186, 195
Service sector, 119
Shah of Iran, 140
Shalev, Michael, 97
Shils, Edward A., 47–50, 54, 207–208
Sindico, Domenico, 165
Slovenia (Yugoslavia), 194
Smith, Adam, 155, 156, 157
Social change, 139
Social classes, 48
Social control, 50–53, 54, 55, 56, 57, 58(nn 12, 13)
Social Democratic Center (CDS) (Portugal), 186
Social Democrats (PSD) (Portugal), 186
Socialism, 64, 67, 72, 98, 159, 171